THOR HEYERDAHL

AKU-AKU

Illustrated with Photographs in Color

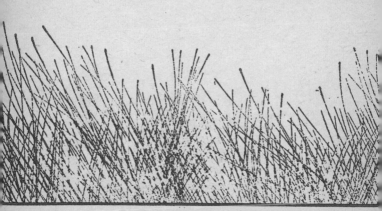

AKU-AKU

American edition published by Rand McNally, September, 1958

Book-of-the-Month Club edition published September, 1958

CARDINAL GIANT edition published January, 1960
1st printing....................November, 1959

AKU-AKU, originally published in Norwegian by Gyldendal Norsk Forlag, Oslo, with simultaneous editions in Swedish, Danish and Finnish, ©, Thor Heyerdahl, 1957. English edition published in London, ©, George Allen & Unwin Ltd., 1958.

CARDINAL GIANT editions are distributed in the U.S. by Affiliated Publishers, Inc., 630 Fifth Avenue, New York 20, N.Y.

AKU-AKU is the fascinating account of a scientific expedition to solve the mysteries of Easter Island. That lonely speck in the Southeast Pacific is dotted with colossal statues of long-eared men—weird relics of a people who have vanished from the earth.

When and how were these fifty-ton giants carved? How were they moved for miles without machinery? How were they erected? What toppled some of them over? And what happened to the men who made them?

To Thor Heyerdahl, famous Norwegian explorer who thrilled the world with his dangerous voyage on the raft *Kon-Tiki,* this new expedition was to prove even more exciting.

The house-high statues were only part of the amazing secrets of Easter Island. Underground, Heyerdahl found caves guarded by suspicious natives, caves filled with revealing objects and fantastic clues to the skills and customs of the pale-skinned, red-haired "long-ears."

AKU-AKU is lavishly illustrated with 32 pages of full-color photographs plus maps and diagrams. It was published originally by Rand McNally & Company at $6.95.

THE SECRET OF EASTER ISLAND

POCKET BOOKS, INC. • NEW YORK

Contents

Illustrations

ILLUSTRATIONS

MAPS AND DRAWINGS

AKU-
AKU

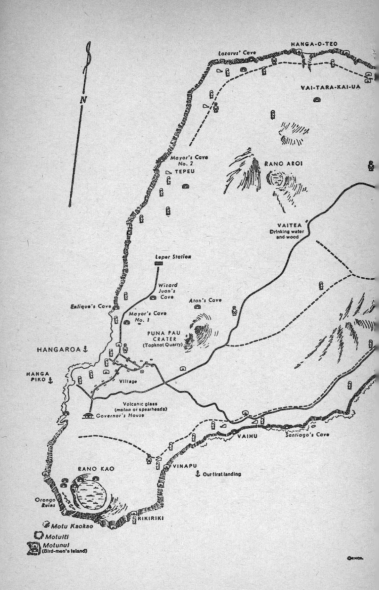

N

HANGA-O-TEO
Lazarus' Cave

VAI-TARA-KAI-UA

*Mayor's Cave
No. 2*
TEPEU

RANO AROI

VAITEA
Drinking water
and wood

Leper Station

*Wizard
Juan's
Cave*

Ealique's Cave

Atan's Cave

*Mayor's Cave
No. 1*

PUNA PAU
CRATER
(Topknot Quarry)

HANGAROA ⚓

HANGA
PIKO ⚓

Village

*Volcanic glass
(mataa or spearheads)*
🏛 *Governor's House*

VAIHU

Santiago's Cave

RANO KAO

VINAPU

⚓ *Our first landing*

*Orongo
Ruins*

RIKIRIKI

Motu Kaokao
Motuiti
Motunui
(Bird-men's Island)

ANAKENA
⚓ Our permanent anchorage

La Pérouse Bay

TE PITO KURA Bay

HEKII

ANA O KEKE
(Cave of the White Virgins)

The three Spanish crosses

The Long-eared Earth Oven

POIKE PENINSULA

KATIKI

RANO RARAKU

Marotiri

HOTUITI

⚓ Our first anchorage

TOATOA

Easter Island
(RAPA NUI)

Miles 0   0.5   1   2

Statues (often in groups)
Statues of unusual type
Important temple platform (ahu)
Cave visited by members of expedition
Presumed location of unexplored cave

Shepherd's hut
Expedition camp
Jeep track
Prehistoric track
Bog

CHAPTER ONE

Detectives Off to the End of the World

I HAD NO *aku-aku*.

Nor did I know what an *aku-aku* was, so I could hardly have used one if I had had it.

Every sensible person on Easter Island has an *aku-aku*. I too got one there, but at the moment I was organizing a voyage to that very place, so I did not possess one. Perhaps that was why arranging the journey was so difficult. Getting home again was much easier.

Easter Island is the loneliest inhabited place in the world. The nearest solid land the islanders can see is above, in the firmament, the moon and the planets. They have to travel farther than any other people to see that there really is land yet closer. Therefore, living nearest the stars, they know more names of stars than of towns and countries in our own world.

On this remote island, east of the sun and west of the moon, mankind once had one of its most curious ideas. No one knows who had it, and no one knows why. For it happened before Columbus led white men to America, and in so doing opened the gate for voyages of exploration out into the great unknown Pacific. While our own race still believed that the world ended at Gibraltar, there were other great navigators who knew better. In advance of their time, they plowed unknown seas in the immense watery void off the desolate west coast of South

America. Far out they found land. The loneliest little island in the world. They landed there, whetted their stone adzes, and set about one of the most remarkable engineering projects of ancient times. They did not build fortresses and castles, or dams and wharves. They made gigantic stone figures in man's likeness, as tall as houses and as heavy as boxcars, and they dragged them in great numbers across country and set them up erect on huge stone terraces all over the island.

How did they manage this, before the age of technique? No one knows. But there stood the figures they had desired, towering into the sky, while the people fell. And they buried their dead at the feet of the colossi they themselves had created. They raised great statues and buried their dead. Then one day the blows of the adz on the rock face fell silent. A sudden silence, for tools were left lying and many of the figures were only half-finished. The mysterious sculptors disappeared into the dark mists of antiquity.

What happened? Yes, what had happened on Easter Island? I bent over my desk for the thousandth time and let my eyes sail over the large-scale chart of the Pacific, that deceiving sheet of paper on which the islands bulk large in capital letters and you travel with the ruler as easily up as down the ocean currents. I was beginning to know this ocean now.[1] There in the wild valleys of the Marquesas group, just south of the Equator, I had lived for a year in native fashion and learned to see nature with Polynesian eyes. There, too, I had heard for the first time old Tei Tetua's stories of the man-god Tiki. And down in the Society Islands, among the palms of Tahiti, the great chief Teriieroo had once been my teacher. He had adopted me as his son and taught me to respect his race as my own. And there, on the coral reef in the Tuamotu group, we had landed with the *Kon-Tiki* raft, and learned that even the salt sea has its unceasing treadmill, the route from South America out to those distant islands. However lonely the islands were, they all lay within the natural range of the Incas' old balsa rafts.

And from over there, from the dry cactus forests of the

[1] The route of the *Kon-Tiki* raft and the sites and dates of Thor Heyerdahl's former scientific visits are noted on the map found on pages 342–43.

Galapagos group, I had other strange memories. We had nearly landed up there with the *Kon-Tiki* raft, so I went later with another expedition to see what secrets this remote group of islands concealed. In a fairy-tale land, among giant lizards and the world's largest tortoises, I had taken part in collecting a veritable Aladdin's lamp, which lay crushed to fragments, buried in an old rubbish heap among the cactus trees. One had only to rub the dirty old fragments to see broad sails on the eastern horizon. It was the Inca Indians' mighty forerunners that we saw, steering out with their rafts from the coast of South America into the wild sea. They crossed the sea once, twice, many times, and came ashore on the waterless cliffs of the Galapagos group. There they encamped, and as time passed they broke one after another of the curious jars they had on board, jars the like of which no other civilized people in the whole world has made. It was fragments of these jars we dug up at the old settlements, and they played the part of Aladdin's lamp, reflecting their owners' maritime feats and casting their light right into the darkness of prehistoric time.

No archaeologist had previously investigated the Galapagos group, and therefore no one had found anything. We were the first to believe that the Indians had sailed so far out to sea, and thus we went out and searched. The archaeologists Reed and Skjölsvold and I had dug up over two thousand of these ancient fragments, from 130 different jars. Leading scientists in the United States analyzed the fragments, as detectives examine fingerprints, and were able to establish that a thousand years before Columbus opened the door into America the Incas' forerunners had thrown open the door of the Pacific and paid repeated visits to the remote Galapagos Islands.[2]

These were the oldest traces of man that had so far been established on the real ocean islands of the Pacific. They announced that before the islands of Polynesia were inhabited, and long before the Vikings set out on their voyage to Iceland, the ancient people of South America had begun to explore the Pacific and had gained a foothold on islands as far from

[2] For further details see: Thor Heyerdahl and Arne Skjölsvold, "Archaeological Evidence of Pre-Spanish Visits to the Galapagos Islands," published in 1956 as Mem. No. 12 of the Society for American Archaeology.

their own coast as Iceland is from Norway. They had fished there, planted native cotton, and left many traces at their settlements before they forsook the inhospitable and waterless islands for an unknown destination.

From the Galapagos the same fierce ocean current rolls on unchecked, swifter than the Amazon and a hundred times as wide, till, only a few weeks later, it rolls its watery masses in among the South Sea Islands.

An uncertain little dot, with a note of interrogation beside it, was marked on the chart out in the middle of the ocean current. Was it land? We had steered right over the spot with the *Kon-Tiki* raft and discovered that it was only eddies. But far to the south, where the southernmost branches of the current turn off, lay another little dot, and this had a name, Easter Island. I had not been there, and it was there I wanted to go. I had always wondered how prehistoric men got themselves to that desolate spot. Now, for a change, I was wondering how I should get myself there. It was rather irrational to try to solve the travel problems of a Stone Age people when I could not solve my own.

As the *Kon-Tiki* drifted with the current far to the north, we had sat on deck in the moonlight and talked about the mystery of Easter Island. At that time I had secretly dreamed of coming back some day to the eastern Pacific and going ashore on that lonely island. Now I was trying to make the dream a reality.

Easter Island belongs to Chile. A warship goes there just once a year with provisions for the inhabitants. Then she turns round and goes back to Chile, which is as far away as Spain is from Canada. Easter Island has no other regular communication with the outside world.

The warship offered no solution to my travel problems. To explore Easter Island in a week, while the warship lay waiting, was of course futile. To be left on the island for a whole year with diligent scientists was an equally senseless plan, for they might find after a month that there was nothing more to do there. It was possible to get there on a balsa raft from South America, drifting with the current and wind, but with such a craft I might not get my archaeologists to go with me, and there was no point in trying to explore Easter Island without them.

So I must get a boat of my own, a kind of expedition ship. But there was no harbor at Easter Island, no reliable anchorage, and no access to a wharf. And there was no oil or water supply. The ship, therefore, must be large enough to carry, in addition to all our supplies, oil and water for the voyage out and home again, and for mobility during our stay. She began at once to be quite a big ship. And suppose the archaeologists found that there was nothing to dig for. In that case it would be poor planning to have come all the way to Easter Island in our own ship unless we could use her to go on to other unexplored South Sea Islands. Well, there were enough of them in the eastern part of Polynesia. A whole string of exciting islands lay awaiting excavation right in that part of the Pacific where the ocean current rolls in from the Galapagos and South America.

About voyages to remote seas I have always consulted my friends Thomas and Wilhelm, of the Fred Olsen Line. One day, while my plans were still only an unspoken secret, we were sitting together in the cozy old shipping office down by the wharves at Oslo. Thomas had smelled a rat when I came in and he produced a fat globe, which he placed between us. I turned it round till it was nearly all blue. That can only happen when the immense South Pacific is swung up so that America and Asia disappear together with Europe onto the back half of the globe. I pointed to Easter Island.

"There," I said. "But how?"

Two days later we were sitting round the globe again, and Wilhelm presented his calculations.

"The best thing for you would be a diesel-propelled boat about 150 feet long with a speed of 12 knots and space for 50 tons of water and 130 tons of oil," he said.

I did not doubt for a moment that this would be the best thing for me. I had learned to rely on Wilhelm's nautical calculations ever since he had helped me estimate the *Kon-Tiki's* drift so exactly that we should have been there to the day if only we had managed to throw a rope ashore to keep from drifting past Angatau.

Wilhelm called me up a few days later. He had an offer from a canning factory at Stavanger. They had a suitable trawler on the Greenland fishing grounds. I could hire her for a year if I took her from September.

I looked at the calendar. It was toward the end of April, and September was only four months away. The offer was "bareboat"—I was to take over the vessel empty, without crew or equipment.

My own navigating experience had never got beyond the balsa-raft stage. Nor could the other fellows from the *Kon-Tiki* voyage man a real ship: licenses and papers were required. It was all much simpler on an Inca raft.

"Our office can help you with all nautical problems," Thomas said.

So we suddenly found ourselves sitting at the big green conference table with the marine superintendent, the signing-on authority, the provisioning authority, the insurance authority, and all the other experts higher and lower. And the result was a real ship. I could almost hear impatient hootings from the big vessel which lay at Stavanger without a spark of life in her funnel, her deck empty of men, and not a thing in the large hold where naked iron girders projected cheerlessly like ribs round an empty stomach.

There is always a good deal to think about when taking the family to the country. And there is just as much to remember when, in addition to the family, you are taking to the South Seas five archaeologists, a doctor, a photographer, a crew of thirteen, a ship containing spare parts, special equipment, and a year's meals for everyone. One feels like a conductor busy eating spaghetti while trying to drive his orchestra through a rhapsody by Liszt. My desk was a complete chaos of passports and papers and licenses, photographs and letters. The furniture was covered with charts and lists and samples of all kinds of gear. This madness soon spread all over the house.

After the newspapers had announced our plans, there was no end to the strange proposals which came by mail. I heard almost daily from people in the most scattered quarters of the world who told me that Easter Island was the last remnant

6

of a sunken continent, a sort of Pacific Atlantis. It was on the bottom of the sea round the island, they said, that we must seek for the key to the mystery, not on land.

There was even a man who proposed that I should give up the whole expedition. "It is a waste of time to travel so far," he wrote. "You can sit in your own study and solve the problem by vibrations. Send me a photograph of an Easter Island statue and a photograph of an old statue from South America, and I'll tell you by the vibrations if they originate from the same people." He added that he had once made a model of Cheops' pyramid in cardboard, with raw meat in it. And after a time it vibrated so horribly that he had to send the whole family to the hospital.

September came. A streamlined Greenland trawler, shining white like a yacht, with the bearded face of the sun-god Kon-Tiki painted in brick red on her funnel, was lying at pier *C* in front of the Oslo city hall. Forward, on the high bow, reinforced against ice, a curious blue emblem was painted, the meaning of which only the initiated knew. It showed two of the sacred bird-men of Easter Island, half-bird and half-human, copied from one of the rare tablets with undeciphered hieroglyphics.

A crew had been signed on in spite of wives' and sweethearts' alarm over a year's absence in the romantic South Seas, and now there was heat in the funnel, and the ship lay full-loaded in the fiord water right up to her blue-painted water line. There was hectic activity on board, and such a dense crowd ashore that it was almost impossible for trucks delivering bundles and parcels at the twelfth hour to get through.

Had we remembered everything? Of course we had food and digging gear, fishhooks and yard goods for barter with the natives, and all that we knew for certain we should need. The danger lay in the unforeseen. Suppose we found, contrary to our expectations, a skeleton under water. Had we the right chemicals to prevent it from disintegrating? Suppose we had to go to an inaccessible rock or ledge, had we the means of reaching it? Or how should we tackle problems of contact and provisioning if the camp was on one side of the island and the ship had suddenly to go round to the other side on account of bad weather? What if the cook burned a hole in a saucepan, the propeller was damaged by a block of coral, or a sailor put his foot on a poisonous sea urchin? And what about all the food if the refrigerator ceased to work? Had we all imaginable special equipment and spare parts? Now there was no more time to think it over. Now we must be prepared to meet all conceivable reverses, for the Greenland trawler was lying vibrant, ready to sail for Easter Island, the loneliest spot in the world, which had not a single workshop or store.

The captain was on the bridge, and the crew were running about the deck battening down hatches and hauling on ropes, while a gigantic mate stood, pencil in hand, checking off items on a long list. At all events, everything he had been told about had come. Even the skipper's Christmas tree was packed away in the refrigerator. The list was in order.

The ship's bell sounded for the last time. Orders rang out from captain to first officer, and there was a fierce blast from the funnel behind the sun-god's shining head. Farewells and last good wishes were exchanged over the ship's rail. Brusquely the gangplank was rolled away, there was a splashing of cables and creaking of winches, and the engineers down below applied their magic: the ship began to move. A cheer rose from the long wall of figures on the pier. Hands waved and handkerchiefs fluttered like treetops in a gale, while the captain made the siren utter a few heart-rending howls.

This chaos was the end of chaos, its climax and full stop.

I was left waving in the turmoil on the pier. It was not that I had forgotten to embark myself, but I had first to fly to the United States to meet three archaeologists who had agreed to join the expedition. And after that I had to pay a courtesy visit to Chile before I went aboard our ship when she came through the Panama Canal.

H.R.H. Crown Prince Olav had most kindly offered to be patron of the expedition, and the Norwegian Foreign Office had obtained permission from the Chilean Government for the expedition to begin digging on Easter Island as long as we did not damage the monuments. Both Great Britain and France had given permission for their islands, so we had the green light for everything we could stumble upon in the eastern Pacific.

When the boat turned her white stern toward us and slid slowly away from the quay, a solitary deck boy stood high astern. As bright as the evening sun with sheer joy, he proudly hauled in the end of a dirty mooring cable, while his classmates stood on shore shouting hip-hip-hurrah for Thor Junior, who was being let off school for a whole year.

Then the little craft slipped behind a big ocean steamer and was lost to sight. She was in a hurry, she was to go halfway round the world with detectives on the track of other seafarers who had a start of several centuries.

CHAPTER TWO

What Awaited Us at the World's Navel

How QUIET!

What perfect peace. The engine had stopped. The lights had been put out. The whole starry firmament, suddenly freed of the artificial dazzle, swung to and fro and in slow circles, clear and glittering round the masthead. I leaned far back in my deck chair and enjoyed this complete harmony. It was as though the plug of an electric line to the mainland had been pulled out and the ceaseless stream of impulses from disturbing stations all over the world had been removed. Nothing remained but the intimate present and naked reality: fresh air, black night, and twinkling stars. Almost imperceptibly sight and hearing opened wide again and let a breeze blow right through my soul.

There were here no impressions to be washed away or suppressed; no city racket with flashing neon signs, restless competition, and noisy amusements which, as though in a race with time itself, strove to force their way in through every opening at the risk of jolting to pieces the sensitive human soul. Here there was quiet so complete that time itself ceased to roll on. It too stopped, stood motionless, and waited. One almost hesitated to cough, as if to do so would break the spell and wake the world's sleeping elements of unrest.

Far off toward the land a faint rushing noise was sometimes heard in the darkness, as of wind or waves breaking at short

10

intervals against a cliff. All on board were curiously silent; the stillness must have given them a feeling of reverence. Only from the cabin hatchway did I hear now and again a short, hushed exchange of words, accompanied by the washing of water in finely graduated tones against the ship's side, and then a quiet rhythmical creak, creak, creak, like a contented grunting from the little vessel as she rocked discreetly in the silence of the night.

We had come under the shelter of land.

We had done with the hurried panting beat of the engines and the seas which thundered against our bow in endless lines and rolled us up and down and sideways before they hissed past us. We had crept into the protecting embrace of a lonely coast before night fell over us and the sea. There, in the darkness, lay Easter Island.

We had stolen up under the land just in time to catch a glimpse of rolling gray-green ridges, steep cliffs along the coast, and, far away in the interior, statues standing scattered up the slope of an extinct volcano, like black caraway seeds against the red evening sky. We had made our way in by echo and ordinary sounding as far as we dared go, and then the skipper had cast anchor.

Not a soul was to be seen on shore, only a deserted, petrified world with motionless stone heads gazing at us from their distant ridge, while other equally motionless stone men lay prostrate in a row at the foot of a long terrace right in the foreground, on the lava blocks along the coast. It was as though we had anchored with a hovering spaceship off the shore of an extinct world, where once had lived beings of a kind other than those on our own earth. The shadows were long, but nothing moved: nothing but the fiery red sun as it descended slowly into the black sea and drew the night down over us.

Strictly speaking, we ought not to have anchored here. We ought really to have pushed on through the seas right round the island and announced our arrival to the governor, who lived with the whole population in a little village on the other side. But it would have been no pleasure either to him or to the native inhabitants of the island if we had arrived just at dusk, at a place where a call from any ship is one of the greatest events of the year. Better to ride out the night here under the lee of the cliffs, even if the bottom was of the worst kind for anchoring. Then we could arrive at the village of Hangaroa early next morning with all flags flying.

The door of our cabin was cautiously opened and a strip of light slanted across the boat deck for a few seconds as Yvonne, my wife, stole out. In the cabin little Anette lay sleeping as peacefully as the night sky itself, with a doll under one arm and a teddy bear under the other.

"We ought to have a little celebration tonight, even if we haven't arrived officially," Yvonne whispered, nodding happily toward the land.

It was the first time for fourteen days of rolling and pitching that she had been on her legs and able to think of anything of the kind. I told her that the steward had had his orders and that the captain was going to assemble all hands on the boat deck in a few minutes. Yvonne remained standing at the rail staring in enchantment landward into the darkness. We could actually feel a few light breaths of mother earth, a curious dry scent of hay or grass, which now and then mingled with the clean salt breeze.

The men began to arrive. Newly shaved, and smartened up till hardly recognizable, they sat down on chairs which had been placed in a ring between the two ship's boats on the upper deck. There was Dr. William Mulloy, or Bill. He came swinging along, broad and thickset, and flung the stub of a cigarette into the sea as he sat down. He stared thoughtfully at the deck. Close behind him came tall, thin Dr. Carlyle Smith. Carl lit up and remained standing, half-hanging from a stay and looking at the stars. They were both professors of archaeology, at Wyoming and Kansas universities respectively. Then there was our old friend Ed, or Edwin Ferdon, from the Museum of New Mexico, the only one of the three American archaeologists I had known before. He leaned over the rail beside Yvonne and sniffed happily toward the contours of the land.

The skipper came down from the bridge, a little man who moved like a bouncing ball. Captain Arne Hartmark had been sailing to distant lands for twenty years, but he had never seen anything like Easter Island through his binoculars. Behind him stood the gigantic mate Sanna, a jovial fellow, hanging onto a stay with each hand, looking like an amiable tame gorilla. And there was Second Officer Larsen, the most good-natured man in the world, who would find something to laugh at even in the electric chair. He was sitting between two inexhaustible humorists, the stout chief engineer, Olsen, his face wrinkled with perpetual smiling, and the skinny second engineer, whose newly acquired chin tuft made him look like a cross between a lay reader and a conjurer.

The doctor, Dr. Gjessing, came up the ladder, bowed, and sat down, and behind him gleamed the spectacles of the expedition's photographer, Erling Schjerven, who lit a small cigar in honor of the occasion. Thor Junior had found room for his lanky, boyish figure between two stout sailors up in a ship's boat, and the cook and steward were sitting there too, side by side, after having silently placed the most exquisite dishes on the table between us. No sea could prevent Gronmyr, the steward, and Hanken, the cook, from performing their culinary miracles on board. Then came the boatswain, the electrician, the deck boy, and the galley boy, with Arne Skjölsvold and Gonzalo. Arne was an archaeologist and head of the new state museum at Elverum. He had taken part in the Galapagos expedition as well. Gonzalo Figueroa was a student of archaeology at Santiago University and the official representative of Chile on the expedition. We had been ready for anything before he came, as I had invited him without an interview, but Gonzalo came up the gangplank at Panama in high spirits, an athletic aristocrat with the chameleonic gift of adapting himself to the most variable conditions of life.

So we were gathered on the boat deck, twenty-three in all, a most versatile party, including men from many walks of life. In the weeks on board we had become close friends, bound by a common desire to set foot on that very island that lay there in the darkness. Now that all were assembled, and the engine had stopped, it was natural to tell them something about other people's experiences on Easter Island so that they might all have a little background for what lay ahead.

"No one really knows the name of that island," I began. "The natives call it *Rapa Nui,* but research workers do not think that this was its original name. In their most ancient

13

legends the natives always call the island *Te Pito o te Henua,*
or 'Navel of the World,' but even that may be an old, poetical
description rather than the island's real name. Later the
natives also called it the 'Eye Which Sees Heaven' or the
'Frontier of Heaven.' The rest of us who live thousands of
miles beyond all the island's horizons have elected to place the
name 'Easter Island' on the map, because it was on the afternoon of Easter Day, 1722, that the Dutchman Roggeveen and
his companions came here, the first Europeans to sail into
these waters. They noticed that unknown people ashore were
sending up smoke signals, and when the Dutchmen cast the
anchors of their two sailing craft at sunset, they had a glimpse
of a strange community before night fell. They were first met
on board their ships by tall, well-built people who, so far as
can be judged, were fair-skinned Polynesians such as we know
them in Tahiti, Hawaii, and the other eastern islands of the
South Seas. But the population did not seem to be absolutely
pure and unmixed, for among the native visitors some were
conspicuous by their darker skins, while others again were
'quite white,' like Europeans. A few were also 'of a reddish
tint, as if somewhat severely tanned by the sun.' Many had
beards.

"On shore the Dutchmen saw gigantic figures thirty feet
high, with great cylinders on the tops of their heads, like a
kind of crown. Roggeveen himself tells that the islanders
lighted fires before these giant gods and then squatted down
before them with the soles of their feet flat against the ground
and their heads bent reverently. They began to raise and
lower their arms with the palms of their hands pressed together. Behrens, who was on board the other ship, tells us
that when the sun rose next morning they could see the natives
on shore lying prostrate and worshiping the sunrise, and they
had lighted hundreds of fires which the Dutchmen thought
were in honor of the gods. This is the only time that anyone
has described active sun worship on Easter Island.

"Among the first who came on board the Dutch ships was
a 'completely white man' who had a more ceremonious air
than the others. He was ornamented with a crown of feathers
on his head, which otherwise was close-shaven, and he had
in his ears round white pegs as large as fists. This white man

showed by his bearing that he was a prominent person in the community, and the Dutchmen thought that he might be a priest. The lobes of his ears were pierced and artificially lengthened so that they hung down to his shoulders, and the Dutch noted that many of the islanders had ears artificially lengthened in this manner. If their long ears got in the way when they were at work, they just took out the pegs and tied the long flap up over the upper edge of the ear.

"Many of the islanders went about stark naked, but with the whole body artistically tattooed in one continuous pattern of birds and strange figures. Others wore cloaks of bark cloth colored red and yellow. Some had waving crowns of feathers on their heads, and others queer reed hats. All were friendly, and the Dutchmen saw no weapons of any kind. Curiously enough there were hardly any women to be seen, although the place swarmed with men. But the few women who showed themselves were more than cordial to the unknown visitors without the men showing the smallest sign of jealousy.

"The inhabitants lived in long, low huts made of reeds—they looked like boats turned bottom upward—with no windows and a door opening so low that one could only just crawl in. Evidently masses of people lived in these without any furniture save a few mats on the floor and a stone for a pillow. Fowls were the only animals they kept. They cultivated bananas, sugar cane, and above all sweet potatoes, which the Dutch called the island's daily bread.

"These lonely islanders could certainly not have been active seafarers, for the largest craft the Dutchmen saw were canoes eight feet long, so narrow that one could barely force both legs in, and so leaky that one spent just as much time bailing as paddling. They were still living in Stone Age fashion, with no metals, and their food was cooked among glowing stones in the earth. It must have seemed to the Dutchmen that there was, in their own century, scarcely any place in the world so backward. It was, therefore, only natural that they were utterly astonished to find, in the midst of these poor people, gigantic statues towering upward, larger than any they had seen in Europe. At first they were intrigued by the feat it must have been to erect these tall statues: they saw no solid wood or strong rope in the inhabitants' possession. They examined the worn surface of one of the weather-beaten colossi, and solved the whole problem to their own satisfaction by declaring that the figures were not of stone, but were modeled from a kind of clay which was afterward stuffed with small stones.

"They rowed back to the ships, which had already lost two of their anchors, and sailed away from the newly discovered island after a single day's visit. They noted in their log that the inhabitants they had found were cheerful, peaceful, and well-mannered, but all were expert thieves. Through a misunderstanding one native visitor was shot on board one of the ships, and a dozen others were shot ashore, while the Europeans got off with the loss of one tablecloth and of a few hats which were stolen while they had them on their heads.

"The natives were left on the shore with their dead and wounded, staring after the great sails disappearing westward. Nearly fifty years were to pass before the next visit from the outer world.

"Next time it was the Spaniards who came. Led by Don Felipe Gonzáles with two ships, they appeared over the horizon of Easter Island in 1770, and they also were attracted by smoke signals sent up by the natives. They went ashore with two priests and a large party of soldiers, and marched in ceremonial procession to the top of a three-humped elevation on the east coast, while great crowds of curious, cheering natives came dancing after them. They planted a cross on each of the three hummocks, sang, fired a salute, and declared the island to be Spanish territory. As proof that all these proceedings were legal, they wrote a declaration addressed to King Charles of Spain, under which the boldest of the natives who stood round were allowed to sign their names, 'with every sign of joy and happiness,' in the form of birds and curious figures which the Spaniards accepted as signatures. So now the island had an owner, the King of Spain, and it received a new name, 'San Carlos Island.'

"The Spaniards were not deceived into thinking the monuments were of clay. They struck one of the statues so hard with a hoe that sparks sprang from it, and thus it was evident that they were of stone. How these colossi were set up was a mystery to the Spaniards, and they even doubted whether they could have been made on this island.

"Both gifts and stolen goods disappeared so completely that the Spaniards suspected the inhabitants of having secret underground hiding places, for the whole country was open and treeless. No children were to be seen anywhere; the whole population seemed to consist of multitudes of grown men and only a few women, but these few decidedly unrestrained.

"The Spaniards met on the island tall, fair men. Two of the biggest were measured and were respectively 6 feet, 6½ inches and 6 feet, 5 inches tall. Many had beards, and the Spaniards found that they were quite like Europeans and not ordinary natives. They noted in their diaries that not all of them had black hair: the hair of some was chestnut brown, and in other cases it was even reddish and cinnamon-colored. And when they actually got the inhabitants to repeat clearly in Spanish, 'Ave Maria, long live Charles III, King of Spain,' all the Spaniards agreed that they were an intelligent people who could easily be civilized. Filled with satisfaction they left their new subjects, never to return.[1]

"It was the English next time, under the command of no less than Captain Cook, and after him came the Frenchman La Pérouse.

"The people of Easter Island were now beginning to have enough of these foreign visitors. When Cook landed, astonishingly few people were to be seen, only a few hundred in all, and these were all under middle height and in a miserable state. They were cheerless and indifferent. Cook's companions thought that some misfortune must have befallen the island since the Spaniards' visit, that the inhabitants were dying off. But Cook himself suspected that the population had gone into hiding underground, for in particular there were remarkably few women to be seen, although patrols were sent all over the island. At several places the Englishmen found heaps of stones with narrow descents to what they thought might be underground caves, but every time they tried to investigate these, the natives refused to admit them. The English-

<hr>

[1] An English translation of old logbooks and original letters in connection with both Roggeveen's and Gonzáles' visits to Easter Island is contained in vol. XIII of the Hakluyt Society, Cambridge, England, 1908.

men, plagued with scurvy, left Easter Island in despair and disappointment, having obtained for themselves nothing but a supply of sweet potatoes, the only important product they saw. But even with these they were cheated, for the cunning natives had filled the baskets with stones, and only laid a few potatoes on the top.

"Only twelve years had passed since Cook's visit when the Frenchman La Pérouse paid a similar lightning visit in 1786. This time people appeared again all over Easter Island. As before, some had light hair, and nearly half were suddenly grown-up women. There were, moreover, swarms of children of all ages, as in any normal community. It really seemed as though they had been spawned up from the interior of the earth into the treeless moonlike landscape of the little island. And that was just what had happened.

"They came crawling up out of subterranean passages, and the Frenchmen obtained free admission into some of the narrow stone tunnels which the English had not been allowed to enter. They confirmed Cook's suspicion that the population had made themselves secret retreats in dark underground chambers. Here the aristocracy had sheltered itself from Captain Cook, and here the children and most of the women had been hidden even when the Dutch discovered the island. La Pérouse understood that it was because Cook and his men had behaved so peaceably that the population of the island now took courage and crept out into the light of day, a couple of thousand in all.

"Even if the greater part of the people were hiding under the earth while Cook was going about on the island, and even if they had hustled all their most important possessions down underground with them, at any rate they had not taken the huge stone figures with them. The statues stood at their posts as stubbornly as ever. Both Cook and La Pérouse were in agreement that these were relics from earlier times: they were in their eyes already very ancient monuments. Cook was not a little impressed by the degree of skill achieved by those unknown builders, who had once raised their colossi on the top ledge of terraced walls without any mechanical contrivances. However it had been done, Cook held it to be proof of intelligence and resourcefulness in a people who had lived on this desolate island in ancient times. For he was sure that the existing population had had nothing to do with it. They had not even attempted to maintain the foundations of the walls, which had long ago begun to fall into decay. Nor did all the statues stand upright in their original places; many had fallen prostrate on the ground at the foot of their own platforms, with every sign of deliberate destruction.

"Cook investigated a few of the great wall terraces on which the statues stood, and was vastly impressed at finding that they were composed of huge stone blocks, so precisely cut and polished that they fitted together without mortar or cement. Cook had never seen more perfect mason's work in any wall, even in the best buildings in England. Yet, he added, 'all this care, pains, and sagacity had not been able to preserve these curious structures from the ravages of all-devouring Time.'

"A Polynesian from Tahiti was on board Cook's ship, and he understood some of the dialect spoken by the population of Easter Island at that time. From the scraps of information thus obtained, the Englishmen got the impression that the statues were not regarded as ordinary images of the gods, but as monuments to earlier *arikis*, memorials of deceased persons of holy and royal birth. Parts of skeletons and bones showed that the platforms on which the statues stood had been regularly used as burial places by those who now lived in the island. It was obvious that they believed in a life after death, for on various occasions they made the clearest signs to explain that while the skeleton lay lifeless on earth, the person's real ego had disappeared up in the direction of the sky.

"An effort to influence the local culture of Easter Island was attempted for the first time when, in the few hours he lay off the coast, La Pérouse landed pigs, goats, and sheep, and sowed a quantity of seed. But all this was eaten up by the hungry natives before it had time to propagate, and the island remained unchanged.

"No one else visited lonely Easter Island till the beginning of the last century. Then our own race suddenly reappeared, and the natives assembled in crowds on the cliffs along the coast and no longer tried to crawl down into their shelters. This time it was the captain of an American schooner, paying a short visit to look for colonists for a proposed sealing station on Juan Fernández, the Robinson Crusoe island off the coast of Chile. After a fierce struggle he succeeded in kidnaping twelve men and ten women and put to sea with them. After three days' sailing he let his prisoners loose on deck. They immediately jumped overboard and began to swim across the sea in the direction of vanished Easter Island. The captain took no notice of them, but put the ship about and carried out a fresh raid on the island.

"The next ships which passed were unable to land men on the steep coast because they met an impenetrable wall of natives throwing stones. A Russian expedition at last succeeded in forcing a landing with the help of powder and shot, but a few hours later they also had to retreat and re-embark.

"Years passed. At last the natives' confidence slowly returned, and at intervals of many years some passing vessels made a brief call. There was gradually less and less stone throwing, and more and more women emerged into the daylight and charmed the visitors. But then there was disaster.

"One day a flotilla of seven Peruvian sailing ships anchored off the coast. A crowd of natives swam out and boarded the ships, where to their gratification they were allowed to inscribe a few flourishes at the foot of a sheet of paper. Thereby they had signed another legal document, but this time it was a contract to go as laborers to the guano islands off the coast of Peru. When, happy and unsuspecting, they wanted to go ashore again, they were bound and taken below.

"Then eight of the slave hunters rowed ashore with clothes and brightly colored presents and threw these down on the shore. Numbers of curious natives who had assembled on the rocks round the bay began slowly to come nearer to admire these tempting objects. When at last several hundred stood crowded together on the beach, the slave hunters attacked. The natives who were kneeling down and picking up the presents were seized and their hands tied behind them, while those who tried to escape over the cliffs or swim out to sea were fired at. Just as the last of the ship's boats was ready to put off, loaded to the gunwales with prisoners, one of the captains discovered two natives who had hidden in a cave.

When he could not persuade them to go with him, he shot them down.

"So it was that on Christmas Eve of 1862 Easter Island lay desolate and depopulated. All who were not lying dead on the rocks by the shore, or below decks out in the bay with their hands bound behind them, had crept down into their subterranean catacombs and rolled stones in front of the openings. An oppressive silence reigned on the treeless island; only the breakers murmured threateningly. The expressions of the giant gods remained unmoved, but from the ships there was cheering and shouting. The visitors did not weigh anchor till they had celebrated Christmas.

"The population of the World's Navel, having experienced white man's Christmas as well as Easter Day, was now to see a little more of the outside world. The ships sailed away with a thousand slaves, who were landed to dig guano on the islands off the coast of Peru. The bishop of Tahiti protested, and the authorities decided that the slaves should be taken back to their own island immediately. But about nine hundred had died of illness and unfamiliar living conditions before the ship was ready to fetch them, and of the hundred survivors who embarked eighty-five died on the voyage, so only fifteen returned to Easter Island alive. They brought with them smallpox, which spread like wildfire at once and made an end of almost the whole population, of even those who hid themselves down in the deepest and narrowest caves. Scarcity and misery prevailed till the population of the whole island fell to 111 in all, adults and children.

"In the meantime the first foreigner had settled on the island. This was a solitary missionary, who honestly did his best to alleviate the misery he found there, but the natives stole from him everything he possessed, even the trousers he was wearing. He got away in the first ship, but returned with several helpers and set up a little mission station. A few years after, when all the surviving islanders had consented to be baptized, a French adventurer arrived and set them against the missionaries. The natives drove out the missionaries and killed the Frenchman, and went on singing hymns on their own account. All other traces of the missionaries were obliterated.

"At the end of the last century the Europeans found that there was excellent grazing for thousands of sheep round the statues on Easter Island, and at last the island was annexed by Chile. Now there are a governor, a priest, and a doctor on the island, and no one lives in caves or reed huts. Civilization has displaced the old culture on Easter Island, just as it has done among inhabitants of all the other South Sea Islands, and the Eskimos and Indians.

"So we haven't come here to study the natives," I concluded. "We've come to dig. If the answers to the riddle of Easter Island exist today, they must be down in the earth."

"Has no one been here and dug before?" someone asked.

"No one thinks there is any earth to dig in. No trees grow on the island. If there was no woodland in old times either, not much earth can have been formed from withering grass alone."

In fact there had been only two archaeological expeditions to this strange island. The first was a British private expedition headed by Katherine Routledge. She came to Easter Island in 1914 in her own sailing yacht and surveyed and mapped everything she saw above ground. In the first instance wall terraces, old roads, and over four hundred gigantic stone statues which lay scattered about all over the island. She had her hands so full with this pioneering work that there was no time for any systematic excavation, apart from clearing up round some of the statues which had been partly covered by sand and gravel carried downhill by rain. Unfortunately all the scientific notes of the Routledge expedition were lost, but in a book on her voyage round the world she writes that the whole island teems with mystery and unsolved problems. Each day she had been filled with continually increasing wonder at the strange unsolved problems which lay behind it all. The shadows of the departed builders still possess the land, she says. One cannot escape from them. They are more active and real than the living population of the island, and reign supreme with their silent giant constructions as vassals. Impelled by motives unknown to us, this people had hacked their way with crude stone picks into the mountainsides and altered the shape of a whole extinct volcano, just to obtain raw material for the fulfillment of their fanatical desire to see gigantic sculptures in human shape erected round about, on all the bays and landing places.

"Everywhere is the wind of heaven; round and above all are boundless sea and sky, infinite space and a great silence. The dweller there is ever listening for he knows not what, feeling unconsciously that he is in the antechamber to something yet more vast which is just beyond his ken." [2] Such was Mrs. Routledge's view of Easter Island. She freely recognized the mystery, soberly presented her own facts, and left the solution to those who would come after.

Twenty years later a Franco-Belgian expedition was landed by a warship and picked up again by another. One of the archaeologists died on the voyage, and while the Frenchman Métraux collected oral information from the natives for a large-scale study of the island's ethnography, the Belgian Lavachery was more than fully occupied in examining thousands of rock carvings and other strange stone works which were to be seen everywhere on the treeless island. So no excavation was done this time either.

The Franco-Belgian expedition had, generally speaking, set itself other objectives on the island than the British, and the statues were not their main concern. But Métraux thought the mystery was exaggerated: ordinary natives from the islands farther west could have come here with the idea of making figures, and because there were no trees to carve they tackled the mountain rock.

Other research workers and numerous circumnavigators have landed on Easter Island both earlier and later; their vessels have waited for a few days, or most often a few hours, and meanwhile they have collected legends and wood carvings from the poor population, or live creatures and plants from its equally poor terrain. The little island east of the sun and west of the moon has been slowly stripped for the benefit of the world's museum cases and souvenir cabinets. Most of what could be taken away has been taken away. Only the giant heads stand on the slopes, with a stony, supercilious smile, and say how-do-you-do and good-by to the Lilliputians who

---

[2] Katherine Scoresby Routledge, *The Mystery of Easter Island: The Story of an Expedition* (London, 1919), pp. 133, 165, 391, etc.

come, stare, and go again as the centuries roll by. A veil of mystery has continued to lie about the island like a haze.

These were the main features of Easter Island's history.

"Isn't it possible that the natives themselves have any unreported legends?" the skipper asked quietly.

"Optimist," I said. "Tomorrow you're going to meet people who are as civilized as you and I. The first person who collected legends among them was an American, Paymaster Thomson, in 1886. At that time natives who had grown up before any white man had settled on the island were still living. They told him that their forefathers had come over the sea from the east in big ships by steering straight toward the sunset for sixty days. Originally two different races had lived together on the island, 'long-ears' and 'short-ears,' but the short-ears had slaughtered almost all the others in a war, and then they ruled on the island alone.

"What ancient legends there were you can read in books today," I added. "There isn't much left of the old South Seas."

"Least of all on Easter Island," Gonzalo put in. "A handful of white people live here now, and even a school and a small hospital have been built."

"Yes, the only benefit we can get from the inhabitants is the extra help we shall need for digging," I added. "And perhaps they can get us a few fresh vegetables."

"Maybe there are some vahines who can teach us a bit of hula," muttered one of the engineers, and there was a lively burst of laughter and approval from one of the ship's boats.

Then we suddenly heard a hoarse, unintelligible remark, and everyone looked round in astonishment. Who had said what? The mate flashed a light over the dark deck. No one was there. Everyone felt rather foolish, and the engineer tried a new joke about hula girls. But at the same moment we heard the voice again. Was it someone overboard? We ran to the rail and turned a light down toward the black water. Instead of water the light played straight into a knot of upturned, staring faces, the faces of the worst gang of pirates we had ever seen. They were standing close-packed in a little boat and gazing up at us.

"*Ia-o-rana.*" I tried the Polynesian greeting.

"*Ia-o-rana,*" they replied in chorus.

So they were Polynesians. But upon my soul they were a mixture of everything else as well.

We flung a ladder down to them, and one by one they came clambering up the ship's side and jumped on board. Most of them were strong, well-built fellows, but almost all were conspicuously ragged and tattered. The first man to appear in the light at the top of the ladder had a red cloth round his head and a bundle hanging between his teeth. He pushed his bare toes over the rail and scrambled on board wearing a torn undershirt and the remains of a rolled-up pair of trousers. Behind him came a big pockmarked, barelegged fellow in an old, green army overcoat, with a large wooden club and a bundle of carved sticks over his shoulder. He was followed closely by the goggle-eyed grinning head of a ghostlike wooden figure, which was maneuvered up the ladder by a native in a white sailor's cap. Once on deck, the ragged fellows shook hands with everyone they could get near, and produced bags and sacks full of curious things. The most bizarre wooden carvings began to circulate from hand to hand, and soon attracted more attention than their owners.

There was one particular weird figure with sloping shoulders which reappeared in all the men's wood carvings. It had a strikingly curved aquiline nose, a goatee beard, long hanging ear lobes, large deep-set eyes, and a face convulsed in a devilish grin. The spine and naked ribs stuck out, while the stomach was completely drawn in. The figure was always exactly the same, whether it was large or small. There were a few other curious wooden figures, notably one of a human body with wings and bird's head; there were elegant clubs and paddles adorned with staring masks; and there were moon-shaped breast ornaments decorated with mysterious hieroglyphs which no person now living could interpret. All the carvings were faultlessly executed, and so highly polished that they were like porcelain to the touch. There were also some copies, a good deal less successful, of the great stone statues, and a handsome feather crown with a dress belonging to it, also made of feathers, artistically bound together.

I had never seen such productiveness on any of the other Polynesian islands, whose inhabitants prefer to take life very easy. Here, indeed, we had been received by a whole team of admirable wood carvers. It looked, moreover, to an uninitiated person as if these fellows with their bizarre works of art must be possessed of untamable fantasy and joy in creation. But on closer inspection one quickly perceived that the same curious shapes reappeared all the time, quite unchanged. There was no variation whatsoever from certain predetermined patterns.

I had just studied Dr. Mostny's collection of modern popular art from Easter Island in the National Museum in Chile, and when the natives began to produce their wooden figures, they were most astonished at my recognizing all the different types by name. In reality they were all perfect copies of carvings which the earliest Europeans found among the natives on Easter Island, and which now exist only in museums. The originals are today immensely valuable, but as they are no longer on the market, the natives see that the trade is kept going with good copies.

The wood carvers pointed with apologetic smiles to their ragged trousers and bare legs, they wanted to barter their goods for clothes and shoes. In a few seconds business was in full swing all over the deck. The crew, impelled both by acquisitiveness and charity, plunged down into their cabins and came up again with all they could spare in the way of clothing. Little Anette suddenly appeared in pyjamas. She stood in the middle of the throng and tugged, quite enthralled, at the leg of a grotesque bird-man which one of the ragged natives held under his arm, and when he saw that she liked the figure, he gave it to her at once. Yvonne hurried off to fetch a parcel for him.

The photographer came up and nudged my arm. "There's a fellow standing over there holding something queer under his shirt. He says it's very, very old—goes back to his great-great-grandfather," he whispered.

I smiled, but accompanied him to a thin, pleasant-mannered man who looked more than anything like a pale Arab with a Hitler mustache.

"Buenos días, Señor," he said, showing off his Spanish, and with an air of mystery drew from his breast a little flat stone with a bird-man obviously quite freshly cut on one side.

Before he had time to mention his great-great-grandfather

again, I said enthusiastically: "No! Did you really do that yourself?"

For a second he was taken aback, and his face contorted in a struggle between a smile and confusion. Then he blushed proudly and looked at his masterpiece as if he thought that, after all, it would be a great pity to give anyone else the credit for it.

"Yes," he said proudly, and was now visibly basking in the consciousness of his own talent. He had no need for regrets, for the photographer liked the stone and took it.

Another boat had suddenly come alongside, and I was told that a white man was on his way up the ladder. It was a smart young naval officer, who presented himself as the governor's assistant. He had come to welcome us. We invited him into the lounge for a drink and explained why we had anchored here. He told us that in any case the weather would have made it impossible to anchor off the village at the moment, but he proposed that we move next morning under the lee of another cape, which was nearer the inhabited area, and then they would try to help us ashore over the rocks.

We were told that it was just six months since the last ship had called; she had been, as might be expected, a Chilean man-of-war. The year before they had had a visit from a big luxury liner. The governor had been asked whether there was an elevator in the hotel and if there was transportation from the landing stage, and when he replied that there was no hotel and no landing stage, the passengers were refused permission to go ashore. Instead, some of the natives were allowed to go on board and sell souvenirs and do a hula dance on deck. And then the ship went on to see more of the Pacific.

"Well, we're going ashore if we have to swim for it," we laughed, without a suspicion of how nearly true this was going to be.

On the way to the ladder the naval officer suggested that we keep one of the natives on board to act as a local guide when we made the trip round next morning. "They steal like magpies," he added. "It might be best for you to keep the mayor. Have you been introduced to him?"

I had not. The mayor was fetched by his proud subordinates, and they led up to me no other than the thin man with

27

the stone. His shirt was now crammed full of the photographer's barter goods.

"There's no chief any longer, but this is the mayor of Easter Island," the naval officer said, clapping the man with the mustache genially on the shoulder. "And he's the best wood carver on the island as well."

"Si, Señor," said the mayor, blushing and laughing and so proud that he did not know whether to look up or down, while his friends crowded round so as not to be deprived of their share of the honor of having a mayor of their own, elected by themselves. Many of the fellows looked extremely alert, and there were several robust leader types among them.

"Si, Señor," the slightly built man repeated, and drew himself up so that one leg of the photographer's old trousers stuck out the front of his shirt. "I've been mayor for twenty-eight years. They elect me again every time."

Queer that they elect such a fool, I thought. There appeared to be better material to choose from.

The naval officer had to use his full authority to get the men to leave the ship with him; only the mayor remained. Little did I suspect that he was to play the chief part in the strangest adventure I had ever had.

Early next morning I was awakened by the rattling of anchor chains. I jumped into my trousers and went out on deck. The sun was already beginning to play over the island, which looked green and yellow and friendly now that its night silhouette had been obliterated and the colors wakened to life again by the morning sun. The unchangeable statues stood far away on the slope. But no one was lighting a fire, no one was worshiping the marvelous sunrise, no one was to be seen at all. The island lay there as lifeless as if we had been taken for a slave ship and everyone had gone underground.

"*Buenos días*, Señor."

There stood the everlasting mayor again, raising his hat. One of our hats. For he had been bareheaded when he came on board the night before.

"*Buenos días*, Mayor. There's not much life to be seen ashore.

"No," he said. "This isn't our country any longer, we live in

28

the village on the other side. This is only for the Navy's sheep. Look there—" and he pointed to a round-backed down on which I now saw clearly a multitude of sheep, looking like a gray carpet.

The ship was moving all the time and the bay where we had anchored was lost to sight behind a bluff. I had asked the captain to steer round the north coast to get a general impression of most of the island before landing. We were gliding along a perpendicular cliff where foaming breakers had eaten their way into the volcanic formation till the coast was sheer and immensely high. There were gleams of reddish-brown and yellowish-gray as in the layers of a cut cake, and high up on the crest over our heads we could see green grass and ancient walls which seemed on the verge of tumbling down the precipice. Mile followed mile of inaccessible cliffs, till the surface of the island changed shape and rolled its stone-strewn fields down toward the sea from round grassy hummocks and hillocks in the interior. The green never came right down to the surf, for there a tumbled barrier of black lava blocks lay like a protecting wall all round the island. Only at one place did the landscape really open up, and there the island smiled at us, revealing a broad sunlit beach. The whole effect was wonderfully beautiful and inviting.

"Anakena." The mayor inclined his head reverently. "Here at Anakena the kings lived in old times. It was on this beach, too, that our first ancestor Hotu Matua landed."

"Who lives there now?"

"Nobody. The shepherds have a hut there."

I called to the skipper and pointed, and he agreed that this was an excellent camping ground.

As the ship slid by, a barren headland closed the view to the bay. Again the same savage lava coast with precipices and loose blocks continued right round the island till, at the western end, the land at last ran down in a gentle slope toward the sea. Here lay all the houses of the village of Hangaroa. Little white-painted houses set in well-kept gardens, sometimes surrounded by solitary palms and scattered trees, and on the ridges there were even some fields planted with eucalyptus. A fence ran right around the village: the rest of the island was the Navy's sheep farm.

"That's my home," said the mayor, glowing with pride. And it was pretty. The mayor could quite justly note that we were all standing and staring landward in enchantment; even Anette sat motionless in Yvonne's arms, gazing as though hypnotized at the little doll's village under the great blue sky. The whole place suddenly began to move: everywhere people were running, or galloping on horseback, all in one direction, the same as ours.

"Did you ever see such a place?" cried Thor Junior. "It's like the theater."

The captain had hoisted all our colors, and the whole ship was bright with a rainbow of bunting as even the code of signals, from cholera to mail, rippled in the breeze. We saluted both by siren and ensign, and someone replied by running up a Chilean flag on a solitary mast on shore.

The mayor dried his eyes with his shirt sleeve.

"Señor," he said. "This is Hotu Matua's country. This is my country. I have been mayor here for twenty-eight years. What would Easter Island have been without me? Nothing. Easter Island, that's me. I am Easter Island." It came with violent emphasis as he struck his chest.

I thought I saw a Hitler behind the little mustache, but no, I was wrong. This fool was infinitely nicer. He was contented with what he had, absolutely contented. He did not even want to take back the land from the sheep on the other side of the fence.

"Señor." More rhetoric followed. "We two are the only famous people on this island. Everyone knows me. Who knows the governor? People have come all the way from Germany to take blood samples from my ear, and letters have come from Glasgow and Austria ordering wood carvings from the mayor of Easter Island. The world knows me. Señor, give me your hand as a friend!"

When I had done this, he asked politely if he might call me Señor Kon-Tiki.

We rounded a fresh cape with unusually high and precipitous sides, and the village disappeared behind a chaos of perpendicular crags and wild little islands of lava which lay like ruined castles and black awls at the foot of the ferocious cliff. There were foaming breakers now, and the ship was rolling where currents met in a race, with a fierce backwash from the rocks. The mayor became seasick and tottered to a deck chair, but he managed to mutter something about its being right there that the bird-men had been active. He pointed to the grotesque wooden figure which Anette had laid in a doll's bed.

Once past the unquiet cape we came to a kind of open bay where the cliffs no longer reached to the sky, although the coast was both high and precipitous. The riders and the crowd of people on foot had taken a short cut across the cape farther inland, and the green slope above the drop to the sea was packed with horses and people. It looked as if some of the swarm had spilled onto a narrow sloping promontory descending like a dragon's crest to some black lava rocks in the foaming breakers, and there they were launching a boat. Another boat was on its way out to fetch us, dancing in the seas. Our captain went as far in as he could and anchored the ship. The mayor was very busy.

"In our own dialect 'Good day everyone' is *Ia-o-rana korua*," he whispered to me. "Call it out when you get ashore, and they'll like you."

It was a rough trip in through the foaming seas, and I had picked only a few men to go along. A frothing crest lifted us up and hurled us in round a huge lava block; here the native coxswain made a masterly turn and got us more or less into shelter before the next cascade came rushing on. There was no harbor, no breakwater, only nature's wild fantasy. Behind the first sheltering blocks projecting like a jetty into the sea stood a long and narrow file of natives up the sloping edge of the ridge of lava which descended from the plateau as a kind of natural stair. They were all standing motionless, staring.

"*Ia-o-rana korua*," I shouted at the top of my voice as we swung into their world.

"*Ia-o-rana korua*," came an avalanche of voices from all the way up the height, and all of a sudden everybody began to move to help us ashore. They were a mixed assembly to greet: it looked as if most of the island's nine hundred inhabitants were there. They were Polynesians, but of very mixed blood, and they had all come in some combination of garments which had a mainland origin. I had hardly got out of the dancing boat when a bent old woman with a kerchief on her head caught hold of me.

"A secret, Señor," she whispered hoarsely and produced a basket of sweet potatoes. She pushed a large potato aside and eyed temptingly the corner of a cloth which lay just under it.

"Thanks for letting me see it," I said and went on. I had not seen anything, but no great secret was likely to be disclosed when the whole cliffside was packed with staring people. Many of the men on the ledges of the cliff had wooden figures and bags, but no one tried to show anything. One by one they muttered *ia-o-rana, ia-o-rana,* as we clambered past them.

The crest above us was black with waiting natives, and in the midst of them stood a solitary white-robed form, his gown fluttering in the wind. I guessed at once who he was: Father Sebastian Englert, the most powerful man in the whole island. He had written a book on Easter Island, and I had heard him spoken of in Chile as the uncrowned king of the island. If one made friends with him, all doors were opened. But woe to the man he did not like, someone had said to me.

Now he stood before me, broad and straight-backed, with legs apart, in a long white robe with a cord round the waist and big, brightly polished boots. He was like an apostle or prophet in his white gown with the hood thrown back, his bare head and flowing beard against an incredibly blue sky.

I looked into a ruddy face with shrewd wrinkles and searching eyes, and held out my hand.

"Welcome to my island," were his first words.

I noticed the possessive adjective.

"Yes, I always say *my* island," he added, smiling all over his face, "for I reckon it as mine and would not sell it for millions."

I understood that, and said we were prepared to place ourselves under his command.

He laughed.

"Do you like natives?" he suddenly asked, and looked at me steadily.

"The more genuine they are, the better," I replied.

His face grew sunny.

"Then we shall be good friends."

I introduced Gonzalo, the captain, the doctor, and one or

two others who had come ashore with me, and then we sauntered off to a jeep which was standing out in the open, among lumps of lava and grazing riding horses. We bumped off across country on a zigzag course till we came to some ruts farther inland, which led us down to the village. We turned off inside the fence and at last stopped before the governor's solitary bungalow.

A wiry little man in a khaki uniform came out and received us cordially, and all formalities were quickly and easily disposed of in his office. Now we sat before the two chief people of the island: the old sage Father Sebastian and the young commandant Arnaldo Curti, the military governor. The first had been there for twenty years and would remain there till the end of his days, the other had come on the last warship to run the island for two years for the Chilean government. Which held the reins—experience or power? We soon learned that they formed an indivisible whole; they put their heads together daily and solved the queerest problems, which can only arise in a most unusual community on the world's loneliest island.

When the captain had submitted the list of the ship's company, and the doctor a certificate of good health, there were no more formalities.

"Good luck with the digging," the governor said, and shook my hand. "We only impose on you two restrictions: you must not give the natives arms or alcohol."

That was fair enough.

"One thing more," he said, scratching his neck. "You're by no means an unknown person among the natives, and you've created something of a real problem for us here on the island."

The priest smiled and stroked his beard.

"Well, at least your ship can take over the guard duties now," he said, laughing.

We did not understand but were given an explanation. When the news reached Easter Island that the *Kon-Tiki* raft had passed far to the north of them and had come to land safely in the South Sea Islands, the natives had been interested. Since their forefathers had been able to survive such adventures, why should they themselves do any worse? There was no timber for a raft on the almost treeless island, but some fellows knocked together a little open plank boat and went far out to sea to fish. The current took them, and Easter Island fell from view. They drifted involuntarily westward just as the *Kon-Tiki* had done, and landed five weeks later, starving and worn-out, on Reao, an atoll in the Tuamotu group, whence they made their way to Tahiti.

This whetted appetites. Some other men also built an open boat and were planning to go to sea, allegedly to fish. The governor had found the boat full of water cans, and he smelled a rat. It was dangerous to let them go in such a craft, and he ordered the boat hauled up on shore. When the natives tried to get away to sea in spite of this, he was obliged to set another native as armed guard over the boat. The result was that one more man took part in the voyage: the guard put out to sea with the others in the dead of night. This boat drifted still farther west than the first, and the natives on board did not see land till they jumped ashore in the best of spirits at Atiu, a long way beyond Tahiti.

Now a regular travel fever had set in on Easter Island. Two crews had built boats, and these were ready far inland. The whole village knew of the intention, and although there were only a handful of white men on the island, the governor was obliged to keep one of them on guard day and night.

"If I can tell them that now we can fetch them back with your ship if they start, I'll be free of all this watch-keeping," said the governor.

I gave him my promise.

"We need guards at other places instead," he said. "The natives steal anything up to two thousand sheep in a year from the other side of the fence. We have a sort of prison for the worst thieves, but it doesn't help much, for the prisoners have to go home for all meals. If we began to serve food in the prison, they'd all think of some crime just to be put there and fed for nothing.

"They're grand fellows in other ways," he continued, and Father Sebastian nodded. "If only one understands them. There's never any serious disturbance or fighting. Stealing has always been their worst quality, but one must remember that they give away just as readily as they steal. Property is a thing which passes through their hands very easily; it doesn't mean so much as it does with us."

Father Sebastian promised to pick out some good fellows as extra diggers. He would figure out a suitable rate of pay and daily rations. Our selection of barter goods had a very high exchange value compared to all kinds of gold and notes, for there was no shop or moviehouse on the island, not even a barber's.

We agreed that Anakena Bay on the other side of the island was the best place for the main camp of the expedition. There were many reasons for this: it was the prettiest place on all the coast; it had the only decent sandy beach on the island, where we could land all the gear by raft; and it was as far as possible from the village, with the minimum risk of thieving and other incidents. Moreover, it was the Valley of Kings, famous in story, where the legendary Hotu Matua had first landed. We could not desire much more.

After a splendid meal in the governor's bungalow, we returned to the ship. There were still swarms of natives on the cliff, and to Father Sebastian's great pleasure all who wished to have a look round on board were allowed to do so. I thought they appeared better turned-out today, clean, and above all not so ragged as when they first came on board. I mentioned this casually to the mayor, who had been home and put on a whole shirt. He gave me a crafty smile.

"That's an old trick of ours," he confessed, giggling. "If we put on old rags, we are much better paid for the wood carvings."

The sea was so rough that not many came out to the ship, and we promised to repeat the invitation another time. Just as we were about to send the last visitors back to the shore, the skipper came hurrying up with the visitors' book.

"We must have the names of the people who have been on board," he proposed, smiling. He gave the book to one of those who looked the brightest, and asked him to get them all to write their names. The fellow took the book and pen and wandered off to the others with a thoughtful look on his face. They put their heads together as though in profound reflection and muttered rapidly to each other. Then he returned gravely with the book, without one signature in it.

"Isn't there anyone who can write his name?" the skipper asked.

"Yes, many," the man said, "but they won't."

Gonzalo heard what was said. He took the book and went up to the crowd, explaining that since he was a Chilean they might understand his Spanish better. But when he tried to make the request, there was loud grumbling, and at last it seemed to be blowing up for a regular brawl—one of the men wanted to throw the visitors' book overboard. I had to exercise all my authority to get Gonzalo out of the crowd, and he came back with the book, untidy and disheveled.

"It's quite incredible," he said, "but they refuse to sign. They declare that was how their ancestors were tricked into going to be slaves in Peru!"

"It isn't possible that they can still have traditions about that," someone said.

But when we began to figure back, we realized that it was these people's grandfathers who had experienced the slave raid, and the fathers of some of them might already have been born at the time.

The visitors' book was hurriedly removed, and I explained to the islanders that they must go ashore now, for we were going to sail. No one went, and blowing the siren and starting the engine, with as much shrieking and general racket as the engineers could produce, was quite ineffective. Finally I had to accompany several of them to the ladder to make them clamber down into the two native boats which were waiting. When I ordered the others to be rounded up, I saw that one boat was rowing off, towing the other, which had suddenly become full of water. I shouted to them and asked them to take the others who were on board too, and they replied that they would come back as soon as they had been ashore and got rid of the passengers and the water.

Time passed, but no one came back for all our siren-blowing. We had to shift our anchorage before darkness fell, and we did not know these waters well enough to land people between the lava blocks in our own boat. Finally we weighed anchor and left with all our new passengers on board. They all took it quite naturally. When our own supper was ready, the cook served food to our sixteen new passengers, who made a hearty meal and then rushed to the rail overcome with sea-sickness, for the ship had begun to roll.

We anchored under the lee of the same cliff as the night before, but not even here did we get rid of our passengers. Night fell and it began to rain a little. We should be thoroughly robbed in the night, I thought, if we let that gang of pirates into the cabins. Accordingly I gave them the choice of sleeping on the hatch on deck, or paddling themselves ashore in the ship's aluminum raft, in two batches. They chose the raft, and we launched it. But then suddenly they all insisted on going in the second group, and at last we had to give up the idea of getting rid of them. Happy and well-fed, they now produced a guitar and began to do a hula dance on the foredeck. This turned out to be a good move. The crew had not been ashore or seen a show for a long time, and they were all enlivened by the music. Now that we had natives on board whether we liked it or not, why not make the best of it? Song and exciting string music, with rhythmical hand-clapping, filled the whole ship, and in the surrounding darkness the ship's lantern had the effect of footlights on the festive scene.

"*He tere te vaka o Hotu Matua. . . .*" The broad humor of our carefree pirates was so infectious that scientists and sea-men alike had no choice but to surrender and join in the dance, singing as best they could.

Then the mayor suddenly appeared out of the darkness, wet and cold. He sat in a little boat with three other natives. After some discussion we quickly agreed that his party of four should come aboard to spend the night on condition that they rowed the sixteen others ashore. To make everyone happy I said that the two parties could remain and play for another hour. The mayor agreed delightedly. On board he asked immediately if his party also could not have a meal such as the others had had.

"Yes," I said diplomatically, "but not till you've taken the other sixteen ashore."

He sauntered cheerfully up to the musicians and clapped in time for half a minute. Then he came hurrying back and said that the others must absolutely go ashore at once. Otherwise they would get wet and cold on the way home.

All my pleading for them was of no avail, and the fact that

the hour had just begun made no difference; he began to shout to stop the music. So I altered my tactics.

"For that matter you can quite well have a meal now," I said.

The mayor rushed straight into the cook's galley without giving the musicians a further thought. He just stuck his head out, with his mouth full of food, to see if the three others were following him.

But he kept his word, and when the hour was over the native boat, full of laughter and music, was tossing about on her way toward the dark coast. It had been a successful party.

"Ohoi! He tere te vaka o Hotu Matua. . . ."

So it happened that we arrived at the Valley of the Kings early next morning, with the mayor of the World's Navel asleep on the lounge table.

CHAPTER THREE

In Volcanic Gas Tunnels

THERE WAS not a soul in the Anakena Valley when our first patrol went round on the plain in from the beach looking for the best place to put up the tents. But as we walked a single rider appeared over the ridge, and a native shepherd jumped off his horse and came up to greet us. He said he had a little whitewashed stone cottage on the western side of the valley and was responsible for the sheep in that part of the island. When we told him we had come to live in the Anakena Valley, he immediately pointed to a little gully with several good-sized caves in it. He told us that they were Hotu Matua's caves. The first king and all his companions had lived there when they landed on the shore. Afterward they had built large huts of fresh-water reeds. He spoke of Hotu Matua as naturally as an Englishman would speak of Queen Victoria. It was unthinkable to him that there were people who did not know about Hotu Matua: he was the alpha and omega in the conceptions of Easter Island, a sort of hybrid between the Adam of religion and the Columbus of history.

When I told him that we had no need to live in caves because we had with us ready-made huts of watertight cloth, he at once pointed in the opposite direction.

"If you've got canvas, you can sleep just across the beach on Hotu Matua's old site," he said.

He accompanied us over the plain to a flat area at the foot

of a little dome-shaped hill. Everywhere were traces of vanished greatness. Inland from the center of the beach, and on each side, were three templelike terraces built of colossal blocks of stone, facing the sea. They lay just above the sandy beach and would have had the appearance of fortresses protecting the plain against attack from the sea if several large yellowish-gray human forms in stone had not lain prostrate on the flat area behind them, showing that the terraces had served as a foundation for the statues. All these colossi had fallen face downward and with the tops of their heads pointing inland, which indicated that before they fell, they must have stood with their backs toward the sea, looking inward across an open temple square. By the central terrace a whole row of fallen giants lay side by side, and huge cylinders of rust-red stone which once had been balanced on the tops of their heads had tumbled off and lay on the plain.

The lofty and imposing terrace in the easternmost corner of the bay had had only a single statue, but lying where it did, with its face buried in the earth, this appeared broader-backed and bulkier than its slender relatives on the next terrace. It was next to this broad giant that King Hotu Matua himself had lived. The shepherd pointed reverently to the solid foundation wall of the king's old house still visible on the ground, and just behind it was a curious five-sided stone oven which indicated the king's own kitchen. Here, of course, we should dig, so we marked out the campsite close by, on the flat temple square in front of the fallen giant's head.

The shepherd looked on with great interest and kept repeating that this was the king's old site, till he was sure that we all completely understood where we were. He got a pack of cigarettes for his help and rode on well pleased.

Soon after this we began to land the equipment. On a tiny raft of aluminum pontoons we first rowed about in the bay with a couple of the natives who had stayed on our ship the night before, to study the rocks and breakers. The beach near the middle of the bay had no stones and the surf was slight, so we landed the photographer with all his camera outfit. Then we went out again toward the landing boat, which was waiting halfway between the ship and ourselves. When we were well under way, we saw a great roller toss the ship's boat

40

high in the air as she made off seaward with her engine at full speed to avoid the clutches of a still bigger sea which was just rising. We rowed after her as hard as we could and weathered the first sea, but the second came rolling toward us ever higher and steeper, and in a moment we were flung up against a perpendicular wall of water and felt the raft whirling round bottom uppermost. I got a nasty bump on the head, but dived to the bottom as quickly as I could to avoid another blow from the pontoons. I kept my eyes shut to keep out the whirling sand and swam as far and as deep as I could before I had to come up for air. By that time the others were already clambering up onto the bottom of the capsized raft, and the seas were as normal as before.

This was a valuable lesson to have had before we began to land indispensable equipment. Even if big seas were rare, we had always to be on the watch for unexpectedly big breakers which now and then came rolling in through Anakena Bay when we least wished it. To avoid them we anchored our largest life raft out in the bay, like a kind of floating pier, well outside the danger zone of the breakers. The landing boat could safely go in as far as this pier with equipment from the ship, and here everything was transferred to the tiny pontoon raft, which could ride with the breakers right onto the beach so long as none of the worst seas were in sight.

The whole transport of personnel and equipment between ship and shore was effected in this manner; the landing boat was directed by blasts of the siren from the ship and flag signals from the shore. On the last lap through the surf there was always cursing and laughter and wet trousers. It was often so rough that the cook and the steward had to swim ashore with their newly baked bread in watertight rubber bags. But if the water was slightly cold, the sandy beach ashore was warm and pleasant, and we were all of us happy in the sun-steeped Valley of the Kings.

Soon one green tent sprang up beside another, and formed a peaceful little village in the temple square between the old fallen giant and the house in which Hotu Matua's dynasty had begun. Our four native friends, who had been helping with the landing of the equipment, were vastly impressed when they came up behind the great wall and saw where we had pitched our tents. The mayor drew a deep breath and said solemnly:

"Señor, Hotu Matua built his first house right there. See, there is the foundation wall and there the kitchen."

Although this was repeated by the natives over and over again, no one seemed to object to our choice of a site. Before night fell the four natives caught some unsaddled horses, and then they thanked us and rode off in the direction of the village.

I was long in getting to sleep that night. I lay gazing at the moonlight on the thin green tent cloth over my head and listening to the surf on the beach where Hotu Matua had landed. I wondered what sort of a craft he had had, what language he had spoken.

What did this valley look like when he came? Were there woods here then, as on all the other South Sea Islands? Was it perhaps Hotu Matua's descendants who had cut the timber and burned the logs, and finally destroyed all the woodland till there was not a single tree to give shade over all the rolling downs? I was a little uneasy when I thought of this complete lack of trees and shrubs on all the plains and hills. Perhaps, after all, it was true that it was useless to dig in the earth of Easter Island. Perhaps it had always looked as it did today, since there were no plants to rot and make the soil rise year by year into strata. But for the sand dunes on the shore and the sheep's dung among the stones, it looked as if the ground, dry and grudging, had lain there unchanged from Hotu Matua's day.

In fact, since Hotu Matua's own foundation wall lay visible above ground and was pointed out as a regular tourist attraction, the soil was obviously meager, and the chances of new discoveries equally so. Louder thunder peals came from some of the breakers on the shore, and I rubbed the bump on my head. Now that we had managed to get here, we would certainly not give up without at least attempting to dig before going on to the other islands on our program.

During our first days ashore the archaeologists went out on reconnaissance tours to the east and west, while the rest of us brought the equipment ashore and organized the details of the expedition's operations. There was not a brook on the whole island, but down in the craters of three of the old volcanoes there were marshes and partially open water, full of reeds. We should have to carry both wood and drinking water four miles from Vaitea, the sheep farm up on the high ground in the middle of the island. Here a little eucalyptus grove had been planted by Europeans in our own century, and here there was drinking water in a pipe from the volcano Rano Aroi. When the first Europeans reached the island they found the land as barren as we know it today, except for some clusters of trees at the bottom of the deepest crater, Rano Kao. Apart from driftwood and modern importation, these original *toro miro* trees at the bottom of the crater have supplied wood-carving material for the Easter Islanders until the present day.

One calm day, when the Greenland trawler had gone round to the anchorage in Hangaroa Bay, the governor lent us a stout homemade lighter which the natives rowed out to the ship, and we succeeded in getting the expedition's jeep brought into the village. With this transportation our wood and water supplies were secured.

There were traces of ancient roads on Easter Island, and the manager of the sheep farm had increased the network of roads by having the worst of the stones moved away so that one could bump along in a jeep right across the island, which is about ten miles long. Father Sebastian and the governor helped us obtain plenty of horses and homemade wooden saddles. Even the poorest natives had at least one riding horse each on this island: nobody went on foot because fragments of lava lay strewn all over the ground like great lumps of reddish-brown and black coke, often so close that only a horse's hoofs could find room between them. Easter Island children learn to ride as soon as they can walk, and we often saw the tiniest of tots galloping over the stony fields bareback, three at a time, each clinging to the next and the one in front holding tight to the horse's mane.

Along the coast there were a number of wells of great antiquity, dug in masterly fashion and lined with cut stone. The original population had accustomed themselves to drinking brackish water, which they obtained by intercepting a few subterranean streams which they had detected as they came out into the sea below the ocean surface. Windmills had now been erected over these ancient stone-lined wells. They pumped the brackish water up to the sheep, and here we watered the horses and fetched a supply to the camp for washing.

Meanwhile the boatswain, who was also the carpenter, made shelves and tables for the big mess tent, where walls of mosquito netting enabled us to eat and work undisturbed by dense swarms of flies, imported long since, which whirled round us.

"We'll have to let down the tent wall on the side the wind comes from," said Yvonne. "There's dust coming in through the mosquito net."

"Dust here on the island?"

"Yes, look here," she said, and made a distinct streak along the bookshelf with her forefinger.

I looked on with great satisfaction. In a hundred years or so there would be a pretty thick layer to brush away. Perhaps it would be worth while to dig on Easter Island after all! Just because there was no woodland, wind and weather probably got a firmer grip on the hills and sent a shower of fine dry earth over the lowlands like a fall of snow. No doubt most of it drifted into the sea, but some of it, perhaps, up onto the grass slopes.

The archaeologists came back from their reconnaissance tours with interesting reports. They had seen old walls which they wished to examine later, because there were indications that possibly two different civilizations had built on the island before the Europeans came. That they might get to know local conditions better, it was decided that they should first undertake some minor excavations near the camp at Anakena before setting about their main tasks.

The first choice was Hotu Matua's five-sided kitchen oven and the boat-shaped foundation wall just beside it. Excavation of this kind is done not with pickax and spade, but with a little mason's trowel whereby one scrapes down into the ground, a fraction of an inch at a time, so as not to injure what is found. The earth which is scraped away is shaken through fine-meshed netting so that anything of interest is left lying on the top of the sieve. The depth beneath the turf is noted exactly, for, of course, the deeper one gets the older the findings are.

Just beneath the turf lay a fragment of an old stone bowl, spearheads, and other sharp implements of black volcanic glass. And as the archaeologists scraped their way down, they found bits of fishhooks made both of human bone and of prettily polished stone. When they had got a foot down into the earth beside Hotu Matua's oven, the trowel scraped against some stones, and as soon as they had cleared the earth away, they saw that it was another five-sided oven, of exactly the same type as that which lay above ground. If the uppermost one was constructed by Hotu Matua, the traditional discoverer of the island, who had been here before and cooked his food in just the same way? The natives did not understand at all. They themselves and all visitors had accepted the ruins above ground as Hotu Matua's, for this was quite certainly the place where he had lived.

We scraped our way farther down and found many fragments of fishhooks, shell, bone splinters, charcoal, and human teeth, till we were far down in the earth beneath the lower oven. We must be far back in antiquity now. Then Bill dug up a pretty blue Venetian pearl, and recognized it as a type Europeans had used in dealing with the Indians two hundred years ago. So we had not got so deep as to be beyond the scope of the first European visits. The earliest date at which the pearl could have been brought to Easter Island was that of its discoverer Roggeveen; we had, therefore, not yet dug farther down than the year 1722.

We looked up Roggeveen's log on the discovery of Easter Island, and found that the first native who boarded his ship had been presented with two strings of blue pearls, a small mirror, and a pair of scissors. Nothing was more natural than that some of these pearls should have found their way to the king's house at Anakena. We dug a little way further down, and then we came upon mere rubble without a sign of human activity.

One thing was certain now: there had been a soil or sand deposit over the years on treeless Easter Island. It would be worth while to dig. We should have to enlist native labor, for one or two of the projects we had in mind required more men than we ourselves could muster.

We had seen very little of the natives in these few days. To avoid thieving and intrigue, Father Sebastian had expressly asked us to keep the camp closed to natives who had no special duties. It was no use trying to prevent our men from becoming acquainted with the merry vahines of the island, and that he fully realized. But if the boys wanted to amuse themselves, they would have to ride over to the village. Otherwise the whole village would soon move over to us. We agreed to this arrangement, and strung a rope all round the camp as a kind of symbolic frontier of the "taboo" area. It was on the whole surprisingly effective. Of course, no one but a handful of shepherds really had any occasion to roam about on this side of the island, for the natives were restricted by the fence on their side, to keep them from stealing sheep. But such limitation of movement was not easy to enforce on a small island.

One of the first nights two water cans were stolen from the camp area, and the tin rope which marked off our "taboo" ground was cut and carried away. Father Sebastian thought it was stolen as gear for one of the small rafts which were preparing to put to sea. The governor then sent Kasimiro and Nicholas to patrol the area. They were the village's two native policemen.

Old Kasimiro was as tall and thin as Nicholas was fat and round; he had, moreover, a striking resemblance to the shambling, round-shouldered, weird figure in the Easter Island collection of wood carvings. If the figure had not already been known in Captain Cook's time, Kasimiro might have been suspected of having sat for it. Kasimiro had a big leather holster at his side, containing an old-fashioned revolver, and if he caught sight of any of his countrymen, irrespective of sex or age, he howled and yelled and brandished his revolver till they disappeared in a cloud of dust. Then he came back, stooping and swaying, and sat down on the "taboo" ground in the shelter of the tent.

We liked old Kasimiro. He seemed a little weak in the head, but was extremely good-natured and modest. Nicholas was a pleasant fellow too, but no one seemed to feel sorry for him.

The daintiest leftovers from the cookhouse always went first to the skinny old man, who ate as he had never done in all his life. He loafed about in the shade of the tent with his trouser pockets full of valuables in the shape of our cigarettes, twirling his big revolver. Kasimiro was in seventh heaven.

One day he thought he must do something in return for all our hospitality. He came to my tent and confided in a low voice that there was a cave with "important things" in it out on the bird-men's island. He had been there when quite a small boy with his father and a few other children. His father had told the children to wait while he went behind a rock where he crawled into a secret cave. Kasimiro had never seen the opening, which was blocked by stones, but if I would take him out there in our boat, without anyone in the village knowing about it, he would point out the spot where he himself had stood waiting, and if I found the cave, we would share the treasure. The old man's eyes shone.

I did not take this too seriously. Both the Routledge expedition and Father Sebastian had received similar offers. When they had gained the natives' confidence, there was always someone who knew of a region in which there was a secret, sealed-up cave. In caves such as these their ancestors had hidden ancient tablets of wood marked with hieroglyphics, *rongo-rongo* in the island language. These *rongo-rongo* tablets were worth a real fortune, for there were only a score of them in all the world's museums put together. The natives knew that quite well, and whenever someone agreed to take a party to such a secret *rongo-rongo* cave, the only result was a lot of futile searching. It was always impossible to find the concealed entrance. A pity, they said, now the opening was gone, covered up by a landslide.

Our first Sunday came.

Father Sebastian had hinted that we should be welcome at the church if we would like to hear the natives sing. I called all the men together, scientist and sailor alike, and explained that church was something very special down here in the South Seas. It was not merely the sole stable element in the natives' world, a center where they found a longed-for replacement for their old belief in Tiki and Make-Make; it was also the only social meeting place where the whole population came together in their best clothes, because there was usually no assembly hall, theater, or market place. On some of the islands the natives were Protestants, on others Catholics or Mormons; it all depended on what missionary had come to the place first and built a church. The natives often became fanatics for their church: if one stayed away on Sunday, one could stay away for the rest of the week too. And if visitors did not attend, it was interpreted as a demonstration, an attack from a hostile quarter. It was easy for an uninformed person to put his foot in it.

"I'm an atheist and never go to church," said one of our men. "But if you think it has any importance, I'll come with pleasure."

So off we went in a crowd, atheists, Protestants, and Catholics, at a gallop on the camp horses with the jeep bumping along in the midst, to assemble outside Father Sebastian's little village church.

The church square sparkled with white and colored dresses: the whole village stood waiting in freshly washed and ironed Sunday clothes. We walked into the little spireless church among reverent men and vahines, children and adults, aged people, newborn and unborn babies. Inside there was such a crowd that those who sat at the end of the rows could get only half of themselves onto the wooden benches. The village now lay empty in the sun, but there was sunshine in Father Sebastian's church too: bright colors, bright faces, and the sun itself sent pencils of light through the gaps between roof and walls. By the same route a few little birds had crept in, and they flew about fearlessly, twittering and singing among the rafters.

Father Sebastian had put on a chasuble of spring green over his white robe and stood there big and amiable, like a kindly grandfather with his great beard. The atmosphere in the church was that of an opera. The climax of the service was singing. The hymns were sung in Polynesian, and most of them to old native tunes. Every single voice in the church took part except our own. We used only our ears, for this was an experience: the perfectly executed singing had rhythm and color which only South Sea natives can achieve.

Father Sebastian's ceremony was simple, and what he said was wise and put clearly. Around us our native friends and all their lively vahines sat squeezed close together, following his every word, as enthralled by what they heard as children watching a cowboy film. There was a special word of welcome for us strangers: Might all go well for the expedition, and might all the men and women on the island do everything in their power to help us, for even if we had not all the same creed as they, we were all Christians with the same ideals.

From that day we became, so to speak, a part of the population: if Father Sebastian accepted us, we were certainly decent people.

After the service all the members of the expedition were invited to a splendid dinner at the governor's. Here, besides our hosts and Father Sebastian, we met the tiny white colony: two of the nuns who managed the leper station north of the village, the Chilean Air Force captain who was preparing plans for a future transoceanic airport on the island, and the governor's two assistants. The only persons not there were the village doctor and the schoolmaster; these two we had never seen, not even in church. I noted that our own doctor was invited to attend the governor, who had heart trouble.

As we were going home to camp in the evening, we were stopped by a little thickset fellow with jet-black eyes and stiff black hair. It was the village doctor, and he invited everyone to a hula dance. This was so popular that it was useless to say no.

The dancing was held in a little house belonging to a sister of the mayor's. It was so packed when we arrived that people had to climb out of the open windows for us to be able to get in at the door. To my alarm I saw that a large pitcher containing a whisky-colored liquid was going round, from which glasses were being filled to the brim. But it proved to be *agua pura*, "pure water," collected from the drips off the roof. The prevailing atmosphere was not the less merry and lively, and roars of laughter and jokes in four languages shook the roof when the vahines dragged shy sailor lads and stiff-legged scientists out on the dance floor and made them wriggle like

49

eels on a hook. Four men were playing the guitar and singing. There was such a racket, and such a crowd that the walls would have bulged out if there had not been still more people outside pressing at them, trying to get a glimpse through the packed windows. In the midst of it all the village doctor pushed up to me, wanting to engage me in deep political discussion.

"My aim is to open the window of the world for these people," he said.

A good thing too, I thought, for there would soon be no air left in the room. But he did not mean it like that, and I had to resign myself to going outside and listening to his earnest words.

He and the schoolmaster were in opposition to the other white people on the island.

"We have Indian blood in our veins," he said, pointing to two flashing black eyes. "We want the natives to get away from this island and learn to know the world on the mainland."

And Father Sebastian doesn't want that, I thought. For he is afraid of their drinking themselves out of their senses when they get to a place where they have unrestricted access to alcohol. He is afraid of their being exploited and going to the dogs.

"We want to raise the standard of living to a modern level," the doctor continued. "We want those who now go barefoot to wear shoes."

And Father Sebastian thinks that's a mistake, I thought. For I had once heard him say that natives who had never worn shoes fared best, both ashore and at sea, on this island where footwear was quickly worn out by the sharp lava stones. Those who had begun to wear white man's shoes got thin skin on their leathery soles, and cut themselves to ribbons every time their shoes gave way. No, I thought, there are two sides to all these questions, and Father Sebastian has had a generation in which to think the matter over, while the young doctor had come with the last warship.

In the meantime the dance went on, shoes or no shoes, and when we finally made for the Valley of the Kings we all agreed we had got to know a truly friendly people.

We had now secured a large body of native workers. Some lived at home in the village and rode over every morning, others moved into caves near the excavations. To free as many of our own people as possible, we had engaged four vahines to help us with camp work and washing. One of them, Eroria, was a first-rate woman and a tireless worker. She looked like a rising thundercloud to those who did not know her. But it was easy to conjure up her good spirits, and then the cloud vanished like morning dew as her rough face lit up with a dazzling smile. She had been Father Sebastian's housekeeper for years, but was lent to us to look after the camp due to her complete reliability.

Eroria and her old gray-haired sister-in-law Mariana were, curiously enough, the keenest cave hunters on the island. They crisscrossed the hills with a pocketful of candles, searching for old dwelling caves, where they dug in the floor with a small iron bar to discover their ancestors' stone and bone tools for Father Sebastian's little collection.

"It's only in the caves there's any use looking for things," said Father Sebastian. "Take Eroria and Mariana and get them to show you all the old caves they've found."

When the rest of our party were well under way with the excavations, we saddled four horses, and the photographer and I, with Eroria and Mariana, rode off to reconnoiter caves. On the first day we were in and out of dark caves from morning till night. Some were quite open, and we could bend down and walk in. Others were carefully blocked up with stones, so that only a little rectangular opening was left through which we could crawl in on all fours. But most of them were mere ratholes, into which we could neither walk nor crawl, but had to push our legs in with stiff knees and keep our arms stretched over the head while wriggling the body like a snake through a long and horribly narrow shaft. The shaft always had smooth walls, often of skillfully cut blocks. In some caves it went in through the rock like a horizontal channel, or sloped downward; but in others it went down into the ground perpendicularly like a chimney, and we had to brake with thighs and shoulders till we came down through the roof into one corner of a pitch-black cave. In most of these caves the roof was so low that we had to stoop, and in some we could only stand doubled up or merely sit.

In these subterranean cave dwellings the old-time population of Easter Island had lived, at any rate in an uneasy period when they did not feel themselves safe in the reed huts up in the fresh air. Here they had taken cover when the early European ships had called. Most of these dwelling caves were of the size of an average bathroom, and it was so dark that we could not see our own hand without stretching it out into the mouth of the narrow shaft. The floor was cold earth, deep and rich from former refuse, and as hard as an automobile tire from the contact of a thousand crawling hands and knees. Roof and walls were naked rock, often improved here and there with artistically laid masonry.

At one place we scrambled down into something which resembled a huge open well with walled sides. At the bottom we had to creep into a narrow hole, and beyond that three spacious caves lay aslant, one above the other in levels. Eroria treated this cave with special reverence. Her own grandfather had lived there; it was her family seat. The floor here had been thoroughly turned up by the two vahines' iron rod. I picked up from the loose earth a sawn-off piece of human bone, bored through at the end as an amulet to hang around the neck.

A little farther down toward the coast Mariana pointed out an overgrown foundation wall, the remains of one of the old boat-shaped reed huts of which we saw traces everywhere. Her own father-in-law, Eroria's father, had been born there. There he had lived during the last generation till the whole population of the island had moved to the village of Hangaroa to be Christianized.

So it's no longer ago than that, I thought, and looked bewildered at the two trousered vahines, who from their appearance and manner might have had ancestors civilized since the time of Noah. The foundation wall was of the shape and dimensions of the rail of a fair-sized rowboat, pointed at both ends and composed of perfectly cut and often prettily curved stones of hard basalt, with rows of deep holes on the top into which pliant boughs had once been stuck to form the crisscross foundation of the curved reed hut. If all the reed huts whose walls we found all over the island had been in use at the same time, Easter Island must once have had a considerable population.

The two vahines had found an immense number of old dwelling caves. In most of them they had already wrought havoc with their iron rod, but they also showed us the way to some holes which were not yet "opened"—that is to say, no one had visited them since the last inhabitant had moved out and rolled lava blocks in front of the opening. Once when I had rolled one of these blocks out of the way to slide down into the narrow hole, a motionless colony of fourteen scorpions lay under the stone. Another time the opening was so narrow between the rocks that I had to empty my pockets and have several tries, without my shirt on, before I was able to force my body through. Down in the darkness my flashlight shone on human bones and a snow-white skull. I tilted the skull cautiously, and under it lay a glistening black obsidian spearpoint and an old wasps' nest. I thanked my stars that the nest was not inhabited, for if it were, I should have been badly swollen before I managed to squeeze myself back up that narrow opening.

On our way home in the afternoon we rode over a stony plateau on the high ground west of the camp. The ground was flat, with a mass of lava stones strewn thickly over the earth, often in low, compact heaps. We dismounted at one of these heaps, for Mariana's son had told her that he had found there the descent to a cave of "the other kind," a refuge cave. How anyone could find the right heap of lava in that large stone-strewn area was more than I could understand, especially as Mariana had only been given the "address" of this cave by word of mouth. But, on the other hand, she might never have been able to find her way about the labyrinth of a city's streets.

By this time the photographer and I had been trained by the two descendants of the cave dwellers to be regular experts in slithering in and out and up and down narrow shafts. We followed blindly their advice always to work our way feet first, with our arms stretched over our heads, and, if the shaft was not perpendicular, always on our backs with our faces turned upward.

But this time old Mariana first shone her light carefully down through the rectangular, perpendicular funnel. Then she asked me to look in a particular direction while working the lower part of my body down into the hole. The force of gravity drew me slowly down while thighs and shoulders braked against the stone-lined shaft. It was so narrow that my arms had to be stretched straight up and held close together over my head. This time the funnel came to a dead end and I stood immured at the bottom with my arms helplessly jammed together pointing upward. There was a rectangular hole at the base of one wall, and I maneuvered my legs into it while I slowly let my body sink down into a stiff-legged sitting position, with heavy masonry above my lap and closely surrounding my head and chest. Next my body had to follow the stiff knees into the narrow side channel, and I wriggled down, with my arms still squeezed behind me, till at last I lay stretched on my back in the horizontal funnel.

Give me a modern apartment building with an elevator!

It is a horrible feeling to lie closely walled-up down underground with rock right in your face and your arms forced back over your head so that you cannot use them. With arms trapped, you feel especially helpless. The solid rock walls seem to press more closely than ever round your head, and they cry, "Hands up, you're a prisoner." You ought not to hear this cry, nor ought you to try to free your arms, for it can't be done. You ought to think of nothing and only shove yourself along feet first by twisting the shoulder blades and dragging with the heels till you notice that you can bend your knees and kick about in an empty space—or that you cannot get any farther along the shaft because the soles of your feet have met solid rock.

If this happens, it means that the funnel makes another right-angle turn, and a man lying there with his arms over his head has to turn onto his stomach and grope along feet first between the narrow rock walls into a new perpendicular shaft which ends in a last cunning turn. Here he remains entombed in a hideous grip until he manages to twist himself round by force to enter a second horizontal funnel, where the walls suddenly disappear. Now at last he is about to enter the cave, and a moment later he can pull his arms down, he is

54

free, he can brush away the sand round his eyes and do what he likes, so long as he does not bump his head against the roof before he turns on his flashlight.

I had been in two or three of these caves before I learned to tow a light along with me. Only then could I see the narrow shaft behind me as I moved along. It was always neatly walled with smooth stone blocks without mortar, and was built with square cross section like a chimney. Some of the stones had symmetrical holes bored in them, and proved to be polished stones taken from the foundation walls of old reed houses. This showed that the builders of these cave entrances had pulled down the idyllic reed houses of their predecessors to construct these wretched rattraps instead.

For this first wriggle down into a cave of "the other kind," my pockets had been carefully emptied. I had not even taken a matchbox with me, and the floor was slippery and full of surprises; so I simply remained where I was, waiting in the dark like a blind man. When I turned my ear toward the shaft, I could hear someone coming down after me. In a few minutes old Mariana stood beside me and lit her trusty candle stump. It was of little use. The flame was so weak in the intense darkness down in the black rock that all I could see was Mariana's flashing eyes, surrounded by deep, shadowy wrinkles and a fluffy cobweb of ashen-gray hair, like a grotesque face against a windowpane. She gave me another candle stump and lit it from her own. When we held the lights up, we could gradually make out bulges and projections in the wall. Some obsidian spearheads lay on the floor.

Now Eroria too arrived. It took some time, with a good deal of scuffling and panting in the shaft, but she came. They told me that this was not an ordinary dwelling: it was a refuge for use in wartime only, for no enemy could reach people here. If so, the wars must have been many and of long duration, judging from the thickness of the hard-trodden layer of refuse at the bottom of the cave. I never understood how anyone dared to crawl down into these ratholes in wartime; the enemy had only to fill up the shaft with stones, and the occupants would be hermetically sealed up forever. But perhaps the trick was to keep these refuges secret. If they did that, and rolled a stone over the little opening behind them, it would be a hard task to find the fugitives.

I found a small channel between the stones in one of the walls, and I crawled in with Mariana and Eroria at my heels. We entered another and larger cave, and after wriggling through a little hole in the back wall of this we came into a large room, so high that we could not see the roof with our candles. We continued on our way through the rock: some places were as high and wide as a railway tunnel, at others we had to crawl among stones and rubble, and at some we had to lie flat on our stomachs and shove ourselves along till the roof rose again in a large room.

Each time I looked round to be sure the others were following, I saw Mariana's wrinkled face close behind me; she would not let me get an inch away from her. She taught me to look out for loose blocks in the roof and holes and cracks in the floor. In one of the rooms there was underground water. It was running across our route and trickling down a side passage into which we also crept. Ancient people had been at work here and cut a narrow gutter in the floor of the cave to collect water, and the gutter led down into several artificially cut depressions—like washtubs. I rinsed my hands in the lowest depression, filled them in the uppermost one, and drank. Compared to tap water this tasted like the choicest wine—cold, clear, and full-flavored. I wondered if the old cave dwellers had not known more about the grading of water than we who only get a third-class quality out of a metal pipe.

Far inside the rock the cave split into branches several times, and the innermost passages took the form of narrow catacombs with a level floor, and roof and walls arched in a pretty curve without a sign of unevenness. It looked like the work of man, but these were only channels made by gas and streams of hot lava forcing their way through the molten rock at the time when Easter Island was just an erupting volcano. For long stretches the smoothly polished archways shrank and became so narrow that they closed round my outstretched body as though tailormade. Some of them terminated far into the rock in small bell-shaped domes, while others were blocked up with stones or became so narrow that it was useless to go on.

Later we visited several of these huge caves with room after room like pearls on a string running down through the underworld. Their entrances were all skillfully walled up, so that one could get down only through the narrow funnels cut with sharp angles or zigzags, in which any assailant would be completely helpless. There was water in some of the largest caves; two of them had regular subterranean ponds, and right down at the bottom of a third we found a walled well of ice-cold water, surrounded by a stone pavement and a well-built terrace some ten feet high.

One of these great refuge caves could have accommodated the whole population of Easter Island, but everything indicated that each cave had belonged to a separate family or group of families at a time when bloody civil wars had raged on the island, and no one could sleep securely in his old reed house. I thought, as I walked about in the first pitch-dark refuge, that it had been foolish of these people living on a sunny South Sea island to choose this way of life in preference to keeping the peace with their neighbors up in the sunshine. But then I came to think of the twentieth-century world, in which we too have gradually begun to bury ourselves and our most important installations in shelters deep down in the earth, frightened because we ourselves and our neighbors have begun to play about with the atom bomb. Then I forgave Eroria's and Mariana's primitive grandparents, and as visions of past and future combined to haunt the darkness around me, I began hurriedly to wriggle up the long zigzag shaft. I felt profoundly happy when I escaped into the dazzling sun of the present, surrounded only by grazing sheep and horses dozing in the salt sea breeze.

It had taken us eighty minutes to crawl and walk through all the passages in this first great cave, and when we came up again we found the photographer, who had had a serious fright. Halfway down the shaft claustrophobia had overtaken him, and he had preferred to struggle up again and wait. Up till then it had never taken us more than a few minutes to look at a cave dwelling, and after waiting patiently for three-quarters of an hour, he had become uneasy, so he put his head down the shaft and called to us. When no one answered from below, he really became anxious. He had yelled and shouted down the hole so that the shaft resounded. But the only person who heard him was old Kasimiro, who came hurrying from a long way off, brandishing his revolver. He stood waiting faithfully at the photographer's side as we came crawling up out of the hole.

Mariana picked up her big reed hat from a stone. She begged us always to take a hat with us, or something else which we could leave behind on the ground if we crept down into these holes alone. Some Chilean treasure seekers had once been down in one of the caves with a native, she told us, and while they were deep below their lamp went out and they lost their way completely in the dark. Their lives were saved by their caps and jackets which they had thrown off up above, for a native found these and realized that the men were underground.

Our archaeologists dug up the floor in a number of caves. The inhabitants had dropped all their rubbish where they sat, and the floor, therefore, had often risen toward the roof. Fish-bones and shells lay there in masses, mingled with bones of fowls and an occasional turtle. Even rats and human beings had figured on the menu, baked among glowing stones in the earth. Cannibals had lived in these caves; apart from the little native rat their two-legged enemies were the only quarry they could capture on land. Sitting in the dark round their stone lamps, they had dropped quantities of fine needles made of human bones among the waste on the floor. These, and a few other primitive implements of human bone, stone, and volcanic glass, and some simple amulets of bone and shells were all we found. Nothing else.

There was something about this that did not make sense. Could these primitive cannibals have been the masters who wrought the classical giant sculptures of aristocratic ruler-types which dominated the countryside on this same island? How could a people of hunted cave dwellers have bred such unique engineers and ingenious artists as the creators of those gigantic monuments? And how could monolithic work have been organized among people who did not even live together in a village, but hid here and there down narrow, underground shafts scattered about the island?

I crept into the funnel leading to a cave where Bill was

sitting in the light of a kerosene lamp digging carefully with a mason's trowel. He had a bag beside him full of burned human bones.

"The same primitive culture," he said, scraping two molars out of the earth at his feet. "Look, these dirty devils have been sitting here eating each other and spitting the teeth on the floor."

It was not only on ceremonial occasions that human flesh had been devoured on this island. The natives have legends to this very day of ancestors who would rather eat their own race than fish or fowl. They have also persistent legends of a still earlier time of greatness when another people, the long-ears, had lived at peace with their ancestors, the short-ears. The long-ears had demanded too much labor of the short-ears, and in the end there had been a war in which nearly all the long-ears were burned in a ditch. From that day no more statues had been made, and many of those which were standing had been pulled down with ropes. Civil war, family feuds, and cannibalism marked the years which followed, right up to the time when Father Eugenio landed two generations ago and collected the inhabitants peacefully round him in the village of Hangaroa.

Father Sebastian was convinced that two different races with separate cultures had come to Easter Island, and the natives were unshakable in their affirmation that this was the case. He had also pointed out that the population differed in many respects from ordinary Pacific natives. Among other things, they contained unmistakable remnants of a white race.[1] It was not only Roggeveen and the first discoverers who had noticed this. Father Sebastian pointed out that according to traditions of the natives themselves, many of their ancestors in olden times had white skin, red hair, and blue eyes. And when Father Eugenio settled among them as the first European, and assembled all the people at Hangaroa, he was surprised to find many completely white people among the brown ones. As recently as the visit of the Routledge expedition forty years ago, the natives still divided their ancestors into two categories according to the color of their skins, and

[1] P. Sebastian Englert, *La Tierra de Hotu Matu'a* (Chile, 1948), pp. 203-5.

they told Mrs. Routledge that even the last king had been a quite white man. The white branch was looked up to with admiration and respect, and just as in the other South Sea Islands some leading personalities had to undergo special bleaching processes to be as much like their deified ancestors as possible.

One day Father Sebastian came to take us with him to Ana o Keke, the holy bleaching place of the *neru* virgins. *Neru* was the name given to specially chosen young maidens who in old days were confined in a deep cave to become as pale and white as possible for special religious festivals when they were to be shown to the public. For a long, long time they might see neither the light of day nor other people, and their food was carried to the cave and pushed through the opening by women appointed for the purpose. The natives could still remember that when the smallpox epidemic raged all over the island after the slaves returned from the mainland, it did not reach the *neru* maidens, but they died of starvation in their cave because there was no longer anyone to bring them food.

The entrance to the virgins' cave Ana o Keke lay at the most easterly point of the island, the Poike Peninsula, and the name means "Cave of the Sun's Inclination." To get there we passed the island's most easterly volcano, Katiki, behind which lay the three hummocks where the Spaniards had once set up their first crosses. There was a cave dwelling there too, and beside it a diabolical giant's head carved in the rock wall itself, where the rainwater was carried into an open mouth so large that I climbed in and concealed myself behind the underlip with the greatest of ease.

Father Sebastian led us farther on, right out to the edge of the frightful precipice which falls into the sea all round this lofty peninsula. Here he began to walk along the very edge of the cliff in such an unconcerned manner that we four who were with him called and begged him to keep farther in. An unusually violent east wind thundered at the cliffs and tore at our clothes, making us feel unsteady and insecure. But our white-clad friend in his long, fluttering robe and big black boots kept on rapidly along the outermost edge; he was searching for the place and did not know exactly where it was. Suddenly his face lighted up and he threw up his arms: ah, here it was! He broke off a piece of the loose yellowish-brown rock to show us that it was quite worn away by weathering, so we must step carefully. Then he went straight to the very edge, a thundering gust of wind took hold of his habit, we gave a yell, and Father Sebastian had gone.

Carl sat down and clutched at his hat in sheer bewilderment. Cautiously I crawled out and looked over the edge. Far below I saw the foot of the cliff, on which white surf was breaking, with the sea behind it stretching away white-crested into infinity. The air was full of the roar of wind and sea. To my relief, on a narrow shelf to my left I saw Father Sebastian's white robe; the wind was whipping it as he pressed himself close to the face of the cliff and moved downward sideways. It was blowing furiously that day: the wind hammered at us violently in gusts, now from one way, now from another, due to the steep barrier that flung it back. I suddenly was overcome with an unbounded admiration for this old priest who climbed with such perfect confidence, and who identified reality with his own faith to such a degree that he had no fear of physical dangers. I almost believe he could have walked on the water.

Now he turned toward me and smiled, pointed lower down beneath his feet, and raised his fingers to his mouth as a sign that I must bring our parcels of food, for we were going to have lunch down there. I felt so unsteady in the uneven gusts of wind that I crawled back from the cliffside and pulled off my fluttering shirt before I fetched the parcels of food and plucked up courage to follow Father Sebastian on the ledge.

When I began to clamber down he had gone on; I could not see a trace of his robe, but I did see six hundred feet straight down into the breakers below. Mountaineering is not my strongest point, and I did not feel very cheerful as I carefully lowered myself onto the ledge, pressed my stomach against the face of the cliff, and with my heart in my mouth set off in Father Sebastian's wake, feeling my way forward step by step to see if the rock would hold. The worst part of it was the wind. I arrived at a slight corner in the cliff where the only support was something which looked like a hard lump of earth, separated from the actual cliff by a crack. If it had borne Father Sebastian, it would bear me. I kicked it cautiously, but dared not kick too hard.

I put my head around the projection and found Father Sebastian again. He was lying with only his head and shoulders projecting from the cave entrance in the face of the cliff. The entrance was about half the height of an opening to a dog kennel. He was laughing. I shall always remember him thus, like an Easter Island Diogenes in his tub, with rimless spectacles on his nose, wide white sleeves, and flowing beard. When he saw me, he raised his arms in a sweeping gesture and cried: "Welcome to my cave!"

I could hardly hear what he said for the noise. Then he lowered his beard toward the narrow shelf and pushed himself back in through the crevice so that there would be room for me too, for under the opening there was a sheer drop. I got across to the shelf in front of the cave and squeezed myself in after him. Noise, wind, and light disappeared. Inside it was very narrow, but soon the roof became higher and there was inviolable peace and security here within the belly of the cliff. A scrap of light found its way in so that we could soon make each other out, and I could see with my pocket flashlight that the curved walls were covered with curious signs and figures.

This was the virgins' cave. Here the poor little girls had sat for weeks, perhaps for months, waiting till their skins became white enough for them to be shown to the people. The cave was less than five feet high, and there was not room for many more than a dozen children if they sat in rows along the walls.

After a while the opening was darkened by someone forcing his way in. It was our native friend. Father Sebastian sent him out again to fetch Carl and the photographer; he would not have them drawing back when he, a man of sixty-eight, had led the way.

We were soon all sitting together enjoying our lunch. Father Sebastian pointed to a small hole in the back wall and said that if we crawled in there we could get four hundred yards farther into the rock. But it was the worst trip he had ever made, and he would never do it again. Halfway in, the passage for a long stretch was so narrow that it was just possible for a man to force his way through, and inside, teeth and remnants of human bones were lying about as in a burial cave. It was a mystery to him how anyone could have carried a dead person in there, for it was impossible to push the corpse in front, and if a man dragged it behind him, it would bar the way back for himself.

I put on my shirt and decided to see the rest of the cave. Father Sebastian roared with laughter at the thought of what I was going to encounter; I would turn back quickly when I saw what it was like in there! Only the native was willing to come with me when I crept in through the hole.

The cave forked, but the branches met again immediately in a narrow passage through which we had to go. Then the roof rose and we found ourselves in a long tunnel, so high and spacious that we could run to save time. The flashlight was miserable and shone with only half its strength. Through an accident in storage the batteries had been damaged, and for safety's sake I carried a stump of candle and a box of matches in my trousers pocket. To save the batteries I continually turned the light off, and we ran, walked, and crawled in the darkness as far as we had seen ahead of us between the flashes. We could not help knocking our heads against the roof two or three times, so that little drop-shaped particles tinkled down like glass through our hair and down our necks. A long way in we came to a place where there was mud and water on the floor. Here the roof fell lower and lower. We had no choice but to stoop down and crawl on our hands and knees in water and ooze, but it became still lower, and at last we had to lie flat on our stomachs and wriggle forward under the rock as ice-cold mud soaked through our shirts and trousers.

"Nice road," I called back.

My companion wallowing in the mud behind me laughed politely. It was beginning to be unpleasant. Now I understood what Father Sebastian meant, but if *he* had managed it, there was little reason for us to give up halfway.

Just after this I almost regretted having started. Although I was lying with my body pressed into water and soft mud, the roof came down so low that again and again I tried without finding a passage. The flashlight was watertight, but it was hopeless to keep the glass free of mud when I myself was lying flat, pressed down in it. Nevertheless, the faint light showed clearly that the passage was not only low and narrow, but that there was no other choice. Father Sebastian had pushed himself through here. I forced my chest in slowly, and felt that it was just possible if only it did not grow worse. With the mud pushed aside and the hard rock pressing me both from below and from above, I squeezed myself in through the crack inch by inch. It was so grotesque that I could not help groaning "nice road" to the poor wretch who was following me, but now his sense of humor was no longer functioning.

"Bad road, Señor," he grunted.

We had to push ourselves forward for five yards through this vise which held our ribs in its hold. Then we were through the needle's eye and reached the part of the cave where the remains of skeletons lay. Here it was dry and the roof gradually became higher, so that again we could alternately crawl on all fours and amble through the passages. The poor *neru* maidens, if they had wanted to get a little exercise during their long stay in the cave, had had no romantic moonlight walk. I was stiff and cold from the wet earth, and when I turned the light behind me to see if my native friend was following, I found that I was pursued by a figure caked in mud, hardly distinguishable from the dark of the cave but for the gleam of his eyes and teeth.

At last the cave ended in a smooth, steep earth slope which led up to a hole in the roof. After much helpless slithering I managed to scratch my way up and came into a little, bell-shaped dome, which had all the appearance of being made by man. But it was only an old gas bubble. Father Sebastian had left a candle stump there. I still had mine in my hip pocket, and my back and hinder parts were comparatively dry. I tried Father Sebastian's candle; it would not burn. There was something wrong with the matches too. Now I felt sweat trickling down my face; the air was bad here. I hastily slipped down the earth slope to my mud-caked companion who stood waiting for me, and then we retraced our steps as quickly as the wretched light and the height of the roof allowed.

We looked like two creatures from Hades as we crouched and crawled along, and we felt like it too, for when we came to the horrible needle's eye, we flung ourselves down in the water and mud with jesting words and pressed ourselves into the crack. The native followed with his head right at my heels, and we forced our way forward inch by inch, feeling our chests crushed in the inexorable mountain jaws which would not open one hairsbreadth extra for two human bodies. It had taken a long time to get in, but it seemed to be taking longer to get out again. We still tried to joke a little, knowing we would soon be out now; but I felt unpleasantly wet and dirty, sweat was drenching my face, and I was rather tired. The air was very bad. After a while we kept silent and only struggled to force our bodies on with outstretched arms, I trying not to let the glass of the light get down into the mud.

Had there been more space under the roof for a moment? If so, now there was less again. It was queer that this narrow passage still continued, that we did not soon emerge into the outer tunnel. My weary brain had been vaguely considering this for some time as I shoved and shoved to get my body through the vise. Then I saw, in the faint glow of the electric bulb, that just in front of my nose there was a sudden little upward bend, and it looked as if I could not get my body up through it. Perhaps this bend had been much easier to pass in the opposite direction, so that I had not realized how difficult it would be to get through on the return journey. Queer that I did not remember anything about it. With all my might I forced myself a little farther forward and tried to look up through the hole in a cramped position, with millions of tons pressing on my back and chest. Then to my terror I saw that there was something wrong: it was impossible to get past this bend.

"We can't get any farther," I said to the man who was lying at my heels. The sweat poured from my face.

"Go on, Señor. There isn't any other way out," he groaned in reply.

I forced myself another fraction of an inch farther, with my head twisted on one side to find room in the narrow gap between the rock surfaces, and with my chest in a devilish squeeze. By turning the light upward I saw that the hole was positively much smaller than my head. It was impossible to get through.

In the same second I switched off the light: now every spark must be saved, for we had trouble ahead. One could think in the dark. I suddenly felt that the whole mighty massif of the Poike Peninsula was lying on my body and pressing hard. It was terribly heavy—heavy—and it was worse if I tried to push against it. The only thing to do was to relax altogether and make oneself as thin as possible. But even then the rock went on pressing, from above and from below.

"Go back," I said to the man who lay right at my heels. "This won't work."

He flatly refused, and begged me to push on; there was no other way out of this hell.

This could not be the case. I switched the light on again and examined the ground before my hands and chest, shoving myself a little farther back as I did so. On this little slope there seemed to be a mixture of earth and half-dry mud; the impression of my shirt and buttons was plainly visible just in front of my chest, and my fingerprints too as far forward as I then had my hands, but immediately ahead was muddy earth and rubble, untouched by man or beast. I switched the light off again. The air was heavy. My chest was in that beastly squeeze. My face and body were dripping with perspiration. Had we caused the old cave passage to collapse by talking or pressing our way through on the way in? If a fall from the roof had blocked the whole passage ahead of us, how could we dig ourselves out into the daylight when there was no room to push earth and stones past us into the cave behind? How long could we hold out in that bad air before the others realized what had happened and were able to dig their way to us? Or could we have made a mistake in crawling and got into another passage which was a blind alley? How could we have done that, when the entire virgins' cave was one single narrow tunnel, hardly wider than a man's body in the part where we were?

The native blocked me completely from behind and tried to force me on. My whole body was caked with mud, and the cliff weighed me down with all its millions of tons—harder and harder the more I thought about it.

"Go back!" I shouted.

He was beginning to press upon my heels in desperation; he had not seen the little hole, and I could not let him past so that he could see for himself.

"Go back! Go back!"

The native was now working himself into a mad panic. I raged at him, "Go! go!" and kicked out with the sole of my foot. That had some effect. He shoved himself back inch by inch, and I followed. We went slowly, one little backward movement at a time; we must not get stuck fast or caught by the head between the rocks. I was most afraid of placing the head wrong, for it would not yield to pressure as the chest did.

Suddenly there was more space above us. I understood nothing: I was quite muddleheaded from the bad air. Could we have got right back to the skeleton place? I used my flashlight again and saw two openings in front of me: the right-hand one went slightly uphill. This was where we had gone wrong; we had crawled to the left instead of up to the right. I called to the native, but he only went on, as if in a stupor, shoving himself backwards.

"Here it is!" I cried, and crawled forward again into the left-hand entrance, the native following me automatically. Our voices sounded very queer in the cave. The passage grew narrower and narrower again. This was ghastly. At last I used my light and saw ahead of me the same impossible little hole as before. Then I realized that my brain was no longer functioning clearly: I had crawled into the wrong hole for the second time, although I knew perfectly well that it was the other hole I should have taken.

"Go back!" I groaned.

And now all our actions seemed purely mechanical. We forced ourselves out again backwards and I thought of only one word: right, right, right. When we saw the two passages again I crept mechanically into the right-hand opening, and soon we could raise ourselves up, we felt gusts of cold, fresh air in the tunnel, we were able to crouch and crawl, and finally we came out of the last hole and into the snug cave with the inscriptions on the walls where our friends were sitting waiting for us. It was heavenly to push oneself out of the cliffside, out into the roaring wind. Heavenly to meet again the blinding sunshine and the limitless space stretching from the precipice sheer below us into the unbounded blue immensity of sea and sky.

"Did you give up?" Father Sebastian asked eagerly, laughing heartily at our appearance.

"No," I said. "But it's understandable that skeletons may be left in a cave like that."

"Did you say you have been in the bleaching cave?" Yvonne asked when we came back to the camp. That was certainly not obvious from our appearance.

I went straight down to the shore and flung myself into the salt surf with all my clothes on.

CHAPTER FOUR

The Mystery of the Easter Island Giants

ANYONE WHO is dreaming of a trip to the moon can get a little foretaste of it by climbing about on the dead volcanic cones of Easter Island. Not only does his own hectic world seem immeasurably distant, but the landscape can easily give the illusion of being on the moon: a friendly little moon hung between sky and sea, where grass and ferns cover treeless craters which lie gaping sleepily toward the sky.

There are a number of these peaceful volcanoes here and there all over the island. They are green outside and green within. The time of eruptions is so long past that at the bottom of some of the largest craters sky-blue lakes with waving green reeds mirror clouds flying before the trade wind.

One of these water-filled volcanoes is called Rano Raraku, and it is here that the men in the moon seem to have been most busily at work. You do not see them; they have fled in haste from what they were doing. But you have a feeling that they have only hidden themselves in concealed holes in the ground, while you yourself walk about in the grass surveying their interrupted tasks.

Rano Raraku remains one of the greatest and most curious monuments of mankind, a monument to the great lost unknown behind us, a warning of the transience of man and civilization. The whole mountain massif has been reshaped, the volcano has been greedily cut up as if it were pastry, although sparks fly when a steel ax is driven against the rock to test its strength. Hundreds of thousands of cubic feet of rock have been cut out and tens of thousands of tons of stone carried away. And in the midst of the mountain's gaping wound lie more than a hundred and fifty gigantic stone men, in all stages from the just begun to the just completed. At the foot of the mountain stand finished stone men side by side like a supernatural army.

You feel miserably small in approaching the vanished sculptors' workshop, whether on horseback or driving in a jeep along the ancient roads. Dismounting from your horse in the shadow of a great block of stone, you see that the block has features on its underside: it is the head of a fallen giant. All twenty-three of our expedition could creep under it and find shelter in a rainstorm. On going up to the foremost figures, which are buried in the earth up to their chests, you are shocked to find that you cannot even reach up to the colossi's chins. And if you try to climb onto those which lie flat on their backs, you feel a regular Lilliputian because often you have the greatest difficulty even in getting up onto their stomachs. And once up on a prostrate Goliath you can walk about freely on his chest and stomach, or stretch yourself out on his nose, which often is as long as an ordinary bed. Thirty feet is no uncommon height for these figures. The largest, which lay unfinished and aslant on the side of the volcano, was sixty-nine feet long, so that, counting a story as ten feet, this stone man was as tall as a seven-story building.

In Rano Raraku you feel the mystery of Easter Island at close quarters. The very air is laden with it. Bent on you is the silent gaze of a hundred and fifty eyeless faces. Nothing moves except the drifting clouds above you. It was so when the sculptors went, and so it will always be. The oldest figures, those which were completed, stand there proud, arrogant, and tight-lipped, as though defiantly conscious that no chisel, no power will ever open their mouths and make them speak.

But even though the giants' mouths are sealed seven times over, anyone going about in the chaos of uncompleted figures up the mountain slope can learn a good deal. Wherever we climbed and wherever we halted, we were surrounded, as in a hall of mirrors, by enormous faces astonishingly alike. All had the same stoical expression and the most peculiar long ears.

We had them above us, beneath us, and on both sides. We clambered over noses and chins and trod on mouths and gigantic brows, while huge bodies lay leaning over us on the ledges higher up. As our eyes gradually became trained to distinguish art from nature, we perceived that the whole mountain was one single swarm of bodies and heads, right from the foot up to the very top of the precipice on the uppermost edge of the volcano. Even up here, five hundred feet above the plain, half-finished giants lay side by side staring up into the firmament, in which only the hawks were sailing. But the swarm of stone men did not stop even up here on the topmost ridge, they went on side by side and above one another in unbroken procession down the inside of the volcano, right down to the lush green reed bed on the edge of the crater lake, like a people of blind robots searching for the water of life.

We were all equally overwhelmed and impressed by the gigantic enterprise which had once been interrupted in Rano Raraku. Only little Anette took it all quite calmly:

"Look at the dolls," she said, enthralled, when I had lifted her down from the pommel at the foot of the volcano.

But when we went closer, the dimensions became too great for her imagination too. She played hide and seek round their necks without suspecting that heads rose into the air on top of them. When her mother helped her up a ledge she could not climb, she did not realize that she was being lifted from the upper lip of a recumbent giant onto the tip of his nose.

When we began to dig, the impression was no less astonishing. The famous Easter Island heads were large enough already, standing on the slope at the foot of the volcano. But when we dug our way down along the throat, the chest appeared, and under the chest the stomach and arms continued and the whole of the huge body right down to the hips, where long thin fingers with enormous curved nails met under a protruding belly. Now and then we found both human bones and remains of fires in the strata of earth down the front of the statue. The heads looked quite different from the pictures in encyclopedias, now that they were standing there with bodies and arms. But this uncovering solved none of the problems of Easter Island; it was merely a fascinating sight which the Routledge expedition had experienced before us.

We had the greatest difficulty in throwing a line over the highest heads, and only the best climbers attempted to struggle up the rope, for when these statues were completely excavated some of them stood as much as forty feet high. The last bit, from the eyebrows upward, was the worst, for here the rope was pressed tight against the giant's forehead and did not afford a decent grip.

It was difficult enough for a man on a rope without encumbrances to ascend the skull of one of these standing giants; how it was possible to carry up a large "hat" which was to be placed right on the top of the head, we could not understand. Especially considering that the hat too was of stone, and could have a volume of two hundred cubic feet, and could weigh as much as two elephants!

How can one lift the weight of two elephants to the level of the roof of a four-story house when there are no cranes and not even a high point in the vicinity? The few men who could find room for themselves up on the figure's skull could not possibly have dragged an enormous stone cylinder up to the small flat space which was their only foothold. And although a crowd of men could stand on the ground at the foot of the statue, they were mere midgets who could not stretch their arms more than a fraction of the way up the lower part of the giant. How then could they have pushed the weight of two elephants high in the air, right up past the chest, and on past the towering head, up to the very top of the skull? Metal was unknown, and the island was practically treeless.

Even the engineers shook their heads resignedly. We felt like a crowd of schoolboys standing helpless before a practical conundrum. The invisible moon dwellers down in their holes seemed to be glorying over us, saying: "Guess how this engineering work was done! Guess how we moved these gigantic figures down the steep walls of the volcano and carried them over the hills to any place in the island we liked!"

There was little use in guessing. We must first have a really good look round to see if the old-time geniuses had been careless enough to leave behind something which could give us even the smallest hint.

To tackle the problem at its root, we first studied the numerous uncompleted figures which lay on the ledges in the quarry itself. It was clear that all work had been broken off suddenly: thousands of primitive unpolished stone picks still lay in the open-air workshop; and as different groups of sculptors had worked simultaneously on many different statues, all stages of carving were represented. The ancient stonecutters had first attacked the bare rock itself and made the face and front part of the statue. Then they had cut alleyways along the sides and made giant ears and arms, always with extremely long and slender fingers curved over the belly. Next they had cut their way underneath the whole figure from both sides, so that the back took the shape of a boat with a narrow keel, attached to the rock.

When the façade of the figure was completed in every minute detail, it was rubbed with a sort of pumice and thoroughly polished: the only thing they took care not to do was to mark in the eye itself under the overhanging brows. For the present the giant was to be blind. Then the keel was hacked away under the back, while the colossus was wedged up with stones to prevent it from slipping away and sliding down into the abyss. It was a matter of utter indifference to the sculptors whether they carved the figure out of a perpendicular wall or a horizontal slab, head upward or downward, for half-finished giants lay bent in every direction. The only consistent thing about them was that the back was the last part to remain attached to the rock.

When the back also had been cut loose, transportation down the cliff to the foot of the volcano began. In some cases colossi weighing many tons had been swung down a perpendicular wall and maneuvered over lower ledges where there were statues on which work was still proceeding. Many were broken in transport, but the overwhelming majority had come down complete—that is to say, complete without legs, for every single statue ended in a flat cut-off foundation just where the abdomen ends and the legs begin. They were sort of lengthened busts with complete torsos.

At the foot of the cliff lay a thick layer of gravel and decomposed rock, often piled up into ridges and regular hillocks. This was the result of thousands of tons of stone splinters which had been carried away from the quarry by the sculptors. Here the giant men had been temporarily raised up into a standing position in holes which had been dug in the rubble. Not till now, with the statues standing thus, did the sculptors set to work on the unfinished back. As the neck and hinder parts took shape, a belt, decorated with rings and symbols, was carved on the waist. This little belt was the only piece of clothing the naked statues wore, and with only one exception all the colossi were male figures.

But the mysterious march of the stone colossi did not end here among the rubble. When the back also was finished, they had to be moved to their wall-less temples. Most of them had already gone: only comparatively few were still on the waiting list for transportation from their holes at the foot of the volcano. All the fully completed giants had moved on, mile by mile right over the island; some had finished their journey up to ten miles from the quarry where they had first been created, and the very smallest weighed from two to ten tons apiece.

Father Sebastian acted as an outdoor museum director in this deserted moon landscape. He had climbed about everywhere and painted a number on all the statues he could find, and there were over six hundred in all. All were of the same grayish-yellow, black-grained stone; all had been hewn in the same gigantic workshop on the steep face of Rano Raraku. It was only there that this special coloring of the rock was found, and knowing this, one could recognize a statue simply by its color even if it was lying prostrate among other huge boulders a long way off.

The strangest thing was that the colossi had been moved about not as shapeless lumps which could stand a knock or two, but as perfectly smooth figures, rubbed and polished fore and aft, from the lobes of their ears to the roots of their nails. Only the eye sockets were still missing. How had it been possible to move the completely finished article across country without rubbing it to pieces? Nobody knew.

At their destination the blind stone men were not erected just by dropping them down into a hole. On the contrary, they were lifted up above the ground and placed on the top of an *ahu,* or temple platform, where they remained standing with their base a couple of yards above the ground. Now at last holes were chiseled for the eyes; now at last the giants might see where they were. And then came the finishing touch. They were to have "hats" put on the tops of their heads—hats which weighed from two to ten tons.

Actually, it is not quite correct to talk about hats, even though everyone does so nowadays. The old native name for this gigantic head decoration is *pukao,* which means "top-knot," the usual coiffure worn by male natives on Easter Island at the time of its discovery. Why did the old masters lift this *pukao* up on top of the giant in the form of an extra block? Why could they not simply cut it out of the same stone with the rest of the figure? Because the important detail was the color of the topknot. They went to the opposite end of the island, seven miles from the stone quarry in Rano Raraku, and here they had hewn their way down into a little over-grown crater where the rock was a very special red. It was this red stone they wanted for the statues' hair. So they had dragged yellowish-gray statues from one side of the island and red topknots from the other, and superimposed one on the other at the upper platform of more than fifty temple terraces all round the coast. Most of these platforms had a couple of statues side by side, a great many had four, five, or six, and one had no fewer than fifteen red-haired giants standing side by side, with their bases twelve feet above the ground.

Not one of these red-haired giants stands in his old place on top of the temple platforms today. Even Captain Cook, and probably Roggeveen also, arrived too late to see them all standing in their old places. But the first explorers did record that many of the statues were still standing at their posts with red *pukaos* on their heads. In the middle of the last century the last giant crashed down from his temple, and the red top-knot rolled like a blood-stained steam roller over the pavement of the temple square. Today only the blind hairless statues in the rubble-filled holes at the foot of the volcano still stand with heads raised defiantly. They stand so deep in the earth that no native enemy succeeded in pulling them down, and a single attempt to cut off one of the heads with an ax was total-ly unsuccessful because the ancient executioner had not managed to cut his way more than a hand's breadth into the giant's neck.

The last statue to fall was dragged down from its *ahu* about 1840 on the occasion of a cannibal feast in a cave nearby. It had a topknot two hundred cubic feet in size on the top of its thirty-two-foot-tall body, which in turn stood on a wall almost the height of a man. It weighed fifty tons and had been transported two and a half miles from the quarry in Rano Raraku.

Let us imagine ourselves taking a ten-ton boxcar and turning it upside down, for the wheel was unknown in Polynesia. Next we capsize another boxcar alongside the first one, and tie the two firmly together. Then we drive twelve full-grown horses into the cars, and after them five large elephants. Now we have got our fifty tons and can begin to pull. We have not merely to move this weight, but drag it for two and a half miles over stony ground without the slightest injury being done to it. Is this impossible without machinery? If so, the oldest inhabitants of Easter Island mastered the impossible.

One thing is certain: this was not the work of a canoeload of Polynesian wood carvers who set to work on the bare rock faces when they landed merely because they could find no trees to whittle. The red-haired giants with the classical features were made by seafarers who came from a land with generations of experience in maneuvering monoliths.

Now that we have got our fifty-ton load to the right place, the three-story stone man must be hoisted onto a wall and made to stand upright. And then the topknot must be put on: in this case it alone weighs ten tons, and has been carried seven miles as the crow flies from the topknot quarry. Seven miles is a long way in country like this, and thirty-two feet in excess of the stone platform is a good height anywhere when the object to be superimposed weighs ten tons, or as much as twenty full-grown horses. But it was done. And the whole thing was pulled down again in 1840 by cannibals, who undermined the foundation stones in the wall and celebrated their deed by eating thirty of their neighbors in a cave.

I stood on the top of the crater of Rano Raraku and had a magnificent view all round of the grass-clad island. Behind me there was a fairly steep slope down into the overgrown interior of the volcano, where the sky-blue lake lay in a broad

When the first Europeans visited Easter Island, several of the statues still had their red-stone topknots balanced on top of their heads. Note the native hat thief. (Old illustration from the visit of La Pérouse.)

frame of the greenest green reeds I ever saw. Perhaps they seemed a brighter green in contrast with the grass all over the island, which now, in the dry season, was beginning to turn yellow. In front of me there was a steep drop down the terraced wall of the quarry to the flat ground at the foot of the volcano, where the members of the expedition were working like ants, excavating the brown earth around the gigantic figures. Their horses stood tethered here and there, looking exceedingly small alongside the burly giants. From here I had a good survey of what had happened in the past. This was the focal point of Easter Island's foremost riddle; this was the statues' maternity home. I myself was standing on a sturdy embryo, watching the swarms of others all down the descents, both before and behind me. And at the foot of the slopes, both outside and inside the crater, the newborn stood erect, blind and hairless, waiting in vain to be hauled away on their long transport.

From up here I could see the course the transport had taken. Two of the figures which were completed inside the crater had been on their way when all work suddenly ceased. One had just come up onto the edge of the crater on its way out, the other had already been on its way down through a gully on the outside, and they both lay, not on their backs, but on their stomachs. Along the old stoneless grass tracks over the plain, as far as the eye could see, others lay abandoned, singly and in irregular groups of two and three. They too were blind and hairless, indicating that they had never been set up where they lay, but had been suddenly left in the midst of being transported from Rano Raraku to the platforms that awaited them.

And far away to the west, beyond the horizon, was the little volcano Puna Pau with the topknot quarry. I could not see it from where I stood, but I had been down into its blood-red interior and seen half a dozen topknots lying like giant stone cylinders in the precipitous little crater. A number of the largest had been conveyed up over the steep slope. These now lay in a dump outside, waiting to be taken further. Others had evidently been abandoned while under way to their future owners, for here and there you saw a solitary topknot on the plain. I measured the largest topknot which had been carried up out of the red crater. It was six hundred fifty cubic feet in size and weighed roughly thirty tons, or as much as sixty full-grown horses.

My own comprehension was insufficient to grasp the ancient Easter Island engineering scheme, and I turned resignedly to the native shepherd who stood by me in silence gazing at the abandoned giants which lay about on the plain.

"Leonardo," I said, "you are a practical man. Can you tell me how these stone giants could have been carried about in old times?"

"They went of themselves," Leonardo replied.

But for his grave, almost reverent air I should have thought he was joking, for Leonardo was no less civilized, and more intelligent, than the average man in the world outside.

"But, Leonardo," I said, "how could they go when they had only heads and bodies and no legs?"

"They wriggled along like this," said Leonardo, and gave a demonstration by working himself along the rock with feet together and stiff knees. "How do *you* think it happened?" he asked indulgently.

I was silenced at once, and as I was certainly not the first white man who had shown Leonardo that he had no comprehension whatever of the mystery, it was really quite reasonable that he should accept the practical explanation of his own father and grandfather. The statues had walked of their own accord. Why set up unnecessary problems when the answer was so simple?

When I got home to the camp, I went over to the kitchen tent to old Mariana, who was sitting peeling potatoes.

"Have you heard how the great *moai* were carried about in the old times?" I asked.

"*Si,* Señor," she said with conviction. "They went of themselves." And Mariana began to tell a long story about an old witch who lived at Rano Raraku at the time when the sculptors made the great figures. It was her magic which breathed life into the stone giants and made them go where they should. But one day the sculptors had eaten a big lobster, and when the witch found the empty shell, and realized none of the contents had been given to her, she was so angry that she made all the walking statues fall flat on their noses, and they have never moved since.

Forty years ago the natives told Mrs. Routledge just the same story about the witch and the lobster, and I found to my astonishment that all the natives I talked to still accepted this easy solution to the mystery. And unless someone could give them a more plausible explanation, they would stick firmly to the witch and lobster version till Doomsday.

In general the natives were certainly not naïve. With or without lawful grounds, they were always thinking of cunning excuses for leaving the village and coming over to the camp to sell wood carvings. Nearly all of them could carve; several of them were real masters, but the best of all was the mayor. Everyone wanted his figures, for although they all invariably offered the same subjects, the graceful lines and perfect polish of his showed that no one could shape a piece of wood better than he. He had far more orders in the camp than he could execute.

American cigarettes, Norwegian fishhooks, and brightly colored English yardgoods ranked highest on the list of barter goods. As on so many of the other islands, the people of Easter Island were absolutely crazy about cigarettes. Those who had come on board the ship and obtained a few packets by barter the first night had not smoked them all themselves. They had galloped off to the village and gone from house to house, there waking up relatives and friends so that everyone could taste a cigarette, for the supply which had come with the last warship had been consumed months ago.

Among the elegant wood carvings there appeared now and then a freshly made but very inferior stone figure, either a naïve copy of the great statues or a shapeless head with only eyes and nose casually indicated. At first the owners tried to make us believe that these were old figures found on the ground or in temple walls. But when we laughed at them, most of them gave up the pretense, and only a few tried to be still smarter.

One of these people, a woman on horseback, came up to me, saying that she had found something curious right in the middle of an old heap of stones. At the place, she began carefully to remove the stones, and right down among them I saw the light fall on a little bright-colored and newly made model of a statue.

"Don't touch it," I said to her. "It's new. Someone has put it there just to play a trick on you!"

The woman's face grew very long, and neither she nor her husband tried to fool us again.

Then there was a fellow who came panting up after dark to tell us that he had found a baby statue buried in the sand while he was fishing in the sea by torchlight. If we wanted to have it, we must come along right now in the dark, even if we could not see very well, for he was on his way home to the village. He was visibly chagrined when we maneuvered the jeep to the spot and turned its headlights full on. There on the grass lay a badly executed little figure, carefully plastered with sand, but otherwise brand-new. While the rest of us stood by laughing, the owner had to pack his miserable production away in a sack and lug it back to the village. A sailor in the next warship would probably get it.

A third variation came from a native who wanted to show me a little open grotto with a water hole and some curious sculptures in the roof. The figures in the roof were genuine enough; there were old bird-men and great staring eyes, and I was really pleased. While I was studying the roof my innocent-looking guide stood and amused himself by casually dropping lumps of earth into the water. Suddenly he gave a shout. I saw a piece of earth slowly dissolving, and a little doll-like stone figure became visible in the water, like a chicken coming out of an egg. It was so comical that I laughed more than the sinner deserved, and he never tried any more games with me.

But in their zeal to secure our popular barter goods some of them really did find old things in the ground. One day a young married couple came and took me to see four curious heads that they had found. The place was close to the sheep fence east of the governor's land, and when we got there we were met by an old woman and a virago of a daughter who I thought were going to scratch our eyes out. They were beside themselves with rage and shouted and shrieked at a rate which is only possible in Polynesian. If our two guides tried to get in a word, a shower of abuse was almost spat in their faces. The photographer and I sat down and waited for the steam to blow off. The old woman cooled down a little.

"Señor Kon-Tiki," she said. "These two are thieves and rascals. These are my stones; no one may dare to touch them. I am descended from Hotu Matua and this has always been my family's land."

"It isn't now," one of our two guides interrupted. "It's the Navy's sheep farm now. The stones are ours because it was we who first found them!"

The old woman went mad with rage again.

"First found them? Liars, thieves! The stones belong to my family, you thieves!"

While the two parties were quarreling savagely over the ownership, I suddenly realized from their gesticulations what stones they were talking about. The old woman and her daughter had now each sat down on one of them, I had unconsciously sat on a third, and our two guides were standing by the last. They looked like ordinary boulders, and not at all like something to quarrel about.

Then I thought of the wise man Solomon, who, when two mothers both laid claim to the same child, took a sword and prepared to cut it in half. I could have done the same now with the help of a sledge hammer. The young couple would just have agreed and said yes if I had raised the hammer to strike. The old woman would have gone out of her mind.

"Let us have a look at your stones," I said to her, "and then we won't touch them."

She did not say a word in reply, but let us roll the great round stones over so that they lay bottom upward. Four grotesque faces with round eyes, large as tea trays, stared blindly up into daylight. They were not in the least like the great classical statues, but rather suggested the round gods' heads in the Marquesas Islands, terrifying and devilish. The two owners of the stones looked desperate, while the two who had found them were triumphant, thinking that they were going to do a good stroke of business.

Both parties looked equally tense as we rolled the grotesque heads back into place, with their faces buried in the earth. Then we thanked them all and went away. The young couple looked after us, open-mouthed. Time would show that the old woman did not forget this.

In the meantime something else happened which puzzled us a good deal. Pottery, or ceramics, was as unknown on Easter Island as everywhere else in Polynesia when our own race came out into the Pacific. This was curious, for the art of pottery was at an early date an important cultural feature in South America, and it was still older among the peoples of Indonesia and Asia. We had found vast quantities of fragments of South American pottery in the Galapagos, but that group of islands lay within range of regular calls from the old seagoing sailing rafts of the mainland, and, furthermore, there was hardly any earth to cover the ancient remains. On Easter Island the conditions were different. It was unlikely that prehistoric voyagers had often found their way from the continent out to Easter Island, and the few jars they might have brought and broken after their arrival would today lie hidden deep under the grass roots. But in any case I had brought a fragment of pottery with me, meaning to ask the natives if they had seen anything like it, for single fragments can tell the detectives of archaeology as much as a written book.

Our first surprise was that several of the old natives, independently of one another, immediately called the fragment *maengo*, a word which was not even in Father Sebastian's lexicon. One of them had heard from his grandfather that *maengo* was an old thing which people had in earlier times. A man had tried to make *maengo* of earth many years ago, but he did not quite succeed. Eroria and Mariana thought they remembered having seen some such fragments in a cave, and they went about for two days trying vainly to find them. The governor's wife had collected some while digging in the garden. And then a native came and told us with an air of mystery that he had a fragment like it at home.

The man, whose name was Andres Haoa, took several days to bring us his ceramic fragment. To our great surprise it was hand-molded in characteristic American Indian fashion, and not turned with the help of a potter's wheel in the European manner. I promised to give him a wealth of cigarettes if he could show us the place where he had found the fragment, so that we ourselves could find more and confirm that the place of discovery was genuine. He then led us to a great *ahu* with a row of fallen statues and a gigantic stepped wall which was strikingly similar to the classical Inca walls in the Andes. He pointed down into the pavement of the upper platform, saying that he had found three pieces of that kind just there several years ago. We carefully raised a number of the slabs with the help of native labor. In one place inside the stone terrace we uncovered two complete skeletons stretched out side by side, a quite unusual form of burial to find on Easter Island. Just beside them we found a descent to two dark chambers, each covered by a gigantic, beautifully cut stone slab, and in both chambers quantities of old skulls lay about higgledy-piggledy. But we found no fragments of pottery, and Andres did not get his full reward.

Next day Carl went back to the place with archaeological equipment and an excavation crew: Ahu Tepeu was obviously a building which in any case deserved closer study. An old native who was with him digging suddenly began to pick up fragments of pottery from the ground; he was the only person who found any, and the bits were so miserably small that it was strange that he had seen them. Then Arne and Gonzalo came galloping up from the village. They had heard from a native woman that the old man had received fragments of pottery from Andres Haoa to help him get his full reward. We compared the new small pieces with the big piece I had formerly got from Andres, and saw at once that one of them was only a corner broken off the big sherd.

Andres was furious at our having discovered his hoax, and would not tell us where he had really found the big piece. He went defiantly to Father Sebastian, who was astonished when three whole ceramic jars were placed on the table before him.

"Look here," said Andres indignantly. "I'm not going to show these to Señor Kon-Tiki because he says I'm a liar. I'm not a liar."

Father Sebastian had never seen any such jars on Easter Island before, and asked Andres where he had found them.

"My father found them once in a cave and said they were good to hold water," Andres replied.

This was obviously a fresh lie, for he had no water in the jars, as he did not even have them in his house. The many

84

friends who wandered in and out and knew every corner of their neighbor's little hut could testify to that.

The three mysterious ceramic jars promptly disappeared without trace, just as they had come, after Father Sebastian alone had had a view of them. And so we had yet another mystery to chew over. The jars did not return to Andres' house. Where did he hide them, and what actually was going on?

In the meantime we had acquired one more problem to tax our brains. I had decided to accept the old policeman Kasimiro's invitation to make a trip out to the bird-men's legendary island to look for his father's secret *rongo-rongo* cave. There was so much whispered gossip among the natives of ancient wooden tablets covered with hieroglyphics, which were still hidden in sealed caves, that anyone long enough on the island was bound gradually to be infected with curiosity.

"We have been offered 100,000 pesos for a *rongo-rongo* tablet, and so one is worth at least a million," the natives said. And I knew in my heart that they were right. But I knew also that if any of them found the entrance to a *rongo-rongo* cave, they would scarcely dare go in. For every *rongo-rongo* tablet had in their ancestors' time been a sacred possession, and the old learned men who had hidden their sacred *rongo-rongo* in caves at the time when Father Eugenio introduced Christianity had put a taboo upon their hieroglyphic boards, so that all who touched them should die. This the natives fully and firmly believed.

There were only some twenty specimens of these wooden tablets in all the museums in the world, and none of the world's scholars had so far been able to make out the inscriptions. They were artistically written symbols of a type not found among any other people: the signs were prettily cut in a row conforming to a continuous serpentine system in which every other line was upside down. The tablets which are preserved today were nearly all handed over by their native owners while they still kept them in their homes. But Father Sebastian was able to tell us about the last which left the island; it had been found in a taboo cave. The native who found it had let himself be tempted by an Englishman whom he took to a place nearby the cave. The Englishman had been told to wait there, and the native had laid a semicircle of small stones before him, which he must not cross. Then the native disappeared and came back with a *rongo-rongo,* which the foreigner bought. A short time afterward the native suddenly went out of his mind, and he actually died. This had done much to increase the natives' old fear of breaking the taboo of a *rongo-rongo* cave, Father Sebastian said.

Whatever the reason may have been, old Kasimiro too drew back when at last I accepted his offer to take me to the cave. He said he did not feel very well, but proposed instead that old Pakomio should show us the place; he had been there too when, as small boys, they had had to stand and wait while Kasimiro's father went to the cave alone. Old Pakomio was a son of the prophetess Angata, who had started so much trouble and superstition when the Routledge expedition was there forty years earlier. I approached him through Father Sebastian, who finally persuaded Pakomio to show us the way.

Old Pakomio reverently climbed on board our motor launch, and we went out to the bird-men's rocky island, Motunui. Behind our backs we had the highest precipice on Easter Island hanging over our heads. On its sharp, topmost crest lay the deserted stone ruins of the ancient cult center Orongo. Ed was digging and surveying up there with his men. We could barely make them out as white dots, and they saw the boat below them as a little grain of rice floating in the blue.

As late as the last century the mightiest men in the island used to sit for weeks on end in the half-subterranean stone houses up on the lofty cliff watching for the year's first migration of sooty terns, which settled on the little rock island of Motunui down below. It was an annual competition to swim out to that island on a reed float and find the very first egg that was laid there. The man who became owner of that egg was exalted to a kind of divinity: he had his head shaved and painted red, he was led in procession to a sacred hut among the statues at the foot of Rano Raraku, and there he had to remain indoors in the shade for a year, without contact with the common people. Food was taken to him by special servants, and he was designated the sacred bird-man of the year. The surface of the whole rock face by the ruins where

Ed was now working was decorated with one confused mass of arch-backed men with long curved birds' beaks, carved as relief sculptures in the rock.

When we went ashore at the legendary bird island, not so much as a feather was to be seen. All the birds had moved to another precipitous rocky island farther along the coast. When we had passed it in the motor launch, a swarm of birds rose up like a smoke cloud over a volcano.

On Motunui we found without trouble the entrances to a number of partially overgrown caves. In a few of them human bones and skulls green with age lay along the walls. In one a carved, diabolical, red-painted head with a goatee beard thrust forward, like a trophy, from the roof. Mrs. Routledge had been in two of these caves. Pakomio stood waiting impatiently outside. He remembered Mrs. Routledge well. But it was not these caves he was to show us. He took us halfway up the cliff and stopped suddenly.

"It was here we baked the chicken," he whispered, pointing to the ground just in front of him.

"What chicken?"

"Kasimiro's father had to bake a chicken in the earth to bring good luck before he went into the cave."

We did not quite get the point, and all Pakomio could add was that this was the custom, and that only the old man had been allowed to stand where he could smell the baked chicken; the children had to keep to the other side of the hearth so that none of the odor could enter their nostrils. They had not even been allowed to see the things that were in the cave, but they knew they were immensely valuable. It had been an experience for Pakomio and Kasimiro just to be allowed to stand nearby and know that the old man was inside inspecting all that wealth.

Of course we did not find the secret cave. When we had made a long and thorough search for the secret entrance among ferns and boulders, Pakomio suggested that the old man might have gone that way just to trick them, and that the cave was sure to be in the opposite direction. When we had clambered about for a while in the opposite direction too, our interest began to flag. The sun was broiling hot, and one by one we gave up the search. Instead we flung ourselves headfirst into a cleft brimful of crystal-clear sea water pumped in by the ocean through a crack in the rock. We dived to the bottom after violet sea urchins, which Pakomio ate raw, and we bumped noses with the queer fish in colors competing with an artist's palette as they glided about. One by one they came gaping out of their hiding places to examine these new additions to Motunui's natural rock aquarium. Glittering rays from above kindled a fireworks display on the marine life down in the sun-filled cleft, where the water was so clear that we felt like bird-men hovering among whirling autumn leaves. It was fantastically beautiful, a Garden of Eden under the sea. We could hardly bring ourselves to climb up onto the dry, hot rocks again, knowing that all the priceless beauty of the pool would be abandoned, perhaps forever, to eyeless sea urchins and color-blind fish.

But we had other uses for our eyes on Easter Island, for picks and spades were beginning to expose to the sunlight things which not even any native had seen for hundreds of years. People began to gossip in the village. They interpreted what was happening with a slight infusion of superstition. How could a foreigner know that old things lay hidden under the turf unless he was in direct contact with the island's own past, with the help of *mana* or supernatural power? At first no one said it in so many words, but one or two came and asked me if I was not really a *kanaka*, a local native, and not a foreigner. My light skin and fair hair meant nothing, for some of their ancestors had been white and red-haired, and the fact that I knew only a few words of Easter Island's Polynesian dialect merely signified that I had been in Tahiti and Norway and other foreign countries so long that I had forgotten most of my old language. At first none of us dreamed that they meant what they said. We took it as a kind of Polynesian compliment. But the more the archaeologists discovered under the turf, the more evident it was to the natives that there was something strange about Señor Kon-Tiki.

It began with Bill's excavation team. Bill had chosen an exciting task. He was the first archaeologist to set to work on the most famous ruin on Easter Island, the great *ahu* at Vinapu. All who have seen this unusual piece of stonemason's work have been struck by its remarkable resemblance to the grand mural constructions of the Inca empire. There is nothing like it on the tens of thousands of other islands in the vast Pacific. Vinapu alone stands as a mirrored reflection of the classical masterpieces of the Incas or their predecessors, and it is all the more striking because it appears on the particular Polynesian island nearest to the Incas' own coast.

Could it have been the master masons from Peru who had been at work out here too? Could it have been scions of their guild who had first landed and begun to chisel gigantic blocks for the Easter Island walls?

The evidence spoke for it. But there was indeed another possibility, which science hitherto had preferred. Technical similarity and geographical proximity could be purely accidental, the result of mere coincidence. The people of Easter Island *could* have produced this masterly and most intricate type of architecture as a result of independent evolution on their own little island. If this was correct, the classical wall at Vinapu was the last phase of a local development, and theoretical research had till now accepted this view without investigating the ruins.

Bill worked at Vinapu for four months with twenty men. But the first few weeks provided the general answer we were eagerly awaiting. The central wall at Vinapu, with the classical stone masonry, belonged to the very oldest building period of Easter Island, contrary to all previous theories. The *ahu* had twice been rebuilt and added to later by far less capable architects who were no longer masters of the complicated Inca type of technique. Ed and Carl, who had been working separately on other *ahus* rebuilt in antiquity, came independently to exactly the same result as Bill.

It was discovered for the first time that there were three clearly separated epochs in Easter Island's enigmatic history. First, a people of highly specialized culture, with the typical South American type of masonry technique, had been at work on Easter Island. Our carbon-14 datings testified that these earliest discoverers of the island had arrived more than a thousand years before the ancestors of the present Polynesian population. The classical buildings had no parallel in the later history of the island. Gigantic blocks of hard basalt were cut like cheese and fitted carefully to one another without a crack or a hole, and these mysterious constructions with their elegant steep walls stood for a long time, looking like altar-shaped and partly stepped fortresses all round the island. But then the second epoch had begun. Most of these early classical structures had been partially pulled down and altered, a paved slope had been built up against the inland wall, and giant figures in human form had been brought from Rano Raraku and erected with their backs to the sea on top of these rebuilt edifices, which now often contained burial chambers.

It was while this gigantic task was at its height in the second epoch that everything came to a sudden and unexpected standstill. Not much more than a century before the Europeans came, led by Roggeveen in 1722, a wave of war and cannibalism swept over the island: with the arrival of the genuine Polynesians, all cultural life came to an abrupt end, and the tragic third phase of Easter Island's history began. No one chiseled great stones now, and the statues were pulled down without reverence. Boulders and shapeless blocks were flung together to make funeral mounds along the walls of the *ahus*, and the great fallen statues were often used as improvised roofs for new burial vaults. The work was makeshift and utterly lacking in technical ability.

As the archaeologists dug and scraped, rents were gradually appearing in the veil of mystery. The history of Easter Island was for the first time beginning to have depth. And one riddle was solved, one piece in the great puzzle placed: we knew now that the specialized South American technique in mural construction was brought to Easter Island in a fully developed form. It was used by the people which had first landed on the island.

Serious natives came in crowds to look at the excavations at Vinapu, where Bill took care to uncover the concealed back wall of the *ahu* so that the stratification of all three epochs was clear to everyone.

While all this was going on, one day Bill stumbled over an unusual red stone on the plain behind the excavation ground. He called me and asked if I shared his impression that the stone had two hands with fingers. It was a long brick-red stone, shaped like a four-sided column, and only the front of it protruded from the turf. It was not at all like the Easter Island statues, either in shape of substance. It was not even of Rano Raraku stone. Nor did the stripes which suggested fingers appear at the very base of the column as in all the six hundred figures known on Easter Island. The natives smiled politely and explained that this was only a *hani-hani,* a red stone.

However, what was visible above the turf reminded me of something very special. It recalled some of the pre-Inca red column statues in the Andes. I had copied the bearded head on the sail of the *Kon-Tiki* raft from just such a four-sided column representing a man, and it too was hewn from a choice red and rough-grained stone exactly like this.

Two-four-five, two-four-five; yes, indeed, those could be fingers. But no head, or other human characteristic, was to be seen.

"Bill," I said, "we must dig. I've seen four-sided red columns similar to that on the shore of Lake Titicaca!"

Father Sebastian had once stopped at this stone when he was going round painting numbers on all the standing and lying statues on Easter Island. Eroria had pointed out the stripes that looked like fingers, but Father Sebastian had shaken his head and gone on with his paintbrush. All the statues on Easter Island were of one type, and none of them looked like the square-cut red stone down there in the earth.

We carefully dug a deep trench in the thick turf all round the stone, and worked our way slowly in toward the sides of the column with a mason's trowel. Were those meant to be fingers, or was it only a stone with accidental furrows? I was so excited that I held my breath as I cut away the first long strip of turf which covered what ought to be a hand. A hand it was! Forearm and upper arm came to light too, continuing all up one side of the statue, and it was the same on the opposite side. The figure even had short legs. It was a statue of a type hitherto unknown on Easter Island; unfortunately the head had been deliberately knocked off and a deep hole bored in the chest where the heart ought to be.

We patted Bill on the shoulder and shook him by the hand. Father Sebastian, the commander of Easter Island's silent old stone guard, was more shaken than anyone else by the unexpected addition to his mighty force of a beheaded, red, four-sided soldier.

"Dr. Mulloy, this is the most important find which has been made on the island in our time," he said. "This statue absolutely does not belong to Easter Island, it belongs to South America."

"But it's been found here," Bill laughed, "and that's what counts."

We raised the red statue with lifting tackle and twenty men to pull, till it stood upright with its short clumsy legs buried in a hole in the earth. The natives who hauled and struggled with the ropes had cause for astonishment, too. It was not a *hani-hani* after all, but how could we foreigners have known?

This was only the beginning. Soon afterward Ed dug a curious little smiling figure up out of the earth in a quite unknown temple he had uncovered near the bird-men's ruined village of Orongo on the top of Rano Kao. Father Sebastian, the governor, and crowds of natives made a pilgrimage up there to see. And where Arne's team was working, at the quarry in Rano Raraku, other peculiar things came to light down in the earth. The most impressive was a bulky giant with a figure as foreign to Easter Island as the red statue at Vinapu. An innocent little corner of a rock with two eyes was all that had been visible when Arne began to dig. Thousands had gone past without seeing that the stone was staring at them, not dreaming that there was more under the soil. The eyes belonged to a burly troll weighing ten tons, which lay hidden with the turf as a quilt.

A thick layer of fine rubble and masses of worn-out stone tools from the abandoned quarry above had buried this giant, and when we brought him to light, he had not a single feature in common with his stiff, blind, and legless neighbors. Both archaeologists and natives stared in equal amazement, and Father Sebastian and the governor had to be fetched again. This figure was so different. It had a fully developed body with complete legs, and it was sculptured in a lifelike kneeling position with a fat backside resting on its heels and with its hands placed on its knees instead of on the belly. It was not naked, like the others, but was wearing a short cloak or *poncho*, with a square opening for the neck. The head was quite round with a peculiar goatee beard and strange eyes with pupils; and the figure stared straight up with an expression which no one had ever seen before on an Easter Island stone giant.

It took us a week to raise this giant, even with the help of the jeep, all our equipment, and multitudes of sailors and mystified natives. But one day it was there, in its humble kneeling position, staring reverently up to the sky. It seemed to be straining its eyes for other planets, for a world which had gone. What had it to do with us, uninitiated aliens? Where were its faithful old servants? And who were those stiff, long-nosed figures up above, whose birth rubble had buried its own person?

When the newly raised figure stood there, as an alien among aliens, the men took their hats off, one by one, and wiped the sweat from their foreheads. Then they drew themselves up to gaze at the figure, as if expecting that something would happen. But the figure just knelt there motionless and ignored us all.

Old Pakomio suggested quietly that it was now time to give the island a new name: it was now no longer Rapa Nui or Easter Island. Everything was changed, he said. Kasimiro and the whole team of excavators agreed, but the mayor added that in that case they would have to find new names for Orongo, Vinapu, and Rano Raraku as well, for nothing was as before. I proposed that they should keep the old names, for the only change was that old sights were now being seen again.

"Old sights are new to us, Señor Kon-Tiki," said Pakomio. "When one has lived on Easter Island all one's life, one remembers every little thing one sees. Now we don't remember all that we see round us, and so it isn't Easter Island any longer."

"Then you can call the island the World's Navel, *Te Pito o te Henua*," I said in fun.

They all brightened up, nodded and laughed as they recognized the name.

"That's what they called our island in old times. So you knew that," said the mayor, with an inquisitive smile.

"Why, everyone knows that," I said.

"Everyone doesn't, but you're a *kanaka*." This came from an old man who was standing behind the statue, nodding slyly to show that he had realized the source of my knowledge.

The natives had never seen anything like this new giant brought up out of the earth to become part of their own little world, kneeling in the hillside. But to Gonzalo and myself it was almost an old friend. We had both been at Tiahuanaco, the oldest pre-Inca cult center by Lake Titicaca, and there we had seen similar kneeling stone giants which could have easily been cut by the same master, so like they were in style, features, and position. They had knelt at Tiahuanaco for over a thousand years, along with the bearded red figure and other stiff four-sided columns depicting mysterious men, surrounded by the most enormous and best cut blocks of masonry which the whole Inca realm can offer.

Indeed, in the whole of ancient America there is nothing to equal this imposing megalithic work. Archaeologists have discovered that the largest cut blocks weigh over a hundred tons. And they too were transported for mile upon mile across the plain. They then were stood up on end and lifted up on top of one another as if they were empty cardboard boxes, and in the midst of these ruins of unroofed walls and terraces the old masters placed all their strange statues in human form. The largest is twenty-five feet high; many others are considerably smaller, but still of superhuman dimensions.

Tiahuanaco lies there in the mountain plains, mysterious and desolate, with all its statues and cut blocks of masonry, and the Incas say that these were there equally deserted and ownerless when the first Inca came into power. At that time, they say, the master sculptors had already migrated into the open Pacific, and left the field to the primitive tribes of the Uru and Aymara Indians. Only the legend of vanished creators of Tiahuanaco lived on. But for the moment we left the legends alone. We were digging in the earth for bare facts, and what we found were mute stone men. Tribal memories may be called upon later to blow life into the nostrils of the dead stone figures.

One of the mysterious things about the Easter Island statues had been that all were of the same type: one was astonishingly like another, and all were quite characteristic of Easter

Island and nowhere else. Outside this one island there was nothing in the whole world which harmonized exactly with them. Before the dawn of history unknown civilizations had abandoned large stone statues in human form all the way from Mexico down to Peru and Bolivia, and on the very nearest islands where the ocean current from Peru reaches the easternmost outposts of Polynesia. But none were precisely of the Easter Island style. And in the central and western Pacific, toward Asia, there are no statues of any kind at all. How could Easter Island's giant figures have been inspired from outside, when there was nothing quite like them anywhere else? Most research workers, therefore, have been led to believe that the idea once arose on this little oceanic island, independently of the outside world, gigantic and incomprehensible as the whole undertaking was. The more imaginative took refuge in the theory of a sunken continent: similar statues must be found on the bottom of the sea.

But now statues of different types were beginning to appear in the soil of Easter Island. Furthermore, inside the walls of several of the *ahus* we found a number of unusual figures, some of which had been smashed to pieces and only used as building stone and filling during the second cultural epoch, at the time when the classical walls had been rebuilt and the gigantic statues from Rano Raraku had been placed as huge monuments on top of them. Father Sebastian also suddenly recollected having stumbled upon a couple of figures the size of a man made of hard black basalt. One of them he had seen walled-in as foundation stone in the façade of an old *ahu;* only the broad back projected. And right in the actual village area Father Sebastian and the natives helped us to put another stout fellow on his legs. This too proved to be a deviating and primitive type, and it was of the same kind of red stone as the headless figure at Vinapu.

Now we were a long way nearer our goal; the second piece in the puzzle was soon in its place. We had discovered that the men who had built the beautiful South American type of walls in the first period had made statues unlike the famous stone giants from Rano Raraku which have made Easter Island so renowned. These alien figures left from the first epoch were generally not much larger than a man. They had round heads, short faces, and large eyes; they were sometimes of red tuff and sometimes black basalt, but also of the yellowish-gray Rano Raraku stone which became all important to the sculptors of the subsequent period. These earliest island statues had few features in common with the famous Easter Island giants except that they too usually held their arms flexed with both hands in a stiff position on their stomachs, so that the fingers pointed toward one another. This was also a peculiarity of a large number of old pre-Inca stone men and of the statues on the neighboring islands in Polynesia.

Now at last we were on speaking terms with the taciturn statues of Easter Island. It was the abased and humiliated walled-up specimens that first loosened their tongues, and they set the haughty and defiant fellows up on the top gossiping too, right up to the quarry in the mountain. The family tree of the stone men had begun with a gust of wind from the other world which brought ideas and technique to the island along with the classical masonry. The stumpy figures which were later pushed as foundation rubble into the walls, the headless red pillar statue on the plain at Vinapu, and the large kneeling one which lay buried under the rubble at the foot of Rano Raraku, belonged to this early period.

Then came another epoch in which local sculptors had invented a more elegant and exclusive style of their own, and bulky colossi with red hair were carved and carried up to the top of the numerous rebuilt walls. As the sculptors gained experience, the new colossi steadily increased in size: they became larger and larger, ever larger. Those which had already been erected on the *ahus* were big enough, but many of those which were left under way were bigger, and some of those which stood at the foot of the volcano waiting to have their backs finally chiseled were bigger still. And the biggest of all was the giant seven stories high who lay unfinished in the quarry itself, with his back as part of the solid rock.

How would this local evolution have ended? Where would the limit of the possible have been ultimately fixed? No one knows, for before the limit was reached the catastrophe came which halted the advance of the marching stone giants, and they were all flung flat on the ground. All because the witch did not get her lobster, the present-day people of the island believed. But the fight was probably for stronger meat, for the march of the stone giants ended just when the third epoch began, and the cannibals suddenly took the stage.

The population of the island today is the freshest shoot sprung from the victorious warrior tribe of the third epoch. It was no peaceful affair when their Polynesian ancestors arrived from the palm islands to westward. Of the battles which followed their arrival, of the statues which fell, of the time when adzes cut their way into men of flesh and blood instead of men of stone, we were soon to hear stories from the living population of the island. For during this epoch their own forefathers had really been present and played the leading part. The third epoch was not quite dead yet, although customs and beliefs of western civilization had been adopted, and although peace and tolerance now reigned on the island.

CHAPTER FIVE

The Long-Ears' Secret

IN THE CAMP at Anakena life followed its usual round. The sun shone on our gleaming white ship anchored outside the rocks in the bay. It seemed to have become a part of Easter Island, a landmark like the bird islands round the coast. No ship had ever remained at the island for so long—none but those which had been washed up against the rocks and now lay at the bottom of the sea with the tops of their masts many fathoms beyond the grasp of the trade wind.

When the on-shore wind thundered too loud on the tent walls, the steward hurried out to the ship and brought ashore an extra supply of provisions, for it sometimes happened that the skipper sounded the siren and told us on the walkie-talkie that he must move out. Then the ship went off round the coast and found shelter under the cliffs behind the cape where we had first anchored, at the foot of Rano Raraku. For a day or two the bay in front of the camp looked painfully empty, like a familiar picture suddenly altered. But then one morning when we crawled out of our tents, the ship would be there, lying in her usual place, pitching in the morning sunshine.

It was always a good feeling to return to Anakena Bay, whether we had been away from camp a day or a week. When we saw the white ship behind the black rocks, and in front of them the green tents on yellow grass and sunny sand dunes, all in a wide blue frame of sea and sky, then we were at home. At the end of the day's toil the breakers called aloud to us to come and bathe, and the steward hammered on his frying pan and invited us to a tasty dinner. In the evening we lay in groups on the grass and talked under the stars or in the brilliant moonlight. Some of us sat near the lamps in the mess tent, reading and writing or listening to the phonograph, while others jumped onto horses and disappeared at a gallop over the ridge. The seamen had become regular cowboys on shore; and when the men were starting for the village of Hangaroa, the old temple square in front of the tents was a regular circus ring full of neighing and rearing horses. The messboy broke an arm by taking a short cut through the scree, and the doctor had to set it. But what sacrifices will a man not make to arrive quickly in a distant village when a real hula dance is the attraction?

We soon knew most of the people in the village. But the black-eyed village doctor was rarely to be seen even by those who went to the hula dancing, and his friend the schoolmaster we never saw. They did not attend Father Sebastian's little church, and so were never present at the Sunday dinners which followed, either at the nuns' house or with the governor and his wife. But one day fate unexpectedly brought the schoolmaster into our world.

The governor had asked several times on behalf of the school if the children might make a trip round the island in the expedition ship: it would mean so much to them all. They could go ashore at Anakena and have a picnic lunch in front of the camp. When Father Sebastian told me that none of them had ever seen their own island from the sea, except from the village bay, I promised to ask the skipper to bring the ship round to the village. In fact, the whole of the main deck was admirably suited to children, for it had high sides curved inward which no child could climb over. Furthermore, as everybody said, the native children could swim like fish; they began to lark about in the bay long before they started school.

We dropped anchor off Hangaroa early one morning in fine weather, and 115 native school children were taken on board:

they were an eighth part of the population of the whole island. The schoolmaster himself, the village doctor and his assistant, the governor's assistant, three nuns, and seven adult natives went along to look after the children. There were cheers and shouting all over the deck, the children sang and were wildly excited. But when the anchor was raised with a clatter and crash, and the siren sounded a farewell to the village, most of them seemed to become quieter and looked almost sadly shoreward toward their homes. It was as though they were going on a voyage round the world instead of a daytime trip around Easter Island. After all, this was their entire world.

When the ship began to pitch gently in a long, shining swell, the children were all seasick without exception. The only one of the guests who was in top form was the schoolmaster. He had been full of energy from the moment he came on board, a portly figure amid the crowd of children. He declared that he had never been seasick, though he had made countless voyages in all kinds of weather. With his raven hair and flashing black eyes the schoolmaster reminded us of his friend the village doctor, and he immediately displayed the same political leanings. But even if his black eyes were as hard as coals when he was preaching politics, something gentle came into his face when he took out his pencil to draw the rolling contours of the coast in his diary, or when he saw a chance of patting one of the children on the head. He stomped about, a solid sturdy figure, consoling his seasick pupils in their own Polynesian language. Now he was sitting with some of them and giving them pills, now he was dancing off to the rails dragging a long, weedy lad whose signs and gestures made it evident to everyone that a clear road was needed.

As we rounded the cape the sea became so quiet that some of the bigger children forgot their seasickness. Instead of following our advice and remaining amidships where there was the least movement, they all wanted to go forward into the bow to watch the seas being plowed aside. Soon the schoolmaster had to step in and drag them back, green and gaping, to a horizontal position on the hatch. There was no further gaiety till we entered Anakena Bay. Then the children suddenly came to life and Polynesian singing again filled the air.

When the ship lay in her usual place off the camp at Anakena, all the children were brought ashore and shown the tent village on Hotu Matua's old site. Then their chaperons took the whole party down to a temple terrace, where they picnicked in the grass at the foot of the wall. A few natives had come over the island on horseback to help, and six lambs were baked in Polynesian fashion between hot stones in the earth. The afternoon passed, and while the children went swimming and diving in the bay, another group, led by a nun, was enthusiastically singing their ancestors' song of Hotu Matua, who had come here to Anakena Bay.

Suddenly the schoolmaster looked at his watch, clapped his hands, and told the children to get ready to leave. The sea was quiet with a gentle rolling swell, and the motor launch lay as usual moored to the large raft anchored a little way from shore. The children had been using it as a diving board. The engineers went out with the first boatload to get everything ready on board, and when the launch came back, the schoolmaster stood on the beach again rounding up pupils for another trip. The second group was rowed out to the large, anchored raft via the little landing raft, and some of the children treated themselves to an extra farewell plunge by swimming alongside. When the launch had gone, for the second time, some rowdy boys swam out on their own and crawled onto the raft to await the next trip. The schoolmaster, therefore, went out to the raft himself to exercise better control, and when the launch started for the ship he was in it. The other grownups in charge of the children remained ashore to divide the rest of them for the last trips.

Then the accident happened, like a bolt from a clear sky. While the launch was chugging peacefully round the outermost point on her way to the ship, the children began to move about. Everybody suddenly wanted to rush forward and see the bow wave. The schoolmaster tried with all his might to keep order among the children, but now they did not even listen to Polynesian. The carpenter put the engine in reverse, and he bellowed at the children to go back, but at the same second catastrophe came in the shape of a leisurely wave. The launch, with a capacity of two tons and only half-loaded, ran her bow deep into the side of the slow surge and filled in an instant. All that was to be seen was the stern and a mass of swimmers' heads.

On the ship a boat was immediately swung out, while the expedition doctor and I jumped onto the landing raft down on the beach. All the others ran out to the far end of the point, which was only about eighty yards from the scene of the disaster. I turned my head as we hurriedly rowed out and saw that some of the children were swimming in toward the point, but most of them were bobbing up and down in one place round the stern of the boat.

We were soon there, and went straight for the carpenter and a native schoolboy who were swimming side by side supporting two helpless creatures. When we hauled them up on the raft, I saw that one was the mayor's thirteen-year-old daughter, a pretty little girl with strikingly white skin and red-gold hair. Then I dived in, while the doctor stayed on the raft to row about and haul children on board.

Now the first swimmers from the point had arrived too, headed by the skipper. We picked up children one by one and shoved them up onto the raft. Most of them were quite apathetic and only let themselves bob up and down without making any attempt to save themselves. When the raft was almost packed full, the skipper and carpenter came swimming up with the schoolmaster whose huge form floated by itself. It took several men to heave the top part of his body onto the raft. Now all our sailors from ashore were at the scene, as well as the village doctor's assistant and half a dozen natives. These swimmers began to push the raft in toward the point while the doctor rowed like fury in spite of all the children on top of him.

The skipper and I went on swimming around to make sure we had overlooked no one. Then the ship's boat arrived, and the engineers dived from her, but there was nothing left at the bottom except discarded clothing. Forty-eight children were on board the ship already, and a count of those ashore showed that no one was missing.

When we reached the point, all the children from the raft had been carried ashore onto the rocks, where our own doctor conducted artificial respiration with the help of the village doctor's assistant and bystanders. The village doctor, who had been standing on the point receiving those arriving on the raft, had jumped on board to take it right into the beach when it proved impossible to haul the heavy schoolmaster up on the sharp lava rocks.

In the harrowing hours which followed, while night sank over the island, the village doctor worked on his friend the schoolmaster on the beach, helped by our biggest and strongest men, while out on the point all the rest worked over the children. Nearly a dozen were in need of treatment. Everywhere people were running about with kerosene lamps, carrying blankets and clothes. Up in the camp Yvonne had thrown all the tents open and was serving hot food. As riders began to stream in from the village, people swarmed into the tents and all around us in the dark.

It was a night of dread which I shall never forget.

An atmosphere of horror hung over Anakena Valley and was emphasized by a strange gray and colorless sort of rainbow which stretched itself gloomily over the black night sky, just where the moon was hidden behind the ridge. The children came back to life one by one and were carried into the tents and put to bed. But the hours passed, and two of them did not move. One was the little red-haired girl. The mayor sat motionless by her side and said in a calm voice:

"She's well off. She's always been good, she's with the Virgin Mary."

I have never felt grief at such close quarters. I have never seen people take it more quietly. Those who had lost their children took our hands silently in both of theirs as if to show us that they knew that we who owned the boat could not help what had happened. Those whose children had been saved flung themselves on our necks and wept.

The last to come up from the beach were eight men carrying the schoolmaster on a stretcher. The sky was black and the gray arch of the colorless rainbow still lay across it as a frame above the eight lanterns swinging in the night. The village doctor looked at me with quiet, coal-black eyes. He said: "The island has lost a good man, Señor. He died at his

103

post and his last words were: '*Kau kau pokil*'—'Tread water, boys!'"

The next time I saw the village doctor was in Father Sebastian's little church. He was standing motionless with bared head beside his friend's bier. The two children had been buried the day before with a simple and beautiful ceremony. The whole village had walked in the funeral procession singing gently of the two who had gone to heaven. Today Father Sebastian's address was short but warm.

"You have loved your pupils," he ended. "May you meet again."

On the way to the burial place, we heard the village doctor muttering: "Tread water, boys. Tread water."

The natives forgot the whole disaster incredibly fast. The relatives at once began to slaughter cattle and sheep for the great feasts which they always held when they lost their dear ones. They even came riding over to us with whole haunches of oxen and large quantities of other meat. But what surprised us most were the conditions inside the tents after everything had been tidied up. For two centuries the most notorious characteristic of the natives of Easter Island has been thieving, the pilfering of everything they can lay their hands on. On that dark, tragic night there had been no guard, all the natives went in and out of the tents as they liked, and everything we owned lay in the open. We did not expect to see a single thing again. But we were completely wrong. Nothing had gone: not a hat, not a comb, not a shoelace. And all the dry clothes and blankets which were lent to the children when they went away on horseback, came back from the village, washed and ironed, in neat piles. Nothing was missing.

However, one of our men had thrown his watch into his hat on shore when he dived in to the rescue. That watch was stolen by a native out on the point while the owner was in the water saving children. It was a shabby action, but of little importance.

I met Father Sebastian in the churchyard for the first time after the disaster. "It was terrible about the children," was all I could say.

"It was worse about the stolen watch," said Father Sebastian without blinking an eyelid.

"What do you mean?" I asked, quite shocked at his answer.

Father Sebastian laid his hand on my shoulder and said calmly: "We all have to die. But we don't have to steal!"

I shall never forget those words. I merely gazed at him quite bewildered until I suddenly realized once again that I had met here on Easter Island a great personality, perhaps the greatest I had ever known. His teachings were to him as real as life itself, not just edifying words reserved for Sundays. To him teachings and beliefs were completely one.

He said no more, and silently we walked back to the village.

A few days later I met Father Sebastian again. I had halted all work during those days, but the natives did not like that. When the sun had risen and set and risen again, yesterday was yesterday, and today today, and they wanted to work for more rations, more daily pay, and more goods. The mayor sat on his steps and carved a bird-man out of a large chunk of wood while the shavings flew thick and fast, and he smiled and waved and showed his work as the jeep passed.

We stopped outside Father Sebastian's little house next to the church, and I saw him through the window. He beckoned to me to come into his little study, where he sat at a table thickly covered with papers and letters. On the wall behind him was a shelf of books written in an impressive number of languages. They formed a colorful and learned frame for the big and bearded old sage who sat in his white robe with turned-down hood behind a small table. The only thing I missed, which would have made the picture perfect, was a large quill pen in an inkstand on the table; Father Sebastian had a fountain pen. But to make up for that, an old stone adz lay there as a paperweight.

This old priest was a man of exception for our own twentieth century. While he was indeed completely at home among us, he might just as easily have represented a learned monk in a medieval painting, or a bust of a Roman sage, or a portrait of a scholar on a Greek vase or on a clay tablet from old Sumeria. Father Sebastian could have lived among any people for thousands of years past and been himself, with no adjustments, and still the joy of life and youth would have shone from his blue eyes.

That day Father Sebastian was full of enthusiasm; he had something particular on his mind. He wanted to ask me to start excavation at a very special place on the island, a place which figured more than any other in the traditions of the natives.

I heard for the twentieth time the legend of Iko's ditch, or the long-ears' earth oven. Everyone who has landed on Easter Island has heard the legend, everyone who has written about the mystery of the island has dealt with it. The natives had shown me the marks in the earth where the ditch had once been, and all had been eager to tell me the story. Father Sebastian had reported the tradition in his own book. Now I heard it from his own lips, with a request that I would set a team to dig in the ditch.

"I believe in the legend," he said. "I know that science has claimed that the ditch is natural, but scientists can make mistakes. I know the natives. The tradition of the ditch is too living to be mere fancy."

The story of the long-ears' defense ditch begins far back in the legends of the present population. It begins where the march of the statues ends, and describes the catastrophe which put an end forever to Easter Island's golden age.

There had then been two peoples on the island, and they lived side by side all over it. One of these peoples had a peculiar appearance: their men and women pierced their ears and put heavy weights into the lobes till the ears were artificially lengthened right down to the shoulders. For this reason they were called *Hanau eepe*, "long-ears," while the other people were the *Hanau momoko*, "short-ears."

The long-ears were an energetic people, filled with plans for improving the island, and the short-ears had to toil to help them make walls and statues. The long-ears' last idea was to rid the whole of Easter Island of superfluous stone, so that all the earth could be cultivated. This work was begun on the Poike Plateau, the easternmost part of the island, and the short-ears had to carry every single loose stone to the edge of the cliff and fling it into the sea. On the grassy peninsula of Poike today there is not a loose stone, while the rest of the island is thickly covered with black and red scree and lava blocks.

Now things were going too far for the short-ears. They were tired of carrying stones for the long-ears. They decided on war. The long-ears fled from every part of the island and established themselves at the easternmost end, on the cleared Poike Peninsula. Under the command of their chief, Iko, they dug a trench nearly two miles long which separated the Poike Plateau from the rest of the island. This trench they filled with a great quantity of branches and tree trunks till it was a gigantic far-flung pyre, ready to be set on fire if the short-ears on the plain below tried to storm the slope leading to the plateau. Poike Peninsula was like a huge fortress, with a sheer drop of six hundred feet all round the coast: thus the long-ears felt themselves secure.

But one of the long-ears had a short-eared wife: her name was Moko Pingei and she was living up on Poike with her husband. She was a traitress and had arranged a signal with the short-ears down on the plain. When they saw her sitting, plaiting a large basket, the short-ears were to steal in a long file past the place where she sat.

One night the short-ears' spies saw Moko Pingei plaiting a basket at one end of Iko's ditch, and they stole one by one past the place where she sat, right at the edge of the cliff. They sneaked on along the outer edge of the plateau till at last they had completely surrounded Poike. Another army of short-ears down on the plain marched openly up toward the ditch. The unsuspecting long-ears lined up to face them and set fire to the whole pyre. Then the other short-ears rushed forward from their hiding places, and in the bloody fight which followed all the long-ears were burned in their own ditch.

Only three of the long-ears succeeded in leaping through the fire and escaping in the direction of Anakena. One of them was called Ororoina and another Vai, but the name of the third is forgotten. They hid in a cave which the inhabitants can point out to this day. There they were found, and two of them were stabbed to death with sharp stakes, while the third and last, Ororoina, was allowed to remain alive as the only surviving long-ear. When the short-ears dragged him out of the cave, he shouted *orro, orro, orro* in his own language, but this was a language which the short-ears did not understand.

Ororoina was taken to the house of one of the short-ears who was named Pipi Horeko and lived at the foot of the hill called Toatoa. There he married a short-ear of the Haoa family and had many descendants, among them Inaki-Luki and Pea. They in turn had a number of descendants, the last of whom are still living among the short-ears on the island now.

This was the tradition of the long-ears' ditch as related by Father Sebastian. I knew that the two expeditions before ours had heard variations of the same tradition, and had been to look at the remains of the ditch. Mrs. Routledge had been doubtful, and was inclined to think that the ditch itself must have been a natural geological depression which the long-ears might have used in self-defense. Métraux went still further. His conclusion was that the ditch was merely a natural formation, that the whole legend was inspired by the natives' urge to explain a geographical peculiarity, that the whole story of the long-ears and short-ears was an invention of the people in fairly recent times.[1]

A professional geologist had also been up to have a look at the long-ears' ditch, and he concluded that the ditch was a natural formation caused in prehuman times by a flow of lava from the center of Easter Island, which had run into an older congealed flow from Poike; where they met, a kind of ditch had been formed.

When the specialists had given their verdict, the natives were bewildered. But they stuck to their guns: this was Iko's defense ditch, the long-ears' earth oven. And Father Sebastian believed in their version.

"It means something to me personally if you will dig there," he said, and he almost leaped with excitement when I agreed.

Carl was to direct the excavation of the long-ears' ditch. We jolted off next day with five natives in the jeep, along a cleared track through the stony plain to Poike. Above us Poike's smooth grassy slopes lay like green carpet, but around us and behind lay the scree, like a covering of black coke. Up on Poike we could have driven freely where we liked

---

[1] Alfred Métraux, *Ethnology of Easter Island* (Honolulu, 1940), pp. 72–74.

A long-ear of Easter Island with beard and feather crown, drawn on the spot during Captain Cook's visit.

with the jeep, but we stopped at the foot of the slope, where all the grass began. All along the hillside from north to south we saw a faint depression in the ground. In some places it was fairly deep, in others it disappeared for short stretches, then became apparent again, continuing right out to the precipices on both sides of the peninsula. Here and there we saw a hummock like a bulwark of earth on the upper side of the depression. This was *Ko te Ava o Iko,* Iko's ditch, or *Ko te Umu o te Hanau eepe,* the long-ears' earth oven.

Carl wanted to test the ground at a few points first before we began to dig in earnest. We walked slowly along the depression and stationed each of the five natives at wide intervals; each of them was told to dig a rectangular hole straight down through the soil. Never have I seen natives take up pick and shovel with greater zeal. As no damage could be done, we went for a short turn along the plateau. When we came back down the slope to look at the first experimental hole, the old fellow digging there was a good six feet down in the ground, hacking and shoveling as the sweat ran off him. In the mustard-yellow earth wall round him we saw a broad red-and-black horizontal stripe. Charcoal and ashes in thick layers! There had once been a great fire down in this earth, and Carl was sure that the heat had been intense, or else the fire had burned for a long time; otherwise the ash would never have become as red as this. Before he could say any more, I was off across the hillside to look into the next hole. Carl hurried after me.

The village sexton, Josef, stuck his smiling face up out of the earth farther on. He had found the same remains of a fire, and showed us a handful of carbonized boughs and pieces of wood. We ran on to the next hole, and the next. At each one we were met by the same sight, the flaming red band of ashes surrounded by black carbonized remains which wound round the walls of the hole.

Father Sebastian was summoned, and he ran from hole to hole to look at the red ash, his white gown fluttering in the breeze. His face was radiant as we rode by the taciturn statues of Rano Raraku on our way to dinner at Anakena. He looked back on the great triumph of the day and forward to good food and good Danish beer, for now we must go to the camp and refresh ourselves for the exciting adventure of the next day, when the real digging would start on Poike.

Next morning a team of diggers was set to uncover an exact cross section of the depression, and in the days that followed Carl started excavations which revealed the whole secret of the ditch. The topmost part of the depression indeed was merely the work of nature and followed the border of an old lava flow. But deeper down industrious men had been at work. They had hewn their way into the rock and constructed an artificial defense ditch with a rectangular bottom, twelve feet deep, about forty feet wide, and nearly two miles long across the hillside. It had been a gigantic undertaking. Slingstones and carved slabs were found down among the ash. Sand and rubble cut away from the bottom of the ditch had been used to build a rampart along the upper side of the ditch, and the deposit of rubble there showed that it had been carried up from the ditch in large plaited baskets.

We knew now that Iko's ditch was a defense work superbly laid out by man all along the hillside and that down in the ditch great quantities of wood had been piled and a huge fire lighted. We looked at the natives. Now it was our turn to stare: this they had known. From generation to generation they had been told that this filled-in depression was the remains of Iko's defense work and the scene of the final slaughter of the long-ears.

One of the easiest things for a modern archaeologist to put a date to is charcoal from an old fire. Its age is fixed within certain limits by measuring its radioactivity, which diminishes at a known rate from year to year. This is known as carbon-14 dating. The great fire in the long-ears' earth oven had burned about three hundred years before our own time. But the whole of the elaborate defense works in the ditch had been built by men long before this final catastrophe, for the ditch was half-filled with sand when the defense pyre against the short-ears was constructed and burned. There were remains of fires farther down, and the original makers of the ditch had flung up the gravel and earth onto a hearth on the ground above, which dated from about 400 A.D. This was the oldest date which had been established so far in any part of Polynesia.

Fresh life had now been breathed into the story of the long-ears, both in the village and in the camp at Anakena. There seemed to be more meaning to the giant statues with their curiously long beaglelike ears.

One evening I strolled among the long-eared statues at the foot of Rano Raraku. I had so much to think about, and one thinks best alone under the stars. One does not really know a place properly till one has slept there. I have slept in the queerest places—on the altar stone in Stonehenge, in a snow-drift on the top of Norway's highest mountain, in adobe chambers in the deserted cave villages of New Mexico, by the ruins of the first Inca's birthplace on the Island of the Sun in Lake Titicaca. Now I wanted to sleep in the old stone quarry in Rano Raraku. Not because I was superstitious and believed that the spirits of the long-ears would come and betray their secrets, but because I would like to assimilate fully the peculiar atmosphere of the place. I clambered over huge stone bodies lying up on the ledges until I was in the midst of a swarm of figures at a place where one giant had been removed from his birthplace. The bed in which he had been born lay empty, like a theater box with a canopy.

From here I had a splendid view of the countryside, and here I should keep dry if it poured rain. For the moment the weather was superb. The sun was about to descend behind the silhouette of Rano Kao's steep volcanic wall at the other end of the island, and red, purple, and lilac cloudbanks had rolled up as a screen before the bed of the retiring sun-god. Nevertheless the sun managed to thrust some silver rays through and down onto the breakers far away, which slowly and noiselessly moved shoreward in their unceasing attack on the distant corner of the island. The rays of the evening sun filled the foaming crests with gleaming silver, and silvery dust hung in the air at the volcano's foot. It was a sight for the gods. And among a multitude of giant gods I sat, a solitary little human being.

I tore off a few stiff tufts of grass and swept the foot of the giant's forsaken bed clear of sand and sheep's dung. Then in the last paling rays of the sun I made myself a good bed of

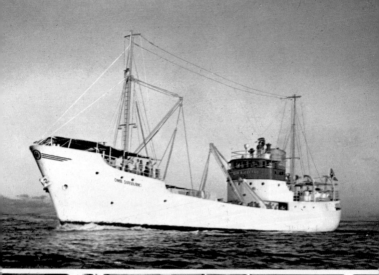

ABOVE: Our expedition sailed to Easter Island in a converted Greenland trawler. BELOW: Lunch on board. From the left: Gonzalo, Bill, myself, Yvonne, Anette, the skipper, Carl, Arne, and Ed.

ABOVE: Thor Junior on the bridge. He was excused from school for an adventurous voyage as deck boy. Little Anette quickly picked up South Sea ways, and soon could sing in Polynesian and dance the hula. BELOW: Our camp at Anakena, on King Hotu Matua's old landing site by the sea.

To measure an Easter Island head, one must be a good climber. The skipper is perched twenty feet above the ground. We wondered how much of the statue was hidden beneath the soil.

ABOVE: Father Sebastian Englert was the uncrowned king of Easter Island and the natives' best friend. Captain Arnaldo Curti was the Chilean governor, who ruled his happy little community, the loneliest in the world, with wisdom and skill. BELOW: Two of the old Pakarati brothers narrating legends to the author by the crater lake in Rano Raraku.

Great topknots of stone were placed, as wigs, on the heads of the statues after they were raised on the *ahu* platforms. The topknots were hewn from a red stone found in a crater seven miles from the quarry where the statues were made. These three which lie abandoned in the shallows were once carried along the coast in large vessels made from *totora* reed.

Easter Island, the isle of a thousand mysteries, had never before been excavated. What secrets lay hidden under the soil? What mysterious navigators had found their way to the world's loneliest island? What had happened, and

when and why and how? At the foot of the extinct volcano of Rano Raraku, the statues' maternity home, stone giants stood silently side by side guarding the ancient secrets, their lips tightly locked.

ABOVE: Proud features once were chiseled from hard stone. What race provided the models for these great heads? BELOW: On the rim of the volcano Rano Kao lay Orongo, the ruined village of the bird-men. Ed and the doctor study strange bird-men carved in the lava outcrops of the crater ruin. The entrance to an underground ceremonial house begins in the hole at the left under Ed's feet.

grass and ferns. Down on the plain below me I heard two girls singing tender Polynesian love songs. A shepherd going to his hut stopped along the way to set fire to the grass. The dry season had long since begun, and the grass was yellow and stiff. It had to be burned away so that new grass might come through fresh and green for the sheep. As long as it was light I saw only the smoke from the grass fires, which lay like a gray fog over the plain. Then night came and the smoke was swallowed up by the darkness, but not the fire. The darker it grew the brighter the flames shone out, and soon the innocent grass fires looked like a thousand red pyres in the night.

Suddenly there was a cold breeze, and I pulled the sleeping bag well up under my chin as I lay listening to the silence of the night, drinking in the whole atmosphere of the long-ears' quarry. The silhouettes of the burly giants round me looked like black theater sets framing a stage. Now the action moved to the dark plain below, where fire continually sprang up in new places. It looked as if a thousand invisible short-ears were stealing in on a wide front, torch in hand, to storm the quarry. Time had again ceased to exist. Night and the stars had always been there, and man who played with fire.

I was just dropping off to sleep with this impression burned into my mind when I suddenly heard something prowling quietly and cautiously in the dry grass. Who could be feeling his way about so carefully up here in the quarry? Natives looking for what I had put down beside me in the dark? There was a pattering noise close by my head, and I twisted myself round and switched on the flashlight. Not a soul. Only monstrous eyebrows and a couple of gigantic noses stuck up out of the grass on the ledge next to me, and threw queer shadows on the rock. It had clouded over and was beginning to rain a little, but not where I lay. I turned off the light and tried to sleep. Again the pattering noise around me, and this time in the glow of the flashlight I caught sight of a brown cockroach as big as my thumb. I fumbled about and got hold of a clumsy stone pick, one of the type strewn about everywhere in the quarry. But before I got in a blow at the creature, I saw another sitting motionless beside it, and another, and another. I had never before seen such large cockroaches on Easter Island. They sat in groups on the rock wall beside me, on the roof over my head, a couple were actually sitting on my sleeping bag. I took the stone pick and killed the largest ones nearest to me, and swept off those which were on the sleeping bag. Suddenly I caught sight of two fearful eyes staring right into my face, with a grinning toothless mouth beneath them. This was sheer nightmare. The horrible face proved to be a rock carving of a terrifying *make-make* spirit which had, in the remote past, been carved on the wall just by my head.

I killed a few more cockroaches, but finally decided to yield to superior numbers; otherwise I should sit there murdering the whole night. I pulled the hood of my sleeping bag well down over my head and tried to doze off. But the rock was uncomfortable. I thought how appallingly hard this rock really was, not to lie on, but to hew. I grasped the stone pick once more and hit the wall of the quarry as hard as I could. I had done it before, and knew well that the pick sprang back from the wall without making any mark but a light dusty patch. In fact, the skipper had been up here with me once and tried his luck with hammer and chisel, and it took him half an hour to chip off a piece the size of his own fist. We had figured that over 700,000 cubic feet had been hewn out of the solid rock just on the ledges visible from where we stood, and the archaeologists thought that this estimate could safely be doubled. It was incomprehensible. Yet an idea that I had been toying with for a long time forced its way back into my mind. Why not start an experiment? The stone picks still lay where the sculptors had flung them down, and the last long-ear still had living descendants in the village. Perhaps work could actually be started in the old quarry again.

Next morning the sun shone golden over the plain, and only a mass of wings and bent legs lay around me to show that the invasion of cockroaches had not been a dream. I saddled my horse and galloped along the ancient grass-grown track which led in the direction of the village bay.

Father Sebastian gave me a roguish smile when I told him where I had come from and what I had in mind. He was at once in favor of the plan, so long as we chose a secluded corner of the quarry and did not spoil the impression of Rano Raraku as seen from the plain below. But I did not want just anyone to help me make a statue. Knowing that Father Sebastian was the leading authority on local family trees, and had published a genealogy of Easter Island, I told him that I was looking for natives who were descended from the last long-ear.

"There's only one family left today which is descended in a direct line from Ororoina," said Father Sebastian. "It's a family which chose the surname Adam when Christianity was introduced in the last century. Or Atan, as the natives of this island pronounce it. You know the eldest of the brothers: he's Pedro Atan, the mayor."

"The mayor!" I was more than a little surprised and could not help smiling.

"Yes, he's rather a buffoon, but he's by no means stupid, and he is a most friendly fellow," Father Sebastian assured me.

"But he doesn't look like a native at all," I said. "His thin lips, his narrow sharp nose, his light skin. . . ."

"He's of pure native blood," Father Sebastian went on. "And there are only eighty or ninety of the native population who can claim that today. Besides, he's a genuine long-ear in direct descent on his father's side."

I was on my horse in a twinkling and rode up on the rough village road to the mayor's little white-painted cottage. He was sitting working at a set of chessmen in the form of statues, bird-men, and other familiar Easter Island subjects.

"This is for you, Señor," he said, proudly displaying his little masterpieces.

"You're an artist, Mayor Don Pedro," I said.

"Yes, the best on the island," was the glib reply.

"Is it true that you're a long-ear too?"

"Yes, Señor," said the mayor with the utmost gravity. He jumped up and stood at attention like a soldier who has been called out of the ranks.

"I'm a long-ear, a genuine long-ear, and I'm proud of it," he said dramatically, striking himself on the chest.

115

"Who made the great statues?"

"The long-ears, Señor," he replied emphatically.

"I've heard some of the other natives say it was the short-ears."

"That's an absolute lie, Señor. They're trying to get credit for what my ancestors did. The long-ears made everything. Haven't you seen that the statues have long ears, Señor? You don't think the short-ears made statues of long-ears? The statues are in memory of the long-ears' own chiefs."

He was so excited that his chest was rising and falling and his thin lips trembling.

"I believe that it was the long-ears who made the statues," I said. "Now I myself want a statue made, and I will only have long-ears do the work. Do you think you can do it?"

The mayor stood motionless for a few moments, with strangely trembling lips; then he drew himself up sharply.

"It shall be done, Señor, it shall be done. How long is the statue to be?"

"Oh, medium-size, fifteen to twenty feet high."

"Then there must be six of us. We are only four brothers, but there are several others who are long-ears on their mother's side. Will that be all right?"

"Quite all right."

I rode up to the governor and got Pedro Atan temporarily released from his duties as mayor, and he and his relatives obtained permission to go to Rano Raraku and carve a statue.

The day before the work was to begin I had been asked to keep a little food ready for the long-ears; I had ordered the statue and I must give the food, that was the custom. The day passed and no one collected the rations. One after another our people began to go to bed, first Yvonne with Anette in the tent beside the fallen giant, and soon the lights were put out all over the camp. Only Gonzalo, Carl, and I sat in the mess tent writing.

Then we heard a curious, faint humming. It grew louder and louder, it was right in the camp. A rhythmic thumping on the grass began. Gonzalo rose, looking bewildered, and Carl opened his eyes wide. I myself listened quite enthralled: I had never heard anything like it during all my experiences in Polynesia. We opened the zipper of the tent and went out into the darkness. The photographer was just staggering out of his tent in pyjamas, and the lanterns were lit in one tent after the other.

In the faint light which showed through the mosquito net of the mess tent, we saw a group of humped figures sitting in the middle of the camp, striking the ground with curiously carved war clubs, dancing paddles, and stone picks. Each of them had a featherlike crown of leaves round his head, and two small figures on the edge of the group had large paper masks drawn over their heads to represent bird-men with large eyes and projecting beaks. They bowed and nodded while the others swayed and sang and beat time on the ground with their feet. But the tune was more impressive than anything we could see: it was a direct greeting from a vanished world. One shrill voice among the deep male choir had an indescribably strange effect; it was the finishing touch to this unearthly chorus. When I grew accustomed to the light, I saw that it came from a very old woman, as thin as a rake.

They were all deeply serious, and the singing went on and on till one of our fellows came out of a tent with a lamp. Then the chorus stopped abruptly, and they all murmured "no," and hid their faces in their hands. When the light disappeared, the song began again; one man started, and then all the rest joined in, the old woman last. I felt far away from the South Sea Islands: strangely enough there was something to the music which reminded me of visits with the Pueblo Indians in New Mexico, and the archaeologists said the same.

When the singing was over I brought a dish of sausages which the steward had put out in the kitchen tent, and the performers retreated into the darkness with the dish. We now saw that the two masked bird-men were little children.

The mayor came back with the empty dish, profoundly serious, still wearing the wreath of ferns round his head. I laughed and complimented him on the performance, but the mayor did not move a muscle of his face.

"It is a very ancient ceremony, it is the old song of the stonecutters," he said gravely. "They sang it to their most important god, Atua, to pray for good fortune in the work they were about to begin."

There was something peculiar about the mayor that night, something about the song and the whole way in which it was presented, which made me realize that this had not been done purely for our entertainment. Everywhere in Polynesia the inhabitants have given up all that is old, except when they appear in straw skirts for tourists. If they play and sing, it is more or less imported hula music; and if they tell stories, these are most often legends they have heard quoted from white authors' books. But there was something special about this little night ceremony which was not meant for us alone. We were only accidentally involved because it was we who had asked them to make the statue.

I deliberately tried to joke with the mayor, but with no success. He took me quietly by the arm and said that in a way the ceremony had been "a bit serious," because it was an old song to God.

"Our ancestors knew no better," he added. "They thought God was called Atua. We know better today, but we must forgive them because no one had taught them what we know now."

Then he vanished into the darkness with his party on the way to Hotu Matua's cave in which they were to spend the night.

Next morning we went up to the quarry in Rano Raraku. There we found the mayor and five of his long-ears, who had arrived early, going round collecting abandoned stone picks. They lay on the ledges literally in hundreds, on the ground, and under it, looking like gigantic eyeteeth with sharp points. Up on the balcony where I had slept was a wide gash in the cliffside, which formed a large, flat side wall not visible from below. Here the old-time sculptors had carved their way in. Through this side wall we were to proceed farther into the rock, where old cutting grooves still stood like huge clawmarks on its face.

Our friends the long-ears knew from the very first exactly what they would have to do. They spread a supply of stone picks along the mountain wall where they were to begin, and each of them had a calabash of water standing beside him. The mayor hurried about with the previous night's wreath of ferns round his head, making sure that everything was ready. Then he took a series of measurements along the rock face, now by means of outstretched arms, now by spreading his fingers. He obviously knew the relative proportions from his own wooden figures. With a stone pick he cut marks at different places on the rock face. But instead of beginning he politely asked us to excuse him, and disappeared with all his men behind a projecting rock.

A new ceremony was evidently in preparation, and we waited eagerly to see what would happen. But then they came slowly back with set faces, and all six drew themselves up along the wall, each holding his stone pick in his hand. Apparently the required ceremony had been held on the other side of the rock. They grasped their picks in their hands like daggers, and at a sign from the mayor they burst into the stonecutters' song of the night before, each man lifting his arm and striking against the rock face in time with the rhythm of the tune. It was fantastic to see and to hear. I missed the old woman's harmony, but the echoing blows of stone against the rock were a good substitute. It was so gripping that all of us who watched stood quite hypnotized.

And now the singers warmed up, they smiled broadly, they sang and hewed, hewed and sang. One tall old man at the end of the line was so inspired that he danced and swayed his hips as he sang and hewed. Stroke followed stroke, the rock was hard; stone against stone, the little pick was the harder and the rock must give way. Clink-clink-clink, the blows of the picks must have been heard far out over the plain. For the first time in centuries the clink of stone was heard in Rano Raraku.

The song died away, but the strokes continued, steady and unbroken. Six long-ears had taken up the tools and the craft their forefathers had been compelled to abandon. Not much of a mark was made by each blow, hardly more than a gray patch of dust, but with another blow, and one more, and still another, something was gained. And at intervals the men grabbed the calabash and splashed water on the rock face, to soften it where they cut and to prevent splinters from flying in their eyes.

So the first day passed. Wherever we went in the area, we heard clinking and hammering up on the cliff among the motionless giants. When I went to bed that night tan muscular backs and sharp picks cutting into rock were still before my eyes, and the blows resounded in my ears although all had long been quiet in the quarry. The mayor and his friends now lay asleep, dead tired in Hotu Matua's cave. The old woman had been over to get a large dish of meat and a sack full of bread, butter, and sugar, so the long-ears slept with full stomachs.

Next day, and the day after, the work went on in the quarry: the men hewed and the sweat streamed down. On the third day the contours of the giant were clearly visible on the rock wall. The long-ears hacked and cut parallel depressions down the face of the rock, then they cut across the edge left between the furrows, breaking it off into pieces. They cut and cut and flung on water. And continually they changed their picks, for the points soon blunted.

Earlier investigators had thought that when a stone pick was worn out it was just thrown away, and that this explained the astonishing number of picks which lay about the quarry. But this proved to be wrong. When they dulled, the mayor grasped one after another by the end like a little club and struck it against another pick on the ground: the splinters flew through the air like sharp flakes, and he produced a new point as easily as a clerk sharpens a pencil.

This taught us that the greater part of the unbroken picks in the quarry had been in use at the same time, but that every sculptor had had a series to work with, one after another. There were not many sculptors needed for each statue. An average figure of fifteen feet would take six men. That was why it had been possible to work on so many statues at once. A couple of hundred men were enough to keep work going on a considerable number. Moreover, work on many of the statues in the quarry had been given up on purely technical grounds before the general stoppage came. In some cases the sculptors had found a disastrous crack in the rock; in others a black stone, hard as flint, had defied the sculptors' tools, and the statue was left unfinished with a great wart on its nose or chin.

The mayor and his men had now shown us the technique of the sculptors. But what interested us most was to know how long it would take to carve such a statue. According to Mrs. Routledge's calculations fifteen days were all that was needed. Métraux too thought that the work on the "soft stone" went more quickly than people believed, even if fifteen days was an underestimate. They had certainly made the same mistake as we ourselves and many others—that of judging the hardness of the rock by the outer surface of a statue. None of us had done what the first Spaniards did when they struck a figure with a pickax so deep that the sparks flew. The figures are as hard as bone inside the outer surface, and so is the rock where the rain has not reached it.

After the third day the tempo of the long-ears' work slowed down. They came to me with calloused fingers and said that although they were wood carvers who worked with adz and chisel all day long, they were not trained *moai* men, statue sculptors; therefore they could not keep the tempo going week after week as their ancestors had done. We sat down quietly on the grass and estimated the time needed by the ancient stonemasons to complete a statue. Each of us made his calculations. The mayor came to the conclusion that it would take twelve months to complete a medium-sized statue with two teams working all day in shifts. The tall old man said fifteen months. Bill made an independent study of the rock and arrived at the same result as the mayor: the work on one statue would take a year, and then the problem of removing it would arise.

The sculptors amused themselves by making fingers and features on the unfinished product, and polished the surface with pumice stone, left behind in the quarry by the old stonemasons.

That evening I took little Anette on my shoulder and, with Yvonne, went over to the long-ears' cave on the other side of the Anakena Valley. When we arrived the men were sitting, each man occupied with his own task, swaying their bodies rhythmically while singing a quiet song about Hotu Matua. This ancient and well-known song of Easter Island was pleasant to hear among the hula singers in the village, but it sounded still better in Hotu Matua's cave. Even Anette, only three years old, knew the tune and all the Polynesian words. She began to sing and dance with two little Polynesian children who came out of the cave. Yvonne and I crawled in and sat down on the reed mat where the long-ears made room for us. They were delighted at having visitors in their cave.

The mayor beamed and, with hands on his stomach, thanked us for the good food they got from the cook daily, and especially for all the cigarettes; they were the best of all. He and two other men were sitting with little adzes carving their traditional wooden figures: one of them was putting eyes of white sharks' vertebrae and black obsidian into the grotesque head of his bearded spook. The old woman who looked after the men sat plaiting a hat. A black kettle stood sputtering on a fire outside.

"Don't you ever rest?" I asked the mayor.

"We long-ears like working. We work all the time. I don't sleep many hours of the night, Señor," he replied.

"Good evening." The words came from a man we had not noticed because he was lying on a fern mattress up in a dark pocket of the cave wall. "Aren't we comfortable here?"

I had to admit that they were. Outside it was beginning to grow dark, and the old woman produced a can with a dent in the bottom. In the dent were mutton tallow and a homemade wick, and this imitation of an old-fashioned stone lamp, when kindled, gave a surprisingly good light. A thin old man explained to us that in the days of their ancestors no one used a light at night for fear of being seen by the enemy.

"The warriors had to accustom themselves to see clearly in the dark," the mayor added. "Nowadays we're so used to kerosene lamps that we're almost blind in the dark."

One remark led to another.

"And in those days they *never* slept like this." The old man lay flat on his back with his mouth open and his arms stretched out, and snored. "They slept like this." He rolled over onto his stomach and curled himself up into a ball, resting his chest on his knees and his forehead on two clenched fists, with the top of his head pointing toward me. He held a sharp-pointed stone in his hand.

"Then they could spring up to meet the enemy and kill him

122

as soon as they were awake," the old man muttered. And to illustrate the action, he suddenly shot forward like an arrow and flung himself upon me with a cannibalistic howl which made Yvonne utter a scream, and the cave resounded with laughter.

"They didn't eat much either in those days," said the old man. "And they never ate hot food. They were afraid of growing fat; they always had to be ready to fight in the time we call *Huri-moai*, or the statue-overthrowing time.'"

"It's called so because then warriors threw down the statues," the man up on the ledge added by way of explanation.

"Why did they, when the long-ears had already been burned?" I asked.

"The short-ears did it against each other," the mayor told me. "They owned everything then, and each family had its particular area. Those who had great statues on their land were proud of having them, and when they went to war, one family pulled down the statues on another's land just to annoy the owner. We long-ears are not so warlike. I've a motto, Señor Kon-Tiki: 'Take it easy.'"

He laid his hand on my shoulder in a pacifying gesture as if to show his peaceful temperament.

"How can you be so sure that you're a long-ear?" I asked cautiously.

The mayor raised his hand in the air and began to count on his fingers.

"Because my father José Abraham Atan was son of Tuputahi who was a long-ear because he was son of Hare Kai Hiva who was son of Aongatu, son of Uhi, son of Motuha, son of Pea, son of Inaki who was son of Ororoina, the only long-ear who was left alive after the war at Iko's ditch."

"That's ten generations," I said.

"Then I've left one out, for I'm number eleven," said the mayor, and he began to count on his fingers again.

"I'm of the eleventh generation too." The words came from the man up on the shelf. "But I'm only a younger son. Pedro is the eldest and knows most, that's why he's the head of our family."

The mayor pointed to his forehead and said with a sly smile: "Pedro has a head. That's why Pedro is chief of the long-ears and mayor of the whole island. I'm not really old, but I like to think of myself as a very old man."

"Why?"

"Because old men are wise; they're the people who know something."

I tried to find out a little about what had happened before the short-ears exterminated the long-ears and the "statue-overthrowing time" began. But nothing was to be learned. Their line began with Ororoina, and what lay behind him no one knew. The long-ears had come with Hotu Matua when the island was discovered: that they knew, but they added that the short-ears said the same of their line, just as they tried to claim the honor of having made the statues. But whether Hotu Matua came from east or west no one remembered any longer. The man up on the shelf suggested that Hotu Matua had come from Austria, but as he got no support from the others, he soon gave way and added that he had heard it from someone on board a ship. They all preferred to talk about the "statue-overthrowing time," which to them was something quite real. When the mayor talked of the treacherous woman with the basket who had betrayed the whole of his race, he became so furious that tears came into his eyes and he had to swallow. That story would live on from father to son for another eleven generations, even with the motto "Take it easy."

"There were handsome people among our ancestors," said the mayor. "There were two kinds of people on this island: some were dark and some were quite fair-skinned, like you from the mainland, and with light hair. Real white people. But they were genuine Easter Islanders, quite genuine. In our family there were many of the fair type, who were called *oho-tea*, or the light-haired. My own mother and my aunt had much redder hair than Señora Kon-Tiki."

"Much redder," his brother on the ledge agreed.

"There were many of that type in our family, all the way back. We brothers are not like that. But my daughter who was drowned had a milk-white skin and completely red hair, and so has my grown-up son Juan. He makes the twelfth generation after Ororoina."

This was quite correct: both of them had hair as red as the topknots on the thin-lipped, long-eared statues which had adorned the *ahus* of the island in the second cultural epoch. Their race was lost at Poike, and the statues were pulled down, but the red hair can be traced from the great stone *pukao*, through living individuals described by the first discoverers and the first missionaries, down to some of the last descendants of Ororoina among the mayor's nearest relatives.

We almost felt like fair-haired long-ears ourselves as we left Hotu Matua's cave and strolled home to the dark camp on the other side of the plain. This had been much too late for Anette.

A few days later I was standing with the mayor looking at the row of fallen statues on the temple square in front of the camp. Bill had just reported from Vinapu that his native diggers had used a curious method to lift a stout block into its place in the wall. This raised afresh the mystery of the transportation and handling of the giant statues. The men had taken the simple method they had employed at Vinapu quite as a matter of course. Perhaps it was a trick they had inherited from their ancestors? Who knows? I remembered that I had once asked the mayor how the statues were moved from the quarry. The answer was the same as that given by all the others: the statues had walked of their own accord. I now took a chance and asked again:

"You're a long-ear, Mayor. Don't you know how these giants were raised?"

"Yes, Señor, I do know. There's nothing to it."

"Nothing to it? It's one of the greatest mysteries of Easter Island!"

"But I know it. I can raise a *moai*."

"Who taught you?"

The mayor grew solemn and drew himself up in front of me.

"Señor, when I was a very little boy I had to sit on the floor, bolt upright, and my grandfather and his old brother-in-law Porotu sat on the floor in front of me. They taught me many things, just as in school nowadays. I know a lot. I had to repeat and repeat it until it was quite right, every single word. I learned the songs too."

The mayor seemed so sincere that I did not know what to believe. He had certainly shown in the quarry that he was no mere lightweight, but at the same time he did have a lively imagination.

"If you know how the statues were raised, why didn't you tell all the people who have been here and asked long before us?" I said skeptically.

"No one asked *me*," the mayor answered proudly. He clearly thought any further explanation unnecessary.

I did not believe him. I coolly offered to give him a hundred dollars on the day when the biggest statue at Anakena stood in its place up on the temple wall. I knew there was not a single statue standing in its place on its old *ahu* in all Easter Island, and I was sure that I would never see one standing either, except the blind figures which had been temporarily raised down in their holes at the foot of Rano Raraku.

"It's a deal, Señor," the mayor said quickly, and gave me his hand. "If I go on a trip to Chile with the next warship, then I shall need dollars."

I laughed and wished him luck. The mayor was a bit of an oddity anyway. Soon afterward the mayor's red-haired son came riding from the village with some notes on a scrap of paper. His father wanted me to talk to the governor and arrange that he and eleven other men should be allowed to go back to Hotu Matua's cave at Anakena to raise the largest statue.

I rode over to see the governor. Both he and Father Sebastian laughed at the mayor and said that it was just empty brag. But Don Pedro, the mayor, stood before us hat in hand, with his lips quivering, and I held to my word. The governor gave his blessing on a piece of paper.

Then the mayor came with two of his brothers and a chosen party of relatives who were all long-ears on their mother's side, the steward doled out rations, and they moved into Hotu Matua's cave again. They were twelve men in all.

Just before sunset the mayor came over and dug a deep round hole in the ground between our tents, and then he disappeared.

When it was pitch-dark and the camp was all quiet, a queer uncanny music began, as the time before, but this time the curious thumping increased in strength together with the humming chorus which grew loud and shrill, led by the old woman's cracked voice. Lights were kindled all over the camp, and all the tents shone a ghostly green. But we all came out into the darkness without bringing our lamps, for we had learned the time before that the song must be sung in the dark.

This was quite a different performance. All the men had decked themselves with leaves and boughs; some of them swayed and danced and stamped as if in an ecstasy, while the old woman, as chief singer, sat with closed eyes and led the choir in a shrill voice. The mayor's youngest brother stood down in the newly dug hole, in which we saw later a container had been placed with a stone slab over it. He was stamping rhythmically with bare feet to produce a hollow drumming noise which helped to create the underworld atmosphere. We could barely make out the ghostly group in the faint green light from the tent walls. But then a slender figure emerged from the dark background, and made all our men open their eyes wide.

She was a young girl with bare legs and long flowing hair, wearing a light, loose-fitting dress. She came gliding into the green circle like a fairy nymph, and light-footed she danced before the drummer without any swaying of hips or hula rhythm. It was such a pretty sight that we hardly dared breathe. She was so serious, a little shy, supple, slim, and graceful, and she seemed scarcely to touch the grass with her bare feet.

Where did she come from? Who was she? When the sailors slowly realized that they were standing on solid earth, that this was not a dream, they began to whisper questions to one another, and to old Mariana and Eroria. They had thought for a long time that they knew every single beauty on the island. Had the long-ears kept this nymph hidden in a bleaching cave? We were told that she was a niece of the mayor's; she was so young that she had never been out to a hula party with the others.

Meanwhile the singing and dancing went on, entirely fascinating. We heard and saw the whole performance three times. We understood only the refrain, which was about a *moai* which was to be erected at Kon-Tiki's command on an *ahu* at Anakena. The tune was quite unlike the stonecutters' song, but just as rhythmical. When the drummer had crawled up out of his hole, and all the leaf-clad dancers were preparing to go, they were again given food to carry off to their cave.

One of our men asked if they could not sing and dance some of the ordinary hula melodies as well, but they all refused to do that. The mayor consented to their singing the stonecutters' song as an encore, but said it was not seemly to sing any other kind of music. These two songs were serious and would bring us good luck in our work; the other songs they could sing on other days, when they would not by so doing profane their ancestors and destroy the good luck which they were now seeking. So we heard the stonecutters' song again before they rustled off across the temple square and vanished into the darkness, the fairy nymph among them.

Early next morning the twelve long-ears came over from the cave to look at the statue and the problem that confronted them. The largest statue at Anakena was the broad fellow who lay with his nose in the soil just beside our tent. He was a strapping, sturdy giant, nearly ten feet wide across the shoulders and weighing between twenty-five and thirty tons. That meant more than two tons for each of the twelve men to lift. It was not surprising that they stood in a circle round the giant scratching their heads, but they seemed to have confidence in the mayor. He walked about and studied the colossus with perfect calm.

Chief Engineer Olsen also scratched his neck, and shook his head and laughed.

"Well, if the mayor can manage that devil, he'll be a helluva fellow."

"He'll never do it."

"No, never!"

In the first place the giant lay at the foot of the wall with his head down a slight incline. In addition he lay with his base four yards from the great slab on which he had originally stood. The mayor showed us some nasty little stones which he said had been wedged under the slab by the short-ears when they upset the statue.

Then he began to organize the work. He did it with great calm and as surely as if he had never done anything else. His only implements were three round poles, which he later reduced to two, a quantity of boulders, and a few big stones which the men had collected in the vicinity. Even though the island is treeless today, apart from a few newly planted clumps of eucalyptus, trees have always grown round the crater lake down in Rano Kao. There the first explorers found woods of *toro miro* and hibiscus, so the three wooden poles lay well within the scope of the permissible.

The figure had its face buried deep in the earth, but the men got the tips of their poles underneath it, and while three or four men hung and pulled on the end of each pole, the mayor lay flat on his stomach and pushed small stones under the huge face.

Occasionally we saw a faint suggestion of movement in the giant when the eleven men got in an extra good heave, but otherwise nothing happened except that the mayor lay there on his stomach grubbing about with stones. As the hours passed, the stones he moved out and shoved in became larger and larger. And when evening came the giant's head had been lifted a good three feet from the ground, while the space beneath was packed tight with stones.

Next day one of the poles was discarded, and five men assembled at each of the others. The mayor set his youngest brother to push the stones in under the statue; he himself stood up on the *ahu* wall with arms outstretched like the conductor of an orchestra, beating the air in time as he shouted to the men:

"*Etahi, erua, etoru!* One, two, three! One, two, three! Hold on, push under! Once more! One, two, three! One, two, three!"

Today they had pushed both poles under the right side of the giant. He tilted imperceptibly; but the imperceptible became millimeters and millimeters became inches, which became feet. Then the two poles were moved over to the left side of the giant. This was treated in the same way as the right, and it too tilted up slowly, while all the time countless stones were carefully pushed in and arranged underneath. After that they turned back to the right side, then to the left again, and the right, and the left. And the statue rose steadily, all the time lying in a horizontal position on a vertically growing heap of stones.

On the ninth day the huge figure lay stretched on its stomach on the top of an elaborately built tower, the highest side of which was nearly twelve feet above the incline. It was quite uncanny to see this giant of nearly thirty tons lying stretched out up there, a whole man's height above the tops of our heads. The ten men could no longer reach the poles on which they hauled: they just hung dangling from ropes which were made fast to the ends. And still the giant had not begun to slant toward a standing position; we had not yet had a glimpse of the face of the figure, as it still lay on its stomach with the whole of its front hidden in the compact stone tower.

This looked deadly dangerous. Anette was no longer allowed to push her doll buggy up to the statue with pebbles for the mayor. Now only strong men came staggering along barefoot, like Neanderthal men, with heavy boulders in their arms. The mayor was extremely careful, checking the position of every stone. The weight of the colossus was so great that some of the stones cracked under the pressure like lumps of sugar: a single carelessly placed stone could mean catastrophe. But it all had been thoroughly thought out, every little move was precisely and logically calculated. We stood with our hearts in our mouths as we saw the men pushing their bare toes in between the stones while clambering up the pile with more big blocks to be placed in position.

Every single man was on the alert, and the mayor did not relax for a second. He had a grasp of the situation and did not utter an unnecessary word. We had not known this side of him. In everyday life he was a rather tiresome buffoon, a boaster and a bore, by no means popular among the men in camp because of his bragging and the shameless prices he put on his wood carvings, though the carvings were far the best in the island. But now he was calm and assured, a born organizer and something of a practical genius. We began to see him with different eyes.

On the tenth day the prone statue lay at its highest. Imperceptibly the long-ears began to jerk it, feet foremost, in the direction of the *ahu* on which it was to stand.

On the eleventh day they began for the first time to work the giant into a sloping position by building the stones up even higher, but only under the face and chest.

On the seventeenth day a shriveled old woman suddenly appeared among the long-ears. Together with the mayor she laid a semicircle of stones as large as eggs at a certain distance in back of the statue's base, on the great slab on which the giant was now beginning to fumble for a foothold. This was preventive magic. The statue was now leaning at a dangerously sharp angle and there was imminent danger of its slipping of its own weight and rolling down the steep wall of the *ahu* toward the beach. Quite apart from a slip of this kind, it could also capsize in any direction when it was suddenly tilted off the stone pile and onto its own base. Accordingly the mayor tied ropes round the giant's forehead, and these were made fast to stakes in the ground on all four sides.

Then the eighteenth working day came. While some hauled on a rope from behind, down on the beach, and others held fast to another rope twisted round a post in the middle of the camp, the last cautious jerks with a wooden pole began. Suddenly the giant began to move quite visibly, and the orders rang out: "Hold on! hold on!"

The giant rose in all his might and began to tilt upright, the supporting pile was left standing without a counterpoise, a rumbling and sliding of stones began, and great blocks came crashing down on top of one another in a cloud of smoke and dust. But the colossus only wobbled and came quietly to rest in an upright position. There it stood stiff and broad-shouldered, gazing out over the camp, unaffected by the change of scene since last it stood on the same foundation looking across the same temple square.

The giant bulked so huge that the whole landscape was changed. The broad back was a landmark which could be seen far out to sea. We who lay in the tents at the foot of the wall and in the shadow of the giant's countenance no longer felt ourselves quite at home on Hotu Matua's old site. Wherever we went we saw the broad head close to us, towering over all the tent tops. When we moved about in the camp at night, the burly ogre seemed to come rolling forward out of the starry sky, ready to stride over the green tents in the darkness.

For the first time since past centuries one of the Easter Island giants stood in his place on the top of an *ahu*. The governor with his family, and the priest and the nuns came over by jeep. Horses' hoofs clattered outside the tents; everyone who could come from the village made a pilgrimage to Anakena to look at the mayor's work. The long-ears proudly removed the heap of stones, and the mayor basked placidly in universal praise. He had known that he could provide the answer to one of Easter Island's oldest riddles. Had anyone expected anything less of him, Don Pedro Atan, a sage of long standing, mayor of the island, and senior long-ear? If only he was paid for it, he would put up every single statue on every single *ahu* in the whole island, and everything would be as in the good old days. What he earned now he would share with his friends, but if he were allowed to go to Chile when the next warship came, he would get the President in person to throw wads of notes onto the table so that all the statues could be raised. He had raised this giant in eighteen days with eleven helpers and two poles! What could he not do with more men and more time?

I took the mayor away to a quiet spot and stood him ceremoniously in front of me, with a hand on each of his shoulders. He stood there like a good little schoolboy, looking at me eagerly.

"Don Pedro, Mayor," I said, "now perhaps you can tell me how your ancestors moved the figures round about on the island."

"They went of themselves, they walked," the mayor replied glibly.

"Rubbish," I said, disappointed and slightly irritated.

"Take it easy! I believe that they walked, and we must respect our forefathers who have said that they walked. But the forefathers who told me that had not seen it with their own eyes, so who knows if their forefathers did not use a *miro manga erua?*"

"What's that?"

The mayor drew on the ground a Y-shaped figure with crosspieces, and explained that it was a sledge made from a forked tree trunk.

"At any rate they used those to drag the big blocks for the wall," he added by way of a concession. "And they made thick ropes from the tough bark of the *hau-hau* tree, as thick as the hawsers you have on board. I can make you a specimen. I can make a *miro manga erua* too."

A few paces from the camp one of the archaeologists had just dug out a statue which had been completely hidden in the sand and therefore had never been given any number by Father Sebastian. It had no eyes, and consequently had been abandoned before it had been set up at its destination. I pointed to it.

"Can you draw that *moai* across the plain with your men?"

"No, the other people in the village will have to help, and they won't. We haven't enough people, even with all your men."

The statue was not at all large: it was if anything below medium size. I had an idea. The mayor helped me to get hold of two sturdy oxen in the village. They were slaughtered and placed by the long-ears between hot stones in a large earth oven. We sent out invitations to a great feast for the natives from the village, and soon the whole plain beyond the tents was swarming with people.

The long-ears carefully dug away the sand which covered the oxen, and a steaming mat of juicy banana leaves came to light. When this inedible vegetable carpet was rolled away, the steaming, well-cooked carcasses appeared, and the savor of the world's juiciest beefsteak spread among the gay crowd. Men and women gathered in groups all over the grass with their hands full of large steaming pieces of meat, and the long-ears served heaps of newly baked sweet potatoes, corn-on-the-cob, and pumpkins which had all been baked along with the oxen in the same airtight underground oven. All round the party saddled black and brown horses grazed. Guitars were produced, and there was song and laughter and hula dancing on the temple square.

Meanwhile the long-ears had made preparations for moving the blind statue, and 180 natives, sated and jubilant, took their places on the long rope which was made fast round the statue's neck. The mayor was in great form, wearing a new white shirt and striped tie.

"One, two, three! One, two, three!"

Pang! The rope broke, and there was wild laughter as men and vahines rolled over one another on the ground in chaos. The mayor gave an embarrassed laugh, and ordered the rope to be doubled and made fast to the figure. Now the giant began to move—first in short jerks, but then suddenly it seemed to break loose. As it slid away over the plain, Lazarus, the mayor's assistant, jumped onto the giant's face and stood waving his arms and cheering like a gladiator in a triumphal procession, while the long lines of natives hauled patiently and yelled at the tops of their voices with enthusiasm. It moved as quickly as if they each were hauling an empty soapbox.

We stopped the whole cavalcade a little way out on the plain. We had established that 180 natives with full stomachs could draw a twelve-ton statue across the plain, and if we had had many more people, we could have drawn a much larger figure.

At last we had seen how water and stone picks could gnaw the statues out of the solid rock, if only one had sufficient time; we had seen how ropes and runners could move the giants from place to place, if only there were enough hands to pull; we had seen how the colossi could be lifted to the tops of the walls and raised on end if only one applied the right technique. There was only one practical mystery left: how was the huge topknot placed on the head of a standing figure? The answer had already presented itself. The stone pile which had helped the giant onto his base could be restored as a pathway to the head, and the red topknot could easily be moved up its slope with the aid of the same simple system. When both statue and topknot were in their place up on the wall, all the stones were taken way. The statue remained there silently awaiting the future, and the mystery was not created until after the sculptors had died.

An industrious and intelligent people had come to this tiny

island with its unlimited peace. Absence of warfare, ample time, and traditions of an old technique were all that were needed to raise the Babel towers of Easter Island. The island's discoverers lived for hundreds of years as a nation with nothing but fish and whale as their neighbors. Our excavations showed us that spearheads, the local weapon, were not made on Easter Island until the third epoch began.

Not far from the tents lay a gigantic cylinder of red stone. It had been brought seven miles from the topknot quarry on the other side of the island. The mayor wanted to trundle it on logs for the few hundred yards which separated it from the camp, and then to place it on the head of the giant he had just set up. But at the very time when the long-ears were raising the giant, a new Easter Island mystery began to develop. It interfered with the whole of our program, and the red topknot was left untouched.

We ourselves had something new to think about.

CHAPTER SIX

Superstition Against Superstition

THE LAMP hung by a string from the tent roof and threw long shadows on the thin, canvas wall. I turned down the wick till the light was barely burning and began to undress. Yvonne had already crept into her sleeping bag on a camp bed along the far wall, and Anette had long been asleep behind a low canvas barrier which divided her little pen from the rest of the tent. The whole camp was dark and silent; only the roar of the surf down on the beach was to be heard. Suddenly there was someone outside scraping the tent cloth with his fingernail, and a faint voice whispered in broken Spanish:

"Señor Kon-Tiki, may I come in?"

I pulled on my trousers again. Cautiously I moved the zipper of the tent flap; in the darkness I could see a dim figure with a bundle under his arm, and behind him the bulky silhouette of our still recumbent giant who was towering toward the starry sky. This was the evening of the seventh day of the long-ears' attempt to raise him.

"May I come in?" the voice whispered again imploringly.

I slowly opened the tent flap and pulled it aside. The figure slipped in and stood stooping, looking round quite enthralled. I recognized him: he was the junior member of the mayor's team, a so-called "mixed long-ear," an unusually good-looking lad of twenty. His name was Estevan Pakarati. The tent was so low that he could not stand upright, and I asked him to sit down on the end of my bed.

He sat for a few moments with an embarrassed smile on his face, searching vainly for words. Then he clumsily pushed at me a round parcel wrapped in crumpled brown paper.

"This is for you," he said.

I unfolded the paper, and out came a hen. A stone hen. It was quite realistically shaped, life-size, and did not remind me of anything which had ever been made on Easter Island.

Before I myself could say a word, he hastened to add: "Everyone in the village says that Señor Kon-Tiki has been sent to us to bring good luck. That is why you have given us so many things. All the people smoke your cigarettes and are grateful."

"But where did you get this stone?"

"It's a *moa,* a hen. My wife said I was to give it to you by way of thanks, because it's she who gets all the cigarettes you give me every day."

Yvonne stretched out of her sleeping bag and took a length of cloth from a suitcase. But Estevan refused emphatically to accept the cloth. No, this was not a barter deal, this was a present for Señor Kon-Tiki.

"And this is a present for your wife," I said.

He gave way reluctantly, thanked me again for all the food and cigarettes, all that he and the other long-ears received every day. Then he left the tent and disappeared into the darkness as quietly as he had arrived. He was going to the village for the night. But before he left he begged me to hide the hen so that no one would see it.

I looked at the well-made hen again. It was a masterly piece of work. Queer, but for some reason the hen smelled a little of smoke. I was rather puzzled by this piece of sculpture which I could not place within the local pattern at all. This was the first time I had seen an Easter Island art object which was not a mere repetition of the standardized wooden figures, or a copy of the large statues or other well-known local forms. I put the remarkable stone hen away under my bed and blew out the light.

Next evening, when all was quiet, the whispering voice was there again. What did he want now? Tonight he had a new stone with him, this time a crouching man with a long bird's bill, holding an egg in one hand. The figure was carved in high relief on a flat stone and was a variation of the sculptures in the rock at the bird-men's ruined village of Orongo. It was a beautiful piece of work. His wife had sent the figure as a present because she had received the cloth from us. It had been carved by her father, Estevan said, but we must not show it to anyone. We sent him off again with a gift for his wife.

When I was putting the new stone away, I noticed that it too smelled very strong of acrid smoke; it was still rather damp and had been thoroughly scrubbed with sand. Something strange was going on. But what?

All next day I puzzled over these stones which smelled so peculiar and were so unusually well made. At last I could restrain myself no longer. Late in the afternoon I called the mayor into my tent and rolled down the walls outside the mosquito net.

"I want to ask you something, but you must promise absolutely not to say a word to anyone."

The mayor, his eyes dancing with curiosity, promised to say nothing.

"What do you think of these?" I asked, pulling the two stones out of a suitcase.

The mayor started back as if he had burned his fingers; his eyes stood out of his head as if he were looking at an evil spirit or into the muzzle of a gun, and he turned quite pale.

"Where did you get those? *Where* did you get those?" he whispered hoarsely.

"I can't tell you, but what do you say to them?"

The mayor still sat staring, drawn back against the tent wall.

"There's no one on the island but myself who can make figures like those," he said, looking as if he suddenly stood face to face with his own soul. As he sat staring at the figures something seemed to dawn on him. He took a closer look, and I felt he was becoming convinced of something which was still beyond me. Then he turned quietly to me and said:

"Pack up both stones and get them on board the ship so that no one on the island can see them. If you're given any more, just accept them and hide them on board, even if they look new."

"But what are they?"

"They're serious things; they're family stones."

The mayor's odd behavior did not make me much wiser, but I realized that I had involuntarily started to play with fire. Estevan's father-in-law must be engaged in some queer business. I was determined to find out what was really going on.

The next time Estevan came creeping into my tent, I made him sit down on the edge of the bed and tried to engage him in conversation. But he was too excited to listen to me. He had three stones in a sack, and when he rolled them out onto the sleeping bag, I too became speechless.

One stone depicted three curious and highly artistic heads with mustaches and long beards, and the heads were carved in a ring around the stone so that the beard of one imperceptibly blended with the hair of the next; the second stone was a club with eyes and mouth. The third was a man standing with a large rat hanging from his clenched teeth. This was not only a motif and style of art alien to Easter Island; I had never seen anything like it from any part of the globe. I did not believe for a moment that Estevan's father-in-law had made these stones. There was something grim, almost heathenish about them, and this was reflected in the way the lad looked at them and handled them.

"Why has the man a rat in his mouth?" I asked. I could not think of a more sensible question on the spur of the moment.

Estevan drew a little nearer and told me in a hushed voice that it was a mourning custom of his ancestors. When a man lost a wife or one of his children, anyone he was fond of, he had to catch a *kioe,* a native rat of the edible kind that lived on the island before the ship's rats came. Then he had to run all round the coast of the island without resting, with the rat in his mouth, and kill all the people who placed themselves in his path.

"This was how a warrior showed his grief," Estevan explained, with ill-concealed admiration in his voice.

"Who made the mourning man?"

"My wife's grandfather."

"It was her father who made the others?"

139

"I'm not sure. Her father made some and her grandfather others. She has seen her father making them."

"Is her father working for me?"

"No, he is dead. These are holy, serious stones."

This was becoming more and more puzzling. Again he repeated that the villagers said that I had been sent to the island by supernatural powers. The whole thing seemed completely nonsensical.

"But where have you and your wife kept these stones since her father died? In the house?"

He shifted a little where he sat, and then he said: "No, in a cave, a family cave."

I said nothing.

Then he confided that the cave was full of such things. But no one could find it; only his wife knew where the entrance was. She was the only person who could get in. He himself had never seen the cave. But he knew roughly where it was, for he had waited nearby while his wife went in for the stones. She had told him that the cave was quite full.

Now Estevan and I shared a secret. The next night it was easier to talk. He told me that his wife had scrubbed the stones with sand and water before she sent them to me; she was afraid some native might see them and realize that she was taking old things from a family cave. The smell he thought came from the cave, until it occurred to him that the stones had been dried over the kitchen fire after being washed. He would get this washing stopped, since I wished it. His wife had asked if there was anything special I wanted from the cave. But it was not easy for me to know what to ask for, when not even Estevan could tell me what was there. All I knew for certain was that ethnographic art treasures of incalculable value had begun to emerge from a hiding place on the island.

Estevan proposed in a whisper that he try to persuade his wife to take me into the cave with her. Then I myself could choose the stones I liked best, for there were such quantities that it was quite impossible to bring them all to me. But the worst problem, he explained, would be that his wife was strong-willed and hard in this matter, as hard as stone. He himself had never been allowed to go into the cave. But if she

said yes, we must steal into the village in the middle of the
night, for the cave was not far from his house, in the middle
of the village area.

Estevan's visits occurred during the time when the mayor
and the other long-ears were living in Hotu Matua's cave and
working to raise the giant statue. It could have been a simple
matter for the mayor to notice which of his men disappeared
at night, or he may have spied Estevan entering my tent. At
any rate he took me aside one day and confided, with a knowing look, that Estevan's father-in-law had been a good friend
of his till his death many years ago. He was the last man on
the island who had made "serious" stones, the mayor added,
stones which they kept for themselves, and which were not
for sale.

"What did they use the stones for then?" I asked.

"They brought them out and showed them at feasts; they
took them along to the dances."

Nothing more was to be got out of the mayor on that subject.

I had another meeting with Estevan afterward, and that
night he brought several stones from the cave. But then his
nocturnal visits suddenly ceased. At last I sent for him. When
he came into the tent he appeared crestfallen. His wife had
discovered that the two spirits who guarded her cave were
angry at her for having taken so much out, so Estevan had
nothing more to bring me from her cave. And now his wife
flatly refused to take me with her into the cave. He himself
was willing to do anything in the world for me, but she could
not be persuaded. She was so hard, the lad repeated, as hard
as stone. It was just for that reason, he added, that her father
had chosen her to inherit the secret of the family cave.

During the period in which Estevan was paying his nightly
visits, a great deal else was happening on the island. The
archaeologists were continually making new and surprising
finds, and the natives began to display more and more superstition. On the top of Rano Kao Ed had discovered the walls
of a hitherto unknown temple which he was now excavating
with the help of a native team. One day when I was visiting
him, two of the natives came straight out with their latest
gossip.

"Confess that you are one of our family who left Easter Island many generations ago," one of them said.

"We know it. You may just as well tell the truth," added the other.

I laughed and told them that I was a genuine Norwegian and had come from the other side of the globe. But the men would not give in: they had unmasked me, so why could I not admit it? They had heard the legend of a man who had left the island in ancient times and never came back. Besides, if I had never been on the island before, how could I have gone straight to Anakena and set up my camp exactly where Hotu Matua had settled when he first landed?

I tried to laugh the whole thing off, but my denials were of no use.

On the same day Arne got the natives to turn over a large square block of stone close to the path in Rano Raraku. He thought it looked rather queer. Everyone knew that stone, and most of the natives must have sat on it. But it had never been turned over till now, and to everyone's astonishment what appeared was an absolutely strange head with thick lips, a flat nose, and large pouches under the eyes. The large square face had nothing in common with the known style of art of Easter Island: again something new had turned up, something that bewildered the natives. Who had given Señor Arne a tip that it was worth while to turn that particular stone over? Again Arne was told by his workmen that they knew it: Señor Kon-Tiki was in contact with the supernatural.

Then one evening Yvonne and I were over in Hotu Matua's cave with the mayor and his long-ears. They were lying there regaling themselves with thick slices of bread spread with butter and jam, and the coffeepot was simmering outside.

"We only get sweet potatoes and fish at home," said the mayor, patting his stomach with pleasure.

The can with the wick in it was lighted, and again the talk was of old days, of the time when a king named Tuu-ko-ihu had discovered two sleeping ghosts at the foot of the red cliff down in the topknot quarry. Both ghosts were long-ears, with pendulant lobes down to their necks; they had beards and long hooked noses, and were so thin that the ribs stood out from their breasts. The king hastened home to carve their

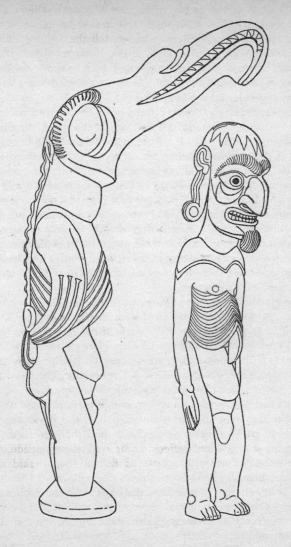

A bird-man figure, which the natives called a *tangata manu,* and a
long-eared ghost-man known as a *moai-kava-kava.*

portrait in wood before he forgot what they looked like. This was the origin of the *moai-kava-kava*, the weird figure which always recurs without variation in the wood carving of Easter Island. No sooner had the men finished their meal than they produced their chunks of wood and began to work on their *moai-kava-kavas*, and their *tangata manus*, or bird-men, while some of the older ones told stories.

Flickering shadows danced round us on the uneven walls of the cave and this opened the door to ghost stories which might well have made the hair of anyone stand on end. We heard of cannibal ghosts which came at night to demand intestines; of a female ghost which resided in the sea and with an immensely long arm drew lone people to her from the cliffs; and of others which went about pushing folk into the sea. Lazarus, the mayor's assistant, said his grandmother had been pushed down a precipice by a malicious ghost. There were also many spirits which were friendly and helped certain people; most of these were friendly to one particular family only, and hostile to everyone else. Such spirits of all kinds were referred to by the natives as *aku-akus*.

One ghost story followed another till they all suddenly recalled something which had happened that very day.

"You were present yourself," one of them said to me, "and you did not look a bit surprised." Then they explained.

Although their ancestors had supernatural help when they moved the statues about on the island, when they erected them they had had to toil with poles and stones; perhaps supernaturals had been present then too, and done part of the work, for today they had all seen something they had never experienced before. An invisible *aku-aku* had helped them in raising the statue. They had had luck because of their singing.

They showed us, with a little figure and two sticks, how they had been working to push up one side of the statue, when suddenly the giant's head had risen several inches by itself, without anyone having touched it.

"Very strange! It was very strange," the man up on the ledge assured us.

At this time Thor Junior was working as assistant to Ed at Orongo, on the rim of the volcano Rano Kao. The ruins up there were to be mapped. Ed and Bill were staying as guests in the governor's bungalow at the foot of the volcano, and the governor's wife, who always showed us boundless hospitality, invited Thor also to stay in the house, as the camp was too far away. But Thor had a boy's longing for adventure; he wanted to stay in the bird-men's village on the top of the cliff. Several of the ancient stone huts were in a habitable state, and even if the floor was hard and the roof low, he would have shelter in all kinds of weather and a view the like of which could not be found in all the kingdoms of the world.

The whole Hangaroa Village and a part of the island lay spread out at his feet, and beyond, the Pacific stretched to the vault of heaven. The bird-men's partly subterranean stone huts lay closely packed side by side next to some curiously sculptured outcrops on the topmost knifelike edge of the volcano. Right in front of their very doorstep the vertical cliff flung itself sheer for a thousand feet down into the sea where the bird-men's islands lay. A few steps in the opposite direction an almost equally giddy drop fell into the gigantic crater which spread a mile wide from edge to edge, and at the bottom lay a dangerous green bog speckled here and there with little open pools.

When Thor went up there with sleeping bag and provisions, the natives became panic-stricken. They begged him to come down for the night; they went to Ed and asked him to order the boy down. I myself received a message at Anakena saying that the boy must not sleep alone in the ruins of Orongo—he would be taken by an *aku-aku*. But warnings were of no avail. Thor had found the castle of his dreams: he would camp alone at Orongo.

At the end of the day, Thor remained on the top while the others came down. Ed's native foreman was so troubled that finally he sent up three volunteers to keep Thor company during the night. When the sun set, and the trade wind roared in the dark abysses, Thor had his first fright. Three shadows came marching into the ruins—three native girls sent to spend the night there. The girls were terrified at being up in the ruins in the dark: one of them was almost crazy with fear. The echo down in the black crater was surely an *aku-aku*. She saw another in a star mirrored in a black pool at the bottom of the crater. There were *aku-akus* everywhere. When daylight came the three girls were only too glad to hurry down to the village again.

On the following nights Thor stayed up on the rim alone. He was sitting there every morning happily admiring the sunrise when Ed and his native workmen came climbing up from the valley. This courage quickly made him a hero in the eyes of the natives, and they deluged him daily with melons, pineapples, and baked fowls. Accordingly Thor could not be persuaded to come down from the clifftop. He lived up there four months, and the *aku-akus* left him in peace. The natives knew why: Kon-Tiki-iti-iti was quite safe up in Orongo alone, he had a protecting power on his side.

This was not the end of superstition, however: quite the contrary.

The next native to approach me was Lazarus, just when I was worming the first secrets of the family cave out of young Estevan. Lazarus was the mayor's right-hand man and, according to both, one of the most important persons on the island. He was one of the natives' three elected representatives and, the mayor said, an extremely wealthy person. The blood of long-ears as well as short-ears flowed in Lazarus' veins, with a slight infusion from casual European visitors. He was a physical masterpiece, yet Darwin might have appropriated his features to support the theory of evolution. But despite the low sloping forehead with projecting brows, the equally protruding lower face with a small chin, large lips with a perfect row of teeth between them, a thick nose, and an animal's watchful eyes, Lazarus was no stupid ape. On the contrary, he was unusually alert, and he had a keen sense of humor. However, he too was highly superstitious.

One day a report came from Ed that he had found several rock carvings of an unknown type on a large slab in the roof of a ruined house in Orongo. At about the same time Arne had found the kneeling statue buried in the earth at the foot of Rano Raraku. Late in the afternoon, when the long-ears had ceased work for the day, Lazarus took me aside with an air of secrecy.

"The only thing you need now is a *rongo-rongo*," he said, slyly studying my face to see the effect of his words.

At once I realized that something special was brewing, and I pretended to be casual.

"There are none left on the island today," I remarked.

"Yes, there are *some*," Lazarus said cautiously.

"But they're rotten and will crumble away if you touch them."

"No, my cousin has touched two."

I did not believe him. He saw it, and asked me to come with him behind the temple wall where the statue was lying on its stone pile. Here he told me in a whisper that he had twin cousins, Daniel and Alberto Ika. Alberto had been born an hour after Daniel, yet it was he who had been chosen to inherit the secret of the entrance to their family cave, which was full of curious things, even some *rongo-rongo*.

Two years ago Alberto had been in the cave and brought out two *rongo-rongo*, which he had taken home. They were of wood, and one of them was shaped like a flat fish with a tail. Both were covered with small figures; they were almost black and extremely hard, though they were very old. Lazarus and many others had seen them. But Alberto had broken the taboo by taking the tablets away from the cave, and in the night while he was asleep an *aku-aku* had come and poked and pinched him till he awoke. Then he had looked out of the window and seen thousands of tiny little men about to climb into his room. He was almost crazy with fear, and had gone straight back to the cave and put both the tablets back in their places. This *rongo-rongo* cave was somewhere near the Hanga-o-Teo Valley, and Lazarus would do everything in his power to make his cousin summon up courage to go in and fetch the tablets again.

I gradually extracted from Lazarus the information that his family had more than one cave. Lazarus himself had access to another cave which was also near the Hanga-o-Teo Valley; there were no *rongo-rongos* there, but many other things. I tried to get Lazarus to take me with him to this cave, but here his co-operation ended. He looked at me with a magisterial eye and declared that it would be the end of both him and me. The family *aku-aku* lived in the cave, and there were also the skeletons of two of his ancestors. If an unauthorized person tried to enter, the *aku-aku* would take a fearful revenge.

The entrance to the cave was the most sacred of all secrets. I tried to laugh at the idea of *aku-akus* and make him, as an intelligent fellow, see reason, but it was like talking to a wall. I got nowhere.

After persistent efforts I did secure a promise from Lazarus that he himself would try to bring me something from the cave. But what would I like to have? A bird-man with or without an egg? The cave contained every possible thing except *rongo-rongo*. I proposed that he should bring several different things, so that I could see for myself and be able to choose. But this was no good. The cave was full of strange things, and he could only risk bringing one single item. Here the conversation was interrupted by a message for me, and Lazarus said goodby and was gone in a twinkling.

Next day I was out watching the long-ears carrying stones to the pile they were building under the statue, when the mayor and Lazarus came up for a chat.

"You realize the *aku-aku* is helping," the mayor said in a low voice. "It would have been impossible for the twelve of us to manage this alone without supernatural help."

They told me how they had baked a fowl that day, in an earth oven near the cave, to make the statue rise more quickly.

I met a flood of protests from Lazarus and the mayor when I scoffed at their superstition. They looked at me as if I was an idiot when I maintained that there were no *aku-akus*. Of course there were. In old days the whole island was full of them. There were not so many now, but they could patter off the names of many places on the island where *aku-akus* of both sexes still lived. People who had talked with them declared that they had a peculiar piping voice, and there were no end of proofs of their existence.

I could not get in a word. I could as easily have persuaded them that there were no fish in the sea or chicken in the village. It was apparent that the islanders were bound to some lunatic form of superstition, and this acted as an immovable barrier to caves with contents hitherto unknown to the outside world.

I drove in to see Father Sebastian. No living person knew Easter Island and its natives as well as he. I knew too that what I told him would remain a confidence between us two.

In his book about the island I had found the following passage:

"There were also secret caves which were the property of particular families, and only the most important persons in a family knew the entrance to their respective secret caves. These served as hiding places for valuable things, such as inscribed tablets, *rongo-rongo,* or statuettes. The secret of the exact situation of the entrance is buried in the graves with the last survivors from the old times. . . ."

I told Father Sebastian that I had reason to believe that secret family caves were still in use on the island. He started back in astonishment and tugged at his beard.

"Oh, no!"

I told him, without mentioning names, of the mysterious stones I had obtained. He was soon ablaze with excitement and wanted to hear where the cave was. I could only tell him the little I knew, and that it was impossible for me to get to the cave because of the crazy ghost stories.

Father Sebastian had been walking briskly up and down the room. He stopped abruptly and clasped his head in despair.

"They are hopelessly superstitious," he said. "Old Mariana came to me the other day and declared quite seriously that you were not a human being. Their superstition is so ingrained that it is no good expecting to get it all out of their heads in one generation. They have an immense respect for their ancestors, and that of course one can understand. Yet they are good Christians. But oh, their superstition!"

He told me quite resignedly that he had not yet been able to relieve his admirable housekeeper Eroria of the belief that she was descended from a whale which had been stranded in Hotuiti Bay. Eroria only replied that he could not possibly know anything about it, even if he was a priest, for she had heard it from her father, who had been told it by his father, who had it from his father, and he was the one who ought to know best, for it was he who had been the whale!

We agreed that I had a hard nut to crack: it would not be easy to get the natives to accompany me to places where they thought devils and evil spirits barred the way. Father Sebastian proposed to lend me some holy water; the natives have a great respect for it, and perhaps they might summon courage if we sprinkled it at the entrance to the cave. However, we agreed that Father Sebastian must not come into the picture openly. He said himself that he was the last person to whom they would come with secrets of this kind. But we must keep in regular contact at all costs; I must come to him even in the middle of the night if I should obtain access to a secret cave.

The insane superstition of the intelligent people of Easter Island was hard to understand until I began to draw parallels with our own familiar world. I have heard of twenty-story buildings which have no thirteenth floor, and of airplanes in which the numbers of the seats jump from twelve to fourteen. Are there people who believe that an evil spirit watches over the number thirteen—a nameless spirit of disaster? All that is wanting to complete the parallel is that we should call it an evil *aku-aku*.

I have also heard of people who are afraid of spilling salt, of breaking a mirror, or who believe that a black cat crossing the road may affect your future. These people believe in an *aku-aku*, only they do not use the name. Is it then so strange that natives of the world's most desolate island suspect their ancestors of wizardry and of walking as ghosts among their giant portraits, which our own race openly calls a mystery? Is there not more excuse for imagining an *aku-aku* among skulls and skeletons in the dark caves of Easter Island than in the skin of a friendly black cat strolling contentedly across the road on a sunny summer day?

Superstition on Easter Island has been ingrained in the people for generations. I had not taken this into account, nor had anyone else done so before me. This oversight had been a major omission which had so far prevented all access to the real mind of the natives. It was no use trying to quench the flames of superstition with reason. All sensible arguments were received like water on a duck's back. Nor can a real forest fire be put out with water: one must start a counterfire. Fire is fire's worst enemy provided it is kept under control.

The natives had inherited from their own parents their belief in evil spirits which reside all over the island. There were certain areas where some of the natives never dared go, least of all at night. The mayor and Lazarus confided to me gloomily that superstition was a real menace to the island.

I racked my brain over the problem, and came to the conclusion that superstition might be superstition's deadliest enemy, if kindled as a counterfire. Those who believed that I was in contact with their ancestors ought to accept as well a message passed on from the same source, a message advising them to abolish all the old and dreaded curses and taboos. Why not? I lay and tossed about in my sleeping bag all night. Yvonne thought it was a crazy plan, but agreed anyway that it ought to be tried.

Next day the mayor, Lazarus, and I had a long meeting up in the rocks behind our camp. It was incredible what I was to learn once I began to chat with them. I told them first—what was quite true—that I knew very well the secret of the taboo, and that I myself was the first who had paddled a canoe in the taboo waters of Vai Po, in an accursed underground cave on Fatu Hiva. There too, without any evil consequences, I had been down in the secret vault of a taboo *pae-pae* or house platform. The mayor and Lazarus listened with eyes wide open: they did not know that there were other islands besides their own which had taboos. I knew enough about the taboo system to impress both of them beyond limits, not least because I could quote stories I myself had heard from natives of Fatu Hiva, describing disasters of the strangest sorts which had overtaken various people who had infringed their forefathers' taboo.

The mayor became pale and shuddered. Then he laughed, slightly ashamed, and confessed that whenever he heard stories of this kind he shivered with cold, even in the baking-hot sun. For Easter Islanders had had exactly, just *exactly*, the same experience of the taboo too. And now I was the one who had to listen quietly to the local examples of the dire effect of the taboo—of a whole family who had become lepers, of a shark which had bitten off an arm, of a fearful flood which had drowned all the people in a reed house, and of many who had gone mad because the *aku-aku* had poked and punched them night after night, all because various attempts had been made to break the taboos of family caves.

"What happened to you on Fatu Hiva?" Lazarus asked, morbidly curious.

"Nothing," I said.

151

Lazarus looked almost disappointed.

"That's because you've got *mana*," he said. *Mana* is the term for a kind of magical quality, a source of supernatural strength.

"Señor Kon-Tiki has not only *mana*," the mayor said slyly to Lazarus, "he has an *aku-aku* which brings good fortune."

I grasped this straw.

"So I can quite well go into a taboo cave without anything happening," I declared.

"Nothing will happen to you, but something will happen to *us* if we show you the cave," said Lazarus, pointing to himself and nodding with a wry grin.

"Not when I am with you. My *aku-aku* is too strong for that," I tried to argue.

But Lazarus found this hard to digest. His family *aku-aku* would take vengeance on him; my *aku-aku* could not prevent that, even if it protected *me*. And I could never in all my life find the opening by myself, even if I stood as near to it as I was to him now.

"Lazarus belongs to a very important family," the mayor boasted on his friend's behalf. "His family has many caves. They are rich."

Lazarus spat proudly.

"But I too have *mana*," the mayor declared, and went on to boast of his own supernatural power. "It's my *aku-aku* which helps us to lift the statue. I have three *aku-akus* inside a small *ahu* in La Pérouse Bay. One is the figure of a bird."

Now we all knew that we were three important persons sitting together up among the rocks. The two others began to vie over who knew the most about the sources of "good luck" and "bad luck." And I found out that quite unknowingly I had passed a test that very day. The mayor told me that he had been looking on when I was tying a knot in the guy rope of the tent, and this had confirmed his suspicion that I knew the secrets of "good luck," for I had tied the knot from the right and not from the left.

With this concession as a bridgehead I delivered my final argument. I said that I knew their family caves had been declared taboo by their ancestors only to protect the valuable contents. The only thing that brought "bad luck" was to trade the figures from the cave to visitors and sailors who might not realize what they were and after a time might throw them away. But it brought "good luck" to trade the same figures with men of science who would preserve them in a museum. A museum was somewhat like a church, a place where people could only walk about quietly and look at the figures behind glass cases, a protected spot where no one could break them or throw them away. The evil spirits would depart from the caves together with the figures, and so there would be nothing more to be afraid of on the island.

I thought I detected that this speech made a special impression on Lazarus, and I was not wrong. That night there was again someone whispering "Kon-Tiki," and scraping the wall of the tent. It was not Estevan this time, but Lazarus. He gave me a sack containing an old flat stone head with the most peculiar features and a long thin mustache. There were spider webs in the holes, and the head had neither been washed nor scrubbed with sand.

I learned a good deal about the cave Lazarus had been in. It was full of sculptures: he had seen a stone bowl with three heads, strange animals and human beings, and models of ships. This cave near Hanga-o-Teo had been inherited from his great-grandfather, and he owned it together with his three sisters. Now that no "bad luck" had befallen him, he was going to talk to his two oldest sisters, to get permission to bring more things from the cave. There was no need for him to say anything to his younger sister; she was only twenty and did not understand such matters.

Lazarus felt himself a hero now that he had been in the cave. His family had four caves. The *rongo-rongo* cave where his cousin Alberto had been was supposed to be near the one from which he had just come, but only Alberto knew the entrance. Then there was one in the cliffs at Vinapu: Lazarus knew that one and would go there another night. The fourth cave was right in the vertical rock face of the statues' mountain Rano Raraku. Three different families each had their own section in this important cave. It was full of skeletons, and he would never dare set foot in it; nor did he know the entrance.

I asked whether, if three families knew the entrance to the same cave, they ever stole from one another. Oh no, he said, that presented no problem. Each family owned its own well-defined section, and had its own *aku-aku* there to look after it.

Lazarus received dress material for his two older sisters and disappeared into the night.

Next day the mayor stood as calm as ever in his place on the *ahu* wall, directing his long-ears as they hung and swung at the end of their lofty poles. The day before he had not betrayed by one gesture that he too had a cave. All that he had boasted of was his own helpful *aku-aku* and three small colleagues in the spirit world who lived in an *ahu* in La Pérouse Bay. I watched him standing there cool and confident, organizing the work like a trained engineer. It would be strange if Lazarus' family had four caves, and the chief of the long-ears himself had not a single one. But stronger medicine was required to make the mayor talk.

Later in the day I saw a chance of getting the two men aside once more. I had no idea whether the mayor had a cave, but at any rate he must know a good deal about their existence on the island. I asked in the course of conversation if many families had secret caves. The mayor admitted that there were some who had, but said that hardly anyone got to know anything about other people's caves. Usually only one member of the family at a time had the whole responsibility of knowing the entrance. Sometimes this person died before a successor had been initiated into the secret, and the system was so ingenious that no one could ever find the opening again. A great number of family caves had been lost in this way, and both the mayor and Lazarus stressed that such a loss brought "bad luck."

"That is just what ought to be stopped," I put in. "That is why the things ought to be moved to a safe museum, where no one can steal them and where they cannot be lost. A watchman is always there to look after them."

The mayor reflected a little. He did not feel quite convinced. Those who had made the things had said that they were to be hidden in secret caves, not kept in houses.

"That was because the reed huts of their day were not safe," I explained. "The caves were the safest places they had, but they are not really safe since everything is lost whenever the entrance is forgotten. There's no danger of anyone forgetting the location of a museum door."

The mayor did not entirely accept my way of reasoning. His forefathers' commandments had more power than all the *mana* he attributed to me. After all, he had both *mana* and *aku-aku* himself, and he had not seen any sign of his forefathers having changed their view on the taboos.

I was stuck. Even Lazarus seemed to waver. There must be some way to show the superstitious mayor an impressive sign which would convince him that his forefathers had now abolished their deadly taboo. I decided to carry out a crazy plan.

At the foot of the plain and right next to the camp lay an *ahu* with fallen statues. The original wall had been sadly damaged during the rebuilding period of the second epoch: the work had never been completed. Later, destructive hands had been at work: blocks and boulders in great numbers lay strewn about in front of the façade. Bill had been over one Sunday to look at the damaged wall, and as he was brushing the sand away from a slab he saw something which he thought was a whale's nose cut in relief on the stone. A large block lay on top of the stone and covered the rest of the figure. Before riding back to Vinapu Bill mentioned it to me. The photographer and I went over to the heap of stones and searched till we found what Bill had seen, and when we removed the block over it, a figure clearly representing a whale about three feet long came to light. The slab slipped from us and rolled down onto the sand below us. It now lay with the shapeless back of the stone upward, looking like all the other rocks which were strewn about in the area.

This gave me an idea. No one had noticed what we had done. I would ask the mayor and Lazarus to come to the camp about midnight when everything was dark and quiet. We would then hold a magical séance and get their ancestors to send a work of art made by them up out of the earth as a sign that they were no longer afraid to have their old secrets disclosed. The days of taboo would be over.

The mayor and Lazarus were eager for the meeting, and when it was dark they came stealing into the camp. Just before they arrived, Estevan had left my tent after his last visit.

Yvonne was frightened at the thought of what might happen, and was lying wide-awake, listening. Everyone else was asleep. I explained to the two men that we must stand in a line and hold onto each other's shoulders, and then walk slowly in a wide ring. Next morning we should find within that ring something which their forefathers themselves had made and laid there as a sign that I was right in saying that no one would any longer be punished by *aku-akus* for breaking old taboos.

So off we went, I myself ahead with my arms crossed, then the mayor with his hands on my shoulders, and Lazarus behind him. I could not see at all where I was putting my feet, and was so convulsed with suppressed laughter that I nearly stumbled over every stone. But the two I had in tow were so solemn and so absorbed by the ceremony that they might have been following me on a leash. When the circle was completed and we stood before my tent again, we bowed deeply to one another without exchanging a word, and each of us went quietly to his own sleeping quarters.

The mayor was on the spot as soon as daylight broke, and told me of two mysterious lights which had appeared outside Hotu Matua's cave in the night. They did not come from the jeep, so they were certainly some sign of "good luck." As soon as the day's program had been organized for the rest of the expedition, I asked the mayor and Lazarus to bring the best and most honorable man they had to help us search inside the ring we had made the night before. The mayor promptly chose his youngest brother Atan Atan, a little fellow with a mustache and large innocent eyes, who himself naïvely assured me that the choice was well made: he was a good fellow with a heart of gold, and if I did not believe him I could ask anyone in the village. We took Atan over to the heap of stones and began to search. I asked them to turn over every single stone which lay strewn over the sandy ground, to see if one of them was a work of art made by their ancestors. To make it more dramatic I started them at the opposite side of the circle, so as not to find the whale immediately.

Atan happened to be the first to find something—a curious red stone object. Then I myself found an old stone file and a pretty little obsidian adz. Soon after we heard a shout from Atan, who had turned up a large slab and brushed away the sand from its underside. The mayor, Lazarus, and I rushed up: on the slab was a beautiful relief figure of a whale. But it was a different whale from the one I had turned upside down, so there must be two of them.

All the long-ears working at the stone statue rushed over to see, and from the camp the cook, steward, and photographer came running. The mayor's eyes were popping out of his head, and his chest was heaving as if he had just finished a hard sprint. Both he and Atan were filled with admiration and murmured praise of my *aku-aku's* power. Lazarus became very serious. He said that this area had belonged to his own family and their *aku-aku*. The mayor shivered. All the natives looked at me as if I were a strange animal. I knew myself that I had now a still greater surprise in reserve.

"Have you seen a sculpture like that before?" I asked.

No, nobody had. But this was a picture of a *mamama niuhi*, a dolphin, they could all see that.

"Then I'll make another of the very same sort come up inside the circle," I said.

The mayor sent his men back to collect boulders for the statue, while we four went on searching. Stone after stone was turned over, and we were nearing the goal. Then the steward called out that lunch was ready. I asked the others to wait till I came back. It was I who would make the whale appear.

While I was sitting in the mess tent eating, I heard shouts and arguments from the distance, and the mayor came running to get me, quite desperate. Unseen by him, two of the younger men had gone inside the circle and searched on their own. They had found the whale and were carrying it off between them to Hotu Matua's cave. They were going to sell it to me. The mayor was seriously agitated. I stood rubbing my nose. What the devil could I do now? Those two fellows had carried off the honors of the day, and now I should not be able to conjure up the whale I had already guaranteed I would produce myself. I returned to the area.

Lazarus was bringing the two men back: they came reluctantly, dragging the whale, and laid it down where they had found it. But surely they were laying it in the wrong place? I went up with the mayor, and now it was my turn to be puzzled and speechless. My own whale still lay bottom upward; no one had yet touched it. Those two fellows who now stood before us, frightened, had found a third whale, a rather small one. Everything was all right, I reassured them. We would continue as soon as I had my lunch; then I would produce a still larger and finer whale.

When we continued the search and came to the last sector of the circle, I noticed that all three carefully passed by the right stone, while they turned over every single one of the others. At last the circle was completed.

"There are no more," the mayor said, a little astonished.

"You haven't turned over that one," I said, and pointed to the all-important stone.

"Yes, we did turn it over. Don't you see it's lying with the pale side uppermost?" said Lazarus.

I suddenly realized that these children of nature could tell merely by looking at a stone whether it was lying with its old sunburned side up. This one lay with its pale, shaded side showing, and they thought they had turned it over themselves.

"It doesn't matter whether you've turned it over or not," I said. "Turn it over once more. You remember what happened when Señor Arne turned over the big stone you all knew so well up at Rano Raraku."

Lazarus helped me to get a good hold, and we rolled the stone over.

"Look!" was all Lazarus managed to gasp out. He simply stood staring and smiling foolishly, while Atan cheered loudly.

The mayor seemed electrified and could only stammer: "Very important—very important. What a strong *aku-aku!*"

Both the long-ears from the statue and our own people from the camp came rushing up again to stare at the third whale. Even the two young rascals who had found a little whale of their own were vastly impressed, and the photographer and I, who had started the whole business, found it hard to keep a straight face, for this was the last word in queer coincidences.

Eroria just shook her head and told me quietly that I had "good luck," real "good luck." She gazed enraptured at the three whales, and I thought to myself that for her this was a regular family portrait gallery, for it was she who had learned from her father that she was directly descended from a whale. But old Mariana had something more to tell me. She lived with the shepherd Leonardo in a stone hut on the other side of the valley, and Leonardo's old brother Domingo had spent the last night with them. When the old man woke up that morning, he told them of a dream he had had: he had dreamed that Señor Kon-Tiki had caught five tunnies.

"Then we're two short," the mayor said quickly, and before I knew what was happening the whole crowd began to turn all the stones on end once more; some of them in their eagerness undoubtedly went outside the circle. They were all absolutely determined to find the two required to make Domingo's dream come true. Late in the afternoon two obscure fish carvings came to light. Both were at once accepted as whales, and the natives triumphantly laid the five figures in a row on the sand.

The mayor took up a little stone and drew an arc in the sand in front of the figures. Then he made a little hole in the middle of the arc and said: "That's done."

He and Lazarus stood in front of the arc and sang a snatch of Hotu Matua's old song, their hips swaying rhythmically in hula fashion. They sang another snatch, then fell silent, and continued in this manner with short breaks, until at last evening came and everyone went home.

Early next morning Lazarus was on the spot with a sack over his shoulder. This he smuggled into my tent unobserved by anyone outside. When he laid it down there was a clatter of stones. From that day onward Lazarus was a frequent night visitor to my tent. He worked with the others in the daytime and lay down to sleep with them in the cave when evening came. But in the darkness of the night he crept out over sleeping forms, got onto his horse, and disappeared over the ridge to the west. . . . Next morning there was another sack on the floor of my tent.

The mayor was on tenterhooks for three days following, and then he too could control himself no longer. We went up into the scree and had a long talk. He told me he had a friend with a large red statue hidden in his garden; it had no number on it, and his friend had promised that I could take it on board ship with me for "good luck." I explained that no one was allowed to have monuments of this kind; they were protected. The mayor was visibly disappointed; his contribution had not proved the success he had hoped.

Clearly itching to win my favor, at long last he said quietly that he would talk to his own men. Several of them had family caves, and he would try to persuade them to bring me cave stones. But I must not allow myself to be misled if anyone brought me strange stones which looked newly scrubbed, even if the owners lied and declared that they themselves had found or made them.

"For people are afraid to talk openly about these things," the mayor said. "Besides, they wash the cave stones and keep them clean."

I said emphatically that they must never do that. It ruined the stones.

Then the mayor made his first slip: His father had expressly asked him to wash the stones, he assured me.

"You must only blow the dust away," I explained, "or the surface will wear away."

The mayor thought this was a sensible idea. I knew a lot, he said, and he would pass on this information. But he was worried about small roots and insects' eggs getting into the porous lava stone. In caves which were not looked after there were many figures which were cracked and damaged. Before he realized what he had said, he had revealed that he washed all his figures at monthly intervals.

I received this piece of information without any visible surprise, and as a result the mayor's tongue really started to wag. It took him fifteen nights to finish a washing ceremony, he confided, for as eldest brother he was responsible for four caves. His wife had to go fishing while he was busy with the stones; she could not help, as she belonged to another family.

He always had to go into the cave alone and never make a sound while he was inside. He had to be quick and just snatch up a few stones—one here, one there—and then hurry out to wash them. He had money, too, in one of the caves. Iron money. But the caves were rather damp, so there were no wooden figures there. He had inherited two caves of the other kind, too, *ana miro*, and they were full of wooden things. But so far he had not been able to find the concealed openings leading to the two caves. He had been right on the spot three times and baked a chicken in an earth oven so that the smell would help him to find the way to the hidden entrances. So far it had not worked, but now he would have another try.

Finally he told me that his own *aku-aku* had recently advised him to take things from the other caves and give them to Señor Kon-Tiki, in spite of his own father having told him never, never, never to take anything away from the caves. If I gave him a pair of trousers, a shirt, a tiny little scrap of cloth, and just a few dollars, he would hide them in the cave and take them out when a relative really needed them. And then we could await events.

The mayor got what he asked for, but for a time nothing happened. Meanwhile the work of raising the statue had reached its sixteenth day, and before long the giant would tilt into position. The long-ears were working against time now, for the governor had been notified by wireless that the warship *Pinto* was on her way to Easter Island. We were well into February, and the annual visit to the island was impending.

The mayor was most anxious to get the statue raised so that the captain of the warship would see with his own eyes that it was really standing. The captain acted as the supreme authority on the island from the moment he set foot ashore, and the mayor hoped he would give a favorable report to the Chilean President.

On the sixteenth day the mayor asked for rope to pull and counterbalance the statue when it was being raised erect. All the rope brought by the expedition was now in use on other parts of the island, and that evening we drove over to see the governor and ask him if he had any rope to spare. When we got there, he told us a radio message had come saying that the *Pinto* would arrive the very next day. She had been ten days under way. The mayor's face fell. Now he would not be able to complete the raising of the statue, for when the *Pinto* arrived everyone would be kept busy loading wool and unloading flour and sugar and certain sorely needed commodities for the coming year. The governor was sorry, too, but the long-ears and all my native workers would have to report to him next day.

We drove on crestfallen through the village to Father Sebastian's, to give him the latest report on the progress of the work. I whispered in his ear that all efforts to get into a family cave were still of no avail, apart from the fact that I now had a remarkable collection of sculptures on board the ship.

On our way to the priest's the mayor had suddenly proposed that both of us should sit and concentrate on our respective *aku-akus*, asking them to help us hold up the *Pinto* so that he would have another day in which to complete the work. He sat on the toolbox, silent and reverent, between the photographer and myself, bouncing up and down and hanging on grimly to stop his head from hitting the roof. Returning from Father Sebastian's we passed right through the village once again, and were about to turn left at the crossroads where the jeep tracks ran off toward Anakena. There stood the governor in the beam of the headlights, pointing to a coil of rope lying by the roadside. He had just received another message: the *Pinto* would not be arriving until the day after tomorrow.

I leaned back in my seat, helpless with silent laughter. The photographer sat chuckling at the wheel. This was really the queerest coincidence of the lot. Only the mayor accepted it as a matter of course.

"There you are," he murmured in my ear.

I had nothing more to say. I merely sat shaking my head in amazement as we bumped along in the dark. What no one knew as yet was that the long-ears would need *two* more working days instead of one. But the mayor, oblivious of this, sat rejoicing in the strength of our combined *aku-akus*. His complacent mood gave way after a while to a sneaking suspicion that probably my *aku-aku* rather than his had really done the trick; for he began, quite unprompted, to whisper to me about all the incredible things he had in his caves. Never, never had he taken from the caves anything he had inherited, but now he was being tempted more and more by his own *aku-aku*.

The next day was the seventeenth working day on the statue. Everyone expected it to be raised that day. It was then that the ancient crone turned up and laid her magic semicircle of stones on the huge slab on which the statue was to stand. Afterward she presented me with a large fishhook of black stone, exquisitely shaped and polished as bright as ebony. She had "found" it that very day as a sign of "good luck." I had never seen this old gray-haired woman before. She was a bent, fragile little creature, but behind her wrinkles one could see traces of a truly handsome, aristocratic face, and two shrewd, flashing eyes. The mayor whispered to me that she was the last surviving sister of his father. Her name was Victoria, but she preferred to be called *Tahu-tahu,* which meant "sorcery." She had been dancing for them all night in front of the cave to bring them "good luck" and to prevent the giant from falling over when it was suddenly tilted free of the stone pile.

The giant did not capsize, but neither did it tip up into the vertical. When the seventeenth day was over, it still lay aslant. Next day it would most certainly have tilted into position, for only a little more maneuvering was needed. But next day the long-ears had to be in the village for the great event of the year, the visit of the warship. To the disappointment of the mayor, the giant was doomed to remain in his undignified position, reclining drunkenly with the stone pile up to its nose, when the ship's captain made his personal tour of inspection.

When night came only our guards were left in camp. The rest of us had gone on board, for at daybreak we were to put out to sea and escort the warship into the village bay. The constant emptiness of the endless ocean surrounding us made the horizon appear to be a delicate spider's thread suspended between two shades of blue. But tomorrow morning when the village population woke there would be a fly and a midge hanging on the thread, and as they increased in size our two ships would soon be anchored side by side off the village.

There was a third vessel too which in the last few days had occupied the natives more than usual. She was not armored with steel, but plaited together with golden fresh-water reeds, and the natives themselves had launched her at Anakena. Now she lay on our ship's deck gleaming like gold in the sun. She had been built as a practical experiment, but once she was launched, she too sailed right into the web of secrecy surrounding the family caves.

This phase of the mystery began early in the week of raising the statue. Ed, crawling about under the stone slabs in the narrow ruins up on the cliff edge in Orongo, had discovered wall carvings different from those already found on the island. The most curious were a typical American Indian weeping-eye motif, and several ceiling sculptures of crescent-shaped reed boats with masts. One of the reed boats had lateral lashings and a large square sail.

We knew that at the time of the earliest European visits the inhabitants of Easter Island had made for themselves the same curious one- and two-man reed boats that Inca Indians and their predecessors have used along the coast of Peru since time immemorial. But no one had ever heard of the old Easter Islanders making reed boats large enough to carry sail. I myself had special reasons for being interested. I had sailed on Lake Titicaca in reed boats of this kind, with mountain Indians from the Tiahuanaco plain as my crew. I knew that they were splendid craft of incredible carrying capacity and speed. At the time of the Spanish conquests large reed boats of this kind were in use on the open sea off the coast of Peru, and drawings[1] on jars from pre-Inca times show that during the oldest period of Peruvian civilization people had built regular ships out of reeds, just as the old Egyptians had built crafts of papyrus. Rafts of balsa logs and boat-shaped vessels of fresh-water reeds were an unsinkable means of conveyance, which the people of Peru preferred for all sea traffic. I knew too that the reed boats would float for many months without getting waterlogged, and a reed boat from Lake Titicaca which Peruvian friends had brought down to the Pacific took to the seas like a swan and went twice as fast as a balsa raft.

And now we were suddenly confronted with illustrations of reed boats among old ceiling paintings in Ed's ruined house No. 19, on the edge of the crater of Easter Island's largest volcano. We not only found pictures of the boats, but we also found a surviving supply of the boatmen's reeds. From the ceremonial center where Ed found his paintings we could

---

[1] See Plate LXXXI and figures on pp. 588–89 of Thor Heyerdahl, *American Indians in the Pacific* (Oslo, Stockholm, London, Chicago, 1952).

look down in the abyss beneath us at one side and see the ocean spending its fury on the rocks, flinging up the salt spume. But turning around to face the giant caldron of the crater, we looked down upon a calm fresh-water lake completely overgrown with tall reeds. This was the giant reed the old Easter Islanders had used. Every single native could still tell of a little craft they called a *pora*, which each of the competitors had made for himself to use in the race to the bird islands for the first egg of the year.

Actually, this particular reed was something of a botanical curiosity. It was recognized by botanists as an American fresh-water reed, and in fact the very reed that grows round Lake Titicaca. It was therefore most surprising to find it here, down in a crater lake on Easter Island. This was the reed used by the Peruvian Indians to build their strange vessels on the shores of Lake Titicaca; and it was laboriously cultivated in artificially irrigated swamps along the desert coast of Peru in areas where access to balsa logs for raft building was difficult. How had this highly important American reed, a fresh-water plant, come all the way to Easter Island?

The natives had their own answer. According to a tradition already collected by Father Sebastian, the reed was not originally a wild plant, like certain other plants on the island. This reed had been brought along and carefully planted down in the volcano by one of their first ancestors, Uru by name. He had gone down into Rano Kao crater with rootstocks and planted the first reed, and when it spread he had taken new rootstocks, first to the crater lake at Rano Raraku, and then to Rano Aroi. The tall reed became one of the most important plants on the island. It was used not only to construct vessels, but also to build houses and make mats, baskets, and hats. To this very day the natives go down regularly to cut reeds in the crater lakes. And down in a shining pool in the middle of the Rano Kao swamp below us we saw through our glasses a large reed raft, which the children had made for a swimming barge.

I wanted to make a *pora*. Apart from a drawing by one of the early European visitors, no modern-day person had ever seen what it was like and how it was used in the open sea off the island.

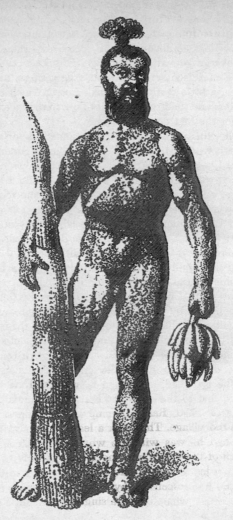

From an old drawing of an Easter Island native with topknot and full beard. He came swimming on a small reed *pora* to visit the ship of Petit-Thouar, one of the early European visitors.

"The Pakarati brothers should be able to help you," said Father Sebastian, interested in the new problem I had brought him. "They're four amusing old fellows who know all about boats and fishing."

Yes, said Pedro and Santiago and Domingo and Timoteo, they could make a *pora*. But I must give them each a good knife and enough time for the reeds to dry. The four old men were given their knives, and went down to the crater lake in Rano Raraku. There were two kinds of reed boat, old Timoteo explained. One kind was for a single person setting out for the bird islands in search of eggs; the other was for two persons fishing in the open sea. I asked them to make one of each kind. The reeds, which were much taller than the men themselves, were cut off at the roots and laid to dry beside the lake at the bottom of the inner statue quarry. Then the four old fellows rode round the island looking for *mahute* and *hauhau* bushes; from the bark of these they would make old-time ropes so that the reeds could be bound in the traditional way.

It was an eternity before the old men got their reeds ready, for no sooner did they leave the crater where they had laid them out to dry, than other natives went in with horses and rode off with large bundles. The reeds were popular for mats and mattresses, and it was so much simpler to supply oneself with reeds ready-cut than with those still growing in the swamp. And so the old fellows had to set to work with their knives again.

One day, while the green reeds were still being dried in the Rano Raraku crater, I took a tent with me and went down into the volcano of Rano Kao; up on the rim was the birdmen's ruined village. Thor took a leave of absence from helping Ed, and he was with me when I clambered down the steep wall of the crater into the interior of the volcano. This was the wildest sight we had seen anywhere on the island. When we had descended by the only possible path down the crater wall, there was not a single foot of solid flat ground to be found. Stretched out before us was a vast oozing quagmire which lay like green spinach at the bottom of a giant caldron with walls rising steeply into the sky on every side. The photographer, who was with us too, could tackle peaks and cliffs with the agility of a mountain goat, but he was not at his ease down by the bog here at the bottom of the crater. The base of the slope on which we stood was very steep, and if we set foot on the bog either we stepped into water or the whole surface swayed under us like a rocking boat.

At the bottom of the slope we had to build a small platform of boughs, carpeted with reeds, before we had enough level ground to pitch our tent without rolling into the bog. Wherever we moved either there was sheer precipice above our heads, or else there were endless screes, so steep that any attempt to scramble up was liable to start a rockfall. In the few places where the slopes were not too steep for us to climb, trees and bushes had got in ahead of us and formed a dense scrub. It was from the depths of this crater that the people of Easter Island had obtained their wood right up to our own time. For once, with plenty of firewood on hand, we enjoyed the luxury of a blazing campfire, a friendly spark re-kindled in an extinct volcano. When we finally retired to our tent for the night, we praised the unknown navigator Uru who had given us such a wonderful reed mattress.

Till now no one had carried out any test boring for a study of this gigantic swamp, and with this purpose in mind, we expected to be down in the volcano several days and nights. After all, according to legend it was here that the boat-building reeds—which we knew had come from South America—had first been planted. The very first Spaniards who came to the island from Peru had recognized this important fresh-water reed as the *totora* of the Incas, and modern botanists have shown that they were right. It was now our intention to bore down into the marsh, as far as our special twenty-five-foot bore could reach, for samples of turf. We knew that a bog like this was just the place in which all kinds of pollen would be hermetically preserved for all time. On our return Professor Olof Selling of Stockholm was going to analyze the samples and determine the ancient vegetable life throughout the history of Easter Island.

If we were lucky the pollen would tell us whether Easter Island had ever been covered with forests, and also when the South American fresh-water reed was first introduced into the crater lake. Anyone could see that it was a long time ago, for the great crater lake was over three hundred acres in extent, and yet so thickly covered with green *totora* that it resembled a huge sugar-cane plantation. Occasionally brown, yellow, and black patches of moss, mud, and tangled dead reeds broke the expanse of green.

It looked as if any movement on this surface would be dangerous, but the natives, feeling their way for generations across the swamp, had got to know the safe places and paths leading to some of the open water holes. When the villagers were suffering from drought, they had to ascend the lofty volcano and then climb down into this deep crater to fetch water from the marsh. The natives believed the lake was bottomless, and Father Sebastian told us that someone had let down a 500-foot line in one of the open pools without touching bottom.

The morning sun was late in reaching the depths of the volcano, and as we lay blowing at the smoking fire for our morning coffee, Ed's native foreman Tepano came clambering down to guide us out into the quagmire. We wanted to reach a series of areas which I had chosen for test borings. He took us on a queer walk. As soon as we had set foot on the heaving bog, we had first to force our way through a jungle of giant reeds standing eight feet high and as close-packed as the bristles of a brush. These lush green reeds grew up from a tangle of dead reed fibers whose tough coils wound about our limbs and pulled us down into an endless web. From these seemingly bottomless snares we could only raise ourselves by pushing thick bundles of fresh reeds beneath our bellies as we crawled.

When we got through this dense barricade which skirted the edge of the overgrown lake, the whole crater marsh spread out before us like a patchwork quilt of brown, yellow, green, blue, and black. At some places we had to wade through surface water while the turf beneath teetered and swung; at others we sank up to our knees in moss and mud. At every step we felt that we should be dragged down into unplumbed depths if we did not immediately put the other foot forward and move on. Here and there were breaks in the floating surface marsh with open coffee-colored water between, and the whole mass lurched violently as we jumped across.

In many places giant reeds grew in small thickets, and

when we forced our way out of one of these, the photographer saw Tepano, Thor, and me in a single step disappear into a water hole completely coated over with green slime. Tepano assured us that there was no danger so long as we could swim.

The sun blazed down fiercely into that windless witches' caldron, and as we crawled out of the trap mud and green slime were baked onto our hair and bodies, making us look like dried-up water sprites. At last even the black, open water pools tempted us to take a dip and clean up. The water was quite tepid on the surface, but ice-cold farther down. Tepano begged us insistently to keep our heads above water; once a native had dived near the edge and never found his way up again because he had got lost under the floating turf.

We found no suitable places for boring. If we put the bore in, it went straight through the turf and down into open water. Often the turf was ten or twelve feet thick and consisted of a tangled mass of dead reeds. If we sounded in the water holes, we recorded the most varying depths, and we never got down to the bottom of the crater lake, for there was always some underwater tangle in the way. Tepano told us that these water holes were never in quite the same place: they shifted from year to year. Everything was in motion down in the witches' caldron.

Before evening came Tepano went back over the edge of the crater, and the photographer left us too. Thor and I were to remain down in the crater a few days longer, to see if we could get better borings. We now knew the secrets of the crater bog; we could tell from the coloring and substance what to expect when we put our feet down.

Next day we made our way right across the marsh to the crater face on the other side. There we caught sight of a stone wall twelve feet high, built on the very edge of the swamp. It was overgrown with scrub and straggling wisps of greenery, and when we climbed up it we reached an old man-made platform. From there we could see that four or five other walls continued as terraces, one above the other, along the side of the crater. And when we began to look about, we found low rectangular openings leading to underground stone houses of the type hitherto known only at the bird-men's ruined village up on the cliff at Orongo. We had come upon a collection of ruins unknown even to the natives; at any rate they had never said a word about it to any white man.

A number of the stones in the walls were covered with half-effaced relief carvings of human beings, birds, and fabulous creatures. There were grotesque faces and magical eyes. The most conspicuous were a couple of bird-men and a four-legged beast with a human head. Ed later worked this site with his team from Orongo. He found that the terraces had once been built for agriculture, and at the foot of the lowest wall we took numerous samples of turf and soil for the pollen tests.

On our fourth day down in the crater we were sitting sealing up all our test tubes with melted paraffin when our skipper came clambering down into the volcano with the news that Arne had made a new discovery at Rano Raraku. He had dug out the body of a giant statue which had been standing with its head above ground, and on the chest of the figure was a picture of a large reed boat with three masts and several sails. From the deck of the boat a long line ran down to a turtle carved on the giant's stomach.

We packed our things and left behind us the crater bottom of Rano Kao. While Thor went up to Ed's ruined village, I drove to Rano Raraku with the skipper. Arne showed us his new find. All his native workers stood by, beaming with pride and veneration at the ancient vessel's catching a turtle on the *moai's* stomach. They were all sure that this was Hotu Matua's own ship, for he had landed on the island with several hundred men on board two vessels so large that Oroi, Hotu Matua's worst enemy, had made the passage as a stowaway. There were no *honu*, or turtles, on the island today, but when Hotu Matua came, one of his men had been injured trying to catch a big one on the beach at Anakena.

As so often before, stories of the great feats of their ancestors were recalled and I was treated to fragments of well-known Hotu Matua legends which had actually been recorded by Father Roussel and Paymaster Thomson at the end of the last century. We could all see that this was an unusual ship and certainly not a European craft. But it was strange to realize that the Easter Island statue makers built themselves vessels so large that there was room to step more than a single mast. And yet, who would have thought that the same people could have erected gigantic human figures as high as four-story buildings, but for the fact that these statues still remained, thanks to the imperishable stone in which they were carved? It was obvious that these tireless engineering geniuses were not merely expert builders in stone: after all it was as mariners in the world class that they had been able to find their way out to this exceedingly lonely haven, where they had created their statues in peace for centuries. Since they had the *totora* reed, and used it to make small rafts, there was really no reason why, by lashing more and larger bundles together, they should not have been able to increase the size according to requirements.

When the first Europeans came to Easter Island they saw nobody building ships, but neither did they see anyone making statues. The only craft the Europeans saw were tiny narrow canoes which could just hold from two to four men in a smooth sea, and even smaller reed rafts. But the Europeans came to the island in the third, or barbarian, period when war had destroyed all the old culture and bloody feuds prevented collaboration between the various family groups. In these chaotic times a divided people, spending most of their time in and around their refuge caves, were hardly likely to get together and build ships.

This explains why historic records of only two miserable little types of craft in Easter Island have come down to us— a little Polynesian outrigger canoe, the *vaka ama*, and a little South American reed raft, the *pora*, both of them too small ever to have brought man to the world's most solitary island. But native legends contain vivid descriptions of large vessels used for long voyages by their ancestors in the golden age of long ago. In the last century Father Roussel was told of great ships which could carry four hundred passengers and had the lofty bow raised like a swan's neck, while the stern, equally high, was split into two separate parts. Many of the reed boats we find depicted on ancient jars in Peru are just like this. But Easter Island traditions also tell of other old types. Father Sebastian had learned that there was a large vessel shaped like a flat raft or barge. It was called a *vaka poepoe*, and was also used when the navigators set out on long voyages with many people on board.

Now that Ed and Arne had each found a picture of a reed boat, we were on the alert every time we saw a boat-shaped figure. We found several on the statues and in the quarry itself with the bundles of reeds clearly defined, and Bill found one with a mast and a square sail. On the underside of a fallen statue over thirty feet long Carl found a reed boat with a mast running straight up the figure's stomach in such a way that the navel formed a circular sail; and up in Orongo Ed found a ceiling painting of another, with a little round sail on the middle mast of her three.

It so happened that we were to obtain yet more tangible evidence that such large vessels had existed. In many parts of the island we had seen wide paved roads which disappeared straight down into the sea. These mysterious constructions had in the course of time stimulated a great number of vivid speculations. They have been one of the main supports for all who believe that Easter Island is the remains of a sunken continent. The paved roads, it has been said, undoubtedly continued along the ocean floor, and if one could follow them, the ruins of the sunken continent of Mu could be reached.

We could easily follow them: we had a frogman among our crew. And with him we rode to the nearest roadway which vanished down into the depths. It was a priceless sight to see the frogman in his green uniform, with Martian helmet and oxygen mask, marching down the road to Mu with his frog fins flapping on the smooth paving stones. He swung in his hand a flame-colored camera container, resembling a lantern, and he waved a graceful farewell as he left the dry pavement and strode on into the sea.

Soon we saw only the oxygen containers on his back and two splashing feet, and then the frogman disappeared entirely. Only scattered air bubbles breaking on the surface told us which way he was going. But clearly the frogman was not finding any short cut to Mu. Soon we saw the bubbles moving to the left, then they changed direction and struck off to the right; and as we watched the bubbles wandered to and fro in rings and spirals till the frogman poked his snouted helmet up out of the water to take a fresh bearing from the road ashore. Then he continued his underwater search, zigzagging in a seaward direction, till he gave up and swam ashore to report.

"Weren't there any signposts down there?"

"Didn't you meet a mermaid who could tell you the way?"

Questions rained down upon the poor frogman. He had seen no road. The paving went no further than the water's edge; beyond there were only ledges and boulders, mushroom corals, and deep crevices, till the rocky ocean floor shelved steeply into hazy blue depths at a spot where he had seen some big fish.

We were not particularly surprised. Oceanographers had long since established, on the basis of deposits taken from the bottom of the Pacific, that in the Polynesian part of that ocean the land masses had neither risen nor fallen so long as man has existed.

Once again I had recourse to the natives. No one could remember what the broad paved roads leading down to the sea had been used for, but they had a name: they were called *apapa*. *Apapa* means "unload." This confirmed our suspicion: they were unloading places or landing ramps where large vessels coming in from the sea were drawn up.

One *apapa* ran down to a shallow inlet at the foot of a large temple platform on the south coast. The inlet was so full of boulders that the old navigators had had to clear a wide channel to enable craft to come alongside the landing stage. And in the shallows of this channel lay three gigantic red topknots, abandoned in the water. Two of these *pukao* lay so close together that they must have been on board the same vessel. This was the first evidence we had come across suggesting that the sculptors had sent some of their heavy cargoes by sea along the coast. We had now established that they actually had vessels which could transport twenty tons, and without a cargo they would have been able to carry a crew of nearly two hundred. Later we found proof that even individual statues had been carried by sea and landed at a spot where only a reed boat or log raft of very shallow draft could have come in with so heavy a cargo.

While we were beginning, bit by bit, to get a clearer picture of the remarkable maritime achievements of the earliest islanders, the four old men were working away with their *totora* reeds in the Rano Raraku crater. When the reeds were dried, each of them swiftly made his own *pora*. By using a special lashing, they achieved a curved, pointed shape, exactly like a huge tusk. It was eerie to see them going down to the water, each with his own craft, because what they were carrying were perfect copies of the peculiar one-man boat which had been a characteristic feature of the Peruvian coast for centuries. And as we knew, it was even made from the same South American fresh-water reed.

When the four old men were about to start building the larger two-man boat, Timoteo directed operations with complete assurance; the other three seemed helpless without his orders. This was so obvious that I asked the reason, and was told that Timoteo was the oldest, and therefore the only one who knew what the boat should look like. I was a little surprised at the reply, but it was not till some time afterward that I began to suspect the reason.

When the canoe-shaped, two-man boat was launched at Anakena, she strongly recalled, in all her construction, the reed boats of Lake Titicaca. The only difference was that the bow and stern were drawn out in a long point sticking up into the air at an angle, just as in the most ancient reed boats on the coast of Peru. The two older brothers jumped on board, each with his paddle, and the curious, flexible craft danced easily over high foaming breakers, heading for the open sea. On top of it rode the two old men dry and safe. The other two plunged into the breakers, each with his one-man *pora,* and confidently faced the sea. They lay with their torsos up on the thick end of the stout, tusk-shaped bundle of reeds, and pushed themselves forward through the water by swimming with arms and legs. The two-man boat, farther out, took the seas so safely and gracefully that when she returned from her trial trip, all four brothers crawled on board and headed again into the roughest seas.

Father Sebastian and the mayor stood with me on the shore. We were, all three, equally fascinated and excited. Just behind us was the back of the long-ears' giant statue which had begun to rise above the tops of the tents, but the mayor had eyes only for the golden-yellow boat with the four men paddling in unison out on the sea. He just stared and stared, with tears in his eyes.

"Our grandparents have told us of boats like this, exactly like this, but this is the first time any of us has seen one, and it brings our ancestors so near to us," he said. "I feel it here," he added, thumping his chest with emotion.

When Timoteo's two-man boat came in again with four men paddling, one of our biggest sailors clambered onto the stern without the craft showing a sign of sinking. If the little hastily built reed boat could carry five grown men, there could hardly have been anything to stop the ancient local engineers from cutting enough reeds in the three craters of the island to build themselves sizable ships.

Father Sebastian was quite fascinated. He had had these strange boats described to him before, by old people on the island, but only now did he understand what they had meant. Now he remembered that they had also shown him a picture of such a craft, painted in a cave on Poike.

"This is a fishing boat," said the mayor, and pointed proudly to the golden vessel. "Think what sort of boats the ancient kings had for their long voyages."

I asked if he knew whether they were large enough to use sails, and to my astonishment he replied that they had sails of reed matting. Once more I was amazed at the mayor as he calmly began to draw in the sand a sail made of reeds which ran perpendicularly. It was easy to make such a sail, he said. One had only to bind the reeds together side by side, as Domingo had done quite recently when he made a mat for me.

I myself had seen how the *totora* boats on Lake Titicaca use reed sails to this very day, the only difference being that in them the reeds were sewn together horizontally instead of upright.

"How do you know the boats had reed sails?" I asked, rather puzzled.

"Aha, Don Pedro knows a lot," he replied with a proud, secretive smile.

The reed-boat launching took place during the time Estevan was still bringing me his wife's cave stones, and it was the

Down in the earth great naked stone bodies appeared as we
excavated round the giants' heads. Centuries of blowing sand
and shifting gravel had gradually buried the old giants up
to their necks.

A man feels very small when digging his way down along the body of an Easter Island statue. But how had the unknown sculptors of antiquity transported and erected these giants with no mechanical equipment?

ABOVE: The natives demonstrate the use of reed floats, or *poras*, in the Rano Raraku crater lake. BELOW: The reed fishing boat was another incredible craft. It had a balsa raft's advantage of being unsinkable and rode the sea like a swan.

ABOVE: All the stone giants which once had been set up at their temple sites many miles from the quarry now lie with their noses in the sand, overthrown in the third epoch of the island's history. The red topknots have rolled into the temple square. BELOW: We went to work like Snow White's dwarfs at the foot of the quarry. Here the statues had been temporarily erected for their backs to be completed before transport began.

ABOVE: A niche in the quarry with an uncompleted figure, the end view. The old sculptors had hewn their way with stone picks into the hard rock as if it were cheese. BELOW: A half-finished giant left in the mountain wall. The whole rock face had been cut away by small hand picks. Work in the quarry had stopped quite suddenly, so that unfinished statues in all stages of completion lay about everywhere.

ABOVE AND BELOW: A giant on a keel. Unfinished statues in the quarry showed that the back was the last part to be cut loose from the rock. The sculptors' stone hand picks lay where they had left them, evidence of what primitive tools they had for work on the iron-hard rock. The number 252 was painted on by Father Sebastian when he made a record of all the stone giants which lay about all over the island.

ABOVE: Even high up on the mountain completed statues lay wedged with loose stones, waiting to be transported down the steep slopes and on to a destination beyond the ridges on the horizon. BELOW: An old statue from the island's earliest period showed his face for the first time when we set him up near the village. Father Sebastian and the skipper leaning against the statue behind him are surrounded by a group of Easter Islanders.

Alien gods, unknown even to the natives, emerged from the bosom of the earth as we carried on our excavations. ABOVE: This kneeling giant, sitting on his heels with his hands on his thighs, was unlike anything previously known on Easter Island. BELOW: The kneeling giant just as he was being dug out of the rubble at the foot of the statue quarry.

How did ancient Easter Islanders raise a statue without modern apparatus? The long-ears' descendants, led by the mayor, agreed to disclose the secret. ABOVE: First three wooden poles lift the statue by fractions of an inch as the mayor shoves small stones beneath it. As more stones are added, their size increases. BELOW: As the work progresses, the statue is lifted into the air on an ever-growing tower of stones.

With a heap of stones under its stomach the figure moves upward and backward until it stands in its old place on the wall.
Twelve men with poles and stones set it up in eighteen days.

On the last day the giant is held by ropes to prevent it from toppling off the high wall when it is tilted into the standing position.

Lazarus and I before the only giant on the island now standing at his post. This is the huge statue raised by the long-ears in the Anakena Valley at King Hotu Matua's site. Hundreds of statues once stood on walls all round the island, but all of them were flung down during the civil wars in the third epoch of Easter Island's history.

ABOVE: Little Atan was the first to show us a secret family cave. The entrances to these caves were carefully concealed, camouflaged with stones, earth, and straw. The caves hid stone sculptures of an unusual style, unlike any art form seen on the island before. BELOW: Enlique too had his private treasure chamber deep down underground. Yvonne and I inspect the curious sculptures which lay piled up along the walls.

The cave stones, hidden in secret family caves and handed down from one generation to the next, were a variety of designs. The skull was a "key" stone which gave access to the secret opening of the cave. A powder made of human bones was placed in the hole in its forehead to kill intruders by pure magic. Note also the three-masted reed boat, a slab with ideograms, a long-eared head, and a foot.

I was the first outsider to see these curious cave stones, which the owners hid from other natives as well. Here are a beast with a human head; a bearded face; a mythical whale with a reed hut and a typical Easter Island earth oven on its back and six balls under its belly; a woman with a fish roped to her shoulders; and the profile of a head.

ABOVE: The magic guardian on the right was the most powerful
aku-aku of the cave belonging to Estevan's wife. It is a recumbent bust of a devil with a humped back, swellings on its head,
and a beard. BELOW: Juan the Wizard, Tumu, and Andres
Haoa, in the wizard's cave. Juan thought himself endowed with
supernatural qualities, and had appropriated the Norwegian
table flag, believing it represented my "power."

previous night that Lazarus brought his very first head from the cave. He was so excited now that he could not restrain himself, and told me that among all the other things he had seen in the cave, there were small models of ships. Some of them reminded him of those which Timoteo had built.

As soon as I heard this, I took a gamble. Estevan had just asked on behalf of his wife if there was anything special I wanted from her cave. I had not known what to request, since I did not know what was there. Now Lazarus had let out that his cave had models of boats. Getting Estevan aside, I fired a long shot at him. I told him to ask his wife to give me "the boats" she had in the cave. Estevan stared at me round-eyed, but when the day's work was over, he galloped off in the direction of the village. Late that night he was back again with five amazing sculptures in a sack. The first, which he unpacked from some dry banana leaves, was a pretty little crescent-shaped model of a reed boat. He added that according to his wife there was a still finer boat left in the cave: it had fine lashings and was high and pointed both fore and aft, and it also had a figurehead at each end.

I listened to him on tenterhooks, for this was the night when I expected Lazarus and the mayor to come and walk in a circle round the hidden whale. When Estevan slipped out into the darkness, I did not know that his wife, scared by the *aku-akus*, would stop him from bringing anything more for many nights to come.

Lazarus himself did not get away to fetch a boat that night, for when he and the mayor had returned to their sleeping friends in Hotu Matua's cave after the nocturnal ceremony, the restless mayor lay with his eyes open and saw mysterious lights and other omens outside the entrance to the cave. But the next night, after all the whales had been found, Lazarus saw his chance of stealing out over his sleeping friends. One of them had waked and drawn his legs up quickly, for on Easter Island it's bad luck to have a person step over you. He had asked what Lazarus was up to, and Lazarus had said that he had to go out to obey a call of nature. But he had his horse standing saddled behind a rock, and had ridden off toward the cave at Hanga-o-Teo.

Early in the morning Lazarus pushed a sack into my tent.

He squatted down on the canvas floor and proudly drew from the sack a stone model of a tusk-shaped, one-man *pora* with lashings. Then came a monster resembling an alligator, and an excellent red-stone bowl with three human heads sculptured in high relief round the edge. He said there were three more boats in the same cave, but none of them were so like those which Timoteo and his men had made as the one he had brought with him.

Lazarus was well rewarded for what he had brought, and I asked him to bring the other boat sculptures with him next time. This he did three nights later. One was a model of a good-sized ship with a broad deck and high bow and stern, and both deck and sides were made of thick bundles of reeds lashed together. The other craft was a *vaka poepoe*, as broad and flat as a raft, with a mast and sail and two inexplicable domes side by side on the forward deck. The third was not a real boat, it was more like a long dish, but it was carved as if made of reeds, with a hole for a mast in the middle. At each end there was a most curious head, placed inside the hull at bow and stern and staring toward the masthole. One of the heads had blown-out cheeks and pursed lips, resembling a cherub sending a puff of wind into the sail. The hair was blended with the reeds on the outside of the vessel.

The sculptures were old, and both the subject and the style were completely foreign to Easter Island. When I questioned Lazarus closely about the stones he brought me, he just flung up his hands and was unable to give any explanation. The stones were like that, he could say no more. But there were masses and masses of other queer things left in the cave, and as he had now seen that no disaster followed, he would take me with him one day after the visit of the warship. His one condition was that not a soul in the village should know what we were doing as long as I was still on the island.

The mayor had so far not brought me anything, apart from his own eternally repeated wooden figures. On the last evening before the warship came, I called him into my tent. This was my last chance. Arrangements for his trip had been made; when the warship left, the mayor was going with it, and no one else on the island, not even his own wife, knew the entrance to his secret caves.

When he came into the tent, I had prepared a really pleasant surprise for him, partly because he deserved an extra reward for all he had taught us, but also in the selfish hope that he might produce an equally pleasant surprise for me. I rolled down the tent walls, screwed down the lampwick till it was half-dark, and leaned toward him, whispering. I had the impression that his hair was already beginning to stand on end: he clearly realized that something of a mystical nature was going to happen.

I told him that my *aku-aku* had said to me that the mayor needed a good many things for his first voyage from Easter Island, and I was going to take my *aku-aku's* advice and give him just what it had told me he needed. Thereupon I brought out my best suitcase which I presented to him, and in it I placed a blanket, sheets, towels, a warm jersey, two pairs of new khaki trousers, shirts, various ties, socks, handkerchiefs, shoes, and all kinds of toilet articles from comb and soap to toothbrush and razor. He also got a rucksack full of kitchen utensils and camping equipment, so that he could fend for himself. Several cartons of his favorite cigarettes followed, and a wallet full of Chilean pesos to keep him going if he struck hard times in the great unknown world. He received one of Yvonne's best dresses as a farewell present to his wife, and various children's garments.

The last thing I produced was a stuffed baby cayman, or South American alligator, a foot long, which a Panama native had induced me to buy for a small sum. Both Estevan and Lazarus had brought me a similar reptile in stone from their respective family caves; and the same animal, referred to as *moko*, was also depicted in a well-known wood carving on the island. The *moko* is known throughout Polynesia as a ferocious legendary creature, although the only resemblance to it on these islands are tiny innocent lizards. This has led many people to believe that the *moko* of Easter Island was a recollection of caymans which the old navigators had seen on the tropical coast of South America.

I handed the little stuffed beast to the mayor, saying: "You can put this in your cave as an *aku-aku* guardian while you yourself are on the mainland."

The mayor had grown so excited as the gifts were handed to

him one by one that his eyes nearly popped out of his head; now he went completely mad. He whispered hoarsely that he had a stone exactly like that creature in his cave, and he would bring it to me. Then he no longer could find words. He shook my hand with both his, and managed only to reiterate that my *aku-aku* was *"muy bueno, muy, muy, muy bueno."*

It was black night before he crept out of the tent, a very happy man, and called to his faithful friend Lazarus to help carry the heavy spoils to the waiting horses. Then they dashed off to catch up with all their friends on the way to the village.

So the cave mystery remained a confused and unsolved riddle, and the sturdy giant stood aslant by the tents with a humiliating stone pile up to his nose, as the Anakena Valley was emptied of people. After seventeen days' working on the statue, one day short of completion, the long-ears rode home to be ready for the work and festivities of tomorrow. We ourselves temporarily abandoned the tents and went on board our ship, which lay in the bay spick-and-span and freshly painted, ready to put to sea to meet the *Pinto.*

CHAPTER SEVEN

Meeting the Caves' Dumb Guardians

THE BIG CHILEAN warship appeared on the horizon as the morning sun still hung low over the sea, bathing the cliffs along the coast in gold and haunting shadows. Broad and flat, and all gray, supporting a bristling pyramid of the tools of modern warfare, she grew in size as she approached us—a greeting from the world outside, the first reminder that there was still land beyond the horizon. The winds had filled in Iko's ditch, man had changed his weapons.

We met the *Pinto* just outside the bird islands. On every deck of the great ship towering above us people were lined up at the rails. As soon as we were alongside, Captain Hartmark gave a blast of the siren, and we welcomed our hosts by dipping our ensign. The warship replied by firing one of her guns and running up the Norwegian flag on her mainmast. This was more friendly than we had dared to hope. We came about smartly, putting on all the speed our engines would stand, and the little Greenland trawler escorted the gray leviathan to her anchorage off Hangaroa Village. The whole population was down at the pier. The *Pinto* fired again, this time twenty-one salutes, and then the launch came out from the shore bringing the governor to bid the captain welcome to his naval protectorate.

Twenty minutes after the governor had gone aboard, I went over in our launch with the skipper and the expedition doctor, as had been agreed. We had a most cordial reception. We were piped aboard, and the captain and governor stood at the head of the ladder to receive us. Up in the captain's cabin we met a Chilean surgeon-admiral and the American naval attaché with his wife; he was to explore the possibility of constructing a large-scale airfield on Easter Island, thereby opening an air route between South America and Australia. Over a cocktail I gave thanks in a little speech for the wonderful hospitality the governor and his people had shown us during our stay, and the captain most cordially followed up by wishing us as good fortune in the future as we had hitherto had on the island. He offered us supplies if there was anything we lacked, and turned over to us two large mailbags on which our skipper and the doctor laid eager hands. The formalities were thus disposed of and the foundation laid for a pleasant relationship.

Soon after the door opened again, and in came the mayor wearing a freshly ironed shirt and tie, marching ahead of Lazarus and half a dozen chosen natives. The mayor rushed straight up to the grave, gold-braided captain, shook him vigorously by the hand, and in a loud voice announced to us all that this was the right kind of captain—he knew how things ought to be done, he was the first who had fired a salute when he came to the island. Then he drew himself up as straight as a ruler, with his fingers pointed down along the sides of his trousers, and, with his men standing stiffly at attention behind him, he sang the Chilean national anthem with full bravura squarely into the stoic captain's face. The very second this was over all the natives relaxed completely, and with flexed arms and swaying shoulders and hips they burst into their rhythmical royal song about Hotu Matua's landing at Anakena. The mayor had hardly finished the last verse when he caught sight of me. He stiffened like a cat about to spring, pointed, and exclaimed: "*Mi amigo,* Señor Kon-Tiki!"

As if on a signal, he and all his friends stuck their hands deep into their pockets and pulled out packs of American cigarettes, which they held up under the captain's nose. Here he could inspect samples of the good brands Señor Kon-Tiki had brought to the island. That was how it ought to be done!

The captain listened with admirable patience, and when

the cocktail tray came in again, drinks were offered to the new arrivals too. The mayor's eyes shone with pleasure: this captain was a damned sensible fellow after all. It didn't matter that the cigarettes he brought were not as good as Señor Kon-Tiki's.

I watched with anxiety as the cocktail disappeared into the mayor at a single gulp. He gave me a sidelong look of satisfaction and said with a reassuring nod that I need not be alarmed, he knew what it was to drink good wine. Then he and his colleagues strolled cheerfully out of the captain's cabin to inspect the big ship.

The next time I saw the mayor he was standing surrounded by an admiring crowd down in the bar of the officers' mess. There were a number of special passengers on board this trip, including two professors, Wilhelm and Peña, and a party of Chilean students of archaeology who had come out to look at our excavations. I knew the two friendly professors from Chile, and was heartily embraced in Latin fashion. Both they and the students listened with great interest to our report of the discovery of Easter Island's different epochs, and of the statues of an alien type which we had dug out of the earth.

I dared not say a word in the bar about the curious sculptures I had obtained from secret family caves: a single careless word now would ruin all my chances of solving the riddle. The whole project of getting into one of them still hung by a thread, and if anything leaked out to the natives now, they would be frightened and seal their mouths shut, and thereby their caves.

But when I rose to go, I had a real shock. From the bar I heard the mayor's bragging voice rise in a new and peculiar tone. And when I saw the manner in which he put down his empty glass, I realized that the counter was somewhat out of focus. Then the mayor said, loud and clear: "My friends, I'm a rich man. I have a cave."

I stood for a moment or two as though nailed to the floor, waiting to hear what would happen next. Nothing happened. The others went on talking and drinking, and the mayor did not say another word. Either no one heard him, or it had been taken merely as drunken talk, if in fact anyone understood there was anything special about having a cave. The mayor must have come to and been frightened at his loose tongue, for no sooner had I returned to our own ship than he was on his way to the shore in another boat.

This year a poor stock of wood carvings was offered to the crew and passengers of the *Pinto*. The best had already been traded to the members of our expedition. Accordingly Professor Peña went straight up to the mayor's own hut, where he found an ample choice of finished and half-finished wooden figures of the best quality. But the mayor refused to sell; all had been made for Señor Kon-Tiki, and now he had more orders from Kon-Tiki's ship than he could handle.

Peña had to accept this. The mayor continued to prattle, next about Kon-Tiki's "good luck." Whenever Kon-Tiki's men turned over a stone or stuck a spade into the earth something strange came to light. Peña listened patiently to this too, but when the garrulous mayor got going, still not free from the influence of the cocktail hour, there was absolutely no end to all the things the Kon-Tiki people had found in the earth. At last Professor Peña became alarmed. The mayor's description was bound to give anyone the impression that the grass of Easter Island grew upon a solid mass of art treasures. He quite forgot to mention that all we had found of real value underground were ruins and giant figures, all of which were still left in place. Peña could not but believe that the expedition ship was full of excavated treasures and museum pieces, which we had discovered because we were the first to dig in the earth of the barren island.

That evening, when Professor Peña came ashore for the second time, he went round with a radiogram in his hand. Several who had seen it came to me in dismay, telling me that it was from the Chilean Minister of Education, who was now authorizing Peña to confiscate the expedition's archaeological discoveries and take them back with him in the warship. The governor was extremely disturbed, the captain was equally unhappy but had no power to intervene, and Father Sebastian was completely bewildered. If indeed this was direct authority from the Minister of Education, no one on the island could stop Peña. In that case the expedition would have to surrender every splinter of bone and every sample of charcoal which the archaeologists had laboriously excavated in the past few months.

Our despairing Chilean friends promised to do all they could to clear up the matter, and it was decided to have a meeting with Professor Peña at Father Sebastian's. Everyone sincerely hoped that the affair would be settled in such a way that the expedition material would not be confiscated.

In the meantime the news had spread to the natives. They came to me trembling with anger and assured me that they could do what they liked with their own property, no one could take from me what I had bought from them. Estevan and Lazarus in particular were in mortal fear for their cave stones. But Lazarus added that if I sought help from my *aku-aku*, it was certain that no one could touch a thing on board my ship. The mayor was profoundly distressed and realized that it was all his fault. He would go straight to Peña, he said, and explain that the only things of value I had taken on board the ship were personal property that I had bought from people in the village, and that I had looted nothing from the earth.

"We can give or sell our own things to whom we like," said the mayor, and he went off looking for Peña.

In the meantime it was decided that the captain of the *Pinto* and his party would drive round in the jeep and inspect the work of the expedition throughout the island. Not until a few days later were we to meet at the conference which had been arranged. The *Pinto* was to remain for over a week. Gonzalo would conduct Peña and the students on horseback round the island, and later, under the professional guidance of Bill, they were to begin their own excavation of an ancient reed-house site on the Tepeu Plain.

Next day the sea was rough and the breakers thundered in toward the coast. The *Pinto's* other passengers could not come ashore, and those who were ashore had to stay there. The marooned passengers sought out Father Sebastian, of whom they had all heard as a legendary personality, the uncrowned king of the island. At last Father Sebastian grew so tired of questions and posing for pictures that he came to ask me if we could not go out to our ship. There we could sit by ourselves undisturbed by this swarm of people. Father Sebastian was not worried about the surf so long as someone who knew the reefs would take us out. Down at the pier, where steep breakers came frothing in one after another, the mayor stood with a sad face and asked humbly if he might come too. He must speak to me now.

"Don Pedro may come with us," Father Sebastian said kindly, and crawled on board the dancing launch, with a helping hand from the skipper.

On board the ship the others had finished dinner, so the steward laid a cold smörgåsbord for Father Sebastian, the mayor, the skipper, and me. Father Sebastian loved good food, and a smörgåsbord with beer was the best thing he knew. I too have an excellent appetite and count a good meal among the great material pleasures of life; and in the two guests now on board I had the most congenial company. They ate and ate, till they were in a regular glow, while the ship rolled slowly in the swell, to and fro, to and fro.

We had canned beer on board, and Father Sebastian gave a friendly nod as a sign that the mayor might have a can too; we both knew that he could now buy wine from the *Pinto*. The mayor was overjoyed and went on eating and filling his glass from the can. But Father Sebastian was beginning to chew more slowly; then he smiled awkwardly and asked us to excuse him. The swell was rather heavier than he had thought. The skipper went out with him to the rail to get a breath of fresh air. The mayor, quite unaffected, went on to consume another helping of the good things from the table.

As soon as we were alone, he leaned toward me munching and began to talk of *aku-aku*. I need not be afraid of anyone taking anything from me. Why, our combined *aku-akus* had held back that great warship out there for a whole day. I picked up the thread and whispered that my *aku-aku* had now revealed to me what the mayor had hidden in his secret cave, in addition to the *moko* he had told me about. I described in the most cautious terms the appearance of some of the cave stones which had proved to be common to both Estevan's and Lázarus' caves. I assumed that features common to both of them were likely to be found in the mayor's cave also.

The mayor stiffened in his chair and forgot to munch. Had my *aku-aku* been in his secret cave? He had to admit that I was right, and went on chewing feverishly while questioning me to determine what else I had found out. I told him I had not asked my *aku-aku* about anything more, for now I counted on the mayor being willing to show me the cave himself, before he sailed with the *Pinto*. That calmed him down and he said no more, only ate.

The steward came and refilled the dishes. The mayor loaded his plate afresh, and devoted himself once more to the unaccustomed joys of the smörgåsbord. He lifted the beer can and looked at me sadly. It was empty, and so were all the other cans. I had just decided to go out and ask Father Sebastian how he was, when I saw the steward had put down a newly opened can of beer on an oil drum beside the door. In one action I stepped over the coaming on my way out, grabbed the new can, leaned back to place it before the voraciously eating mayor, and tossed the empty one into the sea as I proceeded onto the deck.

While I was standing at the rail talking to Father Sebastian, who felt better in the breeze, we suddenly heard a terrified bellow from the mayor. I was at the door in a trice: there he sat as though transfixed to the bulkhead, pointing to the beer can, his face convulsed and his eyes popping out of his head!

"Who put it there? Who put it there?" he yelled like a madman.

It occurred to me that there might have been something wrong with the can, some had fermented, and perhaps the mayor thought we were trying to poison him. I smelled it.

"Who put it there? All the cans were empty when you went out," he continued, as hysterically as if he were surrounded by spirits. I suddenly realized that he might not have seen me make the exchange.

"Has no one been here since I went out?" I asked cautiously.

"No! not a soul!"

"Well, then it must have been my *aku-aku*."

The mayor did not doubt it for a moment. He had never seen such an *aku-aku*: he looked quite enviously at me, the owner of an invisible servant who could fetch beer whenever I wanted some. He slowly calmed down and went on eating, keeping a sharp lookout for any more mysterious happenings.

Then he had had enough. After wrapping the last pat of butter in his paper napkin and putting it in his pocket, he went to join the rest outside. The skipper had weighed anchor and was carefully moving the ship closer under land, where a tiny cape gave us more shelter.

The episode with the beer can had made a greater impression on the mayor than the stone whales and everything else he had seen till then. Again on shore late in the afternoon he took me aside and whispered that his own *aku-aku* was now begging him to go to the cave and fetch something for me. He too wanted to do it, but he must get his grandmother's consent first. I had no idea that he had a grandmother, and asked where she was.

"Up there, above Hanga Piko, close to the road and under a block of cement," he replied.

I started, and for a fraction of a second I had a vision of an old woman sprawling helplessly under something which had been overturned, but then I realized that she was dead and had been buried up there. The mayor confided to me in a whisper that he could not ask her in the daytime or by moonlight: it must be pitch-dark. He was going to ask her tonight, and if she agreed, he would go to the cave as his *aku-aku* proposed.

Next day we weighed anchor and returned to the camp at Anakena, while the *Pinto* began to unload. Gonzalo set out on his tour with Professor Peña and the students, and the archaeologists of our expedition, who now had no diggers, were at their posts and showed the visitors around the excavations. These were sociable days, with dinner for us on board the *Pinto*, and for the captain and his staff at the governor's, and later with us at Anakena. When Peña and the students reached the camp on horseback, there was another lively party, and they stayed the night with us. One of the students was a Bolivian archaeologist, and his enthusiasm knew no bounds when he saw the red pillar statue at Vinapu and the kneeling giant at Rano Raraku. He had dug at Tiahuanaco himself and immediately recognized both these types from his own country.

Peña was in the highest of spirits. He was wildly excited over all that he had seen, but he whispered to me that unfortunately he had a "disagreeable mission." He had been looking for me in vain to arrange a meeting in connection with a very unpleasant telegram. I told him that the meeting was already arranged, and we remained as friendly as ever.

A couple of days later I had a message from the mayor asking me to send the jeep over to the village to fetch "a heavy sack with important objects." The skipper drove over; he was going anyhow to pick up the nuns who were to sail in the *Pinto* and were anxious before they left to see the statue which the mayor had almost set up. When the jeep came bumping back, fully loaded with nuns and a priest from the *Pinto*, the mayor and Lazarus, with queer poker faces, were sitting on the top of a large mysterious-looking sack in the back of the vehicle.

While the others were taken sight-seeing, the two natives came into my tent with the sack between them. The mayor had cracked at last. He had been to the cave "with his own grandmother," and was so profoundly agitated that he seemed almost irritable. Lazarus, on the other hand, was obviously relieved: I felt that he breathed more freely now that he thought he was no longer the only man who had removed stones from a family cave. They had both been terrified when they had got the infernal sack into the jeep and the skipper had told them that he was going on to fetch the nuns. But all had gone smoothly: they had had "good luck."

In the sack was a large parcel containing five stones: they came from Lazarus' second cave, which was at Vinapu: from this cave he was now bringing stones for the first time. All the other thirteen stones were from the mayor's own cave. They were the most exquisite sculptures I had yet seen on the island. One figure was a gaping, snarling dog's head with bared teeth and slanting eyes, so wild that it suggested a wolf or fox rather than a domesticated dog. It was a perfect piece of sculpture: I never grew tired of looking at it. There were also several dogs or doglike animals; the length from the snout to the tail of one was so great that it would have resembled a crocodile but for its legs which held it clear of the ground. There was a crawling *moko* with a broad head, huge jaws, and a dentated ridge along its back, a genuine reproduction of a cayman. And there were birds and bird-men, and a very curious stone head. Lazarus' sculptures also represented queer figures, and among them was a flat stone showing two copulating snakes carved in relief.

In the natives' eyes I was bound to know all the answers, so I had to be extremely careful not to reveal that I was a complete outsider by asking stupid questions. But now I was so absorbed that I blurted out a question about the purpose of these stones. My friends too were so deeply engaged that my blunder raised no suspicion.

"They give power to actual things," the mayor whispered eagerly. He produced a very realistic sculpture of a lobster, or to be more correct, a Pacific *langouste*, with its legs curved under as in nature and its feelers stretched flat along its back.

"This gives power to the lobster, so that they multiply along the coast."

Then he pointed to the two snakes and explained that double figures gave double power. I knew that the snake was completely unknown throughout this part of Polynesia, and to try them I asked if this one gave double power to the "eel." But this did not work. These were not eels, they said, for the eel had no slender neck behind its broad head as these two had. These were land creatures similar to what the Chileans called a *culebra*. A gigantic one of the same kind was carved in the rock on the way to the Hanga-o-Teo Valley.

I suddenly remembered that Father Sebastian had once told me this, and had asked me to go and look at it with the archaeologists. Eroria knew where the place was, but so far I had not managed to make the trip.

Lazarus observed with pride and satisfaction that this was the first time anyone had talked openly with anyone else about things like these. He had admitted first to the mayor that he had been in his cave several times to get figures for me, and then the mayor had said that he had decided to do the same. They had confided in one another, and found that much of what they had in their caves was common to them both.

I knew that in Polynesia magical power had once been attributed to human hair, and this knowledge gave me another opportunity to impress the mayor and Lazarus. Both of them said that they knew all about it. In fact the mayor kept locks of hair from all his dead relatives in a stone bowl in the cave, even from his little red-haired daughter. Then he made a fearful grimace, and shuddering, confided that there was also a head in the cave, a real head. There were masses of skulls in every possible hiding place on the island, so I realized that he did not mean a skull, and asked if he meant a stone head. Oh, no, this was a regular head, a human head, he added, shuddering afresh, as he pulled his hair. Could he have a mummified head in the cave, as on some of the other Polynesian islands?

Lazarus admitted that there were neither hair nor heads in the two of his family caves in which he had been: there were only skulls and bones of his own forefathers.

The mayor confided to me that there must be at least fifteen family caves on the island which were still in use, and many, many more which had been lost. To the best of his knowledge it was only the descendants of long-ears, and people who had some long-ear blood in them, who had such caves. He did not think that genuine short-ears had caves. He had inherited his own most important cave in a direct line from Ororoina. He had taken over the cave on the death of his father, to whom it had been handed down from his ancestors going right back to the war eleven generations ago, when Ororoina and the other long-ears had hidden all their treasures in secret caves so as not to be robbed by the short-ears. From the age of five he had worked to learn family tradition from his elders, but his father had found him unworthy of seeing anything till he was fifteen. Then he was allowed to accompany him to a point near the cave, where he waited while his father entered it to fetch some special objects which the boy was allowed to see. That had been the practice for eleven generations.

The mayor paused. Then he said: "This is the first time I have told this to anyone. But afterward, before I went through the cave's entrance, my father cut a lock of hair from my head."

He plucked at the hair on the top of his head, and Lazarus followed his least movement so intently that I realized this was as new to him as it was to me. The mayor went on to describe how his father had rolled up the lock of hair in part of a banana leaf, tied on the outside with string, in which eleven knots were made. Then his father took the little parcel into the cave to a stone bowl on which another stone bowl served as lid. All the ordinary family hair lay in another bowl beside it, but in this special bowl there were until now only ten small packets of hair, most of them red. The first had one knot and belonged to Ororoina, the second had two knots and belonged to Ororoina's son, and so on down to one with ten knots which belonged to the mayor's own father. Now the last, his own with eleven knots, was added.

After his hair had been placed in the bowl, his father returned and a ceremony was held in honor of the *aku-aku* who was guardian of the place. The *aku-aku* was now told that another person was properly authorized to enter. And then he learned for the first time the secret of the cave's entrance and was allowed to go in and see Ororoina's own cave.

For a whole generation he alone had possessed the ancient secret, but now a problem with serious bearing on the future had arisen. His own red-haired son Juan was a child of his time who no longer understood the old ways. He was grown-up and married, but nevertheless he could not be relied on in such serious and secret matters. If Juan found out where the opening was, he would be tempted to make himself a very rich man by selling the contents of the cave to the first ship that came by. The mayor added sadly that he might therefore be compelled in time to let the cave go to his youngest brother Atan Atan, who had respect for the teachings of their forefathers.

We were expecting guests from the warship to dinner, and I had to break off our conversation. The mayor concluded by emphasizing that he and Lazarus and I were now united as brothers, and it was the same with our *aku-akus,* which were present at that very moment.

"Mine's there," the mayor said merrily, pointing down at his left side to a spot on a level with his own knee. We all left the tent in a crowd, presumably with the *aku-akus* toddling between our legs—unless the invisible little things went straight through the tent walls, for these *aku-akus* have their own ways of getting about. The mayor had told me that his own could travel to Chile and back in the course of two minutes.

After dinner I accompanied our Chilean guests back to the village, as we were to have the meeting with Professor Peña in Father Sebastian's house. Father Sebastian himself was in bed with a fever, but his little study was made available and was more than crowded when all who were to take part in the proceedings were seated.

The captain from the warship presided, as he was now the highest authority on the island. Like the governor himself, he too was most favorably disposed to our case, especially since he had seen the work of the archaeologists. He now wanted to radio the supreme command of the Chilean Navy and try to get us permission to take a whole statue away from the island. He knew that we had applied earlier and been refused because the statues were protected monuments, but he had seen himself that we had brought to light formerly unknown statues, and that there would thus be more statues when we left than when we came.

Beside the captain and his adjutant sat the governor, Professor Wilhelm, Professor Peña, and a student; then there was Gonzalo as the expedition's official liaison officer, Ed, and myself.

Peña opened the proceedings by expressing gratitude and admiration for the expedition's work on the island. And then he regretfully produced his authority to confiscate all our archaeological material.

Professor Wilhelm, who was an anthropologist of international reputation, rose immediately and defended our case. He explained that it would be impossible for the archaeologists of the expedition to complete their work if they could not take their own scientific discoveries with them to their laboratories. And why, he asked, had nobody mentioned this before? Heyerdahl himself had been in Chile to settle all problems before the expedition came to Easter Island to dig.

Peña admitted this, but said the whole thing was due to a deplorable blunder in the administration. The Foreign Department had given the permission, although the decision lay with the Department of Education.

I put in that I had also been to the Minister of Education in person. He had been extremely kind and told me to let him know if I came up against any problems and needed his help.

Wilhelm hastened to emphasize that everyone wanted to help, it was only a matter of finding a legal way of doing so. And that could be done, for he himself had been on the committee which had drafted the law in question, and there was a loophole in it.

Then Peña's student quickly rose and asked if he might speak. He declared that the lack of Easter Island material in Chilean museums made this confiscation necessary. "No country has so little from Easter Island as we who own the island," he assured us, and Peña nodded.

I replied, with support from Ed and Gonzalo, that the excavations had brought to light the monuments and ruins which they had all seen for themselves. These findings we had merely exposed and partly reconstructed. What we had otherwise excavated were primarily bones and charcoal and fragments of old stone tools which were of little value to a museum, but indispensable to our further archaeological study of the island's ancient history. All we had found would be later recorded in our scientific report; what was not included there would be of no value; and anyone thus could control our archaeological findings. I therefore proposed that we should be allowed to take with us everything we had excavated that was not a monument, and let representatives of Chile choose what they liked from the collection after the studies had been completed and the report published.

Both Peña and the student seized upon this. Some such arrangement was just what they had in mind, and the better now that it came as an offer from me.

I added that although we had found no portable museum treasures in the earth, the natives themselves had brought me many curious figures which they claimed were their personal property.

"What the natives have brought you does not interest us," said Peña, "unless—" he leaned toward me smiling slyly—"unless they have brought you a *rongo-rongo*."

"No, I haven't got a *rongo-rongo*," I said, "but they have brought me a lot of other things."

"That does not interest me," said Peña. "I haven't come here as a customs official. The things you have bought from the natives we could all have bought. What concerns us is what you yourself have found in the earth, for no one has dug here before you."

Thereupon an agreement was drawn up by which I was merely deprived of permanent ownership of the archaeological material the expedition itself had found in the earth. I invited Peña to inspect all the expedition's material, both what we had found ourselves and what we had bought or had been given, and the meeting was then closed. While the others remained to make a copy of the agreement, I went out into the darkness where the skipper and chief engineer were waiting in the jeep. As I crept into my seat I gave a start. There was a strange black shadow standing motionless in the dark beside me. It was Lazarus. I whispered to him that all had gone splendidly, but he quickly interrupted me:

"I know. I was standing at the window and listened to everything. If the fat little man had said that he would take anything from you, I'd have run to the mayor and we should have been back with two hundred men!"

I thanked Providence for my own sake and Peña's that we had come to a friendly understanding, and I tried to explain to Lazarus that he must never think of doing such a thing. Farther along the road we met the mayor, visibly nervous, standing outside his garden gate.

"Take it easy, take it easy," he said soothingly, as if he thought we were as agitated as he.

"What happened?" he then asked eagerly.

When he heard that they were not going to take from me as much as a single *moai-kava-kava,* he straightened up and threw out his chest.

"Ha!" he said triumphantly, thumping his chest briskly. "Our combined *aku-akus!*"

Then he tactfully begged the skipper and engineer to remain in the jeep: he had a few words to say to Lazarus and me inside the house.

His living room was furnished with one round table, three chairs, and a corner cupboard. He turned up the kerosene lamp and produced a newly bought bottle of wine, from which he filled three glasses. The mayor had a plan. Lazarus was to keep the two in the jeep company, while the mayor took me to see his grandmother. He wanted to ask her if I might go with him into the cave. After pouring a little of the wine on our fingers and rubbing it in our hair for "good luck," we drank toasts with the rest.

The night was moonless and dark as we strolled out to the others with our hair smelling of wine. We drove on in the jeep to the crossroads by the governor's bungalow, then turned a short way down the road toward the little jetty, stopped and turned off our lights. Only the stars twinkled above us. Some native riders passed, and I could barely make them out although the horses' hoofs clattered by quite close to the open jeep. When they had gone, the mayor explained that he and I were going up the hill to study the stars, and both the skipper and the engineer pretended to believe him.

I followed close on the mayor's heels for some distance to the right of the road till we caught sight of something which in the dark looked like the remains of a stone wall. Here he stopped and whispered that on the other side of the stones he would not be able to say another word to me, only to make signs.

He stole on in silence for another fifty yards, and I followed cautiously, hard on his heels. We came to something which looked like an irregular, flat, whitish stone: it could quite well have been a slab of concrete on the ground, it was too dark for me to see it properly. Here the mayor stopped dead. He pointed to the ground in front of him, made a tremendously deep bow, and stretched out both arms before him with the palms of the hands turned downward. I gathered that he expected me to do the same, so I moved beside him and repeated the bow. Then, tiptoeing noiselessly, he made a full circle round the light patch on the ground. I followed close behind him and could just make out that a regular path had been worn round the spot. When we had made the circuit, we both bowed deeply again, with our arms outstretched as before. This was repeated three times, then he drew himself up silently and stood as a silhouette against the starry sky, with his arms folded. I did exactly the same. In the background I saw the lights of the great warship lying off the coast.

I was now really shaken by what I found myself involved in. This was no longer Easter Island: it was as though I were witnessing a heathen ceremony in some unexplored country a hundred years ago. And yet I knew that the motionless silhouette beside me belonged to the peaceable mayor of the island, who in daily life had a little well-trimmed mustache, and at the moment was actually wearing one of my ties. He did not move, he said nothing, but stood as if concentrating on remote matters. We should never get anywhere with this unless my own *aku-aku* came to the rescue and negotiated a reasonable concession from the obstinate grandmother. I opened my mouth and muttered a few words. I should never have done this.

"That's all, there she went!" said the mayor, and suddenly dashed off at great speed. I followed as quickly as I could, trying not to lose sight of him altogether. He stopped a little way down the hill beyond the stones and stood breathing heavily.

"She said yes," I said.

"She said no," he said, and repeated what he had so often told me, that his own *aku-aku* said yes, yes. He took a box of matches out of his pocket and emptied the whole of the contents into one of his hands.

"You're to empty your cave like this for Señor Kon-Tiki, my *aku-aku* says, but my grandmother says no, no."

He had asked her three times, and she just said no. But now she had said that he was to go to the mainland in the *Pinto*, and when he came back he was to present one of the caves to Señor Kon-Tiki, complete, with everything that was in it.

We stood for some time discussing what his grandmother had actually said, and at last he agreed to ask her once more, but alone, on another night. There were not many days left, however, before the *Pinto* sailed.

Two days later I stopped the jeep outside the mayor's garden gate. I had heard nothing at all from him. I found him and Lazarus over a bottle of wine in the little room with the round table. The mayor hastened to assure me that this was a lucky day for Lazarus, for he had said that he would show me one of his caves two days before the expedition left the island. But for the mayor it was an unlucky day. His grandmother still said no; moreover his own brothers were sure that he would die if he took me to the cave, and since he was their chief, he must not die. On top of this, all the natives had gone on strike. They would not unload the *Pinto* unless they received higher wages, and the mayor had just been told that if he did not succeed in stopping the strike, he would not be allowed to travel in the *Pinto* on her voyage to the mainland.

The strike continued and spread to the Navy's sheep farm, where no one was any longer looking after the windmills which served to pump the brackish water up from ancient native wells for tens of thousands of sheep. The *Pinto's* sailing was delayed.

Meanwhile the Chileans did everything they could for the expedition. Professor Wilhelm saved the expedition's valuable blood samples by replenishing a very special preserving fluid. It had run out when the heat had forced the rubber corks out of the doctor's test tubes. The *Pinto's* radar experts rejuvenated our radar, which had suddenly broken down after excellent service. And our engineer and steward were able to solve many of their problems through fresh supplies from helpful colleagues on board the great warship. They reported that everything should now go without a hitch for another six months. In spite of the strike the launch came in regularly from the *Pinto* with flour and sugar, and large bales of wool were loaded by the Chilean sailors. Finally the sailing date was fixed.

The day before the *Pinto* sailed we brought our ship round once more from Anakena to anchor alongside the warship. Peña came with us on this trip to inspect the archaeologists' cases on deck. As soon as he came on board I took him into my cabin and gave him an envelope. It contained a detailed report to the Minister of Education of the results secured by the expedition up to the *Pinto's* arrival. Peña himself was given a copy in an open envelope, and I asked him to read it. In the report I also described in detail the different types of curious cave stones I had received, and which the natives declared to be inherited property kept hidden in secret family caves. Peña asked if I myself had seen such a cave. I said I had not, but that I expected to be taken to one after the warship had sailed. This did not interest Peña, but he thanked me for the report, and asked to be shown the cases containing the things the archaeologists had found through excavation.

We went down to the foredeck where the first officer had assembled all the archaeologists' cases. When we had opened two, and Peña saw that these contained only plastic bags of charcoal and burned and crushed fragments of bone, he had no wish to see any more. It was with great reluctance that he consented to come to the shelves in my private storeroom to look at the cartons containing what the natives had brought me. The *Pinto* was to leave the island next day, so I knew that there was no longer much danger of anyone talking carelessly in the village. I took out a sculpture of a grotesque head with terrifying open jaws. Peña started, and he excitedly grabbed the stone from my hands. He had never seen anything like it from Easter Island. Had we found any sculptures like that in the earth as well?

We had not. I told him it was always the natives themselves who brought me figures of this type.

Peña lost all interest at once and laid the gaping head back in the carton. He looked admiringly at a large wooden *moai-kava-kava*, and recognized the mayor's work. He regretted the strike which had now prevented that able wood carver from making the voyage to the mainland, for he felt that the mayor could have given him more interesting information than most people on the island.

Now, on no account would Peña inspect anything more; this did not concern him.

In the meantime we had anchored alongside the warship, and the captain and all our friends from the *Pinto* came over in the launch to say good-by. While I was standing talking to Peña, his assistant and two other students approached us. I stood them in front of me ceremoniously, and declared with emphasis that they must listen to me now and never forget what I was to say. Then I told them that there were natives on that island who possessed important secrets.

"The Pakarati brothers," someone quickly put in.

"Perhaps. But also the mayor and many others," I said. I told them that the secrets consisted of superstitious customs which were likely soon to disappear. Moreover, I was quite certain that the inhabitants of the island knew the entrances to secret caves containing small sculptures, although I myself had not yet been allowed to enter such caves.

One of the students interrupted me, saying that I must not pay too much attention to the natives' boasting or to their crazy legends; another said with a knowing smile that the natives were masters in making imitations.

I asked them again to remember what I had said: there were secret caves containing sculptures, and I should do all I could to get into one, but if I did not succeed before I sailed, it was their duty to see that an ethnologist was sent to the island as soon as possible to carry on where I had left off.

Peña clapped me on the shoulder, laughing indulgently. He had offered the natives 100,000 pesos, or 150 dollars, if they would get him a *rongo-rongo*, but it had done no good. One of the students put in that if the *Pinto* had only stayed another five days longer he would have got a *rongo-rongo* from a secret cave.

Soon the ship was full of visitors both from the *Pinto* and from the village, and no more was said on the subject. Now I had laid all my cards on the table, and they could believe what they liked.

The *Pinto* sailed the next afternoon. On board her was our frogman, who had dived to forbidden depths in his spare time and split his eardrums. It was sad to see one of our own party go, but his place was filled by a splendid young Chilean student who had come out with the others in the *Pinto*. Eduardo Sanchez had studied archaeology in Chile and was now to join the expedition as assistant on shore and seaman on board. Gonzalo and he were old friends, and we could not have found a better expedition member.

We followed the big gray ship a little astern on her port side for the whole length of the island. We had many friends now among those in charge on the bridge and the waving crowd that was closely packed on her wide afterdeck. As the sun went down, we bade her farewell with siren and flags. The little Greenland trawler turned off along the dark cliffs of the coast, and the warship glided on into sinister, violet evening clouds which lay ahead of it in the east like the smoke of a fallen shell. Behind us all, on the opposite horizon, a glowing sun sank into the sea like a gun letting out its last burst of fire. So we were once more left alone in the night with the strange little island. Its living population was going to bed in the village on the other side, while on this side only an *aku-aku* or two sat keeping watch over mystic stones on the dark mountain shelves. Far away came a faint glimmer of light from our own camp guard at Anakena.

When the *Pinto's* last light disappeared, the ship itself passed away into unreality. The outer world does not exist for the natives of Easter Island except when it comes into their ocean for a visit. Many are attracted by stories of Tahiti's green palms and Chile's great houses, but life beyond the horizon, like life after death, is something remote and unreal which takes place far beyond the blue vault of heaven. To its native population Easter Island *is* the "Navel of the World" and the center of the universe. The cord of birth binds them to this lonely rock in the ocean. To them even great countries like Chile, the United States, Norway, and Tahiti are either located to the east or to the west. But Easter Island is located right here, at the intersection of east and west, and north and south—that is, the real center of the world.

When the *Pinto* had gone, life on the island quickly fell back into normal grooves. The *cocongo* had not yet begun to spread in earnest. *Cocongo* was the natives' great terror—the annual influenza epidemic which always accompanied contact with the mainland. It came and went with the regularity of clockwork. After the ship's visit it always raged in the village for a month or two. It got into chests, heads, and stomachs; everyone was ill, and there was always a toll of human lives before the *cocongo* passed and left the people in peace for the rest of the year. But this year the epidemic was unusually mild so far. The natives found their explanation at once: the expedition ship had brought the island "good luck." That, of course, was the reason why no one had fallen ill when we ourselves had come to the island.

The governor and Father Sebastian sent our native workers back to us, and at last the statue rose onto its *ahu*. Ed returned to the rim at Orongo, where he had made a number of new finds before the *Pinto* came. When he dug out a small and badly executed *ahu* of the second epoch, which was beside the bird-men's ruined village, he had discovered that it was built above the ruins of an older building with beautiful stones cut in the classic Inca-like style characteristic of the earliest Easter Island period. He had the turf removed for a long way in front, and found that a series of stones had been placed in rows, connecting the newly discovered first-epoch masonry with the smiling head he had found previously. Round about, on all the stones, carvings of large circular eyes stared at him like typical sun symbols; and when, in the middle of the whole complex, Ed also discovered a curious system of holes bored in the rock, he became suspicious.

December 21 was the summer solstice in the Southern Hemisphere, and before the sun rose that day he and the skipper were standing ready with a rod thrust into one of the holes. When the sun rose over the crater rim on the opposite side of the giant caldron, a sharp shadow from the rod fell right into the hole where Ed had expected it. He had thus discovered the first ceremonial solar observatory known in Polynesia. The governor promised to be on the spot at sunrise on the day of the winter solstice, for the expedition would be gone by then. Ed pointed out the hole into which he then expected the shadow to fall, and when the time came and the governor was on the spot, the shadow did fall exactly according to expectations.

At the summer solstice Bill too took his stand, but with surveying instruments down on the great classical *ahu* he had excavated at Vinapu. The sun struck exactly at a right angle to the mighty Inca-style wall. The Incas and their predecessors in Peru were sun worshipers, and once again these new observations recalled to our minds the old cultures of South America. And Bill discovered something more. The level ground where the red pillar statue had been excavated was a gigantic sunken temple square about four hundred by five hundred feet, and formerly surrounded by an earth wall which could still be clearly seen. Charcoal from a man-made fire was found underneath the earthen wall, which laboratory analysis, through carbon-14 testing, dated at about 800 A.D. The corresponding red pillar statue at Tiahuanaco also lay in a similar rectangular, sunken temple square. And in front of the great stone wall Bill found the remains of an ancient crematorium in which a great number of bodies had been burned and buried, some of them with their own bone fishing gear.

Cremation had till now been completely unknown in Easter Island archaeology.

Carl went about mapping and studying old stone constructions. In the *ahu* of Te Pito Kura, where the largest statue on the coast lay overthrown, he excavated a small burial vault in the elaborate wall. Among crumbled human bones he found two of the long-ears' extremely beautiful ear pegs, made from the thickest part of some very large shell.

Arne had several teams at work, and had made interesting discoveries both inside and outside the crater of Rano Raraku. Now he had started a trench through one of the round hillocks which lay at the foot of the volcano. They were so large that the natives had given them place names of their own; and science had hitherto regarded them as natural formations. We were now to see that all these hillocks had been artificially formed. They were rubble from the quarry which had been carried down in large baskets and dumped on the plain, and here good fortune gave us the only conceivable means of scientifically dating the making of the statues. As we cut our way down through the hillock, we found broken stone picks and charcoal from fires. Again the charcoal could be dated by measuring its radioactivity, and we learned that this particular pile received rubble from the sculptors in the quarry until about 1470, or two hundred years before the fatal defensive fire was lighted in the long-ears' ditch on Poike.

As work was resumed on various parts of the island after the *Pinto* had gone, the chief of the long-ears sat calmly on his front steps polishing the hooked nose of a wooden figure. With the aid of his motto, "Take it easy," he did not worry much about the sudden collapse of his dream of travel. The governor let me promise him instead that he should accompany us to Tahiti, Hiva Oa, and Panama when we ourselves left the island, and this made the mayor the happiest man in the world. This was indeed a sign of "good luck."

He visited his grandmother again with fresh courage, silent and alone, but she was stubborn as ever. That night he was continually awakened and finally kept awake altogether because his own *aku-aku* would give him no peace. It kept on repeating, "Go into the cave, go into the cave." At last he could stand it no more: he rose and went into the cave. He had not seen a soul on the way, and had not once needed to take cover. When a man was going to his cave this was a sign of "good luck." When he had passed through the opening, he had grabbed the figure of an animal's head with long teeth, but the *aku-aku* had said, "Take more, take more," and he finally brought a quantity of sculptures out of the cave. These were now waiting in his hut in the village. I must send the jeep as soon as it was dark.

This time the queerest animals were there to greet me. One which continually recurred had a long raised neck and a snout with three front teeth above and three below, its jaws being otherwise toothless. But the prize specimen was a broad reed boat, shaped like an ark, but curved and rounded in all corners. Three masts and thick grooved sails of stone were placed in holes along a bulging deck. It looked like a baker's masterpiece, made of dried lava instead of dough.

"Now you see how I knew that the sails also were made from reeds," said the mayor proudly, pointing to the perpendicular grooves which gave the illusion of reeds.

That day I noticed that the mayor for the first time had begun to clear his throat: the *cocongo* was knocking at his door. As long as he had the suspicion of a cough, he said, he could not visit the cave again, for it was "bad luck" for anyone who was not quite well to enter such a place. A few old people had done so in the past, but it was purposely to hide there and die.

Soon afterward a storm broke out and the skipper had to take the ship to shelter by moving round to the village side of the island for a couple of days. When the storm abated and the ship returned to her old anchorage off our beach, I heard through the walkie-talkie that the skipper had with him a native from the village who insisted on showing me something he had with him on board.

I went out in the launch and found that the native was my young friend Estevan. The lad obviously had something on his mind. Today there was a boyish happiness about his smile which had been absent of late, since his wife had suddenly stopped the cave traffic. He asked politely but eagerly if I had a really dark place on board the ship, for he was now going to initiate me into a great secret. I took him to my own cabin and pulled down the blinds. This was dark enough for Estevan. He disappeared and came back lugging two large bundles. He carefully shut the cabin door behind him and asked me to stand in one corner and just watch what was going to happen.

It was so dark in the cabin that I could barely distinguish Estevan as a dim shadow when he bent over something he had drawn out of the bundles. My first thought was that some phosphorescent object would appear, as he had to have the cabin so dark. But no. What he took out was as black as the darkness round us. I could make out that it was some sort of a costume he was putting on himself. He even put something on his head. So he was going to perform in a dancing mask or some other disguise. I was sure I could see two great ear flaps dangling down beside his head, but it was too dark to be certain. Now he stooped down again and pulled two heavy lumps out of his bundles. One of the objects he left on the floor, the other he laid on the seat beside my bunk. Then he squatted down and I could see that he placed a hand on each side of the object on the floor, as if he was about to enter upon a serious conversation with a dear friend.

And then he began to murmur a stream of Polynesian words in a low and reverent voice. His voice was soft and melodious, but grave and uncannily intense, and I suddenly got a creeping feeling down my spine. A few seconds passed before I realized that the handsome young man was not at all carrying out a demonstration for me, he was busy performing a serious heathen ceremony. I saw that he was becoming more and more moved by the ritual. And when he had finished with the object on the floor and put his hands round the other on the seat, he became so emotional that the whole tone of his voice changed; he began to sniffle and gasp. It was impossible to hear what he was saying, but I gathered that I myself was mentioned several times. Toward the end he had increasing difficulty in suppressing his choking sobs, and at last he was weeping as bitterly as if he had lost a close friend forever.

I was extremely uncomfortable. I felt an intense desire to talk to him and console him, and to find out what was going on. But I thought it wisest not to interfere for the time being. Finally Estevan pulled himself together and began to take off his costume. He asked me to let in the light. When the blinds went up, Estevan stood before me with a grave smile on his face, his eyes red with weeping. I had to give him a handkerchief, which he needed for both his eyes and nose. But in spite of it all he seemed as happy as if he had come to the end of a bad dream.

The clothes he had worn were a thick dark woolen jersey and a regular black polar cap with long hanging ear laps which he must have got from a passing whaler. On the floor sat a large red-stone dog, so thoroughly worn by scrubbing that it looked like a half-melted chocolate figure; and up on the seat there lay outstretched a diabolical creature like Satan himself in the shape of a beast, with a humpback and a goatee beard under an evil grin. It was made of a harder gray stone and was perfectly preserved, in contrast to the overwashed figure on the floor.

Estevan pointed reverently, almost affectionately, to the object on the seat and said that, according to his wife, it was the more powerful of the two. These were two of the four *aku-akus* who guarded his wife's cave. The other two, which were still in the cave, were large heads with strange figures on the top. It was these two guardians now lying before me who had been angry because his wife had taken so much from their section of the cave. She had been suffering from stomach trouble ever since, and she had now decided that the best thing to do was to send the two angry guardians over to me in the hope that they would be pacified when they recovered their sovereignty over their own stones.

Estevan had with him five ordinary cave stones which belonged to the same group: one of them was a double-headed monster which looked much more terrifying than the innocent dog sitting quietly on the carpet in front of the bunk. There were several more figures in the cave which belonged to these two guardians: one was the big boat with figureheads fore and aft, of which he had told me before. Now they were to be mine.

I asked if I could not come to the cave myself to get these things, since they were going to be mine anyhow. Estevan suggested that we should make a joint effort to persuade his wife. I promised to pay them a visit in the village one evening, and said I would bring the doctor to find a remedy for her mysterious illness.

Estevan then turned to his friends the dog and Old Nick on the seat, and emphatically declared that these two guardians were now legally transferred to me. He had done everything his wife had said he should do, for this was the way her father had acted when she took over the cave, and her grandfather had done just the same when handing it over to her father. Now the whole responsibility was on me, and when some day I should hand over the two guardians to another person, I must act exactly as he had done now, preferably in clothing which was not visible in the dark. I could show the guardians to anyone on board, but not to a single person on the island. I must wash them for the first time after three months, and from then on they should be attended to four times a year. It was not enough to wash them clean of dust and growths: I must carefully pick out some white webs which appeared like cotton in the holes of the stone, and every year I must smoke out insects which laid eggs in the pores.

When the two guardians and their stone subjects had been packed away, a heavy responsibility seemed to have been lifted from Estevan's young shoulders. He gave me to understand that he himself was a good Christian, but his ancestors knew no better than to hold converse with devils and had bequeathed a fearful responsibility to those who had to take over the devils and could not escape from their whims.

I asked Estevan if the two creatures he had given me were devils, and he had to admit that in Spanish that would be the name for them, even if his forefathers called them *aku-akus*.

So now I had two *aku-akus* on board the ship. It was nice to know. Estevan gave me clearly to understand that if the decision lay with him I should get the two which were left in the cave as well, and all the others in the island. It would be best if every single *aku-aku* was put on board our ship and taken away from the island forever; then there would be no need to worry about such things again. For all the people on the island today were good Christians and would never have had anything to do with this business if it had not been forced upon them to the danger of their lives and health.

Estevan had been to school, and he could write. In beautiful characters he wrote down for me what he had said in the dark, and explained that I must hand on a similar text to the person who some day would take over the two guardians from me. I read on the scrap of paper:

> *Ko au Ko Kon Tiki he Atua Hiva*
> *Hua viri mai te i Ka uru atua na Ki te*
> *Kaiga Einu Ehoraie Ehiti Ka pura Eurauraga*
> *te Mahinaee. Ka ea Korua Kakai Kahaka*
> *hoa ite umu moa ite umu kokoma ote*
> *atua hiva.*
> *Ko Kon Tiki mo hatu O Ko ia*
> *To Koro Va Ka Tere Ko haho Kogao Vari*
> *one ana Kena O Te Atua hiva Ko Kon Tiki.*

Estevan was unable to give the exact translation, for some of the phrases were old Polynesian; but the gist, he said, was that I, a lord from the outside world, had come from there to here with my party, and here I had caused the four *aku-akus* named Inu, Horaie, Hitikapura, and Urauraga-te-Mahinaee to eat the intestines of a cock baked in an earth oven before the entrance to the cave O Ko ia, while my ship lay swinging at anchor off the sands at Anakena.

I realized that this business with the intestines must have been something Estevan and his wife had already attended to on my behalf.

The doctor and I went to the village a couple of days later, and we slipped into Estevan's little hut unseen. A small table with a bowl full of flowers, together with two stools and two benches, made up the furnishings of the hut, and we guessed that there was a bed behind a curtain along one of the walls. Everything was painted white and light blue, and all was spotlessly clean.

Estevan's wife came out from behind the curtain, and she turned out to be a real beauty. She was pale and well-shaped, with long black hair, grave intelligent eyes, and a quiet, modest bearing. Completely poised, she came forward and greeted us, barefooted, with the dignity of a queen. She did not speak much Spanish, and Estevan helped when we had difficulty in understanding. They apologized for having no chairs, but we were happy to sit down on the benches. I looked at the quiet girl sitting erect with her hands in her lap. She was not the idea I had formed of Estevan's strong-willed wife; I had expected a regular amazon. She answered all the doctor's questions clearly and without hesitation. The consultation indicated that she had developed an abdominal trouble which would be simple to cure if she would go into the little village hospital for treatment.

Estevan himself raised the matter of the cave. His wife's gentle answers to my questions were given as calmly as ever. Her father had said that if a stranger was let into the family cave some near relative of hers would die. She did not want to die, and she did not want anything to happen to Estevan. So she could not take me to the cave. She was completely inflexible on this point. Estevan added unhappily that the first time he had tried to persuade her, she had wept for two days and nights. And when I saw how desperately serious she was about the whole thing, I decided to drop the matter.

I asked instead if she would take a photograph for us in the cave if we taught her how to do it. But no. If she did that, strangers could see the cave in the photograph, and it was the cave which was taboo.

This was a real disappointment. Finally I asked, without much hope of consent, if she could bring the rest of the things in the cave to the house so that we could photograph them there. To my astonishment she agreed without a moment's hesitation. I was still more amazed when Estevan proposed to her that they should put all the stones in an ordinary cave they had in the garden, which had a secret entrance, but was not taboo. Then I could simply photograph everything there. His wife immediately agreed to that too, with two exceptions —the two guardians which had to remain in the family cave.

They looked quite crestfallen when I shook my head and explained that I did not care about the cave unless it was the actual family cave. We finally agreed that the contents of the cave should be brought to the house, and they would let me know when everything was there.

As we were taking our leave, I asked if it was her father who had made the stones. Oh, no! He had only helped with a few of them. Her grandfather, who had received the name

Raimundi Uki when Christianity was introduced, had made almost all of them before he died at the age of 108. She could remember him working to teach her father when she herself was quite a little girl. She had been told that her great-grandfather had originally helped her grandfather with "advice." When the cave was first brought into use she did not know, but some of the things were really old, even though the bulk of them went into the cave in her grandfather's time.

We now knew that at least one of the strange caves on Easter Island had been a growing institution, part of the local life, and not a sealed-off chamber with treasures stored away since the island wars. The cave of Estevan's wife may have been the last on the island which had still been growing; and certainly it was the first to lose any of its contents to the outer world. But I realized, when the young couple let us out into the night, that this particular cave I would never see.

CHAPTER EIGHT

Into the Secret Caves

ONE EVENING at sunset Lazarus and I rode side by side along the old grassy road that led from the statue quarry in Rano Raraku to the camp at Anakena. Behind us the volcano glowed red in the evening sun, before us stretched the stone-covered plain on which the shadows were beginning to lengthen. The quiet of evening lay over sea and sky: all that met the eye breathed of peace. Only two grotesque caricatures of riders followed us in every slightest movement, our own long shadows. I felt once again as if Lazarus and I were riding alone on the moon.

Then I stopped my horse and looked round to the right; the two shadows had suddenly become three. An unknown horseman had appeared close on our heels; lanky and pale, he sat on his horse and stared at us with as grave a mien as death himself. He stopped, as our shadows, the moment we stopped, without saying a word; but as soon as we jogged on, this third shadow followed us too. There was something mysterious about the man and the whole of his demeanor.

Lazarus muttered to me over the horses' bobbing heads that the man who was following us was the sexton's brother. The other day he had told Lazarus that if he got him a job with me he was willing to work without pay. This made the man even more mysterious: I had no desire to have this gloomy horseman among my nearest associates. I felt his eyes on the back of my neck. He did not overtake us if we slowed down, and if we quickened our pace, he did the same. Out of the corner of my eye I saw the gaunt, spidery shadow of him and his horse following us, mile after mile, right down to the camp, when night fell upon us.

Lazarus did not think that the rider had heard what we were talking about. I had said that some time in the future it would be possible to find the secret caves and tunnels of the island by going over the ground with a kind of cavity detector. This had made a strong impression on Lazarus. As we rode along he pointed out several areas in which such an apparatus would be effective because there were supposed to be secret caves under the ground, but the openings had been lost. He declared with dismay that the first person to bring the apparatus to the island would get rich simply by walking among the houses in the village. A secret cave three hundred yards long, which had belonged to one of the last kings, ran underground to the sea from an unknown spot near the most northerly houses. It was found by a man who brought up from the cave some gigantic spearheads, but the *aku-akus* bit and pricked him night after night until he died.

As soon as I came out of the tent next morning I saw the pale, skinny man again. He was lying motionless in the grass right outside my tent, gazing at me from the other side of the rope boundary. The policemen, Nicholas and Kasimiro, had long since ceased to keep watch, for no one touched a thing in the camp any more. All day I had the impression that the thin man was following me like a faithful dog, always at a distance and without having a word to say.

When night fell again, and all the rest of us had gone to bed in the camp, I saw him sitting in the dark on the temple wall near my tent.

There was a regular cloudburst over the island that night. The natives were delighted, for the water tanks in the village were bone-dry and people had begun a laborious search for water in caves and up in the great crater swamp. Now the water poured down in streams, to them a sign of "good luck" right in the middle of the dry season. But for us in the tents it was not so fortunate. After the rain had stopped, a frothing chocolate-colored brook came rolling down the jeep track from the high ground and turned the camp area into a lake.

I was awakened by Anette calling out excitedly in Polynesian, "Look, Mummy, look!" and pointing in delight to her potty, which had begun to bob about among the camp beds. I was less enthusiastic when I saw that the trunks and all our belongings were awash. Outside there was a whirling, gurgling stream, and I heard a beautiful mixture of laughter and swearing from the different tents. The roof of the kitchen tent had collapsed, the wind screens for the gas stoves were full as washtubs, and the food was afloat. The cook and steward stood unsheltered in a sticky mass of flour and sugar, striking the floor with an iron bar to make an outflow into the sand; the cameraman was piling films and equipment onto his bed; and the sailors were bailing out their tents with mugs and buckets as if they were on a sinking ship.

We quickly diverted the rest of the flood by making a ditch and a dam across the roadway. Amid all this chaos the long-ears came over jubilant from their dry cave to congratulate me: this was "good luck"! Now there would be water enough on the island for both man and beast for a long time to come. The skipper reported happily from the ship that they had collected several tons of rain water: the fresh-water tanks had been filled to the brim in a single night. The heavy rain put an end to the shifting winds and treacherous weather of the past few days, and again the sky was blue.

But over in the long-ears' cave a solitary man lay writhing in agony. He had been in the field carrying stones from his family cave for the first time, when he was caught by the cloudburst. I knew nothing about it till late the next night when the doctor and I came home from our meeting with Estevan and his wife in the village. It was long past midnight, and before I crept into my tent, I stood for a moment looking at the silhouette of the newly erected giant against a southern sky ablaze with stars. Suddenly Lazarus appeared out of the darkness, and I saw by the grave expression on his face that something was wrong. He told me that the sexton's brother, the gaunt rider, lay dying in Hotu Matua's cave. Could the doctor come?

We got the doctor as he was crawling into his sleeping bag, and all three of us hurried across the plain to the cave. Lazarus told me on the way that the sick man had confided to him that he had a cave; he had been there the night before and fetched a number of things, which he had hidden in a sack among some big rocks up on the ridge above the Anakena Valley. But during the night, back in Hotu Matua's cave, he had suddenly been taken ill. He grew worse as the day passed and he was now lying doubled up and retching, with a fearful pain in his stomach. He had told Lazarus where the sack was hidden, and asked him to bring it to me if he himself should die.

Long-ears were lying everywhere in the cave trying to sleep, and at the far end the lanky man lay, pale and hollow-cheeked, looking like death itself as he twisted and groaned in pain. They all watched round-eyed while the doctor examined the skinny body fore and aft and gave him a dose of pills. As the night passed the patient became quieter, till it was evident that he was neither in pain nor in danger. When at last we had left the cave, the thin man was so far recovered that he was able to creep out and disappear into the darkness. He went straight up to the ridge for the sack, and hurried from there directly to his cave where he rushed the contents of the sack back into their old places. Then he returned to the village, relieved and empty-handed, and told his friends that he had escaped death by a hairsbreadth. The doctor told me that the man had suffered only a severe attack of colic.

The sexton's pale brother had come and gone almost like a shooting star in the night, but both the torrential rain and the healing of a dying man had made an impression on all his compatriots. When I returned to my tent in the small hours of the morning, a great snarling head lay in my bed, the head of a feline large enough to be a lion or a puma. When I struck a match and looked round in the flickering light, I saw that Yvonne was wide-awake. She whispered that a native had been there and pushed the great head in through the tent opening. She thought she had recognized the mayor's youngest brother.

She was quite right. Next day the little man with the mustache and the large antelope eyes came to me in the tent. It was young Atan, who had turned up the first whale along with the mayor, Lazarus, and me. Lazarus, who now felt

214

quite emancipated, had been trying for a long time to put courage into little Atan. Atan had disclosed to Lazarus that he too had a cave; he had even told Lazarus that he had thought of asking his eldest brother, the mayor, for permission to give Señor Kon-Tiki something from the cave.

After Atan had peered out of the tent and made sure that no one was listening to us, he told me all that he knew. He was a long-ear of pure blood. There were four brothers: the eldest, who was head of the family, was the mayor, Pedro Atan; then came Juan Atan, Estevan Atan, and finally himself, Atan Atan, who bore the additional name Hare Kai Hiva, after an ancestor. Each of the four brothers had received a cave from their rich father. Atan, being the youngest, had the smallest cave with only sixty sculptures. Further, as the youngest, he had nothing to say about his brothers' caves, but they could make decisions about his. He had received the cave from his father, who got it from Maria Mata Poepoe, who got it from Atamo Uhu, who got it from Hare Kai Hiva, and it was he who had made the sculptures. I recognized the name of Hare Kai Hiva from the mayor's family tree: he was a direct descendant of the only surviving long-ear, Ororoina.

To a question, Atan replied rather hesitantly that the great head he had brought me represented a sea lion: these animals sometimes appeared on the coast. I pointed out that a sea lion had no ears. Atan agreed, but thought there might have been other kinds of sea lions in Hare Kai Hiva's time.

Atan was genuinely distressed at the idea that some day people would be able to find his cave with a machine; Lazarus had told him this. If his brothers would allow him, he would rather get rid of the whole thing now, for he was a good Christian and thought it would be best if the whole responsibility was transferred to a protected museum. Atan Atan was a simple, candid soul and not very difficult to influence. He had seen more than enough of my *mana,* and required no further persuasion.

Three evenings later I was invited to his own little hut on the outskirts of the village. There he confided to me that both his old aunt, Tahu-tahu, and his two brothers, Pedro and Juan, had given him a free hand to turn over the cave to me: only one brother's permission was needed, that of Estevan

Atan. I must now help to persuade him. While I sat alone, waiting by the burning candle, Atan stole over to the next hut and got his brother.

Estevan Atan turned out to be a man I had never met. He was the only one of the four brothers who had not been able to join the force of long-ears working for me. Atan naïvely confided to me that his brother was captain of the gang who had built a boat to clear off to Tahiti as soon as the expedition ship was no longer there to keep an eye on them. The new arrival looked rather annoyed, but admitted that this was true. He had never been to sea, but he had learned all about the stars from old islanders, and knew how to find his way across the ocean.

So here was the next village skipper who would soon push off for Tahiti. He was an unusually fine-looking fellow in his thirties, with thin firm lips, honest eyes, and a good bearing. As with the other brothers, there was nothing of the native in his appearance: he would have passed unnoticed in any street in Northern Europe. But he was a genuine long-ear. He also was a man of inquiring mind. He asked about the drift of the *Kon-Tiki* raft and the outside world below the horizon. The night was well advanced before little Atan managed to change the subject to families and caves, but it went quite smoothly. Late at night it was disclosed that the village skipper himself had about a hundred sculptures in his own cave; formerly there had also been a jar or *ipu maengo*[1] among them, but this tiny coffee-colored vessel had been broken. His finest treasure was a "book" with *rongo-rongo* written on all the pages. No one in the island had seen it but himself.

I was told that the family's cave chief was Aunt Tahu-tahu: she was something of a sorceress and had dealings with the devil. She had an immensely important cave, which their cousin would certainly take over at some future date. Old Tahu-tahu had friendly feelings toward me, for I had given her cigarettes and black dress material when she came to Anakena to dance for "good luck" before the men in Hotu Matua's cave.

A few days later things began to move. Rumors first reached the camp that little Atan had suddenly developed blood

[1] *Ipu* means bottle-gourd, or calabash; *maengo*, pottery.

poisoning and was in the village hospital. My heart sank. He was sure to think that this was punishment for having taken the feline head from his cave. Soon afterward Lazarus brought news that the village doctor had lanced Atan's finger: he had had "good luck," for all was going well. And then came a message that Atan awaited me at his hut.

To attract as little attention as possible, I went by jeep to the church late in the evening and stepped in to see Father Sebastian. He was ablaze with excitement when he heard what was brewing. His dearest wish had been to see one of the secret caves of which he had heard so many rumors, and which he thought were now lost. He realized that it was useless for him, as a priest, to come with us. But I again promised to report to him as soon as I had seen anything, even if I had to wake him up at night.

On the last stretch from Father Sebastian's house to Atan's, down a rocky path, I groped my way along a stone wall in pitch-darkness. I found the gate and went in and knocked at the low wooden door. Atan, with his arm in a sling, opened it cautiously and let me squeeze in. He shut the door carefully behind me, and we sat down on each side of a little table with a lighted candle on it. Atan removed a cloth and disclosed a grinning death's-head on the table between us. The head was of lava with horribly realistic features, bared teeth and jawbones and deep dark holes for eyes and nostrils. On the top of the skull were two strange cup-shaped cavities the size of a thumbnail.

"That's for you!" exclaimed Atan, pointing to the skull. "There is the key to the cave. Now the cave is yours."

I was so surprised that I did not know what to do, but before I could say anything stupid, Atan pointed to the two little hollows on the cranium and confided to me that they had been full of powdered bones from an *aku-aku* which would have killed anyone who touched this "key." But old Aunt Tahu-tahu had been in the cave and removed all the bone meal so carefully that I could feel quite safe. Throughout Atan referred to this stone skull as a "key," and said I must keep it under my bed until we went to the cave together two days later. Then I must take the "key" with me.

I shall never forget the sight of Atan with the flickering candle beside the gray skull, and I shuddered inwardly as I saw myself and my shadow grasp the grinning stone "key" which was now mine. Both the light and our voices were so faint that they scarcely reached the walls, but outside I heard the clatter of horses as solitary riders passed up and down the slope. The amount of activity in the village at night was puzzling.

Atan begged to come to the camp for a special meal, a *curando* for "good luck" was the way he put it, on the day he fixed for our nocturnal visit to his cave. When I asked to be allowed to take a friend along, he was at first very reluctant. But his second thought was that the cave was mine now, and if I was going to empty it anyhow, another person might not do much harm. He was relieved when I suggested Ed, for his brother Juan had worked for Ed at Orongo and said he was a good fellow. But three was an unlucky number, so Atan wanted to take his own brother Estevan, the village skipper. Finally I managed to wangle in the photographer as well, but then Atan wanted to have another of his people too, so that we should be six; for two, four, and six were good numbers. Then he asked me meekly not to take more, for we might unintentionally annoy the *aku-aku* of the cave.

On the great day our captain drove over to the village to fetch Atan Atan, and came back bringing also Atan's brother and a young friend, Enlique Teao, who was a member of the mayor's team of long-ears. Dinner was over when they arrived, so we were alone in the mess tent where the steward served a plain smörgåsbord. The village skipper asked me quietly to give a little "good luck" present to his brother Atan today, and another to Aunt Tahu-tahu, who had agreed to his handing over the cave. She had even gone to the cave early that morning and baked a hen for the *aku-aku* near the entrance.

When we sat down to the table, the natives first made the sign of the cross and murmured a little grace. Afterward Atan looked up at me innocently and explained that this was *otra cosa aparte*, "another thing apart." Then he leaned over the table toward the rest of us and said in a whisper that before we began the meal each of us must repeat aloud in Polynesian: "I am a long-ear from Norway. I am eating from the earth oven of the Norwegian long-ears."

When everyone had said this in turn, all further conversation was conducted in whispers. Only afterward did I realize that the meal was in honor of the *aku-akus,* to whom our mutual relationship had just been made known. I knew that Atan had abandoned his former idea that the original inhabitants of the island had come from Austria; both he and the other long-ears were now certain that at least their own tribe had come from Norway. We had on board our ship a big sailor with flaming red hair who was especially mentioned in support of this idea. So now, during the ceremonial *curando,* the *aku-akus* were initiated into this rather complicated relationship.

When Ed came into the tent with a message, I asked if he might participate in the "good luck" meal since he was to visit the cave with us. Then Ed had to repeat in Polynesian, with a broad American accent, that he too was a long-ear from Norway, who was eating from the earth oven of the Norwegian long-ears. The meal continued, profoundly serious, with all conversation in hoarse whispers. The table talk about spirits and caves was as strange to us as the smörgåsbord dishes were to our guests. Atan helped himself liberally to butter with a cake server, and put slices of lemon on his bread instead of into his tea, but they all thoroughly enjoyed the meal. After eating their fill, the three natives went into an empty tent to rest; it was a long time before we were to set out on our secret mission.

A couple of hours after nightfall Atan came to tell me that we could start now. He was grave and solemn; it was clear that he regarded the impending transfer of a cave as a serious event. Personally I had a feeling that I was starting on a long and strange journey when I went into the tent to say good-by to Yvonne and take the grinning death's-head from a bag under the bed. How this magic key was to be used I had no idea, and no one could tell me. Apart from the initiated owners of secret family caves, I was the first person to hold such a stone in my hand. Yvonne handed me an airlines bag with presents for old Tahu-tahu, as I went out into the night to tell Ed and the cameraman that we could start.

We were to go by jeep past the lonely sheep farm at Vaitea, on the high ground in the middle of the island, and from a point between there and the village we were to continue on foot toward the cave. By way of camouflage we filled the back of the jeep with bundles of washing, and our captain drove us up to Vaitea. Here he delivered the washing to Analola, the native manageress at the sheep farm. With some girl friends she had undertaken to do all our washing, since they had access to the only tap on the island; the water was piped from an overgrown crater lake in the volcano of Rano Aroi.

The photographer took the wheel and drove on with the three natives, Ed, and myself. We had started in glittering starlight, but now a shower came. Atan, who was sitting solemnly on the toolbox between the photographer and me, looked uneasy and began to whisper to me about the need for some "good luck." I heard the village skipper mutter to Ed in a gloomy voice that it looked as if the wind was changing. Strained as the natives were tonight, I could not judge with certainty whether anything in particular worried them, or whether they were merely oppressed by the gravity of the occasion. I feared that something might happen to make them draw back at the eleventh hour. The sexton's brother was fresh in my memory.

In the back seat Ed and the two natives were no longer exchanging a single word. The photographer at the wheel was silent of necessity. He understood neither Spanish nor Polynesian and could converse with the natives only through pantomime. When he suddenly stopped the jeep and got out to look at all the wheels, the two Atan brothers were terrified and asked what was wrong. I tried to calm them, saying that everything was all right. Obviously they were both in a jittery state, looking for all sorts of omens and signs. I was almost in a panic myself lest the jeep for once should break down because the photographer, ignorant of our conversation, next began to gesticulate wildly, explaining with a worried look that he thought the engine was running on only three cylinders.

But the jeep bumped on in the deep crooked ruts, and the stars again glittered above us between the scudding clouds. The two brothers still sat as if on pins, and when we came to the appointed place, Atan suddenly changed the program. It would be better if we drove on right into Hangaroa and waited in his house till the whole village was asleep.

When we approached the village, he changed his mind again: his *aku-aku* had said we were to drive to his brother's house instead of to his own. We drove straight through the village with our lights on, swung down toward the coast in front of the church, and went on for a short way northward along a stone wall. Here we were told to turn the lights off and stop, and Enlique Teao was left to look after the jeep while the rest of us climbed over the wall and walked in a drizzle across a stony field. Small, light lava stones lay strewn so thickly over the ground that walking was difficult, and Atan offered the photographer, the oldest in the party, a shoulder to prevent him from twisting an ankle or falling. He repeatedly whispered to Ed that it was safe for his own friends to go over his land because he had a good heart; his *aku-aku* therefore saw that nothing happened to those who crossed his ground. He naïvely added that he had always been kind to others: he gave food to those who had none and listened to those who asked for help. So his own *aku-aku* was satisfied with him.

In the middle of the stony field was a little whitewashed hut. The village skipper tapped cautiously at both the window and the door before he succeeded in waking his wife. At last the door was opened by a grave woman in her thirties, of almost savage beauty, with long raven-black hair flowing down over a magnificent figure. The village skipper, for all his family pride, had found among the short-ears a worthy wife.

Two benches were drawn up to a small table in the middle of the floor, and here the beauty, gliding round about us like a silent shadow, placed a small candle. The village skipper disappeared; in a little while he came back with a coverless manuscript book which he carefully drew from an old paper cement bag and laid before us in the candlelight.

The notebook, whose leaves were yellow and faded, had once been made as a copybook for children in Chile, but it had been used for quite a different purpose. On every page were pagan *rongo-rongo* signs: small neatly drawn figures of bird-men, demons, and other curious symbols which we knew so well from the mysterious picture writing of Easter Island. When we turned the pages, we saw some with nothing but unreadable lines of hieroglyphics, while others were arranged like a dictionary. The latter *rongo-rongo* symbols were nicely set out in a column down the left-hand side of the page, and to the right of each sign its definition was given in Easter Island Polynesian by means of crude roman letters.

We sat around the candle and looked at the faded *rongo-rongo* book, speechless with astonishment. It was obvious that this was no sham arranged for us by the village skipper; and it was equally clear that if the person who had once written these mysterious signs really possessed the secret of the *rongo-rongo* writing, then this simple coverless book was of enormous value for the interpretation of Easter Island's ancient picture writing.

I noticed that 1936 was written on one of the pages, and asked the village skipper where he had obtained this fine book. He said that his father had given it to him a year before he died. His father could write neither *rongo-rongo* nor modern characters, but he had told his son that nevertheless it was he who had made the book: he had carefully copied an older book which had completely fallen to pieces, and that one had been made by *his* father. The village skipper's grandfather had been a learned man who could carve *rongo-rongo* on slabs of wood and also sing the text. At that time there were some men alive on the island who had learned to write modern letters while they were in exile as slaves in Peru. One of them had helped the old *rongo-rongo* man record the sacred meaning of the ancient signs to prevent their total loss since nearly all the old-time experts had died during the slave raid.

Both Atan and the village skipper's own wife were as amazed at the book as we were, and the owner proudly confided to us that until now he had not let a single person see it. He kept it in a cement bag in his own cave, and only took it out now and then when he wanted to think of his father. He had decided to make a copy before this book too fell to pieces, but he had found that it was a fearful task to copy all the little figures on the forty-one pages of the book. I proposed that the cameraman should borrow the book and make an exact photographic copy for him, and after much hesitation he consented.[2]

It was now growing late by local standards, and I asked if we should not be going soon. The village skipper replied that there was no need to go yet; he would know when it was eleven, for a particular cow always mooed then. I did not hear the cow myself, but not long after we broke up and the black-haired vahine took us to the door with the candle. Again Atan carefully helped the photographer over the stony field. Back at the jeep, our watchman Enlique lay sleeping like a log over the wheel. We shook him awake and went on, following the ruts northward in the direction of the leper station. Soon we swung off inland along a cattle track. It was so dark and the "road" so entirely hypothetical that Atan had to sit the whole time with his hand outstretched, pointing out the course. The souvenir of his blood poisoning, a white rag on his index finger, was highly suitable for showing the way at night.

After half an hour's driving we had left Puna Pau with the topknot quarry behind us, and Atan made signs to stop and leave the jeep. We all six crawled out and stretched our legs after the bumpy ride. The village, far behind us, lay dark and silent. The drizzle had stopped and the stars began a new conquest of the sky. The village skipper looked up and whispered that we had "good luck," for the rain had stopped. It struck both Ed and me that this was a most peculiar remark from an Easter Islander, since in the middle of the dry season a shower was always welcomed by the inhabitants. Little Atan added eagerly that he was sure all would go well, for his Aunt Tahu-tahu had great *mana* power. She had not only told him how he should behave, but she had personally prepared the earth oven at the cave.

Before we began our walk, we had to climb over a high wall of loose stones. Here Atan took all the camera equipment from the photographer and nursed him across the barrier. I was terrified lest someone should tumble down and

---

[2] Thereby the irreplaceable contents of the book were saved for posterity, because one dark night after the expedition ship had left, the village skipper slipped off to sea in his little boat. Nobody knows his fate. Perhaps the book is still hidden in his cave, the entrance to which is lost. Perhaps it accompanied its owner into the distant ocean.

Two pages from the village skipper's *rongo-rongo* book. The text seems to have originated on Easter Island in the latter part of the last century when a Tahitian bishop with the aid of an Easter

(glyph)	henaga kite kurega	(glyph)	ko rara la hoa
(glyph)	kuani a rurua	(glyph)	tagata, mau ahi
(glyph)	kaka rava	(glyph)	ite muku nuku, ahi.
(glyph)	kuahuru tugutu	(glyph)	maitae
(glyph)	kaki rava,	(glyph)	kua vero. kokite mata
(glyph)	noi a rurua	(glyph)	mai tae. oho mai
(glyph)	kovare	(glyph)	havir.e takae.
(glyph)	he motu. uira	(glyph)	kituu
(glyph)	he naga. kite mua ke	(glyph)	oho
(glyph)	hehaka. topa hia mai	(glyph)	herima truga ite puoko
(glyph)	hua oo tetere, ote vana.	(glyph)	hoira hoia ra kua hai ki toona, ma
(glyph)	erua oo na. mata kite puoko.	(glyph)	heoho hekori.
(glyph)	he hou hoi.	(glyph)	kito iho.
(glyph)	hoho rua.		
(glyph)	narua, maori. ote kohou.		
(glyph)	heroki, moiu ite kohou.		
(glyph)	he maori, ete kohou.		
(glyph)	natoru. maori. ote kohou.		
(glyph)	naha, maori. ote kohou.		
(glyph)	garoki reo riva riva, mo kai ite kohou.		
(glyph)	na mai taki, ko e. erepae.		
(glyph)	na mai taki te huru. ote horo		

Islander had attempted to write down a similar list of figures and their equivalents. The book also contains a variety of hitherto unrecorded ancient traditions.

bring the top of the wall with him, for that would obviously be taken as a bad omen. On the other side of the wall we came to a narrow path, and here I was asked to lead the way by carefully shining the flashlight down, but soon I had to stop because the cursed battery gave out. The two brothers asked nervously what had happened, and I tried to calm them. But they were uneasy till the photographer smuggled me his light so I could go on.

The path wound through a cornfield, broken by open stretches of stony ground, leading into an area which Atan later told me was called Matamea. This was the name given by the Easter Islanders to the planet Mars. I tried hard to keep my bearings, but it was so dark outside the range of the light falling before the tips of my toes that I could see nothing but the silhouette of three round hills against the starry sky, one of them straight ahead and the others to the right of us.

It was a strange walk through the night by six silent men, an absurd mixture of ancient and modern times. I myself marched at the head with the village skipper's precious *rongo-rongo* book in the airlines bag over my shoulder and Atan's grinning death's-head in an official mailbag of the Royal Norwegian Foreign Department. Behind me in single file came the others with camera equipment and empty cardboard boxes. Now we had reached a field with tall dry grass. Atan whispered that we were to stop, and he asked me to switch off the light.

The village skipper went fifty yards to the left out of the file, and stood in the long grass with his back to us. Then in subdued tones he began to speak in Polynesian. Out in the field the sudden sound of his voice carried into the night with remarkable resonance; even if the melodious phrases rose in crescendo, he was not using the full strength of his vocal chords. There was not a living soul to talk to in the grass, but Atan whispered excitedly that his brother was talking to the *aku-akus* in the area to make sure that all would go well.

When the village skipper rejoined us, he told us only to whisper when we left the path; and we must not smile, we must look serious. I was again asked to lead the way, this time through the high grass near the place where he had delivered his monologue.

The dry grass lay in scattered patches, and we stopped at a spot where the village skipper squatted down and began to dig in the sand with his hands. At once a shiny green banana leaf appeared; it was here that old Tahu-tahu had been early in the morning to prepare the so-called *umu* or Polynesian earth oven. Layers of banana leaves were removed, each browner than the one before, and steamier and juicier; at last the white flesh of a baked chicken and three sweet potatoes came to light, while a most wonderful and unusual aroma rose up to our nostrils. It was a smell that made our mouths water as it diffused into the night.

Atan sat as though on pins while the earth oven was uncovered, and when the contents appeared in good order he seemed immensely relieved. Tahu-tahu's earth oven had been successful: we had "good luck."

While we all squatted reverently round the earth oven sniffing the mingled aroma, I was asked in a whisper to pinch off the little tail on the rump of the hen and eat it in the presence of the others, while saying aloud a magic Easter Island formula: *Hekai ite umu pare haonga takapu Hanau eepe kai noruego.*

I later discovered that the natives themselves had difficulty in translating some old words in this phrase, the meaning of which was that we were to eat from this ceremonial earth oven of the Norwegian long-ears to get *mana* to enter the cave.

The brothers were still on tenterhooks, and I have never struggled so hard to repeat without stumbling a difficult sentence which I only partially understood. At the same time my knowledge of a fowl's anatomy was strained to the uttermost as I fumbled my way over the contorted and trussed-up hen to the place where its tail was. I noticed that head and claws were still intact although twisted out of position, and the beak of the bird was clipped off at the roots. I recalled that the mayor had once told me how one could kill an enemy by doing something magic with a fowl's beak.

I wrenched off the little tail, put it in my mouth, and chewed. It did not taste at all bad. I was next told to help myself to a small piece of sweet potato. It tasted excellent. But I was left with a round chicken bone in my mouth which I did not know whether to swallow or spit out; and I could not blunder. I sat sucking the bone till Enlique signed to me that I could spit it out, but Atan interfered and asked me to lay it on a banana leaf.

I was now told to break off a piece of chicken and a morsel of sweet potato for each of the others, and each time I who helped and those who ate were to repeat the same complicated sentence. I was in a panic when the photographer, as the first man served, ventured the words, but he mumbled something so indistinctly that no one could have known if they were right or wrong. Ed avoided the issue by just swallowing the titbit as soon as I had said the difficult sentence for him.

When we had managed this hurdle, Atan whispered that now the *aku-akus* were pleased. Since they had seen us eating in their honor, we could help ourselves freely and eat up the whole chicken for good luck.

Never have I known a meal to smell better, and never have I come across chicken and sweet potatoes prepared in more masterly fashion than in those banana leaves in old Tahutahu's earth oven. In this one respect the old dancing specter was a true sorceress who could, without cookbook or spices, outdo the most highly trained *chef de cuisine*. But then no restaurant could compete by spreading such a starry sky above its guests, with a wall tapestry alive with waving silhouettes of grass, while spices were wafted in upon the food as a fragrant scent from an open meadow and a burned-out fire.

Yet we who sat here in a circle enjoying our chicken bones were not the guests of honor at the meal. The ceremony was held for other guests, who had no stomachs and therefore lacked our splendid appetites: they just rejoiced to see how good the meal was tasting. I felt almost sorry for the *aku-akus* who sat around us in the grass, if at least they had the sense of smell. Atan whispered that now and then we must throw a gnawed bone over our shoulders and say: "Eat, family *aku-aku!*"

We spoke aloud to the *aku-akus* but only whispered among

ourselves. Apparently the stomachless guests of honor did not
hear very well; sight must have been their keenest sense.

At the height of the meal a disgusting green blowfly buzzed
in and landed plumb in the middle of the food. I was just
about to drive it away from the chicken, but hesitated for a
second. It was as well I did, for Atan stared hard at the fly
and whispered eagerly:

"That's the *aku-aku* singing. It's good luck!"

He grew more cheerful as the meal progressed. When only
part of a large sweet potato was left, I was told to break it
up and strew the pieces round about us, on the banana leaves,
and in the empty hearth.

When this was done, Atan whispered that everything was
ready. He rose and asked me to bring the "key": now we
were to open the entrance to the cave. Never before had I
felt so excited about something I was going to see. We walked
only fifteen or twenty paces west; then Atan stopped. We
both squatted down. I sat there with the grinning death's-head
on my knee.

"Now ask your *aku-aku* where the entrance is," Atan suddenly whispered in an almost challenging tone.

My heart leaped to my throat. We were in the middle of a
plain as flat as the floor of a room; there was not a hill in sight
except the three distant silhouettes against the stars. How
could there be a cave here? There wasn't a sizable rock in
the vicinity.

"No," I replied. "I cannot ask that. It is wrong to ask about
the entrance to other people's private property."

Fortunately Atan agreed, and pointed straight to the ground
at the tips of my shoes. I saw there a small flat stone half-
covered with sand and loose straw, exactly like ten million
others nearby. He asked me in a whisper to bend down toward
the stone, with the death's-head in front of me, and say in a
loud voice: "Open the door of the cave!"

I felt a fool, but did as he said. I bent down toward the
earth with the grinning "key" in my hands, and repeated the
magic words as Atan himself had said them: "*Mataki ite ana
kahaata mai!*"

Then he took the stone head from me and told me to enter.
I brushed away the sand and straw till the whole of the stone

appeared: it proved to be the size of a teatray. I felt it, and it was loose. When I turned it up, a gaping black hole appeared in the earth. It was too narrow for anyone to force his way down. One by one I loosened four other slabs which appeared below, being extremely careful not to let sand or straw slip into the hole. At last the opening was just big enough for a man to drop through.

"Now go in!" Atan commanded.

I sat on the ground with my legs in the hole. It was impossible to see anything down in the black opening, and as I lowered my body I held on with my elbows and stretched down with my toes to feel if I could touch bottom. I could not, and on a signal from Atan I loosed my hold and let myself fall down into the unknown. In the fraction of a second before I let go, I had a curious feeling of having done this before. I remembered a night during the war when I had sat with my legs down a dark hole. That time it was a sergeant who bade me let go, but then I had a parachute on my back and knew that I should land among friends on a training ground in England. Now little Atan, looking at me with his strange big eyes, was the only person who knew where I was going to land, and he seemed vaguely uncertain about the friendliness of the *aku-akus* down below.

I let go and fell down through the darkness, but not far, and my fall was remarkably soft and light. I could not see a thing, and had no idea what I was standing on. Only above me was there light of sorts: a small round hole in the roof with a few brilliant stars. The black shadow of a head appeared, and an arm which handed me the flashlight. When I turned it on, it revealed two shining white skulls at my feet. One of them had a patch of verdigris over its forehead, and a threatening black obsidian spear point lay on top of each. I was standing on a mat of yellow *totora* reeds plaited together with twisted bark: it was so thick and soft that it was like standing on a mattress. The cave around me was small, with rock walls rising solid in front of me, to the right, and behind me, but under a sagging fold of lava it continued inward to the left. There I could see a confused mass of grotesque faces and figures as far as my feeble light could reach. The figures seemed to be standing along the walls on the same kind of mats as that under my feet.

I was able to take only a quick look around before Atan handed down the stone "key"; then he turned about and wriggled his legs and backside into the hole. I noticed that right above me the roof round the opening was artificially constructed of large slabs, but farther in it continued as a natural tunnel with round folds of solidified lava hanging down from the roof.

I moved aside so that little Atan could let himself drop. The first thing he did when he landed like a ball on the mat was to bow gravely to the two skulls, after which he bowed to a stone skull lying a little farther on in the tunnel, exactly like the one I now had in my hands. He whispered that I must put the "key" down beside this other "guardian," and then say in a low voice that I was a long-ear from Norway who had come here with my brother. Afterward he showed me that his aunt had removed the magic bone meal from the holes in the other stone skull also. He took a quick look round and whispered that there was no longer any danger. His aunt had arranged everything, he had meticulously carried out her orders, and the *aku-aku* were satisfied.

I turned my flashlight into the corners where diabolical faces and strange twisted figures of stone were drawn up for review.

"This is your house," Atan assured me. "Now you can walk about in it as you like."

He added that the name of the cave was Raakau, and explained that to the best of his knowledge *raakau* was a rather special name for the moon. Atan and I crept farther into the cave to make room for the photographer and Ed, who were now coming down through the hole. We went along a narrow passage between two wide ledges built of loose stones and covered with yellow reed mats. All the way the strangest sculptures lay closely packed on the mats on both sides of us. The tunnel was not very long, after a few yards it ended abruptly in an irregular wall; but Atan's "moon-cave" was indeed the most fabulous underground treasure chamber. Here were curiosities which would make an art dealer tear his hair with excitement. No museum in the world had figures of this kind: each object was an ethnographic novelty which gave us the strangest impression of the Easter Islanders' secret and bizarre world of imagination.

Every single figure in this myriad of underground sculptures was quite different from what we had seen before. The only traditional Easter Island motif I recognized was a long-beaked bird-man standing erect with his hands behind him; but hitherto such figures had been seen only in wood, no one had yet heard of a *tangata manu* statuette in stone. There were also small stone models of the peculiar Easter Island paddles. Indeed, everything was represented, from human beings and mammals to birds, fish, reptiles, and invertebrates. Nor were fantastic hybrids lacking. Here and there were groups of figures carved on the same stone, such as two bird-men holding between them a strange catlike animal. There were also many distorted monsters with an occasional head here and there, and some sculptures which none of us understood at all.

The central passage between the reed mats was thickly carpeted with dry hay. Atan said that his aunt Tahu-tahu had taken care of the cave for him when he was a little boy, and she still came down here and slept whenever she was depressed and was missing those who had gone. She had been there the same morning and attended to the stones. I noticed that two of them were wet.

As the time passed Atan felt more and more at ease, and in half an hour he suddenly said to me with his voice at normal pitch: "It's all right now. We can talk and do what we like, in *your* home, my brother."

Atan obviously felt that he had carried out the last of his aunt's instructions: the cave with its pleasures, dangers, and obligations was legally transferred. Now it was I who had all the responsibility, he himself was out of the danger zone. His own agitation had reached its climax when the earth oven was uncovered and Tahu-tahu's cooking had proved successful. Now his last anxiety had disappeared, he had escaped from the whole uncanny business. Whether his great relief was solely due to his freedom from responsibility, or whether he also thought the *aku-akus* had resigned their office and moved to a more peaceful habitation, was not quite clear to me. But despite a certain formal respect for the stones, Atan now gave the impression of a completely free man. He only asked us politely to leave the two human skulls where they were, as they were the heads of two of his own family. Otherwise we could take away as many cave stones as we could carry in the cardboard boxes we had brought.

We had entered the ground at midnight, and we emerged again at two o'clock. We helped one another up out of the hole, and it was a relief after the stuffy cave to inhale deep draughts of fresh night air. The village skipper picked a juicy melon which we consumed. Then we covered the hole but did not conceal it with sand and straw because members of the expedition were coming back next day for the rest of the stones. Silently groping our way back in the darkness, we suddenly aroused an invisible drove of horses, whose hoof-beats drummed away with a hollow sound across the field. We saw neither lights nor people. Atan pushed ahead without troubling about the photographer, who now had to fend for himself. It seemed that *aku-akus* were no longer lying in ambush.

Ed asked Atan what he intended to do with his cave when the stones were no longer there.

"I've got to keep it," said Atan. "I shall need it in case of war."

There was not much sleep in the tent that night. The kerosene lamp glowed over the pages of my diary until the eastern sky began to redden, and I managed only a little nap before the steward hammered on the frying pan, the signal of another busy day. Lazarus was on the spot already, hanging about inquisitively while I had my morning wash behind the tents.

The mayor had once told me that if several people entered a secret cave together, the *aku-akus* would move to another place. Without an *aku-aku* the secret entrance would lose its magic, and strangers passing would be able to find it at once. I began to see the practical value of this superstition. For the saying, "What one person knows no one knows, but what two people know all know," is more applicable on Easter Island than anywhere else. No sooner had Enlique been told

233

that he was to enter Atan's cave than he had boasted of this impending event to Lazarus, and even in the village people were beginning to talk.

Some days earlier, before sunrise, Lazarus had come to my tent with some cave stones. He seemed rather upset and said nothing, only silently took from his sack a large bird exactly like a penguin. It was life-size and the likeness was so striking that I was utterly astonished, for I knew that, apart from the icy regions of the Antarctic, the penguin was found only in the Galapagos Islands. Lazarus reached into the sack again, and this time extracted the head of a purely imaginary bird, its beak full of sharp pointed teeth. Finally he produced the head of a beast of prey whose muzzle had been badly scraped on the journey.

He sat silent for a long time, studying me belligerently. At last he told me that he had escaped death that night by a hairsbreadth. To fetch the sculptures, he had twice made a zigzag descent of the precipice leading to his cave; on the second ascent a small projecting rock broke off in his hand. Below him was a sheer drop of a hundred feet, and he was left bent backward with whirling arms, on the point of falling into the abyss. By the merest chance he had grabbed hold of another projection with his left hand, had regained his balance, and had cautiously climbed up the remaining fifty feet to the rim of the plateau. When he had reached the top safe and sound, he had sat for a long time thinking. Why this piece of bad luck? Was it wrong to take stones from the cave?

Lazarus had asked himself this question again and again on his way back to Anakena that night, and now he put it directly to me with a suspicious air.

"It's sheer madness to climb about on a precipice alone at night," I said. "Surely you must realize *that!*"

Lazarus looked at me skeptically, without visible reaction. It was clear that he was accustomed to such climbs, always alone, and always at night.

"Besides, it wasn't *bad* luck," I added. "On the contrary you really had incredibly *good* luck in grasping the other bit of rock!"

This gave Lazarus something to think about, and he began to look a bit brighter. Yes, indeed, he had not fallen; his was an extraordinary piece of good fortune to be sitting there without a scratch. But, he asked, why should he have suffered this frightening experience?

This was not so easy to answer. I sat silent and stared at his sculptures on the bed. Lazarus' stones were never washed or scrubbed, but today the head of the snarling beast had a nasty wound on its dark muzzle. I pointed to this, and Lazarus looked at the fresh scratch with concern.

"Do you think you treat your stones well?" I asked, trying to turn the conversation. "How would *you* like being shaken about in a sack with other contents without any grass around you to take the knocks?"

Lazarus' conscience was uneasy, and it looked as if he had found sufficient reason for the suffering of the night. Nevertheless, we agreed that he should not continue to fetch more stones. As this cave was in such a dangerous place, he must not risk these visits alone at night. And so Lazarus had crept out into the red glow of early morning, fully reassured that after all the night's adventure had been just another proof of "good luck."

The night when our party was preparing to set off for Atan's cave, Lazarus had been lurking about the tents. When he saw me alone for a moment, he said that he knew what we were about, and that he too had decided to take me to his cave after I had been to Atan's. Now, the morning after, Lazarus could not refrain from trying to get a word with me as I stood behind the tents, my head down in a washbasin. He asked no pointed questions: he just sensed that no disaster had befallen any of us during the night. Then he disappeared. •

At that time Lazarus and several of the long-ears were working for Arne in Rano Raraku, returning on horseback to eat and sleep in Hotu Matua's cave. All our native workers had their daily rations, and those who lived in the Anakena Valley also got the leavings from the kitchen tent in the camp. But today Lazarus did not seem satisfied with his daily allowance. He came sauntering up at twilight and asked me if I might have a chicken, a live chicken.

The natives had often brought me live fowls as presents, and all those which did not cackle or crow at daybreak had been allowed to live. They walked freely among the tents, while the noisy ones gradually came to a mysterious end. The steward, who rose early, was said to have seen the photographer stealing about among the tents barefoot, in his pyjamas, with a rifle in his hands. One thing was certain: he daily cursed the natives who filled the camp with crowing cocks and cackling hens.

I suspected that Lazarus was up to something, and I told the steward that he could let him have a chicken. The steward crept up on a flock, and flinging himself on his stomach into the cackling, fluttering mob, he managed to grasp a fleeing leg. Lazarus came back, delighted, with a hen under his arm.

"This means good luck," he whispered happily. "The steward caught a *white* hen!"

Before Lazarus disappeared with his white hen, he made sure that we could take the motor launch along the coast next day. He was willing to take me to the cave. Late in the evening the skipper drove to the village to fetch Bill, for Lazarus had agreed that he and the photographer might come too.

The sea was unusually smooth in the bay next morning when we assembled on board the ship. Lazarus followed me down into the hold: he wanted something to put into the cave to replace the stones we would take away. He asked for two unopened rolls of dress material and, in addition, some small article, no matter what. He was very particular about the color of the dress material, but he immediately accepted a pair of scissors as the small object. I guessed that the rolls of material were for his two older sisters, while the *aku-aku* would have to be satisfied with only the scissors.

When we climbed down the ladder into the launch, both the chief engineer and the electrician came too. They were to put the four of us ashore at a place which Lazarus would indicate. We set our course westward along the cliffs on the north coast, congratulating ourselves that the sea was so calm, that we should get ashore easily. But as we moved farther away from Anakena we felt the launch beginning to roll heavily. Only Lazarus took this as a matter of course, saying that the *aku-akus* always whipped up the sea when someone was going to a cave. He sat goggle-eyed and held on tight.

The coast was a chaos of lava blocks where the waves broke at the foot of a steep drop. In a little while Lazarus pointed out a stretch fifty yards long between two enormous piles of rock running down to the sea. There his grandmother, fishing as she went along the rocks, had once surprised another old woman who was washing and drying cave stones. His grandmother had passed by, pretending that she saw nothing. When she returned a little later, the other woman too was fishing, and there was no sign of the stones. So Lazarus knew that there must be a secret cave in that place.

Shortly afterward we passed the lonely windmill in the Hanga-o-Teo Valley, once an important population center, but now abandoned and desolate. Soon Lazarus pointed to another stretch of the wild coast about a hundred yards long. Within this area lay the secret cave where he had once told me his cousin Alberto Ika had been to fetch the *rongo-rongo* tablets, which the *aku-akus* had forced him to bring back to the cave.

Lazarus had scarcely shown us this spot when he became frightened: he could see people. The rest of us saw nothing, but Lazarus, who had the eyes of an eagle by day and those of an owl by night, saw four persons sitting on a rock. Why were they there, and what were they doing? He stared and stared till we rounded the next point.

Now the seas were becoming steadily worse, and we all saw that it was useless to try to land in such conditions. Just under the steep cliff where Lazarus' cave was located, we circled several times close inshore as Lazarus tried to point out to us a tiny ledge on the face of the precipice, behind which the entrance lay. This was an "open" cave, Lazarus explained. He went on pointing till we all thought we saw where it was. But when we checked up on one another, none of us agreed, and at last we gave it up altogether.

The salt spray drenched our faces as the chief engineer put the helm over and set course for home. The launch rose on end and began a mad dance in the choppy sea. The waves grew worse and worse though the wind had not risen, it had merely shifted. It was no longer possible to keep a straight course; the helmsman had continually to turn into the biggest seas, which came rolling at us with foaming crests. Lazarus did not say a word, he just sat holding tight. The rest of us merely followed with our eyes the helmsman's skillful movements and every tumbling sea, while the salt spray dripped from our hair and faces, and our clothes clung to our bodies like wet paper.

Just before we reached the Hanga-o-Teo windmill, we all saw four small dots up on the edge of the plateau. Three of them climbed onto horses and rode in the same direction as ourselves, while the fourth turned about and galloped the other way, toward the village.

"That's Alberto's brother," Lazarus exclaimed in surprise. "The others must be his sons."

We soon lost sight of the horsemen, and no one had time to wonder what they had been doing. Soon the expedition ship appeared beyond a bluff; she too was pitching heavily in the seas, and roaring breakers followed us right into Anakena Bay, where the surf was thundering on the beach.

Lazarus leaped ashore as if the devil himself was at his heels, and together we walked up to the camp in silence, wet as drowned rats. Bill was as serious as Lazarus, and was trying to rub the salt water off his spectacles with a sodden handkerchief. He confided to me that he had felt so terribly seasick that he thought he would die, but he dared not show it for fear Lazarus would interpret it as a bad omen.

After lunch we set off for the cave again. But this time we saddled four horses and followed the remains of an ancient road which wound along the north coast between the screes of the plateau. Beyond the creaking windmill at Hanga-o-Teo, we came to a stretch of the road where the ancient pavement was still intact, resembling the Inca roads in Peru. Soon after Lazarus dismounted and escorted us to a ledge where a huge winding snake with cup-shaped hollows along its raised back was cut into the solid rock. He had told me about this before, and Father Sebastian had mentioned it too. Bill was quite amazed: the fauna of these Pacific islands did not include snakes, so where had the old-time sculptors found their model?

Soon afterward we passed a lone statue which had been abandoned en route to an *ahu* near the north cape. I thought of the transport problem with dismay: seven miles from Rano Raraku as the crow flies, and much more on this rough ground where riding was so difficult. Here we left the ancient trail and proceeded over a wild stony plain just inside the steep drop to the ocean. The endless sea was still dotted with white-caps. As we were riding down into a little gully, one of my stirrup straps broke, but I managed to hide it so that Lazarus noticed nothing, and rode on with only one stirrup into very rough ground, which was getting worse and worse.

As we neared our destination, I observed for the first time that Lazarus was growing nervous. He whipped up his horse with a little stick and begged me to quicken my pace, so that we might arrive before the others. We increased our lead across the stony plain by a couple of hundred yards, and when we came to the foot of two great lava blocks, Lazarus jumped to the ground and tied up his horse, asking me to do the same. Then he pulled off his shirt and trousers at top speed and stood with nothing on but his shorts. He rushed down the slope toward the edge of the precipice with a coil of rope in his hand, begging me as he ran to strip quickly and follow him with the hen. I had no idea where the hen was, and when I asked, I received an irritable, distracted reply as he bounded down the slope. I caught sight of an old bag hanging from his saddle, seized it, and hurried after him —I too completely stripped but for my shorts.

I overtook Lazarus on the very edge of the precipice, and without turning he hastily mumbled a snappish and nervous order that I should eat the chicken tail and give him a little bit when he came up again. Then he vanished down the cliff. When I asked in bewilderment if I was to eat the tail now or wait till he returned, I received no answer.

In the bag I found the hen plucked and baked and packed in banana leaves. I had just wrenched off the little tail stump when Lazarus appeared over the edge again. I stuffed the tail into my mouth and chewed as I tore off a strip of the breast for him, which he gulped down like a wild beast, looking to left and right. It was a strange ceremony we performed on the very edge of the precipice, wearing only our shorts. The others had now reached the rocks and were dismounting. Lazarus asked me to break a few pieces from the hen and lay them on the rocks, and when this was done he suddenly seemed relieved and said that we could now eat freely, and also give some to the other two, who had joined us.

Lazarus was still in a great hurry. He slung the loop of his rope over a stone which was only loosely attached to the rock by a dried lump of earth, and then flung the rest of the rope over the cliff. Now he disappeared over the edge again, without supporting himself by the rope or even testing it to see if it would hold. I looked down at him and asked cautiously if we could be sure that the rope was securely made fast. He gave me a queer look and said that he himself never used a rope, and what had I to be afraid of? He knew that nothing could happen to me.

It is not always pleasant to be regarded as supernatural. I felt that I had only too good use for the rope, but dared not touch it, so badly was it secured. So I maneuvered myself over the edge, as Lazarus had done, while holding the scissors, wrapped in paper, between my teeth: I had been expressly instructed to bring them with me down the cliff. I am no mountaineer, and loathed what I was setting out to do. I lowered myself down till the tips of my toes found a hold on a disgustingly narrow ledge, but it was almost impossible to find a hold for my fingers. There was a perpendicular drop of 150 feet below, and down there foam and green water were whirling and roaring among sharp lava blocks. The ocean itself was as blue as the sky, but all along the rocks beneath us turbulent waves encircled the island like a twisting green monster foaming in fury as it sent licking tongues of water in between the black teeth of sharp lava jaws, greedily agape for anything which might fall down from the cliff above. It was a horrifying maw to contemplate.

We had to keep ourselves tight against the rock wall, for a single careless inch could tip us out of balance. Lazarus, straight-backed and light-footed, moved sideways along the ledge like a tightrope dancer, showing me the way. I suddenly lost all interest in his cave and cursed all *aku-akus*, not least my own, which had landed me in such a situation. My only wish was to clamber up again before it was too late. But I could not quite bring myself to do that either. So I followed slowly in Lazarus' wake, down the slanting ledge, with one cheek, my body, and two outstretched arms pressed close to the rock face so as not to tilt outward.

Never again will I climb on a lava cliff in my underwear!

Both before and after its work on Rapa Iti, the expedition had to call at Tahiti for provisions and equipment. No one on board regretted it, or the hula evenings there. Yvonne, wearing the red skirt, joined the hula girls in the singing.

ABOVE: The song of the South Seas has entranced people of many nations. The last verse is being sung, but that verse will never end as long as palms wave and the evening air is filled with the sweet scent of the *tiare* blossom. BELOW: Heaven or hell? A grunting pig dance in the Taipi Valley of Nuku Hiva.

On
vahi
villa
were

ABOVE: Rapa Iti's green hills were covered with overgrown terraces and mysterious pyramids which could not have been the work of nature. BELOW: All the men of the village going up the hill to take part in the first real excavation ever done on this amazingly unexplored island. Of the twelve artificial hill-tops we chose Morongo Uta.

Morongo Uta lay like a fairy castle in the wild hills of Rapa Iti. Sites of houses and tools appeared in masses when we began to dig. It was found that the original population had once lived in twelve fortified hill villages on the

highest peaks, and had only gone down into the valley
to mind the *taro* fields and catch fish. Another hill village,
unexcavated and green-clad, is seen in the background to
the left.

Work is over. The first fortified mountain village in Polynesia has been excavated. Bill (AT RIGHT), who directed the excavation of Morongo Uta, Yvonne, and I plant the expedition's flag on the ruins of the largest building ever discovered in the whole of Polynesia.

The wide meshes caught on the jagged surface and I hung fast as though nailed to the wall. I had to jerk and pull till I managed to tear myself loose. If Lazarus had wished for a really vicious *aku-aku* to guard his cave, he could have hit upon nothing worse than an invisible one planted on this narrow ledge to catch ignorant intruders by their shorts at the most inconvenient moment. Certain it was that while I staggered along the ledge, engaged in a constant struggle to release myself, Lazarus was tripping along gracefully on the tips of his toes without a single scratch.

We climbed down in zigzags, coming upon the rope again at a steep place where it hung free down the cliffside. I could not quite do without it down to the next ledge, and I pressed fingers and toes against the lava wall wherever I could, letting as little as possible of my weight rest on the rope, till I reached a little shelf on which Lazarus stood. He flattened himself against the wall as stiff as a guardsman, and gave no sign of going further. This was a most uncomfortable parking place; the shelf was a foot wide and there was just room for both of us side by side, with our backs to the rock.

There was no cave here. Lazarus stood motionless, pressed to the cliff, and stared at me with a strange and inscrutable expression. Suddenly he reached out and said quickly:

"Give me your hand!"

He could have asked nothing worse of me right at that moment, as I was standing with the scissors in my mouth, clinging fast to the rock with my fingers, my shorts in shreds. I pressed against the cliff so hard that I felt the rough lava cutting into my back, and held out my right hand to him. He grasped it firmly.

"Promise me not to say a word to anyone on the island about what we're up to now," he begged. "You can talk to your own people, but they must keep their mouths shut as long as they are here."

He did not let go of my hand, as he continued. If his name was mentioned in connection with this affair, his sisters would be beside themselves with fury. When I had left the island, I could talk freely. For if rumors got back to the village through the *Pinto*, he would just say that he had made copies, and in a few months everything would be forgotten.

I promised to do what he asked of me, and then he let go my hand. He told me to bend over the precipice and look down. I stretched out as far as I dared, and gazed in horror at the sharp lava blocks in the whirling foam. There was a small ledge, like that on which we stood, about a man's height below us. And under this the cliff again fell sheer to the bottom.

"Now, where is the entrance?" Lazarus asked with pride.

"Impossible to say," I muttered through the package in my mouth. My only desire was to get all this over.

"There, under your feet," he said, pointing to the small ledge beneath us. He braced me while I cautiously leaned out again. But still I saw nothing.

"You can't get to the opening unless you do exactly as I tell you," Lazarus said. And then he began a course of instruction the like of which I have not experienced since I stood before my first dancing master. I was told to begin with the left foot and then follow with a meticulous series of short steps and half-turns which were to end in my sinking down on my knees and stretching out on my stomach on the shelf below. I was asked to wait where I was while Lazarus gave a demonstration of the difficult dance. I saw how he placed his hands and feet, how he twisted himself round down on the ledge to be able to sink onto his knees and onto his stomach; after that I only saw his kicking legs, and then he was gone.

I stood alone and noticed more than ever how the air was filled with the thundering surf against the cliff. A few hundred yards farther west, on a curve of the coast, I spotted the cameraman standing on the very edge of the plateau, filming in the late afternoon sun. The ocean was still white-crested. It was out there we had been circling that morning, also without seeing this infernal cave.

Then a hand appeared on the shelf below holding a fiendish stone head; Lazarus' own head and body followed, and he slowly repeated, in reverse order, the same carefully studied steps and turns until he was up on the ledge with me again.

"The 'key,'" Lazarus said, holding out the cave stone.

Again I had to press myself hard against the wall, for now Lazarus asked me to give him the scissors. I had to take them out of my mouth and hand them to him, while he gave me the "key" in my other hand. This "key" had human features with great bulging eyes, a bearded chin, and a most hypnotic expression; but a long neck stretched horizontally from the back of the head, as on an animal. Lazarus asked me to put the "key" down on a tiny ledge by my head, and then it was my turn to begin the frightful dance down to the cave.

There was so little room for the maneuver that I soon realized the necessity of following Lazarus' lessons in every detail. When I had turned myself about so that I could crouch down on all fours on the lower ledge, I saw for the first time the opening leading to the cave, hidden under a projection in the rock. The hole was so small that I should never have dreamed of anyone being able to crawl into it. The original discoverers of the cave must have lived quite near, with time to explore every single inch of this terrain. Lazarus had told me that the cave was called Motu Tavake, which means "Cliff of the Tropical Bird"; the locality was called Omohi and lay at the foot of Vai-mataa on the Hanga-o-Teo plain. The cave had belonged to Hatui, who was the grandfather of Lazarus' mother.

I was crouched on all fours on the tiny ledge, but the narrow hole in the rock opened onto a still smaller ledge, on the same level, but a little way off. To get to it I had to stretch forward and take hold of the edge of the other shelf. Lying flat, I got my arms and head into the hole on one ledge, while my knees and legs still lay on the other. My stomach was without support above the abyss and the breakers. The hole through which I was trying to worm my way was so narrow that my shorts were pulled down several times. The rock scratched and cut my back and thighs, for there was hardly any sand, only rough, hard lava.

At first I could make out nothing but a horribly narrow passage and a very faint suggestion of light ahead. I lay for a long time struggling with my legs out over the abyss, and when at last I got my feet inside I felt that the passage was widening a little, without any rise of the low roof. I became aware of various contours around me. And then, next to my ear, I discovered a sculpture representing two mating turtles. On my other side appeared a small statuette of the same type as the giants from Rano Raraku. I crept farther in and found

243

more room. I could soon sit up and look into a cave which was dimly illuminated from some opening I could not yet see. Closely packed along the walls strange sculptures stood or lay, piled up in several rows on the bare, dry rock. There were no mats here and no hay. A few yards in front of me and blocking the way stood a conspicuous figure, unmistakably of the male sex. He was in a straddled position with bent knees and his arms raised threateningly; and he was surrounded by a mass of other figures. There was a little step behind him leading to a lower level, where two human skeletons were lying. A tiny hole in the wall to the right let a dim light fall on the crumbling bones and made it possible to see faintly the outlines of the ghostly treasure chamber.

I heard something breathing. I heard it as clearly as if it were in the corner beside me. But it was only Lazarus outside, squeezing himself in through the narrow opening. The acoustics were incredible: I could hear his bare skin rubbing against the sharp lava. Lazarus came in without ceremony and squatted down beside me. His big eyes and his teeth shone white. Lazarus now was quite himself again, just as I knew him on his nocturnal visits to my tent. He pointed out the big figure which straddled in a warning posture with its arms in the air, towering above the others; it suggested a traffic policeman directing the swarm of mysterious figures around him and along both sides of the cave down toward the opening.

"That's the most important stone," Lazarus explained. "He's the chief of the cave, an old king."

Otherwise Lazarus knew incredibly little: to all my questions about the other figures his only reply was a shrug of the shoulders and "don't know." The only things he seemed to be sure about were two flat stone disks bearing symmetrical symbols: he declared that they represented the sun and the moon. We were not obliged to whisper, but the whole atmosphere and acoustics were such that it was natural to speak in a hushed voice.

Lazarus crawled round with me for a time, then he disappeared out of the passage again to bring Bill down; it was too risky for the photographer to attempt the descent. A short time passed, and then I heard Bill's voice whispering an oath in the narrow hole. Bill had grown up in the heart of the

Rockies, and he did not mind a precipice, but there were no such damned ratholes in the mountains of Wyoming. He managed to wriggle in, and sat in silence for a while, staring with unseeing eyes. Suddenly there was an outburst: he had discovered all the figures round him. Lazarus followed close behind and brought a flashlight, and we could now see the individual figures better. While a great number of the stones in Atan's cave were scratched and rubbed by washing and care, there was no sign of scratches or marks on any of the figures in Lazarus' cave. In Atan's cave I had felt as if I was entering a magician's secret parlor, with the mats on the shelves and the heaps of hay on the floor. Here it was like going into an old warehouse.

We asked Lazarus if he did not wash the stones. No, there was no need to, because there was no growth here. This was a perfectly dry cave due to the current of air.

Over by the little hole we noticed cold, dry air trickling in, and there was not the smallest scrap of green on the iron-hard walls, not even on the crumbling bones of the skeletons. In Atan's cave there was a fine layer of mold and moss on the wall beneath the entrance.

We lost all count of time inside the cave. We chose some of the most interesting sculptures to take this time; we could come back for the rest. Lazarus and Bill crawled out to the ledge to receive the stones, while I was left behind to try to maneuver the stones through the narrow entrance tunnel without marring them. This was much easier said than done. For to transport a lava sculpture without injury when crawling on the stomach in a narrow cave is a hopeless task unless you hold the light at the same time, and an extra hand is really needed for pushing yourself along as well. I realized now how skillful Lazarus had been when he had crawled out of here alone at night without scratching more than the muzzle of one stone beast. When at last I came to the cave mouth, after moving several stones in front of me inch by inch, I heard anxious cries from Bill, but his words were lost in the noise of the breakers. My way was blocked by my own sculptures, and I could not get further till Lazarus removed them from outside. When I peered past the sculptures, I thought I could distinguish his arm, and suddenly I discovered what had happened: outside it was dark. Night had come upon us.

Lazarus removed the stones one by one, and sent them up to Bill. When the opening was clear, I crawled out and found a complete change of scene. It was barely possible to detect the outlines of the cliff in the faint light of a crescent moon. I had gooseflesh all over my body and was trembling at the knees when at last I stood safe up on the plateau. I tried to console myself with the thought that it was only the night chill. For it had been cold in the cave and cold to climb nude in the night wind. Lazarus went down yet again, this time with the two rolls of dress material.

We flung on our clothes and regaled ourselves with hot coffee from a thermos, while the photographer admired the night's haul. I noticed that Lazarus had begun to sniffle a little, and Bill confided to me that he too did not feel well. We both knew that the *cocongo* from the *Pinto* had begun to spread during the last few days; more serious cases were developing. I was really afraid that either Bill or Lazarus would now fall ill, and in that event, Lazarus, instead of gradually overcoming his inherited fear of *aku-aku* and taboo, would become more superstitious than ever. Bill had a jacket, so I gave mine to Lazarus and put the sack with the priceless haul on my back.

Before we walked over to the horses, Lazarus made sure that no scraps of paper or other traces were left on the ground, and then our little caravan set off homeward in the faint moonlight. The sack was heavy and the going was incredibly rough, so I had more than enough to do to keep myself on the horse's back with only one stirrup. But when we came up onto the ancient trail I rode forward alongside Lazarus and said he could see now that there was no *aku-aku* in the cave that wished us any harm.

"That was because I went down beforehand and said the words," Lazarus replied calmly.

What words Lazarus had said I never found out. Nor the object of undressing before going down into the drafty cave. Perhaps the *aku-aku* in the rock was a survivor of earlier times, accustomed to visitors wearing only a small loincloth.

I dared not ask. For Lazarus believed that I knew all about *aku-akus*, just as well as he did, if not a good deal better.

We rode on in silence, and our horses' hoofs clattered in the dark when we passed over the paved section of the road. Just afterward we heard the low creaking of the lonely wind-mill at Hanga-o-Teo. Driving clouds sped across the crescent moon which peered curiously down into my sack. The night was full of mystery. The wind was chilly, and we urged the horses forward as quickly as we could, without watering them at the mill.

For Lazarus was coughing.

CHAPTER NINE

Among Gods and Devils

A DANGEROUS SPECTER was wandering about on Easter Island in company with the *aku-akus* just at the time we were gaining entrance to the secret caves. This specter had appeared some weeks before; it came and went among the houses in the village, and no one could shut it out. It became more and more daring, and soon it appeared too among our people in the tents at Anakena. Creeping in by the mouth and nose, it ran amok through the whole body. It had come to the island as a stowaway on the *Pinto* and sneaked ashore under the name *cocongo*.

The mayor had been to his cave for stones only twice when the *cocongo* knocked at his door. He kept on his feet for several days, though feeling wretched; then he took to his bed. When I went to see him he declared with a bright smile that the *cocongo* was usually much worse and that he would soon be quite well. A week later I went over to see him again, but learned he was in the village hospital. I called on the new village doctor who had come in the *Pinto* to relieve the other, and was shown into the little sickroom where the *cocongo* patients lay coughing. I did not see the mayor among them and was beginning to be anxious when over in a corner an emaciated man raised himself on his elbow and said in a hoarse voice:

"Here I am, Señor Kon-Tiki!"

I was quite horrified when I recognized him.

"Pneumonia," the doctor whispered. "He nearly died, but I think we're going to pull him through."

The mayor lay there pale and hollow-cheeked with a peculiar, forced smile on his thin lips. He summoned me to the bedside with a feeble gesture and whispered in my ear:

"It'll be all right. When I'm well again we'll do great things together. My granddaughter died of *cocongo* yesterday. She'll guide me from heaven, she will. This is no punishment, I realize that. Just wait, Señor, we'll do great things."

I left the hospital sick at heart. It had been terrible seeing the mayor in such a condition. He had been so odd, I did not quite understand what he had meant. Perhaps it was the fever that had given him that queer look in his eyes and made him talk so strangely. That the superstitious man did not believe his illness to be punishment by the *aku-aku* was of course excellent, but it was rather puzzling.

The days passed. This wave of *cocongo* carried off no one except the mayor's granddaughter, and soon he was well enough to go home. When I went to see him, he smiled the same queer smile. He had no fever now, but he repeated all that he had said in the hospital. For the first few weeks he was too weak to return to us and his friends in the cave at Anakena. He stayed at home with his wife, and we regularly sent him butter and other nourishing food to help him to put on a little flesh again.

The mayor's youngest brother, little Atan, slipped through the epidemic with ease; he did not have even a touch of *cocongo* that year. And thus he rid himself of belief in punishment by the *aku-aku*. He had been released from both the duties and menaces of the cave, but instead of punishment he had received a reward large enough to get his family through many a tight place in the future. By local standards he was now a well-to-do man: both cloth and money were hidden in nature's big safe under the ground. And though the mayor had hung between life and death, Atan did not consider his brother's illness to be a cave punishment, either. On the contrary, Atan, who had no idea that his brother had brought me

249

stones from his cave, was continually advising me to ask him
about his cave as soon as he was well, for it was sure to be
the most important cave of all.

Lazarus, however, was on the verge of illness. The morning
after the ride from his cave he was outside my tent at an early
hour. He asked me, coughing and hoarse, how I was.

"Absolutely first-rate," I said, and saw Lazarus' face light
up at once. I was glad he had not asked after Bill, for he was
not at all well that day. Lazarus went about for two or three
days, coughing and taking medicine, and then he was as fit as
ever without ever having gone to bed.

While the village doctor was fighting the *cocongo* at
Hangaroa, the expedition's doctor had his hands full with all
our own workers, now nearly a hundred strong. We were well
supplied with antibiotics and other medicines, which were in-
creasingly popular with the natives. They were also very fond
of headache tablets and ate them as candy if we did not keep
an eye on them. Thus we rode out one wave of *cocongo* after
another. But problems seldom come alone. Early in the epidemic, before we had seen a family cave, something else happened which caused a considerable stir in the village.

On the last day before his illness, when the mayor was sitting in his house with a room full of cave stones waiting for
transport to the camp, he had suffered a bad shock. Just before the captain arrived with the jeep, Gonzalo, our Chilean
representative, had come to the door unexpectedly and caught
sight of a stone lobster before the mayor could hide it away.

"This is *old*," Gonzalo said, eagerly picking up the sculpture
from the floor.

"No, it's *new*," lied the mayor.

"I can see that it's old," said Gonzalo suspiciously.

"I made it myself," the mayor insisted.

At last Gonzalo had had to give way.

When the mayor got to the camp, he told me at once of the
episode with Gonzalo, and repeated that on no account must
I say a single word to anyone about his having taken stones
from the family cave.

"Señor Gonzalo must have known something," the mayor

said, troubled. "He was much too suspicious, and would hardly believe me when I said I had made the lobster myself."

Later Gonzalo came to me in the tent and gave an account of the same episode. He thought he had unveiled the whole mystery of the caves.

"The mayor's deceiving you," Gonzalo said. "I've seen an incredibly fine lobster which he admits he made himself. You must be on your guard if he comes and says it's from the cave."

Gonzalo was astonished when he heard that the mayor had already brought me the lobster and, in addition, had told me all about Gonzalo's visit.

The mayor was now on the alert, and tried to cover himself by continually saying that he personally made curious stone sculptures. When the *cocongo* began to be troublesome and he had just taken to his bed, he had a visit at home one evening from Gonzalo and Ed. They met the mayor's brother-in-law, Riroroko, inside the garden gate. They had hardly greeted him when he began, unprompted, to attest in a boasting fashion to the mayor's skill at carving stone sculptures; he had special tools with which he made lobsters and animals and boats, afterward washing them and whipping them with banana leaves to make them look old.

Neither Ed nor Gonzalo had asked for information about the mayor's stones, and they were therefore all the more amazed at this frank confession. They told me at once what they had heard. Meanwhile the mayor lay helpless in bed with a rising temperature, and was able neither to make nor fetch cave stones. But Gonzalo went about among the natives with ears wide open, trying to find out more. He was staying in the village at the time, working with Bill at Vinapu.

About this time young Estevan's pretty wife, the strong-minded woman who had sent me the first cave stones, had recovered her health. Being cured of her abdominal trouble, she went to the cave with Estevan every night to fetch grotesque figures, which they stacked in a locked outhouse. I no longer asked to be taken into her family cave; in return she gave me important information about some of the stones which came from it.

I had told Gonzalo that I was expecting a load of sculptures from her cave, and one evening when he was walking about and surveying the village, he saw a heap of uncut lava blocks stacked up behind the house of Estevan's neighbor. Smoldering suspicion blazed up. Gonzalo thought they had been left there by Estevan for making sculptures, and he decided to act.

The same day a little nephew of Enlique's had been brought to the village hospital, severely burned by a kettle of melting pig's fat. Enlique too had brought me a little sack with cave sculptures, and it was he who later went with us into Atan's cave. The day after his nephew's accident, Enlique came to me with a gloomy face, which at once suggested that he wanted to blame me for the disaster, since I had persuaded him to go into the cave for stones. Now things were beginning to get complicated. On this island nearly everybody was mutually related in some way or another, and any mishap in the village could be interpreted as a punishment by someone who had broken a taboo.

Enlique asked me to go with him behind the newly raised statue.

"Something awful has happened now," he began in a low voice. "There's trouble in the village. Estevan and his wife do nothing but lie all day in their house weeping. Señor Gonzalo has said that they have cheated Señor Kon-Tiki, that they have made 'stones' themselves."

"Rubbish," I said. "There's nothing for them to cry about. Ride over and tell Estevan and his wife that all is well. I'm not angry."

"All is *not* well," Enlique said despairingly. "The whole village will soon be furious. If the stones are new, everyone will be angry with Estevan and his wife for trying to cheat Señor Kon-Tiki. And if the stones are old, everyone will be still angrier with them for removing things from a family cave. Everyone's bound to be angry with them now."

Enlique said nothing about the child who had had the accident. Evidently he regarded this as his brother's misfortune, not his own. And his brother had *not* brought me any stones, though I later learned that he too had a cave.

That evening I was busy sealing up fresh pollen samples and could not leave the tents, but the next night the captain drove me into the village where we went to Estevan's hut. He was sitting alone on a bench, while his wife was lying on the bed; the eyes of both were red with weeping. We greeted them, but before Estevan could speak he burst into tears again. He declared that for two days and nights they had neither slept nor eaten, they had just wept, for Señor Gonzalo had said that Estevan had made false stones to deceive Señor Kon-Tiki. He had seen a heap of lava stones next door and thought that Estevan had collected materials for making sculptures. What he had not seen was that their neighbor was building an extension to the back of his house, and that the stones were being used to make the wall.

I tried to console them as well as I could. We had brought several presents with us, and when we left, they both promised to have a meal, go to bed, and try to forget the whole thing.

Lower down the path we went in and knocked at the mayor's door. We found him in bed, his good humor completely shattered. He had had a visit from his powerful aunt, Tahu-tahu. She had been in a towering rage and said that he was a good lad, and so was Señor Kon-Tiki, and therefore he ought not to sell me fakes as rumored in the village. He had not been able to tell her that the stones he had given me were old, for he had not yet obtained her consent to take anything from Ororoina's family cave. So he had merely told her that he was a sick man; he would explain everything as soon as he was well again:

"Other people get angry for a short time," said the mayor. "But old people like her get so angry that they can't speak for three days."

He had given her a roll of cloth and a carton of cigarettes as a token of friendship from me, but she had just flung them on the floor and said she would take nothing he had obtained by fraud. Only when he had explained that the things were a direct gift from me to her, had the old woman picked them up again, and made for the door.

We tried to talk the sick mayor into a calmer frame of mind, but this was a waste of time. His old aunt was a generation ahead of him, with all the rights and all the wisdom this implied. Tahu-tahu was a dangerous woman. If she was angry, she could kill a man by burying a chicken's head.

The rumors about Estevan and the mayor caused a great stir in the village. Many of the natives assured us that there were no secret caves in the island: we must not believe anything of the kind. If there had been any, the entrances had been lost long ago. If anybody brought me sculptures, they had made them themselves; there was nothing of the kind on their island. Some of those who came to deny the existence of the caves were so sincere that they obviously believed what they said. But others made the opposite impression because of their nervous, almost panic-stricken efforts to induce us to believe them. Some of the older people in particular quite lost their heads in their eagerness to remove from our minds any suspicion that there was anything on the island today except sheep and statues.

For several days one piece of information nullified another, while all who had contact with the natives cautiously attempted to get to the bottom of the problem.

Ed came down to us one day from Orongo; he had again come round to the opinion that there must be secret family caves on the island; we must only be on our guard against imitations. He had managed to elicit from his native workers that it was usual for whatever was kept in caves to be taken out now and then to dry. Some of the objects were packed in *totora* reeds.

Bill, too, had been utterly confused by all the rumors with which the village had been buzzing. To get more reliable information, he had left the governor's house and was lodging with a native family. He stopped me outside the church one Sunday and whispered:

"I am sorry I can't speak freely, but I can say one thing: there *are* secret caves on this island, and they *do* contain things of the kind you have got."

Arne suddenly recalled having been shown the area of "a lost cave full of small stone sculptures." He went straight back to his informant, old Pakomio, but now the frightened man refused to talk.

The next to come to me was Gonzalo. He felt profoundly unhappy over all the row he had caused in the village. He had been positive he had discovered that the cave sculptures were fraudulent, but something had now happened to make him change his mind: a strange experience of his own. A native boy had confided in him. The boy had been used by an old woman to climb down into a secret cave at Hanga Hemu, from which the woman wished to take figures for Señor Kon-Tiki. The boy had found a sculpture of a hen which lay as a kind of "key" stone in the first room of the cave, along with two skulls. But the tunnel into the next room had been blocked by fallen rock, so he did not get into the chamber where the old woman had said he should fetch some figures wrapped in plaited *totora* reed.

Gonzalo had become very excited when he heard the story, and after much persuasion he secured the boy's promise to show him the place. Gonzalo found the cave exactly as the boy had described it, with the two skulls and an artificial opening in the sidewall, where the tunnel leading farther in was blocked. But he found more. Someone had been there after the boy and had dug desperately both in the floor and the roof over the place where the rocks had fallen. Gonzalo forced his way ten feet into a narrow crack above this spot, and at the end of the passage he found a hole recently dug straight down to the tunnel beneath. He had thrust his arm down into the hole, but managed to grab only a handful of loose earth; in the earth lay pieces of rotten *totora* reed. Someone had already removed the ancient reed packages.

By this time I had been in the first caves. I asked Gonzalo if he knew who the old woman was. Yes, he knew. It was Analola's mother.

For me this was a valuable clue. It was Analola's mother and sister who had defended with tooth and claw the four great overturned stone heads when the young couple had found them in the field outside the village fence and wanted to sell them to me. The old woman had then furiously abused the finders as thieves of her family property, and had been delighted when I merely let the four grotesque faces roll back into position. Did she now want to show her gratitude by bringing me cave stones instead?

I thanked Gonzalo for this important piece of information, and left the village in the jeep together with the captain. I sat chuckling to myself. So Analola's mother had a cave. Fine. I had a special reason to take note of this.

The evening sun had already sunk into the sea, and it was dark when we stopped on the high land at the Vaitea sheep farm on our way home. Analola managed the farm, and she always came out for a friendly chat when we called for water. She was the most influential woman on the island, an intelligent beauty with flowing black hair and smiling brown eyes. Perhaps her nose was too wide and her lips too full to win a beauty contest in our own world, but out here in the Pacific she was the uncrowned queen of Easter Island. She was able and honest: everyone respected Analola.

When we drew up in front of the tap outside the wall at Vaitea, Analola and a couple of her girl friends came out with a light to help us draw the water. It was usually the captain who came to fetch it, and for the past few days Analola had been going on at him about the mayor having cheated Señor Kon-Tiki.

"There are no such things as secret caves. There's no one on the island who has stone figures," Analola had declared. "I was born here and have lived here all my life, *Capitán*. Tell Señor Kon-Tiki that he mustn't believe it."

Analola was an honest soul who never cared for loose talk, and at last the captain began to get upset.

"You see, when Analola says it—" he mused with a worried look. "The mayor *is* a bit of a rascal, you know."

Analola was what the natives called "a child of our time." Of her ancestors' customs but little remained. She was civilized more than in dress and manner. Only once had I seen a spark of superstition in her brown eyes.

"Is it true that you have talked to a stone statue?" she once asked me after the mayor, Lazarus, and I had found all the whales by the *ahu* at Anakena. "My mother says that a stone statue comes into your tent at night and tells you where to search."

"Nonsense," I said. "A stone statue can't come into my tent."

"Well, a little one could," said Analola.

Now she stood shivering in the chill of the evening and held a light for us as we worked the hose from the tap into the hole of our water tank.

"How's your mother, Analola?" I asked cautiously.

"Funny that you should ask that. She's just come to Vaitea to see me, and she's lying in my bed now."

I took Analola gently by the arm and asked her in a whisper to come with me behind the jeep while the others filled the tank. I had suddenly got an idea. I knew the vivid Polynesian imagination and their bent for obscure, allegoric references to sacred things, of which it was not good form to speak openly. I also knew from Gonzalo's report that Analola's mother had taken a stone chicken from her cave, and I guessed that there was probably a sculpture of a dog there too, as these were motifs recurring in the mayor's, Lazarus', and Atan's cave stones.

We went and stood under a dark eucalyptus tree.

"Analola," I whispered, and she looked up at me with a sweet expression. "Go in to your mother and give her this message from me: 'Chicken is good, but dog is better.' "

Analola stood completely bewildered. She stared at me with her lips apart for almost a minute; then she disappeared silently into the house. The water tank was full now. We waved to the other vahines and started off for Anakena.

The next evening the captain went up for water as usual. He returned to camp with a detailed report. Analola had told him all that had happened the previous evening, and the captain repeated it in her own words. She said that I had first spoken to her quietly in the night. Then her heart had told her: "Surely, Señor Kon-Tiki wants to make love." But afterward, when I whispered to her that chicken was good but dog was better, she thought: "Surely, Señor Kon-Tiki must have taken much wine." Nevertheless she had gone in to her mother and given the message. And she had never seen her mother so queer. The old woman had sat up in bed with a jerk and replied: "That's why I'm here. To go into the cave with you and Daniel Ika."

Analola had been utterly perplexed. Nothing of the kind

had ever happened to her before. Her mother was *mama-tia* to Daniel Ika, his aunt on his father's side. Analola had been so upset by what her mother had said that she had not slept all night. Next day her mother had come and asked her for two chickens, a piece of lamb, and four candles. When Analola asked if she was going to give a party, her mother had not replied.

Next evening the skipper came with a fresh report: Daniel Ika had arrived at Vaitea the night before, and had slept at the sheep farm. Analola had peeped through the keyhole to his room and had seen that her mother was there as well. The two of them had been planning the visit to the cave, and Daniel had managed to persuade his aunt not to take Analola. She would bring "bad luck," he had said, for Analola was a child of our time and would give her secrets away to anyone who could win her favors.

They had decided to visit the cave two nights later, and had agreed where they should dig an *umu* to bake the hens. Analola had understood that this cave was at Vai-tara-kai-ua, which was just west of the Anakena Valley.

"That's funny," the chief engineer said when the captain repeated the story at lunch. "The Second and I have often been for an evening walk over to the place with that queer name. It's so pretty there, with a little clump of green trees where wild chickens are often sitting about. Each time we've been there we've seen old Timoteo, the man who made the reed boats. He says he sleeps there at night because he's so fond of chicken."

The night watch on board our ship told us that he had seen faint smoke from that direction the last few mornings.

Then came the night when Analola's mother and Daniel Ika were to steal to the cave. They came back next morning with long faces. Analola told us that they had baked their chickens somewhere up on the plateau, but they had not got to the cave; they had found someone spending the night at Vai-tara-kai-ua.

Exactly the same thing happened the next night. This time they had seen that the mysterious person was old Timoteo, and they guessed that he had a cave there himself and was watching the entrance so that Señor Kon-Tiki's men should not find it. Analola's mother had decided to make a third attempt, and if they were again unlucky, it was a sign that they ought not to enter the cave. In that case she and Daniel would give up and go back to the village.

We learned from Analola when they were next to visit the cave at Vai-tara-kai-ua, and I decided to keep old Timoteo away from the place on that night. When the appointed evening approached, the sea was calm and glassy. Some of our men had been out by moonlight the night before catching rock lobster with native girl friends. This was one of the island's great delicacies: it is really a big lobster without claws. Our frogman could often spear it in underwater caves, but the simplest way was to wade breast-high in the water along the shore at night with flaming torches. The native vahines were very skillful at this. They trod on the great creatures and held them fast with their toes till they could plunge down to pick them up and put them in a sack.

That evening the cook had twenty-one big fellows in his pot, and we were going to have a lobster party in the mess tent. Lazarus had brought us a huge sack of newly gathered pineapples, the juiciest we had ever tasted.

I had kept old Timoteo at work all that day. I sent him out to the ship to repair his own reed boat, which had been knocked about a good deal on deck before we hung it out of the way down in the hold. I now had no further need for the old man, but I wanted to keep him away from the valley. So when evening came, and Timoteo wanted to go ashore, I brought him a large meal and asked him—purely as a ruse—to take the night watch on board.

"We're going to have a *fiesta* in the camp," I explained. "All hands are going ashore tonight to eat lobsters. The sea's quite calm, so nothing can happen."

Timoteo did not look altogether happy. I had a feeling that the old man would be capable of taking a reed *pora* to swim ashore. I therefore took him up to the barometer and placed a chair in front of it.

"If the barometer goes down to that mark," I said, pointing to the bottom figure to be on the safe side, "then you must blow the siren at once."

259

Timoteo took his instructions in dead earnest. He sat down with his nose against the glass of the barometer and his eyes fixed rigidly on the needle while he swallowed his food. I knew that he would not move now. When the night watch and the engineers came on board again, they would see about sleeping quarters for him.

While Timoteo sat dutifully staring at the barometer, we of the expedition were gathered at our lobster party in the mess tent, and up in the hills somewhere above Vai-tara-kai-ua Daniel and Analola's mother were creeping down the valley toward the cave. As I was picking out the meat from the last leg, I thought they must certainly have dug the baked fowl out of the earth oven by now and no doubt were moving on, taking the candles with them for use underground.

The night passed.

Early next morning Timoteo came ashore with the engineers. He said he must ride off at once to talk to his wife.

"Where is she?" I asked.

"In the village," he replied. He turned slowly and looked at me with a peculiar smile. Then he added: "But last night she may have slept at Vai-tara-kai-ua. Who knows?"

This was a curious remark.

"What's your wife's name?" I asked.

"Her name is Victoria Atan. But she likes to call herself Tahu-tahu. And she is a bit *tahu-tahu*." [1]

Timoteo climbed up on his horse and rode off.

The captain drove up to Vaitea for water extra early that day. The report he brought back was that Daniel and Analola's mother had returned to the village. They had given up all hope of getting into the cave at Vai-tara-kai-ua unseen. When they had made their final attempt the night before, Timoteo was gone, but his old wife had been there.

How Timoteo had managed to warn Tahu-tahu we never discovered. She relieved him only for that one night. But the old man continued to guard the little valley zealously so long as we were on the island. The veil of secrecy lies undisturbed over the two family caves at Vai-tara-kai-ua. It is for Timoteo, Tahu-tahu, and Analola's old mother to decide whether they

---

[1] *Tahu-tahu* or *tahu* means "sorcery" or "witchcraft."

will try to hand on the secret to their own "children of our time." And they must decide soon. For if anything happens to these aged people, two caves with all their irreplaceable contents will be lost forever in the depths of Easter Island.

Daniel Ika had a twin and one half-brother. The twin was Alberto: it was he who had shown two *rongo-rongo* tablets in the village and put them back in the cave because he was invaded by *aku-akus* at night. The half-brother was called Enlique Ika: he was of royal blood and had the right to the noble title *Ariki-paka*. Both Father Sebastian and the governor had pointed him out as a unique specimen, because he simply could not tell a lie. This was a rare virtue on Easter Island. Among us in the camp he was known as the "Royal Son," by reason of his proud nature, his stately appearance, and his noble birth. He could not read, but his unshakable honesty had made him the Navy's most respected shepherd, and he lived in a stone hut on the road to Rano Raraku.

One day after the *cocongo* had passed, he came riding in and offered to make a trade. We had some stout pine beams which we used to support the tall statues when we dug around their bases. He wanted to build himself a new house with these. If I was willing to trade I should get a fat ox for every third beam.

"You shall have all the beams if you'll give us cave stones in exchange," I said.

This was quite a random shot, a sudden inspiration. I had no idea whether the "Royal Son" had a cave at all, or even knew what cave stones were. He was completely taken by surprise and wriggled for a moment in a desperate attempt to lead the conversation into other channels. But I stuck to my offer, and as he realized there was no escape, he said firmly:

"But I don't know where the entrance is. I wish I did know, Señor Kon-Tiki."

"Have you tried to bake a chicken in an *umu takapu?*" I asked sternly. "Have you tried to make *tahu* in front of the cave?"

He was utterly flabbergasted. His expression changed completely.

"I'll talk to my brothers," he said at last. "I can't decide myself. I have only a share."

I learned that the entrance to one of his family caves had been lost. But he and his brother Daniel were sort of "sleeping partners" in another cave, the entrance to which only Alberto knew. The "Royal Son" knew that the stones there were in packages of *totora* reeds, and that the cave also contained *rongo-rongo* and some old paddles. But the finest objects were a stone sailing vessel which he referred to as a *vaka oho*, and a statue of smoothly polished black stone, so large that it reached up to a man's stomach.

The "Royal Son" had searched for the cave many a time, for Alberto refused to show the entrance to his brothers. He did not mind sitting in the village describing the position of the cave to them, but he dared not point it out on the spot for fear the *aku-aku* would see him.

Several days passed before the "Royal Son" appeared again. Then one day he came riding in with some large melons, and while he was unloading them he whispered across the back of the horse that he would be able to get me some old figures. His wife had been weeping and complaining for several days because she had an incompetent husband who could not find his own family cave. When nothing availed, and her husband always came home empty-handed, she had set to work on her own old uncle instead, and begged him for help, so that they could get beams for a new house. She had heard from her grandmother that the uncle knew the entrance to a cave in which she herself had a share, because her father was dead. The uncle, who was living with them in the stone hut at the time, grew weary of all this weeping. The upshot of it was that the old man promised to show them the way to the cave.

The uncle was old Santiago Pakarati, who had helped his brother Timoteo build the reed boats. The four old brothers were now working for me as fishermen. Since I had to provide full board for the natives who were digging at Rano Raraku, I carried on the tradition customary in the stonecutters' time: I selected a special team with no other duties than to work in shifts day and night catching fish and lobsters for all the men in the quarry. This helped us to stretch the meat, rice, and sugar, which were coming ashore from the ship in alarming quantities. Finally we had to keep all the flour for our own use. Only the four Pakarati brothers came to the camp regularly to receive stale bread which they dipped in coffee and ate as cake. We had become especially friendly with old Santiago, who was in the camp every day and collected his brothers' bread and tobacco rations.

We had once attempted to simplify the rationing system by making the distribution once a week instead of daily. But such an arrangement was not practicable on Easter Island. The whole native labor force sat up all night eating and smoking, and came to work next day with green faces, having consumed the whole week's ration. They had passed a splendid night, but then Santiago declared that they must have more cigarettes, or they would go for a whole week with nothing to smoke. Everyone was pleased when we introduced daily rations again: saving is an incomprehensible idea. Let the morrow take care of itself. *Haka-le* was the island's motto. It means something like "never mind." A native would say it if he lost his knife, smashed a bowl—or indeed, if his whole house burned down.

In this easygoing atmosphere of *haka-le*, the *aku-akus* seemed sadly out of place. The natives accordingly did all they could to avoid them, though nothing to get rid of them. They lurked on the cliffs, a blot on the general happiness. Old Santiago was a carefree character, always satisfied with life and ready to joke and laugh. But his face fell into gloomy furrows and he grew almost angry when Arne wanted to camp alone by the crater lake in Rano Raraku. Santiago would not at any price have set foot inside the statue crater alone at night, for *aku-akus* lurked behind the statues and they would whistle at him from the reeds in the lake. I was therefore particularly surprised that old "Uncle Santiago" was the one who had now offered to accompany us to a cave.

It was late at night when the jeep stopped at the little stone hut on the road to Rano Raraku. I had chosen Arne among the archaeologists because he knew Santiago best. The captain, the second officer, and Sanchez from Chile were with us too, in the hope that they might also be allowed in the cave.

The "Royal Son" came out of his hut quickly with his wife and a young man who, they explained, was Santiago's son.

"But where is Santiago?"

"He's ill. He can't come. But he has explained to his son where the cave is."

I knew that old story. It was a disappointing change in the program which never led to any result. I went into the hut to see how ill Santiago was. There he sat squatting on the floor in a corner, staring ahead with a sad expression. He gave a dry, forced cough when he saw me come in. Santiago had no sign of fever, and there was nothing else to indicate that the old man was ill. But it was easy to see that he profoundly regretted what he had promised to do.

"Santiago, you're as fit as a tunafish, you old rascal. Surely you aren't afraid of the *aku-akus* when I'm with you?"

Santiago eagerly grabbed a cigarette and whinnied so hard that all the smile wrinkles moved up to his ears like the folds of an accordion.

"I've got a pain in my back, Señor."

"Then you must give up smoking."

"It isn't *that* bad."

I went on chaffing the old man for a long time until, half-resisting, he came out and crawled into the jeep with an uncertain grin. Now we were nine in the jeep. Santiago sat squeezed in by my side, silent and grave, and showed the way. From Rano Raraku we turned off along the south coast and followed some faint cart ruts along the edge of the cliff. We had to hold on tight, for although it was almost impossible to see the track, it was very easy to feel it.

"This isn't a cave for hiding things, Señor," said the old man suddenly, in the hope of my losing interest.

"Isn't there anything in it, then?"

"Oh, yes, a little. I haven't been there since I was seventeen. An old woman showed me the place before she died."

The old man asked us to stop the jeep before we came to Vaihu, and we covered the rest of the way on foot. There was bright moonlight when we went down to the edge of the cliff. Again I saw silver-gray breakers in the night, hammering away at the lava barricade beneath us. Santiago was carrying a homemade rope ladder, composed of two thin ropes with a few irregular sticks as rungs. Right out on the edge of the cliff he was handed a bag by the "Royal Son's" wife, and he took out the familiar baked chicken wrapped in banana leaves. He asked me to eat the tail, because it was "to me" he was showing the cave. There were baked sweet potatoes in the bag too, but only the chicken's bony tail stump was eaten, and I was the only one to taste anything. The rest of the delicious chicken was left behind on a rock.

Then the old man suddenly began to sing a monotonous song in a subdued voice over the cliffside toward the sea. The tune stopped abruptly, as if broken off in the middle. Then he turned quietly to me and said I must promise to leave one thing behind in the cave. It did not matter what it was, but something must be left there. This was "the law," he explained. The cave was his. There were some distant relatives of his lying inside. That was why he had sung the name of the legal owner of the cave for the *aku-aku*.

Santiago slipped the top rung of the rope ladder over a block of lava right on the edge of the plateau, and flung the rest of it over the precipice.

I lay prone with my head over the edge and turned the flashlight downward. We were on an overhang, for the rope ladder was dangling loose in the air just below. Santiago ordered only his son to undress, keeping merely his shorts on. He was to go down first. It was difficult to get a grip where the ropes stretched tight near the edge, and the few rungs were a long way apart. The roaring breakers were only thirty feet below, but a drop of even six feet would have been enough for a man to kill himself on the jagged lava in the surf.

About twelve feet below us the descending man vanished. The rope ladder hung empty. I reached as far out as I could with the light, but saw nobody. He had obviously left the ladder and crept into a hole in the cliff. When the "Royal Son" followed suit, he too disappeared from the ladder at the same place. When I was about to descend, we saw to our astonishment that the "Royal Son" was on the ladder again, climbing up as fast as fingers and toes could get a grip.

"Did you see anything?" I asked.

"Yes, a long tunnel going into a cave."

"And what was in the cave?"

"Oh, I didn't see. I didn't go in, for I'm not used to caves."

"Because he isn't used to caves, he's afraid of the devils," old Santiago explained.

And the "Royal Son" had to admit that this was so. His wife looked at him in alarm and was clearly glad to have him back.

When I was on my way down the rope ladder, I was quite as frightened as my native predecessor. But my fear was due to rather different causes. I thought of the lump of lava which held the ladder as I struggled with the stick rungs which were set wide apart and often were tightly pressed against the rock. Not till I had a knee bent up to my chin could I reach the next rung with the tip of my toe. I was soon down to the point at which the ladder hung suspended in the air away from the rock, and immediately I caught sight of the narrow hole in the cliff face.

Holding tight with a hand on each rope I had to work my body through the dangling ladder till the tips of my toes reached into the little hole. I managed to push my legs in as far as the thighs, but with my whole body swaying in the air and my arms clinging to the ladder, I could get no purchase. The rope ladder only swung farther from the cliff if I pushed at it. I had hardly any back left when at last I had wriggled and squeezed in as far as my waist. Now I could let go of the dangling rope with one hand while I fumbled for a hold on the rock wall with the other. The rope swung away as if it wanted to drag me out of the hole again until finally I let go with the other hand too. There I hung, face upward, half inside the rock and half outside. This part of the trip had been child's play for the "Royal Son." Not till I was inside the rock up to my neck did I feel easy. I breathed a sigh of relief when I had shoved myself some yards into the crack to where it opened into a cave half the height of a man. It was at this very point that the "Royal Son" had become scared and had retreated.

Santiago's son had lit a candle inside. When I sat up in the cave, I saw that we were surrounded by skeletons. Here San-

tiago's distant relatives lay. They had been packed in *totora-*
reed mats which were now brown and quite rotten; they fell
to bits if we touched them. Some of the bones inside had a
curious blue-green color. I saw that small packages of the
same decomposed reed lay alongside two skeletons which
were stretched side by side at my knees. I felt one package
cautiously with my fingers; the reeds were brittle and crumbled at the slightest pressure, but there was something hard
inside.

At this moment we nearly had a fatal accident. Arne was
now busy doing acrobatics at the entrance to the cave. While
struggling desperately to get himself free of the rope ladder
and into the narrow hole, he broke a rib. He broke it so emphatically that he afterward insisted he had heard it crack,
and the pain was so intense that he was barely able to retain
his grip on the ladder.

We got Arne into the cave, and what he saw almost made
him forget his pain. He crawled about patiently in the low,
uncomfortable grotto. It was incomprehensible how in old
days they had managed to get their dead down the cliff and
into the narrow hole.

Father Sebastian had told me of natives who had crawled
into caves like this when they knew death was near. After
Christianity was introduced in the last century, with compulsory burial in the churchyard at Hangaroa, some of the old
people had stolen into their secret caves so that their skeletons
might remain there, hidden forever. The last person who had
succeeded in burying himself alive in his cave was a man
known as Teave, grandfather to people still living.

But the skeletons we had round us now had been wrapped
in reed mats. The relatives must have let these dead down the
cliff with ropes, while other natives, lying in the passage, had
drawn the bodies in after them.

The captain, the second officer, and Sanchez had also come
in. Only Santiago and the disheartened "Royal Son" with his
wife remained on the plateau above us. We photographed
and made sketches as well as we could under the low roof,
and then we began to examine the cave's contents. Here and
there skeletons lay stretched out on the floor, and the only

burial goods which accompanied them were evidently the small parcels of reeds. A few of the parcels were already completely disintegrated, so we could see what was inside.

The largest parcel contained a female figure carved in stone. From another a double face peered out, with four eyes and two noses which vanished in a curve round the stone and met as spearheads on the other side. At the far end of the cave lay a solitary skeleton with a parcel beside it, and the plaited reeds had kept so well that large pieces held together when we took it all with us. Inside the parcel was a sculpture of a lobster, like the one which had started all the row about the mayor's cave stones. Perhaps it was an old fisherman who lay here in the corner with his favorite magic stone, since a fisherman would have a special interest in increasing the power and fertility of lobsters.

There were only ten sculptures in this cave and all had been packed in reeds. Two of them were almost alike, a small statue of a standing man with a bird's beak. We left one of these behind in accordance with our promise to old Santiago.

To crawl out into the cool night again, we had to lie on our backs and kick ourselves along headfirst. Next, to reach the rope ladder, we had to edge ourselves out of the hole until the back was unsupported from the waist up, our arms stretched over our heads. Then we had to swing ourselves out and up the dangling ladder. It was an unpleasant piece of acrobatics with the surf below us and only the moon providing light. Unpleasant was a mild word when Arne's turn came, with his broken rib. But all went well, and the three who stood waiting anxiously up on the cliff thought merely that Arne was stiff after his climb.

We had carefully packed the contents of the cave, and now we hauled them up with the aid of ropes. When the last load was up, and Santiago had made sure that we had left one thing down below, I caught sight of the chicken which lay on the rock. The smell tempted me irresistibly. I was not going to let the *aku-aku* have this. And the *aku-aku* took no revenge when I helped myself freely to his portion and shared it with my men. But the natives refused to touch a scrap of it and kept away with worried looks until the last gnawed bone was hurled into the sea. Then the woman began to pluck up courage. She laughed with contempt at her husband for having been afraid to crawl into the cave. The farther she got from the cliff, the bolder she became. And as we sat squeezed together in the jeep, bumping home in the moonlight, I felt sorry for the proud man in the back seat. His wife jeered and laughed and teased him till he could not help smiling at himself. He shook his head and declared that he would never be so silly again. Now he knew better. Never again in his life would he let himself be frightened by ghosts and devils. He would go straight home and build the family a new house.

There was another person on the island who was more accustomed to converse with devils than the "Royal Son." As it happened, it was the mayor's youngest brother, little Atan, who introduced me to him and unconsciously dragged me right into a hornets' nest. When he had disposed of his own cave and obtained more useful things in exchange, he was no longer in doubt that it brought "good luck" to get rid of the underground business altogether. Atan had many friends in the village, everyone liked Atan, and he tried with the greatest caution to worm out of them information as to who had a cave.

One evening I was on my way, with other members of the expedition, to a party at the governor's house. Atan and the mayor were with us in the jeep; we had offered to drop them off at the village. Atan had recently told me that he had long suspected his brother-in-law, Andres Haoa, of having a cave. Now at last his suspicion had been confirmed.

"Do you remember Andres Haoa, Señor Kon-Tiki?" he had said. "It was he who showed you fragments of *ipu maengo*. All the time he has had those pieces, and the whole jars he showed to Father Sebastian, hidden in his cave."

For Andres Haoa to be the man was a most unfortunate circumstance. He had been greatly offended by me because I had accused him of trickery, and not given him the full reward the time he had strewn tiny bits of pottery fragments in our excavation at Ahu Tepeu. Little Atan realized this, but proposed that I should send Andres Haoa a present, which he felt sure would put things straight. I handed Atan two cartons of cigarettes and a few dollars, and it was agreed that I should come to Atan's house when the governor's party was over late that night. Meanwhile Atan would try to arrange a meeting.

Just before midnight I left the governor's bungalow. I had informed him that I was taking part in secret trips to the island underworld, but that I was pledged to silence and could give no complete report till it was all over. The governor was grateful for the information and somewhat relieved. He had heard the strange rumors which were going about in the village, but queer things were always being said in Hangaroa, and no one took the native gossip seriously.

At midnight I entered Atan's little hut. He opened the door himself, and the first thing I saw in the light of a flickering candle was my old "enemy" Andres Haoa, unshaven and bristly, staring at me with bloodshot eyes. He jumped up from the bench, embraced me and called me brother, assuring me that he would give me all the help he could. The tiny room was full of big words. Good-natured little Atan flung out his chest and boasted of his own *mana:* it was he who had saved the friendship between us two who now met again in his house. He had inherited his powerful *mana* from his mother. She had chosen him to take over all the strength of her soul; she had liked him best of all her children, although he was the youngest.

He told me that Andres Haoa had been quite beside himself when he saw my gifts of friendship. Andres himself admitted that he had wept for joy when he received the presents and heard the message of reconciliation. He had been in an awkward corner that time when, purely as a friendly act, he had brought me a fragment of real *maengo,* for I had at once demanded that he should show me the place where he had found it. Of course, he could not show me his family cave, and that was where it had come from. He was therefore compelled to take us to another place to draw attention from his cave.

Andres' story did not sound improbable.

And now Andres had heard so much from Atan that he would like to give me the "key," that I might see the pottery with my own eyes. But he had a younger brother who was as hard as flint, and he must first be won over to my side. This younger brother was the chief of the cave. He had been given the "key" by their father, although he was not the eldest. He "lived with" the *aku-aku* and had been very annoyed when Andres had called at his home that evening to suggest they give the "key" to Señor Kon-Tiki.

"Let us go to his brother together," little Atan proposed. "We should be able to persuade him with our combined *mana.*"

I was wearing white tropicals for the party, but now changed into a darker shirt and shorts I had with me, and then we all three sneaked out into the night away from the village in a northerly direction. We walked and walked in the moonlight, and the more we walked and whispered, the more fervent became the talk of friendship and brotherhood. Atan had unlimited confidence in our combined *mana,* and he declared that he himself was a more genuine Norwegian long-ear than I.

During the conversation both of them cautioned me that if Andres' younger brother, Juan Haoa, tried to lead me into a trap by giving me the "key" to the cave, I was to say no, and cross my arms. If he then gave the "key" to his older brother Andres, I was to accept it with thanks from him.

Outside the village we came to a desolate region, where at last we stopped before a high stone wall. Behind the wall great glistening banana leaves stretched up stiff and motionless against the moon, and half-hidden among the trees lay a low whitewashed stone hut. There were no windows and the place had a sinister, uninhabited look. Nothing indicated that anyone lived there. A rotten ladder, with some of its rungs broken, led up the stone wall and over the other side.

Little Atan braced himself: he was to go in first and announce our arrival. The ladder gave a nasty creak as he climbed over the wall; a moment later he was at the door, knocking slowly and cautiously. We saw a glimmer of light from the crack of the door as someone let him in.

Atan was gone for five minutes. He came out alone, and when he was with us again, he looked forlorn and miserable.

Andres' younger brother had been terribly difficult. We must all three go in and get our combined *aku-akus* to work on him. We climbed over the wall and went up to the hut together. I entered first, with the other two at my heels. In a room furnished with nothing but a white-painted table and three short benches we were confronted by two tough-looking fellows who stared at us with hostile expressions. They appeared ready for anything except a joke. One might have been about thirty, the other a little over forty.

I said good evening, and they returned my greeting without stirring, without moving even a muscle of their faces. The younger stood erect, head back, with a grave expression, like an Indian in a Wild West film. He had piercing black eyes, and round his mouth and chin he had a black stubbly beard, just as his brother behind me. It was unusual to see a beard on the island, even if the mayor, Atan, and some others had managed to grow mustaches. He stood straddle-legged with his arms inside the opening of his shirt, so that part of his chest was bare. He gave me a penetrating look with half-shut eyes and said, slowly and intensely, like a man in a trance:

"Watch my *aku-aku*. This is the *aku-aku's* house."

Now I should have to keep a cool head. I had put my foot into it, and the expressions of those fellows showed unmistakably that I was in it up to my neck.

"I know," I said, "I can see."

He brushed my remark aside as if in irritation, and took a few slow steps toward me in a challenging manner till he was looking right into my face. Then he almost hissed, with suppressed, quivering anger: "Show me your *aku-aku's* power!"

It was evident that Atan had been talking big about me and my *aku-aku:* the four men expected to see a miracle. Their expressions were eager and tense, with contemptuous challenge too in the bearded face which was now so close to my own. He gave the impression of being drunk, but he was not. He was in a state of self-hypnosis, almost in a trance. He *was* his own *aku-aku*.

I went two inches nearer till our chests almost touched, and then took a deep breath to be equal to the situation.

"If your *aku-aku* is as powerful as mine," I said, putting the same note of suppressed contempt into my voice, "you can send him out through the door. Send him up to the top of Orongo. Down into the crater of Rano Kao. Across the plain at Vinapu. To the statues in Rano Raraku. To Anakena, Hangaroa, all round the island. Ask him if the island is changed. Ask him if everything has not become better. Ask him if old walls and buildings have not reappeared, and unknown statues risen up out of the ground. When you get your *aku-aku's* answer, I'll ask you: Do you need any more proof of my *aku-aku's* power?"

The man did not hesitate for a moment. He promptly agreed. He asked me to sit beside him on one of the benches.

Little Atan felt quite confident again. He and Andres at once began to ask the brother to give me the "key," and soon the other fellow joined them too and politely suggested that I ought to get it. But the principal player sitting beside me did not move a muscle and did not condescend to listen to what they said. He sat with folded arms as on a golden throne, bolt upright with mouth shut tight and lips protruding exactly like the great statues! Through pure autosuggestion he had inflated himself in his own and his friends' eyes, like a self-worshiping medicine man or priest-king brought out of the mists of antiquity and thrust into shirt and trousers.

The other three stood before him begging him for the "key," but he ignored them completely. They kept on begging him with hands outstretched as in humble prayer: one of them, indeed, went down on his knees before him in supplication.

The man beside me sat for a long time enjoying the others' obeisance. He sat there as if basking in sunlight, slowly turning his head from one side to the other. Now and again he turned to me stiffly and emphasized his claim to immense spiritual power, to *mana*. His supernatural strength came from many sources, for he had in his veins blood of two of the most important tribes. And this was the *aku-aku's* house. He was surrounded by *aku-akus* who protected him on all sides. Behind him he had the mightiest *aku-aku* in the island: he lived in front of old Tahu-tahu's hut, and she was his wife's aunt. The two had no other living neighbors. A little farther down to the right was a deserted hut; it belonged to a woman who had died, and only an *aku-aku* lived there now. He had one behind him, one on each side, and one in the house.

An uncanny glow came into the bearded fellow's eyes. The more he blew himself up the more dangerous and fanatical he became, so I hastened to interrupt him. Now I started to brag: it was just as if I had borrowed his pump and was using it to inflate my own reputation. The air gradually went out of my neighbor as he listened.

I told him that I had inherited a powerful *mana* from Teriieroo, my mighty father by adoption, the last great chief of Tahiti. Before he died he gave me the royal name Terai Mateata, or "Blue Sky." And when our raft landed on Raroia ten years later, I got still more *mana*, for a feast was held in memory of Tikaroa, the first island king, and I was adopted as *Varoa Tikaroa*, the "Spirit of Tikaroa."

No more was needed; the bearded fanatic at last gave way. He rose slowly, and the rest of us did the same. Then he pointed to his big solemn friend and said:

"Tumu, bear witness!"

I had read of the word *tumu* before. It was not a name, but a title. Earlier explorers had mentioned it as a mystic word dating from the original social system of Easter Island, a word which even the natives no longer quite understood and could not explain. Now a *tumu* stood before me in the flesh. His functions were not buried with the past: here he was in full activity. Atan told me afterward that this man, Juan Nahoe, was *tumu* for the Haoa family. He was arbitrator and judge in the brothers' family affairs.

The bearded fanatic drew himself up close in front of me, and Tumu stepped silently beside him.

"Hereby I transfer to you the 'key' to one of my two caves," he said in a sepulchral voice, as if pronouncing a sentence of death.

The others stood silent as the grave and even the flame of the candle did not flicker.

Now this was a dilemma. Was *this* the moment when I was supposed to fold my arms and say *no*? Verbally he offered me the "key"; but he did not hand it to me, nor did I see it. I hesitated for a moment, and then replied dryly, "Thank you," without moving a finger. He stood motionless for a long time, peering at me with his jet-black eyes. Then he quickly turned and marched out of the door with such stern pride in his bearing that he almost leaned backwards.

The other three seemed unspeakably relieved. Little Atan wiped away the sweat trickling down his brow, though the only source of warmth was the little candle now flickering in the wake of the departed man. Eagerly gesticulating and relaxed, the three left in the room were a marked contrast to the one who had just stalked out.

A few minutes passed, and then the unpleasant fellow came back with a light flat parcel under his arm, and a heavy basket in his hand. Both were made of plaited *totora* reed. He gave the flat parcel to his brother, who laid it on the table, and then he stood motionless in front of me again, holding the basket. I also remained entirely motionless, with no expression but defiant contempt and utter indifference.

He turned abruptly to his elder brother Andres and gave him the basket. Andres handed it on to me, and I accepted it, thanking the younger brother for having first given the "key" to his elder brother and not directly to me. The aggressive fellow did not seem to be at all mollified. He stood for another moment or two without speaking. Then he pointed to the parcel on the table and subjected me to a new ordeal.

"What is inside this parcel?" he demanded. "Show your *aku-aku's* power!"

Once more all four were standing round me, staring and tense. I racked my brains. It was like a horrible nightmare; I felt that anything might happen if I did not pass the test. The parcel was as large as a briefcase and much too flat to contain any stone or wooden object. It was made of nicely plaited reeds and had seemed as light as a large envelope when Andres laid it on the table. I realized that what I had in my hand must be the "key" to the cave, and I took it for granted that the parcel on the table also came from the cave. The plaiting of both parcel and basket were exactly the same.

I thought of the pretty feather work the natives had often brought us. They were copies of old feather hats and long strings of feathers used in dancing. Early visitors to Easter

Island had seen prominent men with waving crowns of feathers on their heads, wearing feather cloaks, just like the kings in ancient Mexico and South America. Was it possible that there was something of this kind, but more recent, in Andres' cave? Feather work was certainly not a bad guess. But if so, was it a headdress or what? The others waited, faces taut with excitement. I must stand the test.

"My *aku-aku* says *con pluma,* 'with feather,' " I said cautiously, trying not to be too specific.

"No!" the fanatic snarled. "*No!*" he repeated in a frenzy. "Ask your *aku-aku* again!"

Triumphant, he crouched forward like a cat about to spring, and enjoyed the situation with an angry grin on his face. Little Atan wiped away the beads of sweat and looked quite desperate. He gazed at me entreatingly, as if to tell me that now I must do everything I could to make my *aku-aku* see reason.

Tumu and Andres seemed menacingly suspicious, and they too had slowly drawn nearer. I did not like the situation. These people were fanatical, and I had, uninvited, poked my nose into the most inflammable recesses of their private lives. If anything happened, not a soul knew where I was. From this remote hut not a sound would reach the village. My friends would think that I had fallen over a cliff or been trapped in a secret cave. Nowhere in the world were there so many hiding places in which a man could disappear forever without leaving a trace.

I had no idea what the parcel contained. It could only be pure guesswork. Could it be *tapa,* or bark cloth?

"Something to wear," I hazarded.

"No! Ask your *aku-aku* once more and ask well!"

They all drew closer to me in a threatening manner, and half my brain weighed the chances of fighting my way out, while the other half went on speculating what there could be in the parcel.

"A material," I tried as a last way out, using the technique of "animal, vegetable, or mineral" of the radio programs.

A queer grunt was the reply, and I was asked to open the parcel while they all stood round me black as thunderclouds. I untied a string of reed fiber and drew out an unbound book full of *rongo-rongo* signs. It was something like the priceless book I had been shown by the village skipper. The hieroglyphic ideograms were drawn in ink, ink that had faded with age.

Suddenly it flashed into my mind that in Spanish the word for "pen" was the same as for "feather." I slammed the book down on the table so hard that I almost put out the light, and drew myself up indignantly.

"My *aku-aku* was right!" I said. "He said *con pluma,* and this indeed is written *con pluma!*"

All their faces changed immediately. They drew themselves away and looked at each other foolishly. It was they who had been wrong. Even the savage fellow with the stubbly beard and the flashing eyes had changed completely. He had not thought of it in that way. Little Atan broke the spell. He was so astonished, he could only stammer:

"Oh, what a powerful *aku-aku* you have!"

This kindled a spark of jealousy in my bearded opponent.

"Look at the *aku-aku* in the book," he said. "Look at it!"

He turned over large pages like those of a fantastic picture book till he came to a place at which he laid it open. The left-hand page was covered with mysterious picture writing without explanation. On the right twenty picture signs were repeated and translated into the natives' own tongue in clumsy lettering. At the bottom of the page a separate line was written in faded brown ink.

"There's the *aku-aku,*" he grunted, pointing to the single line.

I read: *Kokava aro, kokava tua, te igoa o te akuaku, erua.*

" 'When worn out at the front and worn out at the back, make a new one,' " the owner said proudly in Spanish. "That's the name of the *aku-aku* in the book."

It struck me that this was very clever. The original maker of the book had added a piece of practical advice, so that his heirs would never dare to let the book fall to pieces and the text be lost. He had turned his advice into an *aku-aku,* so that no one would fail to respect it.

"There's the *aku-aku,*" the man repeated, placing his finger on the sentence, that we might all admire it.

"It's a powerful book," I said, and realized that I had chosen the right adjective instead of saying "interesting," "pretty," or "well-made." It appeared that the man could not read the contents, but regarded the book as pure magic.

From this moment on we were all the best of friends: I was called brother and received admiring looks from all sides. But still I did not feel wholly secure.

"Now we are brothers," the man said, placing both his hands on my shoulders. "Now we will drink each other's blood!"

Little Atan looked at him with mingled fear and admiration. I hardened myself in soul and body and tried not to show any feeling. After the mental anguish I had endured, no one was going to frighten me that night with a scratch from a knife. But the thought of drinking that fellow's blood was unendurable. I remembered the mayor and Atan once telling Ed and me that they sometimes mixed their ancestors' bone meal with water and drank it to get "power." Presumably it was something of the kind we were going to do now.

The grim man marched as stiff as a post into a little back room, and I expected him to return with a knife. Instead he came back with a bottle and five glasses. He opened the bottle and poured some into each glass; the others only got a red splash at the bottom, but I got a full glass. Then each of us had to repeat the magic word *takapu* again and again. Atan had told me before that this was a word which gave *mana,* so that the *aku-aku* could see. Earlier investigators have translated this Easter Island word as "ceremonial earth oven," but this is wrong. The word has nothing to do with an earth oven unless *umu* precedes it, and then it is *umu* that means "earth oven."

When we had repeated the magic word often enough, I sniffed at the dirty glass unnoticed. It was red wine he had procured on board the *Pinto.* Before we drank, the leader said in a gruesome voice:

"Now we will drink our mingled blood."

The idea that wine was blood he must have acquired from the church. We emptied our glasses and he filled them again, an inch for himself and the others and a full glass for me.

"You are our leading brother, drink well," said the bearded fellow in good humor, and I was glad that he was not the one to drink freely. Now there was big talk of *aku-akus* and brotherhood. I was their chief, and I had the "key"—the "key" to their cave and to "good luck" for all five of us. As far as I could understand, Tumu was now responsible for the second cave, but even that was mine if I came back and settled down among them for good.

The bottle was soon empty, and I had had the benefit of most of it.

"Look at my beard," said the black-stubbled bandit who had now become my younger brother. "That's where my strength lies," he said triumphantly.

I was sorry they had not seen me as I looked when I had been on the raft for 101 days. But they had now accepted my strength even though I was clean-shaven.

I had never enjoyed a drink so much, or needed it so badly. I felt in excellent form and looked at my watch. It was three in the morning. It was a long way to the camp, and I must see about getting home. As I was picking up the valuable *rongo-rongo* book and the basket containing the "key" to the cave, my brothers said that they would come and see me at the camp next day, and then we must have a meal of my food together. I bade them all welcome, and walked out into the fresh cool night with Tumu, Andres, and Atan.

Next day my new brothers called for me and took me to the top of a hill. Here the fanatic clambered up onto a mound and began a speech in a hushed voice to an invisible audience out over the sea to right and left of him. He held the *rongo-rongo* book in the reed case under his left arm, while he gesticulated heavenward with his right. He spoke in Polynesian in a low, almost inaudible voice, but looked like an orator mounted on a soapbox at a street corner. He pointed toward the sky and toward us, as excited as if he was trying to hold the attention of some great invisible crowd gathered on the sea and the plain below us. He stood there with open shirt and unbuttoned jacket fluttering in the wind, with one foot far away in antiquity and one foot with us—typifying a people in transition.

When the speech was over, he presented me with a fine wood carving of a sailfish. Then, still in an emotional state, he took out the *rongo-rongo* book and turned the pages vigorously till he came to the page where the *aku-aku* was. He delivered another speech in a hushed voice to all the invisible people round him, keeping his finger on the line. And then he asked me to take the book from him and read the *aku-aku* aloud.

With the three men standing reverently beside me, and overlooking a great part of the strange island below us, I read again:

Kokava aro, kokava tua, te igoa o te akuaku, erua.

They listened reverently and with admiration, and then the ceremony was at an end. Their forefathers had been called upon to witness that the book was now legally made over to me. We climbed down from the hill, down to the green tents, where the steward had laid a cold lunch for us.

The meal which followed recalled the lunch before we went to little Atan's cave. But the ceremony was even more grotesque and the hoarse voices even more harsh as they whispered compliments about the "power" and "strength" of the dishes. And that day each of us had his own vahine with him. Yvonne was terrified when I myself began to speak in the same unpleasant harsh voice and behave as queerly as the rest. She told me afterward that she had been quite sure I had gone out of my mind.

Toward the end of the meal my sinister brother rose and pointed to the little Norwegian table flag, while stroking his black-stubbled chin.

"That is your strength, my brother," he suddenly said to me, and seized the flag. "That is your strength, I must have it."

I gave him the flag and also a little model of the *Kon-Tiki* raft in a cellophane case, which he wanted. And carrying these two presents triumphantly under his arm, he led his party on horseback in the direction of the village.

That evening I managed to get a few hours' sleep before midnight when another cave was to be visited. Enlique Teao, who had been with us in Atan's cave, had talked. This time

Yvonne, Carl, the photographer, and Thor Junior were coming, besides Atan. The cave was most skillfully concealed, but easily accessible through a rockfall at the foot of a bluff on the west coast. Again I had to eat the tail stump of a hen and crawl down a narrow shaft into the underworld. In an underground anteroom we were received by two skulls lying on a newly raked floor. Inside was a kind of bay decorated rather like a Christmas crèche, with hay on the floor, and yellow reed mats, ranged in the form of a horseshoe round the walls, covered with fantastic stone figures. It was really cozy in this inner cave. Enlique was friendly and naïve, like a child proud of a doll's house, and I felt pleasantly relaxed, in contrast to last night's visit with the fanatical brothers. The moon shone on us round and smooth when we came up to the surface again, its silvery light reflecting on the gentle swell of the dark sea.

Next day we had arranged a huge barbecue and dancing for the village population on the plain at Anakena. Our doctor and the village doctor were sitting in the mess tent squeezing drops of blood from the ear lobes of those of our guests whom Father Sebastian had pointed out as purebred. When the turn of the mayor and his family came, they gave their blood as proudly as if the doctors were picking diamonds from their ears. There was no doubt in their minds that a drop of blood from a genuine long-ear's ear lobe could be sold for dizzy prices to museum owners. When they saw how carefully the little red drops were mixed with chemicals and conveyed to the ship's refrigerator in special containers, their expressions showed that they had no doubt about it: we were swindling them hopelessly. But what would they not do for us in friendship's name?

The scene was one of life and gaiety; the mayor himself went round in a straw hat collecting the chosen in order. We were surrounded by songs and laughter, twanging guitars and neighing horses. I had just been to the firepit and helped myself to a juicy piece of meat when a scraggy old man in a discarded army overcoat halted his horse in front of me. He was ragged and toothless and his sunken cheeks were covered with gray stubble. He gave me a friendly greeting, and I asked him to dismount and help himself from the open earth oven. But he only leaned down toward me and muttered in a low voice:

"This is why I'm here: to say you will have double luck. *El brujo,* the wizard, has told me you will have luck at midnight on Sunday if you come to the house. After that good luck will follow you."

The old man would not reply to my questions; he merely gave a jerk to his reins and rode off into the crowd, and I did not see him again. I had never heard of *el brujo* before: as far as I knew only old Tahu-tahu was concerned with *tahu* and witchcraft. But I quickly guessed that the wizard must be my strange new brother, Juan Haoa, if there was anyone on the island who deserved such a designation. He had behaved exactly as if he considered himself a medicine man. He lived in the *aku-aku's* house, in front of old Tahu-tahu's lonely hut, and thought himself surrounded by devils.

When Sunday came, we went over to the little church as usual. The birds flew in and out under the roof and twittered as freely as ever. Father Sebastian, as always, stood in the chancel wearing his handsome chasuble. But we were no longer surrounded by a mass of native heads which blended into an unfamiliar whole. We now knew most of the faces. Friends sat on every bench. There sat the "policemen," Nicholas and Kasimiro. There sat old Pakomio with Lazarus and young Estevan; the village skipper and the "Royal Son" and the four old Pakarati brothers. And Atan and Enlique, Alberto and Daniel. And together with all the rest, the trio Tumu, Andres, and Juan the Wizard. At midnight today, Sunday, I was to see them again, according to the old horseman. Time and again I caught myself staring at the trio. There they sat, quietly reverent, drinking in every word that Father Sebastian spoke. And they sang the Polynesian hymns with the same fervor as the others. The devilish look in their eyes had gone, they had a positively beatific appearance, and the black stubble no longer made them look like bandits, but rather like saints doing penance.

If I had approached them and asked why they were in Father Sebastian's church when they had dealings with *aku-akus* and underground devilry, they would certainly have been surprised and probably replied, like little Atan: "We are good Christians. All that is *otra cosa aparte,* 'another thing apart.' "

Today there was to be a christening in the church. I was to be godfather and sat on the first bench on the women's side. Behind me sat Analola with her old mother and the whole colorful crowd of vahines. Beside me sat the mayor beaming, all dressed up, with his wife, his red-haired son, and his old black-clad aunt, Tahu-tahu. This was the mayor's great day. He had become a grandfather. His daughter-in-law had presented him with a strapping grandson as compensation for the little girl who had died of the *cocongo*. The mayor was overflowing with happiness and wanted to call his grandchild after me. When Father Sebastian asked beforehand what the child was to be named, the mayor replied:

"Thor Heyerdahl Kon-Tiki El Salvador de Niños Atan."

Father Sebastian tugged at his beard in desperation and begged for a shorter name. When the child was held over the font, the grandfather nudged me delightedly in the ribs.

"Look at his hair," he said.

The little boy's skull was covered with stiff, flaming-red hair.

And the child was christened Salvador Atan. He was the latest scion of the long-ears' race. He was the thirteenth generation after Ororoina, who escaped alive from the battle at Iko's ditch.

When night came and the whole village was dark and still, a candle was blown out in the mayor's house and two shapes crept out of the door unseen. Both the jeep and the horses of the expedition's party had returned from the Sunday festivities to Anakena long before. In the village and in the camp people had been asleep for some hours, for it was nearly midnight.

But the jeep had returned to the village unseen and was standing without lights at the mayor's garden gate. The red-haired father of the newly baptized child sat at the wheel and little Uncle Atan was waiting at his side. They made room for the two shadows which came out of the house.

Quietly, and without lights, the jeep rolled along the village

street to the church, then down to the sea and up along the
coast toward the leper station.

The two shadows were Ed and I. We had not returned
to camp; rather we had stayed behind, quite secretly, in the
mayor's house to get some sleep before another nightly mission. When the village was left behind us, and we approached
the area of the "wizard's" house, I began to feel uneasy as
to what might come. A few hundred yards from the wizard's
house the jeep stopped. Here Ed was to wait with the red-
haired boy, while I was to walk on with Atan in the dark.

After a while we came up to the wall with the half-rotten
ladder and again I saw the ghostly house between the great
shining banana leaves. Atan hesitated.

"You must go in alone first," he whispered to me. "You
are our leading brother. You must knock at the door and
say: 'Wizard Juan, stand up for good luck!'"

I climbed over the creaking ladder and went up to the
house. It was silent as the grave. I raised my fist and with my
knuckles tapped cautiously three times on the old door.

"Wizard Juan, stand up for good luck!" I said in a measured tone.

No answer. Not a movement within. Only the wind blowing round the ghostly house caused a faint rustling of the
great glistening banana leaves that reached like giant fingers
toward the full moon. In the distance I heard the faint
washing of the sea.

"Try once more," little Atan whispered from the other
side of the wall.

I knocked again and repeated the phrase. Only the wind
replied.

Now I became suspicious. Perhaps this was another trap.
Perhaps at this very moment they were putting me to a new
test. Atan saw that I was hesitating. He whispered that I
must try once more: they must have gone to sleep inside
for good luck. It seemed impossible that all three would
be sound asleep, just when they were to receive us. I was
beginning to feel defeated. Were they standing behind the
door and waiting for my *aku-aku* to see them? Incidentally,
it was remarkable how much rustling there was over there
to the left, where the great waving leaves caught all the

moonlight so that the ground beneath was masked in darkness. Had they hidden there in the brush to see if I got any help from my *aku-aku?* I thought once or twice, too, that I heard a faint sound from within, but no one came. When I had tried six times, I gave up and turned to go. Then I distinctly heard a quiet movement behind the door. I turned and knocked for the last time.

"Wizard Juan, stand up for good luck!"

The door opened slowly. A young woman came out carrying a homemade tallow lamp. I looked over her shoulder, but saw no one else was there, only the empty wooden benches round the little table at which I had received the *rongo-rongo* book and the "key" to the cave.

The three men had gone, she told me. She thought they had gone to the cave.

That was it. Presumably they would now wait for my *aku-aku* to follow their track so that we could meet at the cave.

Atan decided to go into the village to look for Andres. He quickly set off across the field to the south. The woman put out her lamp and sat down on a wooden bench along the wall. She asked me to join her. I had recognized her at once. She was Juan Haoa's wife and the mayor's youngest sister. I could not help noticing her lovely profile in the moonlight. There was nothing in the least Polynesian about her. She reminded me of an Arab or Semitic beauty. It was a classic profile with a narrow, slightly curved nose and thin lips. Her skin was pale. Yet she was a pure-bred Easter Islander. Actually she was a genuine long-ear. We had a sample of her blood on board the ship.

She was an intelligent woman, and I had no difficulty in carrying on a conversation with her. We were left alone for a long time, for one o'clock came, and two, and Atan had not returned. I got a good deal of information from her as we sat there on the bench, chatting in the moonlight. The three men had decided that I ought to have a sort of *aku-aku* of feathers, she told me, because we had talked about feathers the last time. But to give it power they had been up at old Tahu-tahu's, and she had killed a chicken and made a feather crown for me to wear on my head. They had placed it on the table a few hours ago, when she herself went to bed, but now it was gone. She thought, therefore, that they were waiting for me in the cave with the feather crown. The whereabouts of the cave she did not know; all she could say was that her husband went north when he visited the cave at night. She knew a good deal about caves and cave customs, but had never seen a cave herself.

This information about the feather crown could prove very useful in the event the three put me to another test, I thought. I could surprise them with my own knowledge.

Another hour passed, and when it was three o'clock little Atan came trotting across country, from the village. He had at last found both Andres and Juan in their sister's house, and Tumu was with them. Tumu had demanded that they talk to their sister too about giving me the cave, as she had a share along with the brothers. Now she was furious because the brothers had asked her after instead of before giving me the "key." They tried to mollify her by holding handsome presents from me in prospect, but she was still in a rage and threatened to make trouble if they gave away the cave. She would not even listen to Atan. The three men had been in complete despair, not the least Tumu, who was with them to find a solution which would satisfy all three. They had begged me to excuse the delay, but I must just wait.

We waited till four, when I went off to reassure the two who were still waiting in the jeep. We decided to give it up, and the jeep had already started for the village when we heard the hoofs of a galloping horse behind us. It was Juan the Wizard, riding after us at breakneck speed. He came from the north and not from the village, and said that we must turn and follow him. He seemed overwrought. We turned the jeep, and while Juan rode ahead, we followed without lights along the coast in the moonlight, nearer and nearer to the leper station. I thought soon they would surely hear us up there. Our guide motioned to us to stop and get out in the dark shade of some big lava blocks.

As I crawled out of the jeep, sleepy and cold and stiff, two figures rushed out from a hiding place behind the rocks and were upon me in a single bound. Before I could do anything they stretched their arms up and placed a crown of waving feathers on my head. Juan the Wizard leaped from his horse, tethered it to a stone, and swiftly hung a long string of feathers bandolier-wise over his chest. He explained that this was to show that while I was the chief brother, he came next in rank. He asked me to follow him, and we set off across the stony plain as fast as we could go, with Ed, Tumu, Andres, and Atan at our heels. The red-haired boy remained to watch the jeep.

Tahu-tahu's waving feather crown was a faithful copy of a *ha'u teke-teke,* formerly a well-known headdress among the population of Easter Island: specimens exist in several museums. I felt rather an idiot striding across the stony field with the waving crown on my head; it was as though I had returned to childhood and was running about playing Indians in the moonlight. Things seemed no less crazy when soon after I was squatting down and eating the tail stumps of two hens.

Soon afterward we raised a few stones amid the remains of an old crumbling lava flow, and I slipped through the shaft ahead of the others with the feather crown still on my head. Down below we entered a roomy cave, but it was low under an undulating roof. Again the floor was carpeted with old hay. To the right of the entrance was a little altar covered with a reed mat, and on it was a large and majestic stone head, flanked by two death's-heads. One of the skulls was real, the other was of stone and had a curiously sucker-shaped mouth which was twisted forward and up, ending as a small bowl or oil lamp into which it stared with great hollow eyes. Facing this gruesome trio lay another white skull and a slender stone pestle with a head at the upper end.

In the middle of the floor was a low stone platform, coated with a cushion of hay covered by a reed mat. Juan the Wizard asked me to sit there and look in a given direction, as his grandfather had always done. Round the walls was another platform which supported the most extraordinary figures, some patterned from reality and some from a world of dreams. In addition there was a yellow reed parcel on each side of the platform on which I sat enthroned.

The first thing Juan the Wizard did was to produce the little model raft and the Norwegian table flag.

"This is your blood," he whispered to me in a hoarse voice, gripping the flag tightly. "And there you have new power yourself, there you have *ipu maengo!*" he added, pointing to the parcels.

I was so excited that I held my breath as I removed the wrappings and stared at the contents. In each of them lay a brown unglazed earthenware jar. These must be two of the three mysterious jars Andres had defiantly shown Father Sebastian at the time when he was angry with me.

"He's got many of different kinds in the other cave," Tumu put in. "It's full of *maengo,* and it'll be yours when you come back to us."

One of the two brown jars had a simple band of incised ornamentation. Juan declared that a "grandfather" had made it, and that the incisions represented men who had gone to the wars. The jars had been placed here so that the dead might drink when they wished to.

When we unpacked the two jars later in the camp, only Gonzalo recognized the type. He had seen jars like them in Chile, where the Indians had made them for generations and where they are probably still made in remote regions today. These hand-molded jars had not been turned out by the potter's wheel; they had been made of coils of clay pressed together in the true American Indian manner. How did this exceptional type of native jar find its way to Easter Island, either in ancient or modern times? And what was there about these jars that made them worthy of a place among the figures in the family cave? Why did Juan not put water for the spirits into a glass, a can, or a coffeepot? Earthenware was unknown in the native huts, and yet he must possess more, for we found that neither of the two jars answered the description of the three Andres had shown to Father Sebastian.

Only on one other occasion did I hear of a cave on Easter Island with old jars in it. This belonged to a cousin of Enlique's, but he had left for Chile in the *Pinto.*

Day was breaking and the cocks crowing when I slipped

quietly through the mayor's garden gate and into his house. Not a soul was to be seen, and my bed was as I had left it. Someone had put out fruit and a roast chicken, but best of all was being able to relax between the fresh white sheets which I had presented to the master of the house when he was planning a voyage in the *Pinto*.

"Don Pedro, Mayor," I said when my smiling friend tiptoed in with a bowl of water later that morning, "thank you for a splendid night's hospitality. But when will you show me your cave?"

"Take it easy, Señor. Surely you weren't out last night without good luck?"

"I had good luck. But I shall be leaving the island very soon. When can I see Ororoina's cave?"

"Take it easy, Señor. You've had the 'key' from me. Isn't it lying under your bed?"

It was. And I could not help smiling inwardly when I thought of it, for what I kept under the bed was a long-eared head of a rather different type from what I had expected.

But there had been so much that was unexpected about the mayor before I received the "key." Ever since he had come out of the hospital, he had been a little queer, and I did not recognize him as quite the man I had known. He had grown thin and wan, as was to be expected, but above the sunken cheeks a new gleam had entered the cunning eyes. He seemed exalted and overoptimistic, full of fantastic plans. He was no longer afraid of his grandmother. Now we would empty the cave and both of us would become multimillionaires. He was going to buy a small steamer and start regular tourist traffic from the mainland. His brother, the village skipper, could steer by the stars, and his red-haired son, who had learned to drive a jeep, could look after the engines. Everyone on the island would become incredibly rich, for the tourists he brought would buy more bird-men and *moai-kava-kavas* than the whole population could produce.

I had tried to dampen the mayor's colossal optimism, but it had been quite useless. For "good luck" I must not talk like that, he said. But in spite of all his boasting and big promises the mayor did not bring me a single stone after he had recovered. Nor did he come to work for me. Suddenly he had no time for anything at all. After all, he was mayor, and therefore a fearfully busy man.

But then one day, quite unexpectedly, he had come rushing to meet me outside his garden gate. "Good luck!" he said.

This was a day of real good luck, he whispered excitedly. And then he told me, quite openly and in the captain's presence, that Tahu-tahu had agreed to his giving me the "key" of Ororoina's cave on one condition: that I should take Tahu-tahu's oldest son, as well as the mayor and his son, with me when I left the island. I promised to talk to the governor about it, and the mayor positively jumped for joy. He eagerly invited the captain and me to come into the house at once. At the round table where I had so often sat, we found a brutish-looking fellow with a flat, broad nose and curly hair. He did not seem particularly amiable, even though he tried to smile. Two empty glasses and an opened bottle of Chilean peppermint stood on the table. The man who sat there with bloodshot eyes looked as if he had made certain of the lion's share of the contents. But he was not drunk, and he rose and genially stretched out a large hand in greeting.

The mayor assured us unctuously that here was a good fellow; he was his own cousin, the son of Tahu-tahu. But his father's family had come from the Tuamotu Islands.

"He has helped us," the mayor assured me. "He has persuaded Tahu-tahu."

Then he had dragged up a bag, held it out in front of him, and whispered mysteriously that the "key" stone was a head with three small holes in it: these had been filled with a deadly meal made from his ancestors' bones. The man with the bloodshot eyes nodded gloomily. Now they had carefully removed all the bone meal, and the head was no longer dangerous.

This detail was a feature shared with little Atan's cave. But when the mayor took the "key" out of the bag, it was no grinning death's-head that appeared. On the contrary, it was a jovial pig's head of stone, with an amiable snout, round cheeks, and long hanging ears, exactly like the most cheerful of the three little pigs in the children's story, the one who danced before the wolf and built his house of straw. But unlike the nice little pig in the story, this cave pig had curved teeth, worse than a wolf's, and three holes for human bone meal on the top of his head.

The mayor and his cousin had turned their gloomy gaze from the "key" stone up to us. I tried to look as grave as they were, but the mayor must have detected a suppressed gleam in my eye, for he suddenly smiled and gave the pig's head an affectionate kiss on the snout. Both the captain and I had been on the verge of collapse. I hastened to thank the mayor gravely for the pig's head, the captain took a cardboard box full of other sculptures, and we made for the door. The mayor then asked me to wait in patience for a few days with the pig's head under my bed; for several nights running he must bake chickens in *umu* so that all would go well when we entered the cave.

Days had now become weeks. The mayor seemed never to have finished baking his chickens. And the pig's head was by no means safe from Anette under the bed. She was always crawling under it to play with Daddy's piggy-wig. The figures from all the other caves had been taken on board the ship as the donors had requested, and also because we did not like to have them lying in the tent, for scorpions often crept out of the holes in the stones.

"Yes, indeed, I had good luck last night," I repeated, getting out of bed to take the washbowl from the mayor's hands. "And the 'key' stone is in my tent. But I must take it on board now. We're going at the end of this week."

When the mayor heard this, he had apparently baked enough chickens, for he set a night to enter the cave. Bill was permitted to come, and the photographer, but he would have no more.

On the afternoon of the day the mayor had chosen, we had a number of native visitors to the camp. The first party to arrive brought their traditional wood carvings for sale, and there was lively bartering outside the tents. Among the horsemen was a taciturn halfwit who came over to my tent with six weather-worn stone figures tied up in a cloth. On one of them moss was growing.

"Who made these?" I asked.

"I," the boy replied apathetically.

"You can't have. There's moss growing on this one."

The boy did not answer, but his mouth fell, and it looked as if he was going to weep. Then he told me that his father would give him a thrashing if he heard about it. For the boy knew the entrance to his grandfather's cave.

I gave him a lot of presents for himself and his father, and the lad rode home overcome with happiness. He probably knew of a cave which no one tended, and we never heard another word about the matter.

The wood carvers remained in the camp till dark, then they all rode home in a crowd. They had scarcely left when a solitary horseman came down from the hills. He tethered his horse and came to my tent. It was Juan the Wizard. He looked grave and troubled, embraced me and called me brother; then he gave me an urgent warning. If anyone came to me with more stones, I must not accept them; it would bring me "bad luck." What I had now was all right, but it must go no further. I must not accept a single stone from now on. His *aku-aku* knew everything that happened in the village. If I accepted one more stone, he would get to know of it, and for our brotherhood's sake I must promise to do as he begged me. If I did not, I should regret it, and I should never see his other cave with *ipu maengo* in it.

He gave me a wonderful sculpture of a reed boat with a figurehead and two sails. He had taken it from the second cave, so that I might not forget. He was so sincere in his warning, almost imploring, that I realized that he had discovered something which he could not disclose.

As soon as Juan the Wizard had discharged his peculiar mission, he went back to his horse and vanished into the night.

A little later in the evening a young couple came riding along the jeep tracks from the village. They were two of the most humble and decent natives in the island. The man's name was Moices Secundo Tuki, and he was one of my best workers. His wife, Rosa Paoa, was as quiet and simple as her husband. I had never talked about caves to them, and I was surprised when they silently unloaded a heavy sack from one of the horses and asked if they might show me the contents privately. When they had emptied the bag, seventeen fantastic stone sculptures lay in a row on my bed. A figure of a woman with a large fish roped over her back strikingly recalled a typical motif in ceramics from old desert graves in Peru.

Rosa answered all questions freely. Her father, a short-ear of the Ngaruti clan, named Simon, had given her the sculptures to barter with me. He had inherited them from his great-grandfather, whose name she did not know. But the stones came from a closed cave in the cliff near Orongo, and the cave was called Mata te Paina or the "Eye of the Straw Image." Another family had hidden their sculptures in the same cave, but no one had washed them after Marta Haoa had died.

I was eager to obtain these unique sculptures. But respect for Juan the Wizard and his urgent warning were fresh in my mind and kept me on my guard. Who could know if he was hiding in the darkness and spying on me? There was some mysterious reason for the hurried visit he had paid me. But I did not want to lose these stones. I told the couple that my *aku-aku* warned me against accepting stones just now. But he might change his mind. Therefore they must hide the sack well and come to me again the day our ship was to leave the island.

The couple looked most distressed and puzzled. They remained seated, their faces like two question marks. But when I gave them some presents as a mark of friendship, they stuffed them gratefully into the sack with the stones and crept out of the tent.

I scratched my head in an endeavor to understand what was going on, then blew out the lamp and tried to get some sleep before the appointment with the mayor at midnight. It seemed I had little more than a nap before the cameraman came and told me that the jeep was ready. We were to pick up Bill at a rendezvous in the village, and we were giving a lift to the mate Sanne. He was going on another secret mission. An old native had confided to me that he knew of a red-haired human head in a cave. He himself dared not touch the head, but he was willing to point out the place to anyone who was not afraid of a swim in the sea at night. And the mate Sanne was not afraid of anything. The mayor too had once spoken of such a head which was supposed to be in his cave. Could there be mummified heads in any of these caves? We should soon find the answers.

It was long past midnight when our little party of six sneaked quietly up to Tahu-tahu's house. In addition to the mayor, his red-haired son, and his cousin, there were Bill, the photographer, and myself. In the scree just below her little hut I smelled the well-known odor of chicken in an earth oven, and we were soon squatting in a circle devouring the delicacy, I first with the chicken's tail. The ceremony at an *umu takapu* was beginning to be familiar to me, but never one so cheerful as that night. The natives were not nervous, and the mayor seemed almost theatrically self-confident as he sat at his ease, tossing chicken bones to the *aku-akus* as nonchalantly as if they were dogs standing round us begging for morsels. When he had had enough, he went a little way to one side and lit a cigarette; then he came up and proposed in a friendly way that we should go to the cave.

This time the entrance was not just a few steps away. We clambered over walls, stumbled forward over rough stony fields, and followed winding tracks. We must have walked for ten minutes, and the place where we had eaten was far behind us when at last the mayor stopped by a pile of stones. Once we stood and examined it, it was easy to detect that the stones in the middle had recently been moved.

The mayor asked me to produce the "key" stone which I had in the bag. I must try to find the entrance with its help, he said. When I found it, I must shout three times into the pile that I was a long-ear from Norway, open the door!

I walked straight up to the stones, with the pig's head in front of me like a mine detector, and tilted its snout down toward the suspicious-looking stones, repeating the mayor's magic words. A moment afterward I had removed a number of stones and was on my way feet first down a narrow shaft.

At the bottom I slowly came out of the shaft and was just about to straighten up, cautiously like a blind man, when I felt a sharp bump against my neck. It was not the roof I had hit: I had run into some moving object. There must be someone in the cave. Before I had time to think, I had flung myself aside and around, switching on my flashlight as I did so. It was as I thought, there was something moving. But what on earth was it? The light fell on a large bird of prey with outspread wings and a hooked bill, carrying a human skull on its back. It was of stone, and it was swinging from the roof by a string. But the bird looked strangely bright and new to have hung there for eleven generations since Ororoina's time, and the piece of fiber string which supported it was new.

I turned my light around. The cave was not at all large. Three reed mats with parallel rows of round flat stones lay on the earth floor; on each stone was carved one magnified figure of the symbols which made up the *rongo-rongo* writing. A small head with a goatee beard lay on each mat as guardian. I saw at once that this cave could not have been the source of the varied choice sculptures the mayor had brought me. The only outstanding objects here were a vessel with sails and a large stone bowl over in a corner. Both were well done, but looked as conspicuously fresh as the bird hanging from the roof.

I looked into the bowl. In it lay eleven small locks of human hair of every range of color from red to black. Most of the locks were red, and were bound together separately with thin strips of bark with elaborate knots. But the locks of hair were not at all dry and dull as on mummies: they must have been cut recently from living persons, for they were still pliable and glossy.

The suspicion that had lurked in my mind since seeing the bird that swung from the roof was now definitely confirmed. The sculptures in this cave were not old. They had been made quite recently, and the whole cave was sheer contrivance. We had walked straight into a trap. My first thought was to get out. This was what Juan the Wizard had meant to warn me against.

Bill's legs were already feeling their way through the shaft opening in the wall of the cave, and it was too late to stop him. Behind him came the photographer. It was no use making a row now, for if the three natives up there realized that we had seen through the plot, they would probably be terrified. And if, for this reason, they panicked and filled in the shaft above us with stones, we should be in a nice spot here under the solid rock.

"We've been tricked," I said to Bill as soon as his head was clear of the shaft. "Let's get out of this as quickly as we can. It isn't a family cave. These are not old stones."

Bill looked astonished and quite uncomprehending. He crept across to the *rongo-rongo* stones to take a closer look.

"There's nothing necessarily old here," he whispered back to me.

"Look at the bird and the boat and the bowl with the hair in it," I replied.

Bill swung the light round him and agreed. Now I saw the bloodshot eyes of the mayor's cousin behind me. He was studying me intently, but did not understand what we were whispering to each other in English. Then I saw the mayor's face in the light too. He was dripping with sweat from sheer nervousness. His son peered round him with large eyes. The shaft must now be clear.

"The air is bad down here," I said to the mayor, rubbing my forehead.

He cordially agreed and wiped away the perspiration.

"We'll go up and have a bit of a talk," I said, and made for the shaft.

"Agreed," said the mayor and headed for the same hole.

I felt a thrill of relief when I stood under the open sky and saw the others climb out of the entrance one by one.

"We'll go now," I said curtly, picking up the damned pig's head which lay on the stone pile looking at me with a crooked smile.

"Agreed," said the mayor and jumped as if to confirm that this was no place to remain.

And so the little procession went back the way it had come, in silence: not a single word was exchanged. I led the way, sleepy and tired and cursing inwardly, with the mayor close at my heels. Behind him came Bill and the rest. The mayor's cousin lost little time in making off in the dark, and soon after the son had gone too.

On the outskirts of the village, the photographer and I said good night to Bill. It was two o'clock, and he had to get home to the native house where he was living. On parting he whispered that if I could persuade the mayor to take us to his real cave right away tonight, he would not have time to prepare another hoax.

In the village I asked the photographer to wait with the jeep and marched straight up the garden path to the mayor's house with the mayor himself close at my heels like a dog.

I went in and sat down at the round table without a word. The mayor immediately sat down beside me and let his eyes wander innocently round at the walls. I drummed with my fingers. He shifted slightly in his chair. I tried to make him look me in the eye. He returned my gaze for a moment or two with large innocent eyes, then he gazed round at the walls again. We could have sat like this for the rest of the night. He was unwilling to accept defeat. He clung to the hope that the game was not yet lost.

"That was bad luck, Pedro Atan," I began, and noticed that my own voice shook. "Bad luck for you, for me, and for your trip."

The mayor's chest began to heave. He held his breath. Then he burst into tears and let his head fall upon his arms. He lay for a while sobbing violently; then he jumped up and rushed into the little side room, where he threw himself on the bed and lay moaning. Then he grew quiet and came back into the room where I sat.

"It was all the fault of my cousin, that bad, bad cousin of mine. I thought as you did that we were going to a cave with old figures."

"But it was you who showed the way—your cave," I reminded him.

He stood for a moment or two collecting his thoughts. Then he burst into tears again.

"It was *his* idea. I should never have listened to him," he bawled. He rushed out the door and into his bed, where he lay for a long time. Then he came back again.

"Señor, you can ask me for anything. Anything. But not for the gate of the cave. Not the gate of the cave. I'd be willing to bring out all the stones to you!"

"You don't *have* to show us the cave, but then no one will believe you. For you're much too clever at making figures."

I nodded angrily toward the accursed pig's head which lay in a bag on the table. It was admirably done, and tired and depressed as I was, I could not help smiling inwardly at the thought of the cunning mayor, who had made me dance round like an idiot holding the pig's snout over the stone pile.

"If you don't take us straight to the real cave tonight, you'll be making a lot of new stones for another hoax," I said.

I rose to go.

"I can take you to *another* secret cave now, tonight," said the mayor, in genuine despair.

"Is it Ororoina's?" I asked.

"No, but it's full of old things."

I took the bag containing the pig's head, the only souvenir of the night's adventure, and walked disinterestedly to the door.

"If you change your mind tonight, you can go and fetch Bill from Rapu's hut. I'm returning to Anakena."

The mayor was standing at his door well-nigh desperate, and cursing his cousin, as I walked down weary and depressed to join the patient photographer in the jeep.

We had scarcely disappeared along the road when the unhappy mayor went straight off to Rapu's hut. He woke Bill and offered to take him to a genuine cave then and there. Bill was very sleepy and utterly sick of the mayor, and when he heard the photographer and I had returned to Anakena, he would not go to the cave either.

The mayor had to go home alone just before dawn.

About the same time the mate Sanne swam ashore not very far from the leper station. The old man had refused to let him use a boat, and he had had to swim in the starlight out to a bare lava island. Here, following the directions the native had given him, he had found his way to a couple of burial caves. In one of them he had actually come upon a human head with red hair. A thick tuft of uncommonly fine reddish-brown hair had come off on one side, and he had put this in a bag and taken it with him when he swam back to the rocks on the coast. The hair had no sheen and was bone-dry and brittle.

This was how the hair in the mayor's bowl ought to have looked if he had not gone round, after recovering from his illness, cutting locks from the heads of his red- and black-haired relatives. That confounded *cocongo!* It had evidently given the mayor a bad shock and restored his faith in his dead grandmother and the *aku-akus,* while I myself had been degraded to the rank of a quite ordinary person who had tried to cheat him. The result was that he had decided to cheat me in return, to stop me from pestering him about his own cave. But in order not to irritate unknown *aku-akus* unnecessarily, he had made his sham *umu* far away from all caves and close under the wall of Tahu-tahu's house, where he counted on sympathy and protection.

The following afternoon the mayor's red-haired son Juan came riding to the camp alone, looking very grave. Juan was an exceptionally handsome and well-built lad; as with the rest of the long-ear Atan family, there was nothing in the least Polynesian in his appearance. He told me gloomily that he thought his father was going to die. He refused to see his wife, he refused to eat or drink. He just lay in bed and moaned and wept and talked of "bad luck." Juan had seen by my face the night before that there was something wrong with the cave. He had never been in a cave of this kind before, so he had thought everything was all right.

When I told him what had happened, not a muscle in his face moved, but the tears gushed out and ran down his cheeks. He said that his father had gone straight to Señor Bill afterward to show him another cave, but Señor Bill would not go without a message from Señor Kon-Tiki. But if I would write a message to Señor Bill, the boy would try to find out from his father where the other cave was, and so he himself and Señor Bill would bring "good luck" back to the island.

I wrote a note to Bill, and the boy galloped back to the village.

After Bill had received my note, he was shadowed for the rest of the day by two men. The natives had begun to shadow Lazarus too, so that I never got into his second cave, which was at Vinapu. At midnight Bill managed to elude his shadowers and met Juan at an agreed place. With him the boy had a crude map drawn by his father.

It appeared from the map that they must first go to Ahu Tepeu, which lay far away in the stony region on the coast north of the leper station. Juan had obtained two saddled horses and a long coil of rope, and they set off in the dark. When late at night they reached the great *ahu,* the map had to come out again. They were to go on over a high sheep fence, where they had to leave the horses. The next landmark was some big lava outcrops to the right. Directly below them, on the edge of the coastal cliff, was a firmly set stone which would hold the rope secure. They were to climb down almost to the end of the long rope, and there they would find the cave.

They found the fence, the lava outcrops, and a round stone on the edge of the plateau; and when the rope was made fast Juan climbed down in the dark. They did not eat chicken first and made no *umu takapu*. There was no kind of ceremony. Juan was down for a long time and came up tired out: there was no cave there. They found another stone and tried that, with the same negative result. They moved the rope from stone to stone along the coast, till at last the boy came up completely exhausted. He could just pull himself up over the edge with Bill's help. But this time he had found the place.

Bill set off down the rope in the dark. First he went down a sheer drop to a ledge with a decent foothold. But from there the rope dangled in space. He went on down, and heard breakers far below him in the dark. He could see nothing. Then suddenly as he hung in mid-air he saw a horizontal crack in the rock just in front of his nose. He thought he could make out something inside, but it was too far in for him to reach it, and the crack was so narrow that he would not try to get his head in. With the help of a flashlight he and Juan, in turn, had at last been able to see that the narrow cave was packed with figures buried under a thick layer of dust. Juan managed to squeeze his legs into the crack and had drawn out with his foot a hook-nosed head with a flowing beard, the style of which recalled a medieval ecclesiastical sculpture. They were both so weary after their descents that each had barely been able to climb the sixty feet up the rope to the top of the cliff.

Neither could risk another descent.

Next morning Bill sent me a note. His impression was that this cave hit the bull's-eye. So far as he could see, there was every reason to think that this time it was the real thing.

I examined the remarkable head they had brought with

them. It was certainly different from the fresh sculptures we had been shown the night before last. This was old.

I picked two of our best climbers, the cook and the second engineer. In pouring rain, with Juan and Bill leading the way, we rode off in broad daylight to the cave at Ahu Tepeu. At last we were at the sheep fence, where we dismounted from our wet horses. When we reached the spot the rain stopped. We stripped naked to wring out our clothes, and I ran to and fro on the edge of the cliff to keep myself warm.

Suddenly the breeze filled my nostrils with a familiar smell. I would have recognized it among a thousand scents. It was *umu takapu*, with chicken and sweet potatoes. I called Bill's attention to it, but being a heavy smoker he noticed nothing. I could see neither smoke nor people, but someone had been here and done something mysterious. It was not natural for the village people to come out here with chickens and cook an ordinary dinner for themselves on the cliff.

Juan made the rope fast and flung it down the cliffside. I was quite horrified when I saw where Bill had been climbing; and Bill himself went pale and silent when he saw the place by daylight. There was a drop of some three hundred feet down into the sea, and the cave was a good sixty feet below the edge of the plateau.

Bill had no desire to make the descent again, and I was glad that we had two skilled climbers with us. I had experienced enough of such trips for the present, and I gladly left the pleasure to others since this time I did not have my *akuaku's* reputation to defend. The climbers had with them a sack and a stick with a net on the end to fish the figures out of the rock. And soon the sack began to come up full and go down empty.

Out of the sack came the most incredible sculptures of men, animals, and demons. Suddenly I heard a violent outburst from Bill. He held in his hand a large stone jar: a tall and gracefully curved water jar with a handle. An almost obliterated demon's face and two flying birds in the Easter Island style could faintly be seen in relief when we blew away the fine dust.

"This is exactly what I had expected to find," Bill exclaimed. "Not real pottery, but something like this in stone, with pottery as its prototype, showing some memory of that art."

Bill was a quiet man, never prodigal of superlatives. But now he was afire with excitement. This cave would have been a quite logical place to hide sculptures from Ahu Tepeu when civil war and devastation reached that imposing structure and the great statues on the *ahu* were overthrown.

Now the sack came up again. There was another stone jar with a handle, but this one was much smaller. There were also a phallic figure with three incised human heads and a warrior in a long feather cloak sitting on the back of a turtle. But the most remarkable figure was a whale with grinning jaws full of teeth; its tail terminated in a death's-head, and on its back was a model of the boat-shaped Easter Island reed house, with a square door in the side and a five-sided kitchen *umu* behind. Six round balls as large as oranges projected under its belly, and along its side ran parallel lines which suggested a kind of fabulous boat lashed together with bundles of reeds. A short flight of steps, or road, ran from the house and down along the side of the whale to what might be regarded as the water line of a ship.

Juan could give no explanation of any of the strange things that came up the cliff; all he knew was that his father had once been shown the cave by an old aunt.

Finally the cook and second engineer came up with the last sackful. They had taken the sculptures out of a little room inside the crack. The larger figures had stood behind the smaller ones. All the things were covered with a thick layer of fine dust and over some were spider webs. There were neither mats nor skeletons in this cave; it contained only sculptures, twenty-six in all.

On the way home from the cave in the cliffside the red-haired young man rode up alongside me. There was a question in his eyes.

"This was excellent," I said. "And it will be well rewarded. But tell your father for me that it was not Ororoina's cave."

We unloaded all the stones at Rapu's house where Bill was living, and as we passed the village church I slipped in to see Father Sebastian. He clasped his hands together and marched up and down the floor, quite carried away when he heard that the mayor had now shown us a genuine cave. He had been truly distressed by the episode of the sham cave. Father Sebastian had been kept in bed for a long time with the aftermath of a serious attack of *cocongo;* his case had developed before the *Pinto* sailed away. But even on his sickbed he had followed closely all the strange things that were going on. Whenever I stole in to see him at the most outlandish hours of the night, he sat up in bed in his nightshirt and listened wide-eyed to what I had to tell him. And he always had interesting supplementary information to give me. Today he told me he had heard from old people that there were several caves with "something" in them in those very cliffs on the coast north of Ahu Tepeu.

The events of the last days quickly became known in the village, and the strangest things began to happen. The people all went for the unfortunate mayor and shouted *reoreo*—liar— as soon as he set foot outside his door. Everyone tried to exploit the situation to his own benefit.

Some of the worst in abusing the mayor went home to carve stone figures in secrecy. Now that the secret cave-stone motifs had been revealed by others, they saw no reason to sit and toil at the everlastingly repeated wooden figures. When they now tried their hands at stonework, they no longer produced models of the great statues, or naïve boulders with a nose and eyes. A distinctive and quite mature style had suddenly burst into full flower under the hands of several natives at the same time. It was clear that a new industry had been opened up, based on an old form of art which had been taboo to the unprivileged.

Till now no one had tried to sell a cave stone. All deals had taken the form of an exchange of presents. But the new stones ranked with the wooden figures which were offered for sale. Some rubbed the stones thoroughly with earth, others whipped them with rotten banana leaves to give them the appearance of having once been wrapped in parcels of decayed leaves. Several men came sneaking into the camp with these products to try their luck. Perhaps, after all, Señor Kon-Tiki's *aku-aku* was not all-knowing, for if it had been, would he have let himself be enticed into the mayor's false cave?

On Easter Island anything may be expected. While some men brought new sculptures and said they were old, some tried the opposite line in the last days before the boat sailed. They did as the halfwit had done: they offered old figures and said they had made them themselves. They hit upon the strangest explanations if we pointed to moss and broken surfaces, or found signs of weathering which they themselves had not seen. They declared that their style and motifs were taken from photographs in old books on Easter Island, despite the fact that no sculpture of the cave-stone type had been seen by any explorer or writer before we came. And when I asked if they had seen them in Lavachery's book, they fell into the trap and said yes, that that was the very book.

I could not understand what was going on, but it soon became clear. Respect for taboos had begun to crumble. Some of the village people had become much less afraid of *aku-akus* after all that had happened. Señor Kon-Tiki had no all-knowing *aku-aku*, but neither had the caves. Superstition had been matched against superstition, and in many a village hut it had been extinguished, as a forest blaze would be by a counterfire. But although the respect for the *aku-akus* was dwindling, there was still something which troubled the native mind: the dread of a neighbor's criticism if it became known that a man had broken a taboo and taken stones from his family cave.

Only the mayor was silent and stayed in his house. As we were striking camp, I had another visit from his son. He said his father was tired of being branded as a liar. He had not lied to me from the time of our landing till we went to that unlucky cave. Now he would show my friends and me that everything he had told us about Ororoina's cave was true. Father Sebastian and the governor could come too and see that he had not lied. He would take us all to the cave. For Don Pedro Atan was not a poor creature, not a *reoreo* who went in for loose talk.

The night on which we were to visit Ororoina's cave was set. I drove into the village late in the evening with Bill, Ed, Carl, and Arne to pick up the governor and Father Sebastian. They accompanied us to the mayor's house. He received us at the door with open arms, loud-voiced and smiling, and took us into the sitting room. The round table was drawn back and the floor was covered with sculptures. The mayor had changed his mind at the last moment, and had hurriedly got hold of forty sculptures. He explained to Father Sebastian that he could not take us into Ororoina's cave after all because there was such an enormous number of figures in the cave. There were too many for him to be able to hand them all over to me; and if he took us to the cave entrance, the secret would no longer exist, and he would have no place in which to keep the great collection.

A fair number of the stones on the floor looked really old, but most of them were obviously quite fresh. I at once noticed some figures of recent make which had already been offered to us by some other person. There were also a few clear attempts to copy sculptures from his own little cave in the steep rock at Ahu Tepeu. What on earth was the mayor up to now? This was a second and absolutely futile attempt to deceive us.

"What are you playing at?" I asked him. "Why haven't you kept your promise to take us to Ororoina's cave, if it is true that you have it?"

"It *is* true, Señor. But when I was in Ororoina's cave last night, I saw that there was such a colossal quantity of figures in the cave that I could not hand so much over to you," he repeated.

"You must have known that before. Didn't you tell me that you washed all the stones regularly?"

"Yes, but all those I found tonight lay farther inside the cave. I hadn't seen them before. They were completely covered with dust."

"But you told me once, didn't you, that you had a kind of account book in which you had put down every single sculpture you owned?"

"Not every single *sculpture*, Señor. Every single *cave*."

"You mean that you put down in the book only the number of caves you owned?"

"Yes, certainly, Señor. It's quite a tiny, tiny book," the mayor said amiably, holding up a finger and thumb to show its size—that of a small postage stamp.

I gave up.

I was extremely sad as I walked down the steps from the little house, followed by the rest of the group. The mayor, quite forlorn, stood alone in the doorway with all the stones on the floor behind him. That was the last I saw of the mayor, Don Pedro Atan, the strangest personality on Easter Island, the last standard-bearer of the long-ears—the man whose head was so full of secrets that he himself hardly knew where fantasy began and truth ended. If the island was once upon a time inhabited by a few thousand like him, it was not surprising that giant statues on the verge of the unreal crawled out of the quarry and walked about to set themselves up on temple platforms. Nor was it strange that *aku-akus* had been invented and invisible treasure chambers established as bank vaults for a surplus of imagination in the form of queer sculptures small enough for sinful humans to carry off.

The following day was our last on Easter Island.

When orders from the bridge brought the anchor chain rattling up from the depths, and the bell to the engine room set wheels and pistons humming and beating down in the ship's bowels, there were few cheerful hearts either on board or ashore. We had been accepted by the little community and had become a part of it. The green tents had seemed completely at home on the king's site at Anakena. Now the newly erected giant stood in solitude, once more betrayed, staring out over a sun-filled valley where no one lived any longer. He looked so lonely when we struck the last tent that we felt he was asking to be overturned again, nose down in the sand, as he had lain for the last few centuries.

But the giant at Anakena was of stone, while at Hangaroa we left a giant of flesh and blood. Father Sebastian, bareheaded and in his white robe, towered above the swarm of natives down on the quay. We felt that he belonged to the expedition as much as any of us. But he had both feet firmly planted on the soil of Easter Island. He did not stand alone like the giant at Anakena; he stood as the central figure of the living population of the island, a unifying force and an inspiration. King Hotu Matua had once so stood among their ancestors when first he brought them ashore on this remote island.

We had to go round and say good-by to every single native. And last of all the members of the expedition had, one by one, to take leave of Father Sebastian. After Yvonne and little Anette, it was my turn. I stood shaking Father Sebastian's hand. We did not say much in the way of good-bys. It is easier to find words at a railway station than bid farewell forever to a friend on the shore of the world's loneliest island.

Father Sebastian turned away abruptly and the natives made room for him as he tramped off alone to the top of the hill. The red jeep, his now, was waiting for him there. As long as its tires held out, the old priest would be able to spare his shoe leather on his errands of mercy to the sick and suffering which took him as far as the leper station among the stony plateaus to the north.

The governor and his family had got aboard the launch to escort us out. I was turning to jump in after the others, when old Pakomio took me gently by the arm and led me aside. It was he who had first gone out with me to the birdmen's island to show me a secret cave which we never found. After that he had become Arne's right-hand man and foreman of the diggers in Rano Raraku. When Arne had dug up a tiny statuette at the base of one of the giants, Pakomio offered in a whisper to show him a cave full of similar figures. But after all the row about the caves started, Pakomio was frightened and withdrew his offer. Then he was the first to come running after me, feverishly assuring me that there was nothing of the kind nowadays. In their fathers' time such caves had existed, but now all entrances were forgotten, and if anyone had stone sculptures today they were only copies of those that had been lost.

With the others silent in the background, Pakomio stood before me bareheaded, awkwardly twisting his homemade reed hat.

"Will you come back to our island, Señor?" he asked quietly.

"That depends on the stones I have with me. If it's all lies

307

and humbug, as you say, the stones will bring me bad luck. Then I shall have nothing to return for."

Pakomio looked down. He stood fingering a wreath of white feathers round his hat. Then he looked up calmly and said in a low voice:

"Not all the stones you have are lies. They will bring you good luck, Señor."

As the old man spoke, his eyes were large and timid, yet friendly. We shook hands for the last time, and then I jumped down into the launch.

The natives streamed along the coast, on foot and on horseback, to wave at the ship till the last moment. I fancied there was a hollow drumming under the horses' hoofs on shore, for Easter Island is a world in two levels. But all I could really hear now was the surf breaking against the steep cliffs.

CHAPTER TEN

A Ruined City in the Clouds

IN THE ANCIENT fairy tale you must travel far and wide beyond seven seas and seven billowing ridges to reach the golden castle of your dreams. But who believes in fairy tales nowadays? We did, when we breasted the last ridge at Rapa Iti and looked at Morongo Uta.

Round us on all sides lay the sea—the endless sea, which we had crossed in our little ship from the other side of the globe. Below us lay deep green valleys encircling a bay as smooth as glass; we looked right down into the funnel of the small vessel which had brought us here from Easter Island. On the next summit, straight ahead of us, lay the fairy-tale castle, lulled in the slumber of centuries, like the Sleeping Beauty. As in a spell, its towers and walls overgrown with brushwood and foliage, it lay there just as the king and all his men had left it in the days when the world still believed in fairy tales.

I was tense with excitement as we climbed along the last ridge and approached the foot of the castle. It bulked vast and majestic before us, against a background of drifting clouds and purple peaks and spires. Although it stood free and heaven-soaring beneath the blue sky, there was something earthbound—almost subterranean—about this ancient edifice, which seemed to rise from underground in a vain attempt to push its way through turf and vegetation.

309

A big blue bird swooped down the cliff with a shrill cry. As we drew nearer, three white goats rose out of the greenery on one of the walls, leaped down into a moat, and disappeared.

Considering that Easter Island is the world's loneliest piece of land, it is perhaps not so remarkable that this is one of its nearest neighbors, and yet the distance between the two is the same as from New York to South America. Here among the green hills we felt farther away from the madding crowd than ever. This must be the most secluded corner of the Pacific. Who ever heard of Rapa Iti? The little island had almost been gnawed in two by the vast ocean round it. Too steep for a foothold, the ridge we stood on sloped down on both sides to two sheltered bays, which in turn reflected the dream castle as the wind changed. And if we looked about us, we saw no less than twelve castle-like formations, all equally curious, on the other green hilltops roundabout. But there was no sign of life. Down by the shore of the bay where the ship lay anchored, we saw smoke rising from a little village of reed-thatched bamboo huts and a handful of whitewashed houses. Here lived the entire population of the island, 278 native Polynesians all told.

But who had built this lofty dream castle, and its counterparts on all the other hilltops? And what purpose had these buildings really served? No living soul on the island could tell us.

When Captain Vancouver discovered this remote speck of land in 1791, he thought he saw people running about on top of one of them; he thought he saw, too, a blockhouse and palisades farther down the slope, and presumed that it was a man-made fort. But he never went ashore to examine it. When the famous South Seas missionary Ellis came to the island some years later, he declared that Vancouver had been mistaken: the strange contours up in the hills which looked like forts were simply natural formations. After Ellis, came the well-known explorer Moerenhout. He praised Rapa Iti's strange mountain scenery, with its peaks that resembled towers, castles, and fortified Indian villages. But he too failed to go up and have a closer look at these extraordinary formations.

Twenty-five years ago Caillot wrote a little book about this lonely island.[1] Both he and others climbed up into the hills and saw here and there sections of masonry protruding through the greenery. These were thought to be the walls of some strange and long-forgotten forts, though others believed them to be the remains of old agricultural terraces. Only one ethnologist ever went ashore to study the customs of the natives: his name was Stokes, and his unpublished manuscript has been preserved in the Bishop Museum in Honolulu.

No archaeologists had ever before set foot on the island. When we stood looking out over hill and valley, we knew we were in virgin country. We could begin just where we liked. No archaeologist had dug here before us; no one knew what we might find.

There was once a legend current among the natives of Rapa Iti, recorded nearly a hundred years ago, describing the original settlement of the island. According to this legend Rapa Iti was first settled by women who arrived from Easter Island after sailing their primitive craft across the sea. Many of them were pregnant, and from them sprang the population of this island.

From the fairy-tale castle up in the mountains we could see for many miles across the sea. Far away to the south the sky was black and gloomy. Somewhere down there cold ocean currents, moving *east*, skirted the drift ice of the Antarctic. That was a dangerous region full of storms and dense fogbanks, empty of islands and human life. But to the north the sky stretched bright and blue, flecked with little feathery trade-wind clouds drifting *west*, in company with the mild and all-embracing Humboldt Current that laps the countless islands on its way, including this lonely outpost of Rapa Iti. It would have been quite natural for primitive craft to have drifted this way from Easter Island. That was why we had now followed the very same route to Rapa Iti.

Day after day before reaching Rapa Iti we had plowed the rolling ocean in a westward race with the current and drifting clouds. Day after day we had stood on the bridge, or on deck, or at the rail, gazing into the boundless blue. It

[1] Eugène Caillot, *Histoire de l'Île Oparo ou Rapa* (Paris, 1932).

was remarkable to note how many of us would often wander aft and stand staring where the seething wake ran like a green highway through the blue expanse, marking the way back to Easter Island. It looked as if many would like to be back there. Some, perhaps, were dreaming of vahines, others of unsolved mysteries and untrodden paths now left behind. Certain it is that very few indeed stood in the bow longing for the romantic palm-fringed islands ahead.

Farthest aft of all stood Rapu, Bill's native friend and foreman of his team of excavators at Vinapu. Bill had trained this bright fellow and asked if he might bring him along to help with the surveying. Rapu had embarked on his journey into the outside world with the smile of a movie star. But his heart was tied to the World's Navel, and when it sank into the sea astern, his heart sank with it. When there was nothing left but sky and sea, no one would have recognized the dashing Rapu.

He had a flair for the mechanical, and we first gave him a trial as handyman down in the engine room. But the ship's noisy underworld was not the place for Rapu. He assured the engineers that below deck the ship was full of *diablos*, and the easygoing chief let him spend his watches sitting on a chair at the top of the engine-room ladder. But the sea breeze sent Rapu to sleep as soon as he sat down, and the engineers suggested that he was better suited to keeping watch on the bridge. He quickly learned to steer the ship by compass, and the mate went into the chartroom to attend to his own work. Then the wake astern began to assume a peculiar shape, and hopeful souls on deck thought the skipper and I had come to our senses and decided to return to Easter Island. But Rapu was quite innocent. He had curled up on the bench and gone to sleep, while the ship sailed her own course. What was the point of steering, when the eternal horizon was just as empty whichever way you looked?

Rapu was not particularly superstitious. He was "a child of our time," as the natives on Easter Island put it. But to be on the safe side he too pulled his blanket right up over his head when he slept, as was the custom among all the natives on his island. Arne had asked them the reason, and the answer was that they wanted to avoid seeing all the nasty things that were about at night. Not many of Rapu's friends would have put up a better show than he, if they had set out into the great blue immensity in a ship whose cargo was a thousand cave stones, "key" stones, skulls, and bones. The Flying Dutchman was nothing compared to us. We were faring across the ocean in a ship laden with *aku-akus*.

Pitcairn had risen out of the sea, dead ahead. We had reached the island of the *Bounty* mutineers. The sky behind it was aflame with a low, red sun, as though the desperate fugitives were still burning their ship behind them. Rapu woke up here. Now he too stood in the bow. He counted the coconut palms—one, two—no, he had never seen so many in all Easter Island. Wild goats on the hills, bananas, oranges, and all sorts of southern fruit he had never seen. This must be the Garden of Eden. Rapu would come here with his wife as soon as he got home to Easter Island and could build himself a boat.

Now we saw red roofs amid all the tropical luxuriance up on the forbidding cliffs. A huge boat with six pairs of oars, gleaming in the light as they swung in time, emerged from a little cove set behind a point. The descendants of the *Bounty* mutineers hailed us. The islanders climbed on board—robust, barelegged, picturesque characters, some of them types usually only encountered in historical films from Hollywood. A gray-haired giant clambered aboard ahead of the others: Parkin Christian, great-great-grandson of Fletcher Christian, who had led the historic mutiny. It was Fletcher who had set Captain Bligh adrift in a ship's boat that sailed west nearly as far as Asia, while Christian himself tacked against the wind and ran the *Bounty* ashore off this desolate island. Not a soul lived here when the mutineers burned their ship in the bay and established themselves with their pretty vahines from Tahiti. Yet they found abandoned temple platforms with skulls and a few small statues which faintly recalled the giants on Easter Island. Who had been there before them? Nobody knows. And till now no archaeologist had been ashore on Pitcairn for more than a few hours.

Parkin Christian invited me and my family to stay in his own house, while the others were distributed among all the other homes. We had a splendid reception from a truly hospitable little British community, which spoke English very much as their ancestors had done when they landed here in 1790, but with a mixture of Tahitian phrases and a local accent.

We enjoyed a carefree existence on the mutineers' island for several days. While the archaeologists wandered round and dug and poked about, the sailors visited Christian's cave and Adams' grave, and the frogman went down and had a look at the scanty traces of the *Bounty*. The inhabitants helped us to locate the ballast from this famous old sailing ship which lay in a crack on the sea floor at the bottom of Bounty Bay, a rusty heap of iron bars.

The inhabitants were constantly finding stone adzes in the soil. And there were rock carvings at the foot of a fearsome precipice on the north coast. But generally speaking Pitcairn was poor in archaeological remains. The mutineers' descendants, as God-fearing Christians, had leveled the temple platforms to the ground, smashed the small red statues, and thrown them into the sea to rid their island of heathen images. Arne and Gonzalo, with the aid of the inhabitants, found a cave quarry in a sheer cliff face, where judging by appearances, the red statues had been hewn out of the rock. Worn-out stone adzes from the quarry still lay where they had been flung among the rock chippings on the floor of the cave.

Strangers rarely set foot on this island. The surf pounds the cliffs at the narrow, hazardous landing place. But the shipping route from New Zealand to Panama passes close by, and whenever a passenger liner is expected the natives row out to sea and sell wood carvings of flying fish and turtles, or little models of their ancestors' proud ship. This trade has proved so brisk that Pitcairn has run out of *miro* trees, which they need for their vitally important wood carvings.

In return for their hospitality we took the whole male population of the island, and a good many of their women-folk, aboard our ship and made for the uninhabited Henderson Island. On its shores our sixty passengers felled twenty-five tons of *miro* wood in a single day. The palm-fringed beach looked like the scene of a pirate battle as the colorful throng of Pitcairn people of all ages dashed into the surf with

crooked branches, and maneuvered the logs out to the boats
rearing and plunging on the reef. Laden to the gunwales,
these were rowed off to the ship, to return empty for another
load. To anyone not accustomed to the breakers and backwash, which alternately covered and exposed the coral reef
off the tropical island, disaster seemed repeatedly imminent.
But men and women on the reef clung to the boat each time
the breakers foamed over them and lifted them off their feet,
and a bellowing giant at the tiller shouted orders to twelve
toiling oarsmen who kept the craft afloat, braced against the
onslaughts of the sea.

Next day, as we unloaded the ship at Pitcairn, a smiling
Parkin Christian assured us that his people now had enough
miro wood to carve *Bounty* models and flying fish for another
four years to come.

From Pitcairn we set a course for Mangareva. We anchored in crystal-clear water above a wildly colored coral
garden set with pearl shells and peopled with myriads of
queer fish. Rugged mountains girdled the pretty lagoon.
The only statue we saw in this palm-clad South Seas paradise
was on a painting in the church, where it lay broken in two
under the foot of a triumphant missionary. The French ad-
ministrator was away, but his capable wife drummed the
natives together for a big welcome party, which included a
dance in honor of the legendary King Tupa.

With a grotesque mask fashioned from a hollow palm stem
drawn over his head, "King Tupa" danced at the head of
his warriors. According to legend he had come to the island
from the east with a whole flotilla of large sailing rafts. After
a stay of some months he had returned to his mighty kingdom to the east, never to reappear in Mangareva. In time
and place this legend tallies astonishingly well with the
Incas' legend of their own great ruler Tupac, who caused
an immense flotilla of balsa sailing rafts to be built and set
out to visit distant inhabited islands he had heard of from
his own seafaring merchants. According to Inca historians,
Tupac spent almost a year on his cruise in the open Pacific,
and returned to Peru with prisoners and booty after visiting
two inhabited islands. I knew now, thanks to experiments
we had carried out subsequent to the Kon-Tiki expedition,

that such a raft cruise was entirely feasible, as we had finally rediscovered the lost Inca art of navigating a balsa raft with their *guara* or centerboard method. This enabled a raft to work to windward just as readily as any sailing boat. And Inca Tupac may well have been the Tupa remembered at Mangareva.

The next land we sighted was Rapa Iti. It lay among the cloudbanks to the southwest, like a dreamland sailing on the sea. From far off we could see through our binoculars that there was something unusual about the highest summits. They looked like overgrown pyramids from Mexico, or like stepped Inca fortifications in the wild mountains of Peru. This was surely something worth investigating.

With our hearts in our mouths we stood on the bridge as the skipper, with incredible skill, felt his way through a maze of rents and gaps in the live and growing coral reef which barred the entrance to a wide bay in the heart of the island. He maneuvered the ship right into a smooth lagoon formed by a sunken crater lake encircled by jagged peaks and lofty ridges. Little Anette stood looking in fascination at the skipper as, at short intervals, he swung the handle of the engine-room telegraph back and forth between "stop," "slow ahead," and "astern," and the ship glided imperceptibly forward between the corals. Suddenly Anette rose on tiptoe, took a resolute grip of the handle, and pulled it down to "full speed ahead." "Full speed ahead," the engine room replied, and we would have run smack into the reef like an ice-breaker, had not the skipper hastily swung the telegraph in the opposite direction.

We breathed a sigh of relief when we rode securely at anchor in the unruffled water off the picturesque little village, whose inhabitants came paddling out in tiny canoes to stare at us.

And now at last we had ascended to the topmost crest of the mountain chain after a climb among steep ravines and ridges.

"Morongo Uta," muttered a native who had shown us the way.

"Who built it?" I asked.

He shrugged his shoulders. "Perhaps a king. Who knows?"

We walked across and began to peer about among the dense vegetation. Here and there elaborately built walls projected. I heard a shout from Ed, who was investigating a steep terrace where a section of platform had fallen away, leaving an open earth bank full of shells and fishbones. In the midst of the debris the slender and graceful outlines of a bell-shaped mortar appeared; it was made of flint-hard basalt and had been turned and polished to complete perfection in a remarkably skillful fashion. I had not seen a finer piece of stone work in all Polynesia.

Bill, too, came up to the crest.

"This is terrific," he said, and stared in amazement at the gigantic structure before us. "We must dig here!"

We held a meeting on board the ship. We were beginning to run short of certain supplies. The large native staff of workers and our cave friends on Easter Island had stripped the ship of all our trade goods and the bulk of our provisions—indeed, most of our requirements for the months ahead. The only thing we could do was to weigh anchor, proceed to Tahiti, and provision the ship; then we could come straight back here and attack the castle on the hill.

We battled our way through rough weather till the familiar contours of Tahiti rose out of the sea. My old adoptive father, Chief Teriieroo, was no more. His house stood empty among the tall palm trunks. But Tahiti was full of old friends, and no one had time to be bored, day or night, till we laid our course straight back to the waiting island down near the fringe of the fog belt.

As we once more crept cautiously through the dangerous reef of Rapa Iti, Arne and Gonzalo were no longer on board. We had stopped at Raivavae on our way back from Tahiti, and they had been left there to explore the overgrown ruins of some taboo temples in which we had discovered a number of little stone statues. But there was no extra space on board, as we had taken on passengers from Tahiti. One was my old friend Henri Jacquier, curator of the museum at Papeete and president of the *Société des Études Océaniennes*. He was joining the expedition at my invitation. There was also a native family with us. The authorities at Tahiti had asked me if I would take them back to Rapa Iti, which was their original home.

Jacquier came on board with one suitcase, but we had to swing out the cargo boom for our native passengers. They brought innumerable crates, boxes, parcels, sacks, chairs, tables, chests-of-drawers, cupboards, two double beds, a quantity of planks and beams, bales of corrugated iron, live animals, and huge clusters of bananas, till we could hardly move on board. It was a full-scale operation getting all this stuff ashore when we reached smooth water at Rapa Iti a week later. As transport had been free of charge, the owner valued it accordingly and never even bothered to say thank you, and paddled ashore with his family in a canoe while the rest of us looked after the unloading.

On shore we had already met a remarkable couple. The woman, called Lea, was a high-spirited, humorous vahine, half-Tahitian and half-Corsican. She had been sent to the island as a schoolmistress, to teach both grownups and children to read. Her husband, called Money, was one huge grin from ear to ear, Tahitian by birth with a dash of Chinese in the corners of his eyes. He had been a bus driver in Tahiti; now in roadless Rapa Iti he lounged about doing nothing.

As Lea could both speak and write French, she was the old chief's right hand. If any problem arose, Lea's advice was sought, and she settled the case with great dispatch. She was the life and soul of the little community. Firmly planted on her feet, arms akimbo, and with bristling plaits, she reported for duty when I came ashore. Money stood modestly behind her, well-fed and happy, wreathed in smiles.

I asked Lea if she could get me twenty strong men to dig in the hills.

"When do you want them?" she asked.

"At seven tomorrow morning," I said, expecting that at best a dozen fellows would come wandering in during the next week.

When I came out on deck next morning to stretch myself and watch the sunrise, I caught sight of Lea standing on the shore with twenty men drawn up beside her. I swallowed a glass of fruit juice, crammed a slice of bread in my mouth, and hurried ashore in the launch. We agreed on Tahiti wages and working hours, and by the time the sun was at the zenith we were high up in the hills with Money and twenty strong fellows cutting ledges and steps in the steep hillside so that we could reach Morongo Uta without daily peril to life and limb.

Money led the way, giggling and laughing, and infecting the whole team with his high spirits. They sang and shouted and worked with a will, for this was something new: they were not accustomed to work on this island. Whom else should they work for? Certainly not for their own families. It was the women who cultivated the *taro* in the fields, it was the women who brought the *taro* home and kneaded it to a fermented dough which they ate for a whole week. And once a week when they grew tired of this *popoi* porridge, they went out fishing in the lagoon, and with raw fish and *popoi* on the bill of fare they could retire into the shade and sleep and make love for another week. Once a year a native trading schooner from Tahiti called. Then some of the men spent a few days in the woods gathering wild coffee berries which had already fallen to the ground, and which they bartered for minor commodities on board the schooner.

In our cheerful working team there was only one man, always the last one in line, who shirked as much as he could and encouraged the others to go slow. When Money protested, the shirker inquired in surprise what he was worrying about, as Money was not paying for the work. The man at the rear was the returned traveler from Tahiti, whom we ourselves had brought free of charge, complete with family and luggage.

Up on the sharp ridge which formed the watershed there was a saddle-shaped depression; the brushwood had crept up into it from the other side and obtained a foothold. Here we cleared a camp ground on a ledge just wide enough for a two-man tent. It was so narrow that Bill literally could sit in his tent and spit orange pips down the steep slopes on either side of the island. He was to have his base here. Bill had been given the task of directing the excavation of Morongo Uta.

When we were ready to go up into the hills next day, not a single one of our merry workers had shown up. Money was standing gloomily on the shore struggling with the corners of his mouth, which otherwise would have curled up in his customary smile, and Lea, looking like a thundercloud, came rushing out of a large bamboo hut in the village.

"If only I'd had a machine gun!" Lea cried in a rage, swinging round and aiming at the bamboo hut with outstretched arm and one finger crooked under her eye.

"What's happened?" I asked in alarm, thanking heaven that the enraged woman was unarmed.

"They're holding a council of war in there," Lea explained. "That fellow you brought from Tahiti says it's unfair to the others simply to pick out twenty men to work. They now want to decide themselves how many are to work. Anyone who wants to, shall be allowed to; they say they won't stand for any dictatorship. And if you don't let them decide who is to work, they'll stop your going up into the hills again. They'll drive you away from the island. There are *fifty* of them who want to work."

Lea was really furious. The natives, she added, had solemnly invited us to a meeting in the big hut after sunset. For the time being we must return to the ship.

By six o'clock the sun had set, and we were engulfed in darkness intensified by the stupendous cliffs which rose just behind the village and walled in the old crater-lake bay. The skipper put Jacquier and myself ashore alone, and we walked up to the dark village by the light of our flashlights. Three natives stepped out of the night without a word of greeting and followed us noiselessly on their bare feet.

Not a soul was to be seen in the village. The only sign of life was an occasional heap of embers glimpsed through the doorway of an oval, thatched bamboo hut. But the glare of a kerosene lamp led us toward the assembly hut, where we stooped under the straw roof and walked in, onto soft mats of plaited pandanus leaves. On the floor round three of the walls squatted thirty native men as grim as warriors before a battle. In the middle of the floor, in solitary splendor, sat a large fat woman with a map spread out between her bare legs.

We greeted the gathering with a cheerful *ia-o-rana* as we straightened up inside the door, and received a murmured reply from all those sitting there. Lea and the native pastor were standing by the fourth wall. Lea stood with folded arms, dark and menacing, but flashed a smile of welcome as we entered. Money was not there. Lea pointed to four empty chairs which had been placed for her, the pastor, Jacquier, and myself.

She asked Jacquier to speak first, as officially representing the French Colonial Ministry. He rose and read a speech in French, very slowly and very quietly. One or two of the natives seemed to understand, for they nodded and looked pleased. All the others watched inquiringly, with their eyes fixed steadily on us, for they obviously did not understand a word.

Jacquier told them that he was head of the *Société des Études Océaniennes,* at which the large matron in the middle of the floor nodded, visibly impressed, and pointed to the map. He went on to say that he had been sent by the Governor of French Oceania for the sole purpose of helping us. He had left his family and museum in Tahiti for that very reason. And I—pointing to me—was no tourist. I was the man who had traveled to Raroia with my friends on a *paepae.* And now I had come here with some learned men just to study their ancient buildings. People from many countries had come to work peaceably with the inhabitants of Rapa Iti —from Norway, America, Chile, Easter Island, and France. We had come to learn about their forefathers. We had just visited Rapa Nui—Easter Island. Might we receive as good treatment on Rapa Iti—"Little Rapa"—as we had in Rapa Nui —"Great Rapa."

Lea translated the speech into the Tahitian dialect, adding a good deal that came from her own heart. She spoke softly, almost daintily, but with emphasis and a note of admonition. Her hearers squatted motionless, hanging on every word, and every one of them seemed to be making an honest attempt to weigh her arguments.

The alert types on the pandanus mats round the low bamboo walls—in fact the whole occasion—gave me an intense feeling of reliving events that were commonplace in the South Seas during the days of Captain Cook and the other early explorers. Here on Rapa Iti generations had gone by like months. The gleaming eyes of the men round the walls reflected so vividly the alertness of uninhibited children of nature that for a moment I forgot that they were wearing ragged shirts and trousers; they might have sat there in the loincloths of their ancestors. I saw only rows of attentive eyes, intelligent eyes, without a trace of the degeneration of the half-civilized, but with a primitive gleam I had seen till now only in isolated jungle tribes.

When Lea had finished the old chief rose. He talked to his men almost in a whisper, but we could see from his expression that he took a favorable view. After him another old native jumped up. He spoke for a long time in the Rapa Iti dialect, eloquently and emphatically: he seemed to be the local public orator.

Finally I too rose, with Lea as interpreter, and said that their ancestors might have had good reason to offer resistance and defend their hilltop forts when strange vessels approached. But times had changed. We had come to climb the hills in their company, and remove the earth and brush, so that the forts would be as fine as in the days of their forefathers. I was ready to yield to their demand and give work to all who wanted it, but only on condition that I could send down again any man who did not work well enough to deserve his daily wage.

They all sprang up and rushed toward us, and we had to shake hands with each one in turn. Next day Lea appeared with fifty-six men, while Money stood beside her smiling proudly. This was the entire adult male population of the island, except for two old men who could not climb the hills. Money and I led the army up into the mountains. And Bill nearly fell over backward into the other valley as he sat in front of his tent up on the saddle of the narrow ridge and saw the seemingly endless procession that came climbing round a corner of the cliff just below him, yelling and shouting and swinging axes and long machetes.

Like a great battle, the work began up on the walls of Morongo Uta and went on as easy as child's play. Hibiscus and pandanus and giant tree ferns were powerless to withstand the assault; heavy tree trunks crashed down from the walls and went thundering into the depths, followed by leaves and ferns and brush.

When evening approached, the besieging army retired without a single casualty. They cheered and danced like boys as they scrambled down the hill. They had hardly taken a breather, apart from their midday rest when they had opened the bundles of large green leaves they had brought with them. Inside lay the grayish-white dough called *popoi*, which they ate with two fingers. Money descended the slope and came up twice as fat as usual, having stuffed his shirt full of big wild oranges, which he distributed to all who wanted them.

While the rest of us went down to the village or the ship, the second officer stayed up in the tent with Bill. We were to keep contact every evening by walkie-talkie. But long before contact time we saw light signals flash out from the mountain fort in the dark night. The second mate was sending an SOS: the camp was being attacked by a million rats.

"The second mate always exaggerates," the skipper reassured us. "If he says there are a million, you can bet your boots there are not more than a thousand."

Next morning our army paraded afresh, and picks, spades, netting screens, and all kinds of excavating gear were carried up the hill. The two rats which had visited the camp had gorged themselves on *popoi* and returned to their own orange trees.

For a few days the work went splendidly. But then one morning, all of a sudden, not one of our fifty-six natives turned up. Through the field glasses we could see the figures of Bill and Larsen silhouetted on the hilltop, while Lea stood on the shore waving to us. More trouble. I went ashore in the motor launch.

"They're on strike," said Lea as I landed.

"Why?" I asked in astonishment.

"That man you brought back from Tahiti has told them that everyone who works must strike."

Flabbergasted at the news, I went up to the village where some of the toughest fellows were standing with their hands in their trouser pockets, looking truculent and surly. The rest had withdrawn into the huts. All I could see were a few eyes peeping through chinks in the doors.

"Why are you on strike?" I asked, addressing one of the men directly.

"I'm not the one that knows," the man replied, looking round for support. But he got none. And as I went from man to man, none of them could answer my question. They just stood there looking discontented and grumpy.

"There's a man who knows," a fat woman called from one of the doors. "But he's not here."

I told them to go and fetch him, and several of the men rushed off. They came back escorting a half-reluctant fellow, with a brutish-looking face, wearing an old green army overcoat with no buttons, barefooted like the others, and with one of our cigarettes drooping from his lips. It was our friend the free passenger.

"Why are you on strike?" I asked again as he stood before me with an arrogant air. Everyone came out of their huts, men and women, and crowded gloomily round us.

"We want more wages for food," he answered, with the cigarette sticking up at the corner of his mouth and his hands in his coat pockets.

"But aren't you getting the wages you asked for yourselves, the same daily wage that is paid in Tahiti?"

"We want more because we provide our own food and lodging."

I saw behind him the green leaf-bags of *popoi* hanging in the trees among the bamboo huts. I knew something about daily wages in French Oceania, and that what he was asking was absurd. If I gave way now, there would be a fresh strike and fresh demands the day after tomorrow.

So I said plainly that I meant to stick to the agreement made on the evening I accepted their previous demand. Their reply was that they were all laying down their tools.

An excited vahine of imposing dimensions was standing beside me, with muscles that might have frightened any man. There were others of the same build nearby, and I had a sudden inspiration. I turned to the vahines:

"Are you women going to let the men lie and sleep in the huts, when for once there's paid work to be had on Rapa

324

Iti? When a ship full of food and clothes and other goods is lying out in the lagoon?"

It was a bull's-eye. The stout matron beside me spotted her own husband in the crowd, and at the mere sight of her pointing finger the man slunk off. A deafening clamor arose among the vahines. Suddenly Lea stepped out in front of the throng of gaping men, like a regular Joan of Arc. And with her hands planted resolutely on her hips, she called out to me:

"Why do you want men to work for you? Why can't you use us?"

This caused a landslide. I looked at all the robust girls gazing at me eagerly and closed the bargain. After all, it was they who were accustomed to doing the work on this island.

Before I knew what was going on, Lea was rushing from hut to hut. She pointed to Morongo Uta and shouted her orders. The women came pouring out. Vahines with infants in arms handed them over to daughters and grandmothers. Others washing in the brook flung down their soapy clothes, and the *taro* fields were left to themselves till the men should grow hungry. And then Lea, erect as a soldier, marched off uphill at the head of her regiment of vahines. Napoleon would have been proud of his Corsican blood if he had seen her striding in front singing the "Marseillaise," which in the rearward files became more and more blurred, gradually blending with local tunes, till those who came last were singing hula melodies, waggling their hips seductively as they danced along. Money and I were the only representatives of the strong sex in the procession, and if Money had been smiling before, he was splitting with laughter now.

Bill and the second mate, up on the ridge, came crawling out of the tent when they heard all the noise, and again I thought Bill would tumble down into the valley on the other side when he saw what was coming.

"Here are the diggers," I shouted. "Bring out the spades."

When Bill had pulled himself together, he seized a pick and handed it to one of the prettiest girls. She was so delighted that she flung herself on his neck and gave him a smacking kiss. Bill managed to save his spectacles and his hat and sank down slowly onto a packing case, wiping his cheek and looking up at me with a bewildered expression.

"In all my career as an archaeologist," he said, "I've missed this. I never knew archaeology could produce so many surprises. What'll you come marching up with next?"

Lea and her women's corps did credit to their sex. Neither in the United States nor in Norway had we seen such a working tempo. Masses of turf and soil were heaved down the cliffside so fast that Bill was run off his feet seeing that everything was done according to his orders. The vahines were intelligent and quick learners, and with Lea as their leader they formed a first-class clearing team. They were as meticulous in working on details with the trowel as they were energetic when their task merely involved getting rid of roots and surplus earth with pick and shovel. Gradually the towers and walls of Morongo Uta began to gleam rust-red and steel-gray in the sunlight. When the vahines had finished for the day, Bill withdrew to his tent, completely exhausted. Nor was there the slightest falling-off in the vahines' tempo in the days that followed.

The men were left sitting in the village eating *popoi*. When payday came, and the vahines kept both money and goods for themselves and all their children, the men began to throw down their *popoi* bags and approach the man from Tahiti with scowling faces. No one had reckoned with this consequence.

All this time the chief and the native pastor had stood by us loyally but helplessly, together with the smiling Money. Now they came with all the men to sue for peace. Everyone was willing to resume work for the original Tahiti wages. We set men and vahines to work on two separate wings of the huge structure. This proved a challenge to the sexes, creating competition, and speed and efficiency now became a matter of prestige. Never was a ruin excavated by a more energetic team of diggers. From the ship down in the bay it looked as if a swarm of locusts had descended on the peak and was eating its way downhill. The vegetation covering Morongo Uta gradually receded and disappeared, and every day the expanse of reddish-brown rock increased. Terraces and walls stood out, and soon the stepped summit was stripped and shone like a chocolate temple against the blue sky.

On the other peaks surrounding us the pyramids still lay like the moss-grown palaces of mountain trolls. But Morongo Uta was not a palace. It was not a castle. Anyone who came up into the hills now could see that it was not a single building. It was the deserted ruins of a whole village. It was as wrong to call it a fort, as it had been wrong to think of it as agricultural terraces. For up there on the topmost heights the whole population of the island had once upon a time had its permanent dwellings.

There was plenty of level ground on the floor of the valleys for those who had first found their way to this island. But instead of settling there, they had climbed up the most inaccessible precipices and established themselves round the topmost peaks. There they had clung fast and built their airy eagles' nests. They had attacked the very rock with stone tools and turned the hilltop into an impregnable tower. Round and below it the whole cliff had been carved out in great terraces, on which the village houses had stood in rows. The ancient fireplaces were still there, full of charcoal and ashes. They were curious built-up stone ovens of a type hitherto known only in Easter Island and not found anywhere else in Polynesia. Bill carefully collected the precious scraps of charcoal in his bags. From them, with the help of carbon-14 testing, it would be possible to determine the date of this strange hill village.

Stone adzes of different kinds, whole and broken, were lying about in great quantities. And equally common was the indispensable stone pounder used by the women of the past for beating *taro* into *popoi*. Some of these *popoi* pounders were so perfectly formed and balanced, with their slender lines, graceful curves, and high polish, that our engineer refused to believe that such work was possible without a modern lathe. Even the charred remains of an old fishing net were carefully dug up out of the earth by Bill's trowel.

Once this must have been a well-fortified village. A huge moat with a rampart on the raised village side barred the way to anyone coming along the southern ridge. Hundreds of thousands of hard basalt stones had been painfully carried up from the bottom of the valley to support the terraces on which the huts rested, so that they should not plunge down into the abyss under Rapa Iti's violent rainstorms. The uncut blocks were fitted together in masterly fashion without mortar; here and there a drainage channel ran out through the wall, or long stones projected and formed a kind of stair from one terrace to the next. There were more than eighty terraces in the Morongo Uta village, and the whole complex was 160 feet high with a span of 1,300 feet. It was thus the largest continuous structure ever discovered in the whole of Polynesia. According to Bill's calculations Morongo Uta alone must have had more inhabitants than the population of the entire island today, which totals 278.

Square stone ovens, wells, and storage pits for *taro* were all that was left of the houses, apart from debris and tools. The local type of dwelling had been an oval hut made of pliant boughs stuck into the ground, bent and bound together on top, and covered with reeds and dried grass, like a haycock. This too was suspiciously reminiscent of Easter Island. These hilltop dwellers had found no room in their mountain village for the huge temples which dominate the ancient architecture of all the other islands. The population of Morongo Uta had solved this problem in a manner so far unknown in the whole Pacific: they had cut small dome-shaped niches in the rock behind the terraces, and there they had built themselves miniature temples, on whose flat floors rows and squares of small stone prisms stood on edge like chessmen. Such ceremonies as could not be performed in front of these pocket-size temples could be carried out on the top-most platform of the pyramid, under the open vault of heaven, in company with sun and moon.

While Bill and his assistants were supervising the excavation of Morongo Uta, Ed and Carl went about with the ship's crew exploring the rest of the island. All the other peculiar hilltops were ruins of fortified villages of the same type as Morongo Uta. The natives called them *pare*. Old house sites lay as close together as space allowed along the narrow edge of the lofty watershed which ran from peak to peak. Deep down in the mountain-girt valleys were the walls of old agricultural terraces. They often continued far up the sides of the valleys like flights of steps, and everywhere could be found the relics of artificial irrigation, with conduits which branched off from streams and conveyed water to hillside terraces which otherwise would have remained dry.

Although the strange community of ancient Rapa Iti had dwelt up on the highest peaks, the villagers had gone down daily along paths cut into the precipitous slopes to cultivate *taro* in the valleys and to catch fish and other seafood in the bays. Few eaglets can have nested in a more exposed eyrie than the children of these Pacific hillmen up on their lofty ledges. What had frightened these people and made them take to the heights? Had those who settled on one summit taken to the hills for fear of those who lived on the others? Hardly. The villages were all connected by house sites strung out along the ridges, forming a continuous defense system that faced the endless sea. Had they fled to the heights for fear that their island was sinking into the sea? Hardly. From the hilltops we could see that the coastline way below us was the same as in their time, for where the sea was shallow for some way out, the stones had been cleared away for landing places, fishtraps, and fishponds which could all still be used today.

The answer was plain enough. The people of Rapa Iti were afraid of a powerful outside enemy, an enemy who was known to them, and whose war canoes might appear above the horizon without warning.

Perhaps they had themselves been driven to this out-of-the-way spot from another island which this enemy had already taken. Could this island have been Easter Island? Could the legend of Rapa Iti have sprung from a grain of truth, like the story of the battle at Iko's ditch? The cannibal battles in the third epoch of Easter Island would be enough to frighten anyone out to sea, even expectant mothers. As recently as the last century a wooden raft with a crew of seven natives landed safely on Rapa Iti, after drifting from Mangareva, which we ourselves had visited on our way here from Easter Island.

There were no statues on Rapa Iti, but there was no room for them on the hilltops. And if Easter Island women and children had been the founders of the island's culture, they would have thought of houses, food, and security rather than flaunting monuments and aggressive campaigns: they would have built themselves curved reed houses and rectilinear stone ovens as on Easter Island, instead of rectilinear houses and round earth ovens as on all the islands in the neighborhood. They would have put secure defenses for their own homes before warlike expeditions to those of others. And if they came from Easter Island, it is less surprising that they had the enterprise to reshape entire mountain peaks with their small stone tools. Curiously enough it is the women of Rapa Iti who keep the community going even to the present day, while the men are coddled and cared for almost like overgrown boys.

It had hitherto been maintained that in Rapa Iti there were neither dressed stone blocks nor human figures carved in stone. Up in the hills we found both. The natives took us to a bluff high above the valley east of Morongo Uta. Here they showed us a remarkable rock chamber where, according to legend, the bodies of kings had lain before their mortal remains were taken off on their last journey. It was an outstanding example of the stonemason's art. A repository shaped like a large sarcophagus had been cut in profile into the face of the bluff, and the open side carefully sealed up by four square blocks of stone fitted together so neatly that it looked as if they were of organic matter and had grown naturally together in the course of time. In the cliff beside it a human figure, as large as a child, had been cut in high relief. It stood with raised arms, ominous and menacing, reminding me of the "king" in Lazarus' burial cave on Easter Island.

According to tradition, when they died, the kings of Rapa Iti were carried up to this burial chamber in broad daylight, with pomp and splendor. Here the king lay, with his head pointing east, until one dark night he was taken away by two of his henchmen, who carried him stealthily over the ridge to the Anarua Valley on the other side. There, from generation to generation, all the past rulers of Rapa Iti were carefully hidden in a secret cave.

We found burial caves on Rapa Iti in other valleys. The largest was in the Anapori Valley, behind a waterfall which fell straight down from the rock thirty feet above. A little stream trickled into the cave, and we had to wade knee-deep in a clayey mass inside the rock till we came to dry ground with burial cairns on the shore of a subterranean lake. The shore beyond could only be reached by swimming seventy-five yards through ice-cold water. Yet here too, in pitch-darkness, lay remains of human skeletons.

In the cliff below Morongo Uta we found a burial cave of more recent times. It was hewn into the friable rock, and the entrance was sealed with a stone slab. Three bodies had been laid in the cave, but we quickly replaced the slab when a native climbed up to tell us that the contents were his closest kin. There were several sealed chambers of the same sort close by, apparently in recent use, and as we did not touch them, the man confided that his own grandfather too reposed in a secret cave in the cliff near where we stood, behind a similar slab. Beside him in the man-made cave lay a great many other people who had been placed there one after the other during a period of generations. To this very day the inhabitants of Rapa Iti adhere as best they can to their old custom: although they now bury their dead in consecrated ground near the village, they immure them in lateral chambers dug in the earth wall at the bottom of the grave.

The man-wrought peaks of Rapa Iti rise out of the sea like some elaborate monument to nameless navigators of a forgotten age—navigators who had many hundreds of miles behind them when they landed on this lonely spot. But many hundreds of miles were not enough to remove their fear that other seafarers might follow in their wake. The ocean is vast, but even the tiniest craft that will stay afloat can get across, given time. Even the smallest stone adz will make the rock yield if persevering hands hammer away long enough. And time was a commodity which this ancient people had in inexhaustible supply. If time is money, they had a larger fortune on their sunny mountain shelves than any modern magnate; then their riches were as plentiful as the stones in the walls of Morongo Uta. And in this philosophic mood, looking at the ruins of the village shimmering in space between sea and sky, one could well imagine that this was the golden castle of the fairy tale, beyond seven seas and seven billowing ridges.

But the Cave of the Kings in the Anarua Valley was something that no one on the island could show us. For the king's henchmen, who had known the way, were themselves now hidden in the rock. And the people of Rapa Iti did not know the trick of finding secret caves.

No one here had an *aku-aku*. No one knew how to eat chicken tails.

CHAPTER ELEVEN

My Aku-Aku Says . . .

THERE WAS a smell of wild pig at the head of the Taipi Valley. But not a sign of life was to be seen, either of man or beast. It was impossible to hear a thing. With a hissing noise a gushing waterfall lost its hold on the sheer rock above me, and hung wavering in thin air for sixty feet before it crashed down into the pool where I was swimming. On three sides I was hemmed in by cliff walls which rose as high as the fall, cushioned thickly with soft green moss, cool and wet and rainbow-tinged from the eternal spray. In the moss were glistening little ferns and evergreen leaves, dripping and waving as they caught and shed their drops of crystal rain into the deep pool which whirled about and vanished over the rim and into the jaws of the green forest god down in the valley below.

Today it was boiling hot in the valley. I reveled in the sheer joy of living, lying in the refreshing pool high up in the hills. I ducked and drank and at last lay half-floating, completely relaxed, with my arms around a stone. There was a magnificent view over the roof of the jungle. Down there I had crawled and waded and jumped from stone to stone, making my way up the middle of the stream through a tangle of live and dead trees which lay across it at all angles, thick with moss, ferns, and creepers.

In this virgin forest no ax could have been at work since

the time when iron was first introduced into the Marquesas
group. The population today lived only under the coconut
palms down by the shore in the largest valleys. This was
true not only here in Nuku Hiva, but also in all the other
islands of the Marquesas group. It is estimated that 100,000
native Polynesians had lived here when the Europeans first
arrived. Now the number was down to two or three thousand.
In former times people lived everywhere, and I had seen
many overgrown house walls peeping through the vegetation
as I made my way up the stream. But now I had the whole
of Herman Melville's famous Taipi Valley to myself, for the
little village near the bay where our ship lay anchored was
hidden behind a distant curve of the valley.

Down there, just around the bend and well up the slope
of the valley, eleven sturdy red shapes stood motionless in a
clearing we ourselves had made in the jungle. Eight of them
had been standing in the undergrowth when we came. But
when we raised the other three, they looked Christian men
in the face for the first time. They had lain on their bellies
with their faces stuck in the ground ever since the days when
people came up to the temple to pray and sacrifice to these
ancestor-gods. When one giant was raised with ropes and
tackles under its armpits, we saw that it was a monster with
two heads: the first statue of its kind to be found in the
Pacific.

While Ed mapped the ruins, Bill started excavating in the
hope of being able to date the old stone figures. Incredible
as it was, this was the first time an archaeological excavation
had been started anywhere in the whole Marquesas group
with its wealth of ancient culture. Only one archaeologist
had carried out a field study in the islands, and he had done
no digging.

Bill was lucky. Underneath the massive stone platform
on which the statue stood he found plenty of datable charcoal, which enabled us to compare the age of the local
statues with the age of Easter Island's. In addition we received a greeting from an old long-ear. Maybe he had been
honorably buried here, maybe he had been sacrificed and
eaten by Marquesan cannibals. All that remained of him
were his large ear-pegs and a handful of crumbling bones

hidden in a shaft in this masonry platform. Our various carbon-14 datings in the Marquesas group were to reveal that the oldest statues were raised in about 1300 A.D., or some nine hundred years after man had first settled on Easter Island. This rules out the theory occasionally propounded that the small Marquesas stone figures might be the ancestors of the Easter Island giants.

While we were at work up in the jungle of Nuku Hiva, Arne and Gonzalo were busy with a team of diggers among the palms on Hiva Oa, an island farther south in the same group. They had completed their survey of Raivavae, and we had then examined all the stone-statue centers which existed in the islands of the open Pacific. Now they had landed on Hiva Oa hoping to obtain an archaeological date there, and to make a cast of the largest statue in the Marquesas group. This measured only some eight feet from head to foot, and was a dwarf by Easter Island standards. They had taken with them the expedition's last bags of dental plaster, which we had brought for this purpose. We had used up most of our three tons on Easter Island, making a cast of a thirty-foot giant to be set up in the Kon-Tiki Museum in Oslo, over a grotto filled with cave stones.

As I lay there in the cool basin, reliving the journey in my mind, I suddenly realized to what remarkable extent the lonely outpost of Easter Island stood out among the rest of the Polynesian islands as a culture center of supreme importance. The eleven grotesque little figures in the valley below me, and the handful of others examined by Arne in the Puamao Valley on Hiva Oa—all the Marquesas group had to offer—seemed almost incidental and insignificant in contrast to the multitude of proud giants erected during the two earliest epochs of Easter Island. In fact they seemed by contrast like crumbs blown from the rich man's table. It was the same with the few figures on Pitcairn and Raivavae. Easter Island, with its deep-rooted culture, towered above the rest, a cornerstone in the prehistory of the East Pacific. No other island could possibly have usurped the proud title: "Navel of the World."

A modern scholar gives the credit for all that happened

on Easter Island to its climate. He considers that the comparatively cool weather did not encourage love life and indolence as in the other islands, and that the lack of trees for wood carving led local settlers to attack the rock instead. As to the love life of Easter Island, we heard a rather different verdict from some of the sailors on board our ship. And if low temperatures and lack of trees suffice to make men raise stone monuments, one would expect to see really enormous statues left by the Vikings who settled Iceland. But no monoliths in human form were ever raised by any of the ancient civilizations of Europe or North America, not even among the Eskimos. On the other hand, they are found in a continuous belt running from Mexico to Peru through the tropical jungles of Central America.

It does not come natural for just anybody to make for the nearest mountainside with a stone in his hand, and set about quarrying the solid rock. No one has ever seen a Polynesian do anything of the kind, even in the coldest parts of New Zealand. Generations of experience in stone carving are normally required for such projects, and experience alone is not enough. People with a fanatical urge to work and create are needed—people of the type of the mayor of Easter Island. He was certainly not a Polynesian type, that confounded mayor. I could still see him in my mind's eye, standing at the door with the whole floor behind him covered with queer figures. Beside him, to the left, and on a level with his knees, stood his little invisible *aku-aku*.

I shivered, and crawled out of the pool to stretch myself on a sun-warmed slab of stone. The misty spray drifting from the waterfall settled on me like dew as I lay there dozing, and made existence beneath the tropical sun fresh and utterly delightful. In my thoughts I was on Easter Island. My thoughts were my *aku-aku*: I could send them anywhere I liked, just as swiftly as the mayor's *aku-aku* could travel to Chile or to other distant lands.

I tried to visualize the mayor's *aku-aku*. It was doubtful whether he himself had any clear picture of its outward appearance. But behind its magic veil it must have been the personification of his own thoughts, conscience, intuition, all

336

that could be put together to convey the idea of an invisible spirit: something free and unconstrained, without bones, which could lead the body to do the strangest things while it lived, and still remain behind alone to guard a man's cave when he himself and his crumbling bones had vanished.

When the mayor asked his *aku-aku* for advice, he stood as still and as silent as when he was talking with his dead grandmother, who disappeared, along with his own train of thought, the moment I allowed myself to speak. He stood deep in meditation, putting questions to his own conscience and listening to his own intuition; he talked to his *aku-aku*. Name it whatever you will—everything in a human body that cannot be measured in feet or pounds—the mayor called it his *aku-aku*. And when he had nowhere else to put it, he let it stand by his left knee. Why not? It was always roaming about in the strangest places anyhow.

I felt sorry for my own *aku-aku*. It had followed me for a year as on a leash, without the freedom to wing its way into the unbounded universe. I thought I could hear its complaining voice.

"You're getting stale, and too prosaic," it said. "You're no longer interested in anything but dry facts. Think a little more of all the romantic aspects of life on these islands in former times. All the human destinies. All the things you can't scrape out of the earth with a trowel."

"This is a scientific expedition," I said. "I've lived most of my life among scientists and have learned their first commandment: the task of science is pure research. No speculation, no attempt to prove one thing or another."

"Break that commandment," said my *aku-aku*. "Tread on their toes!"

"No!" I replied firmly. "I did that when we came to these islands on a raft. This time it's an archaeological expedition."

"Pooh!" said my *aku-aku*. "Archaeologists are human, too. Believe me, I've been on hand and seen them!"

I told my *aku-aku* to be quiet, and splashed a little water at a mosquito which had ventured up here into the mist from the fall. But my *aku-aku* was there again. It could not restrain itself.

337

"Where do you think the red-haired strain on Easter Island came from?" it asked.

"Be quiet," I said again. "I only know they were living there when the first Europeans came. And the mayor is descended from such stock. Besides, all the old statues depict men with red topknots. If we say any more, we shall no longer be on firm ground."

"Nor were the red-haired men when they discovered Easter Island. If they had been, they would never have got there," said my *aku-aku*.

"I don't want to speculate," I replied, turning over on my stomach. "I don't want to say any more than I know."

"Fine. If you can tell me what you know, I'll add what you don't know," said my *aku-aku*. And so we were on talking terms.

"Do you think the red hair, too, was caused by the climate on the island?" it continued. "Or what is your explanation?"

"Nonsense," I said. "People with red hair must of course have landed on the island in the past. At any rate, the aboriginal settlers must have included *some* redheads."

"Were there redheads anywhere in the neighborhood?"

"On several of the islands. In the Marquesas group, for example."

"And on the mainland?"

"In Peru. When the Spaniards discovered the Inca Empire, Pedro Pizarro the chronicler wrote that, while the mass of Andes Indians were small and dark, the members of the Inca family ruling among them were tall and had whiter skins than the Spaniards themselves. He mentions in particular certain individuals in Peru who were white and had red hair. We find the same thing occurring among the mummies. On the Pacific coast, in the desert sand of Paracas, there are large and roomy man-made burial caves in which numerous mummies have been perfectly preserved. When the colorful, still unfaded wrappings are removed, some of the mummies are found to have the thick, stiff, black hair of the present-day Indians, while others, which have been preserved under the same conditions, have red, often chestnut-colored hair, silky and wavy, as found among Europeans. They have long skulls and remarkably tall bodies, and are very different from the Peruvian Indians of today. Hair experts have shown by microscopic analysis that the red hair has all the characteristics that ordinarily distinguish a Nordic hair type from that of Mongols or American Indians."

"What do the legends say? One can't see everything through a microscope."

"Legends?" I said. "They don't prove anything."

"But what do they say?"

"Pizarro asked who the white-skinned redheads were. The Inca Indians replied that they were the last descendants of the *viracochas*. The *viracochas*, they said, were a divine race of white men with beards. They were so like the Europeans that the Europeans were called *viracochas* the moment they came to the Inca Empire. It is a historical fact that this was the reason why Francisco Pizarro, with a handful of Spaniards, was able to march straight into the heart of the Inca domain and capture the Sun-King and all his enormous empire, without the vast and valiant Inca armies daring to touch a hair of their heads. The Incas thought they were the *viracochas* who had come sailing back across the Pacific. According to their principal legend, before the reign of the first Inca, the sun-god Con-Ticci Viracocha had taken leave of his kingdom in Peru and sailed off into the Pacific with all his subjects.

"When the Spaniards came to Lake Titicaca, up in the Andes, they found the mightiest ruins in South America—Tiahuanaco. They saw a hill reshaped by man into a stepped pyramid, classical masonry of enormous blocks beautifully dressed and fitted together, and numerous large stone statues in human form. They asked the Indians to tell them who had left these enormous ruins. The well-known chronicler Cieza de León was told in reply that these things had been made long before the Incas came to power. They were made by white and bearded men like the Spaniards themselves. The white men finally had abandoned their statues and gone with their leader, Con-Ticci Viracocha, first up to Cusco, and then down to the Pacific. They were given the Inca name of *viracocha,* or 'sea foam,' because they were white of skin and vanished like foam over the sea."

"Aha!" said my *aku-aku*. "Now that was interesting."

"But it proves nothing," said I.

"Nothing," said my *aku-aku*.

I had to plunge into the pool and cool off once more but when I came back my *aku-aku* was there again.

"The mayor came from such a red-haired family, too," it said. "And he and his ancestors who had made the great statues on Easter Island called themselves long-ears. Is it not strange that they should bother to lengthen their ears, so that they hung down to their shoulders?"

"It's not so strange," I said. "The same custom existed in the Marquesas Islands too. And in Borneo. And among certain tribes in Africa."

"And in Peru?"

"And in Peru. The Spaniards recorded that the ruling Inca families called themselves *orejones*, or long-ears, because they were allowed to have artificially lengthened ear lobes, in contrast to their subjects. The piercing of the ears to lengthen them was a solemn ceremony. Pedro Pizarro pointed out that it was especially the long-ears who were white-skinned."

"And what does legend say?"

"On Easter Island it says that the custom was imported. Their first king had long-ears with him when he reached the island in a seagoing vessel, after having steered for sixty days toward the setting sun on a journey from the east."

"The east? To the east lay the Inca Empire. What does legend say there?"

"It says that Con-Ticci Viracocha had long-ears with him when he sailed off westward across the sea. The last thing he did before he left Peru was to stop at Cusco in the north on his way from Lake Titicaca down to the Pacific coast. In Cusco he appointed a chief named Alcaviza and ordered that all his successors should lengthen their ears after he himself had left them. When the Spaniards reached the shores of Lake Titicaca, they heard from the Indians there too that Con-Ticci Viracocha had been chief of a long-eared people who sailed on Lake Titicaca in reed boats. They pierced their ears, put thick sheaves of *totora* reed in them, and called themselves *ringrim*, which meant 'ear.' The Indians added that it was these long-ears who helped Con-Ticci Viracocha transport and raise the colossal stone blocks weighing over a hundred tons which lay abandoned at Tiahuanaco."[1]

"How did they maneuver these enormous stones?"

"No one knows," I admitted. "The long-ears of Tiahuanaco did not leave a mayor behind who preserved the secrets; no one who could show posterity how the trick was done. But they had paved roads as on Easter Island. And some of the largest stone blocks must have been carried for thirty miles across Lake Titicaca itself in huge reed boats, as they were hewn from a particular kind of stone found only in the extinct volcano of Kapia on the other side of the lake. Local Indians have shown me the assembly point near the shore where gigantic dressed blocks still lie abandoned at the foot of the volcano, ready to be shipped across the great inland sea. The ruins of a wharf are still there, and the local Indians call it *Taki Tiahuanaco Kama,* 'The Road to Tiahuanaco.' Incidentally, the neighboring mountain they refer to as the "Navel of the World.' "

"Now I'm beginning to like you," said my *aku-aku.* "Now I'm beginning to feel happy."

"But all this has really nothing to do with Easter Island," I said.

"Wasn't the reed they used for building these boats the *Scirpus totora?* Isn't that the unaccountable fresh-water reed which the Easter Islanders planted down in the marshy recesses of their extinct volcanoes?"

"Yes."

"And the most important plant on Easter Island when Roggeveen and Captain Cook came there was the sweet potato, which the Easter Islanders called *kumara?*"

"Yes."

"And the botanists have proved that this plant, too, is South American, that it can only have come to Easter Island if carefully transported by man, and that the same name *kumara* was also used by the Indians in large parts of Peru for exactly the same plant?"

"Yes."

"Then I've only one more question, and I'll tell you the

[1] The various Inca legends of their white and bearded predecessors in Peru are recounted on pp. 224–268 of the author's book *American Indians in the Pacific.*

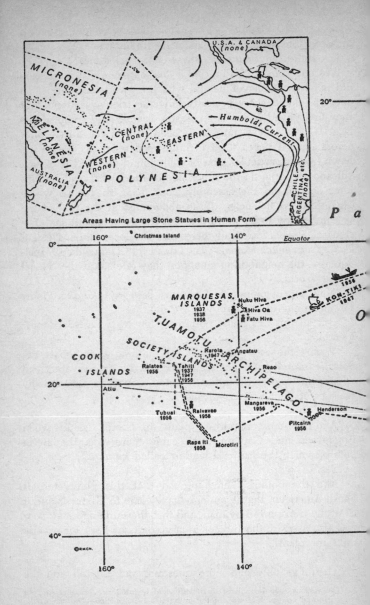

Areas Having Large Stone Statues in Human Form

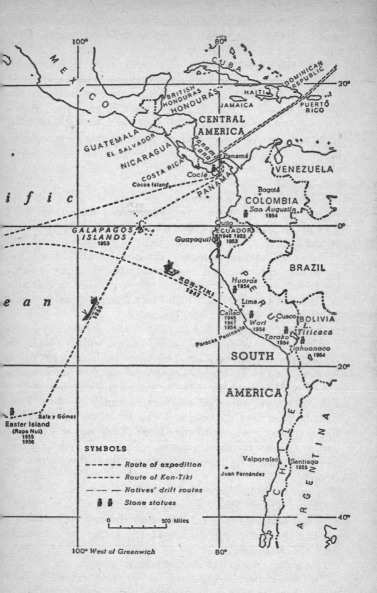

SYMBOLS

- - - - Route of expedition
- - - Route of Kon-Tiki
- - - Natives' drift routes
Stone statues

0   500 Miles

100° West of Greenwich

answer. Can we assume that the Incas' predecessors in Peru were seafarers, just as we know the Incas themselves were when the Spaniards arrived?"

"Yes. We know that they repeatedly called at the Galapagos Islands. And we know, too, that large numbers of raft centerboards, with carved handgrips, are preserved in the pre-Inca graves of Paracas, where the tall, red-haired mummies are found. A centerboard can't be used without sails, and a sail can't be used without a vessel. A single centerboard in a pre-Inca grave can tell us more about the highly developed sailing technique of Old Peru than any dissertation or Inca legend."

"Then I'll tell you something."

"I won't listen to you. You draw conclusions. You don't stick to dry facts. This is a scientific expedition, not a detective agency."

"Granted," said my *aku-aku*. "But how far would the F.B.I. get if they only collected fingerprints without trying to catch the thief?"

That was a question to which I found no ready answer, and my importunate *aku-aku* was off again:

"All right, forget it. But on Easter Island long-eared men with red hair have made long-eared statues with red topknots. Either they did it because they were cold, or they did it because they came from a country where they were accustomed to playing about with big stones and erecting statues. But after them the short-ears came. And they were Polynesians, who were not cold and who found enough wood on Easter Island to carve all they liked. They carved bird-men and models of mysterious spooks with beards and long ears and huge curved Inca noses. Where did these short-ears come from?"

"From the other islands in Polynesia."

"And where did the Polynesians come from?"

"Their language shows that they are distantly related to the small, flat-nosed people in the Malay Archipelago, between Asia and Australia."

"How did they get to Polynesia from there?"

"No one knows. No one has found as much as a single trace either there or on any of the alien island territories that lie in-between. Personally I believe they followed the current along the coast of Asia up to Northwest America. In that area the most striking traces are found on the islands off the coast, and the enormous-decked double canoes there could easily carry men and women on with the same current and wind down to Hawaii and all the other islands. One thing is certain: they must have reached Easter Island last, perhaps only a hundred years or so before the Europeans came," I concluded.

"Then, if the long-ears came from the east and the short-ears came from the west, it must be possible to sail both ways in this ocean?"

"Of course it's possible. Only it's a thousand times easier one way than the other. Look at our own early explorers. Until America was found no one possessed the necessary key to the discovery of the Pacific Islands. The Europeans had maintained a foothold in Indonesia and along the coasts of Asia for a long time without a single ship trying to beat her way ocean-ward against the prevailing wind and current into the open Pacific. It was not till Columbus had brought them to America that Portuguese and Spaniards pushed on from there, with the wind and current at their back, to discover the whole west Pacific.

"Indeed, both Polynesia and Melanesia were first discovered by Spaniards who followed the current from Peru on the advice of Inca mariners. Even Micronesia, with the Palaus and other islands just off the coast of Asia, was first discovered from South America. Expedition upon expedition poured into the open Pacific, all from America, none from Asia. The ships of the time were not even able to return the way they had come across the Pacific. For two centuries all the caravels left Mexico and Peru to cross the tropical belt of the Pacific westward to the coast of Asia; but to get back to America they all had to go north, with the Japan Current following the desolate North Pacific route, well above the islands of Hawaii. We should not expect more of Malay canoes or Inca balsa rafts and reed boats than of European caravels.

"Do you remember the Frenchman, De Bisschop, who was ready to start on his bamboo raft when we called at Tahiti? He once tried to sail from Asia to Polynesia in a primitive craft. It didn't work. Then he tried the opposite way, from Polynesia to Asia. Success, and at a spanking pace. Now he's going to try sailing a raft from Polynesia to America. He'll have to go a long way down into the cold eastbound Antarctic Current. As a European he may withstand the icy gales down there. But if he should ever get safely within a few hundred miles of the South American coast, he'll have the worst part to face, as the eastbound current suddenly turns north. If he can't overcome the current he'll start drifting straight back to Polynesia, the same way as the *Kon-Tiki* raft did, and a solitary American raftsman who followed in our wake.[2] It's one thing to go by steamer, or to travel with a pencil on a chart. It's quite another to travel in primitive craft on the restless ocean."

I listened for my *aku-aku's* reply. It had fallen sound asleep.

"Oh, where did we leave off?" it said, when I shook it awake. "Oh, yes, we were talking about the short-ears. They were distant relatives of the Malays?"

"Right. But very, very distant, for they themselves were certainly no Malays. On their Pacific wanderings they must have stopped off in some inhabited area where they greatly changed their language and entirely changed their race. Physically the Polynesians and Malays are contrasts in every respect, from shape of skull and form of nose to body height and blood type, according to the *race* experts. Only the *language* experts can point to any relationship at all. That is what is so peculiar."

"Dammit, which of them is a poor fellow to believe?"

"Both of them, as long as they simply put their facts down on the table. But neither of them, if they ignore each other and start to piece the whole puzzle together on their own. That's the strength of pure research," I said.

"And that's its greatest weakness," said my *aku-aku*. "In order to penetrate ever further into their subjects, the host of specialists narrow their fields and dig down deeper and deeper till they can't see each other from hole to hole. But the treasures their toil brings to light they place on the ground

---

[2] We subsequently learned that Eric de Bisschop's raft sent out distress signals and her crew was picked up by a warship, while the bamboo raft itself broke up in the fierce northbound Humboldt Current before reaching the Robinson Crusoe island of Juan Fernández.

above. A different kind of specialist should be sitting there, the only one still missing. He would not go down any hole, but would stay on top and piece all the different facts together."

"A job for an *aku-aku*," I said.

"No, a job for a scientist," retorted my *aku-aku*. "But we can give him a useful hint or two."

"We were talking about a possible link between Malays and short-ears," I said. "What would your view be, as an *aku-aku*, if language said yes and race said no?"

"If language suggested that all Americans came from England, I'd back the race experts."

"Let us stick to the Pacific. You're a fool if you ignore the conclusions of the language experts. Language just doesn't blow by itself with the wind."

"Language spreads by devious ways," said my *aku-aku*. "It certainly can't blow by itself *against* the wind. And since the Malays themselves didn't ever reach Polynesia, something strange must have happened en route, whether the migration went east or west, or more indirectly by the shores of the North Pacific."

Far down the valley a solitary horseman was riding. It was our expedition doctor returning across the hills from Taiohae Village with a bag full of test tubes filled with blood. He had collected samples on all the islands where we had been. Chiefs, elders, and local authorities had helped him select those who could still be considered as pure-blooded. We had sent the samples by air in ice-filled thermos bottles from Tahiti to the Commonwealth Serum Laboratories in Melbourne. Our next consignment would be dispatched by air from Panama. The *Pinto* had taken the first. Never before had living blood from the natives of these islands reached a laboratory in such a condition that all the hereditary genes could be studied and determined. Previously only the A-B-O blood group had been studied, revealing that the native tribes of Polynesia lacked the strongly hereditary B factor, which is also absent among all American Indians, while B is dominant in all the peoples of Southeast Asia, from India and China, right through the Malay Archipelago, Melanesia, and Micronesia.

"I wonder what the blood will tell us about the M-N-S, Rh, and other blood groups," I said to my *aku-aku*. I did not know then that Dr. Simmons and his colleagues would expose our samples to the most thorough blood analysis that had ever been applied to any people up to then. Nor did I know that they would find all the hereditary factors directly arguing Polynesian descent from the original population of the American continent, and at the same time clearly separating them from the Malays, Melanesians, Micronesians, and other Asiatic peoples of the West Pacific. Not even my *aku-aku* could have told me this in my—no, in his—wildest dreams.

I began to feel chilly, and put on my clothes. I glanced for the last time up at the cliff where the fall roared and the drops of water trickled through the moss. A few yellow hibiscus flowers came whirling along with the current and danced over the edge down toward the jungle beneath. Now I too was going to descend along with the current to the village. That would be far easier going: moving water was the early traveler's guide to the ocean, and beyond.

A few hours later we were all topside, either on the bridge or on the afterdeck. Even the engineers had come up to gaze spellbound at the scene, as our ship slipped along the precipitous coast and the imposing red mountain wall slowly closed on the lovely Marquesan valley like a giant sliding gate. We could still see the untamed jungle, green and heavy, down the steep slopes of the valley toward the sea. A few slim and elegant coconut palms, as though escaping from the green army behind, lined the beach, waving a friendly welcome to new arrivals and a wistful farewell to those departing. But for them, the island showed no culture: but for them, all was just savage beauty. We drank in the view and the scents. Soon it would all blend and blur into a vague shadow on the blue rim of heaven, before sinking with the sun into the sea behind us.

We stood there in the baking sun with cool, scented wreaths of flowers round our necks. Following the local custom, we were now supposed to throw them into the sea and wish ourselves back to these enchanted islands. But we hesitated to do so, every one of us. When they went overboard, they would lie drifting astern, marking a full stop to our adventure. Twice before I had cast my wreath in farewell to this enticing island world of the South Seas, and I had come back for the third time. I was not sorry for that.

There came the first wreaths, floating through the air to the sea. From the skipper and the mate up on the bridge. From Thor Junior and the mess boy at the top of the highest mast. From archaeologists and sailors, from photographer and doctor, from Yvonne and myself. Up on the boat deck with us little Anette was standing on a chair, peeping over the high rail. She struggled for a while to get the wreath off her neck, raised herself on tiptoe, and flung it with all her might over the rail and straight down.

I lifted her down from the chair and looked overboard. There lay twenty-three red-and-white wreaths, rocking gaily in our green wake. Anette's was not among them. Her little wreath had caught on the rail of the deck below. I stood watching it for a few moments. Then I went quickly down and flipped it overboard. I did not know why. I looked around me satisfied, and went up again to the others. No one had seen me. But I distinctly felt someone was laughing.

"You're as bad as the mayor," said my *aku-aku*.

Readers who wish to know more of Thor Heyerdahl's
theories concerning the origins of the Polynesians
will find them in his book
American Indians in the Pacific.

Appendix
and
Index

Appendix

THIS BOOK is an account of the adventurous aspects of our expedition, of the strange experiences of a group of outsiders who came to look into the ancient history of some of the loneliest islands in the world. Although the natives of Easter Island confronted us with new and baffling mysteries pertaining to the present day, a great many problems of the past were solved, and new facts were added to those already known concerning the early history of the eastern Pacific.

It has not been my intention to burden the reader with more scientific details than those required to understand the story of our expedition. For the scholar, a special monograph on our findings will be published by the School of American Research and the Museum of New Mexico. It is obvious that such discoveries as the old image quarry on Pitcairn, miniature temples and sculptured tombs in the giant hilltop villages of Rapa Iti, aboriginal constructions on the summits of the uninhabited Morotiri group, unknown temples and stone constructions on Raivavae, and statues of unrecorded type in the Marquesas group, combined with numerous carbon datings and excavated tools, all provide new scientific information and add to our general knowledge of the Polynesian past. Yet the interested layman may wonder how much our excavations added to the known history of Easter Island, how much they have changed former speculations on early human voyages in the vast surrounding ocean. To answer this I give the following résumé.

1: Easter Island holds a very special geographical position among all the countless islands of Polynesia: it is much farther

from Asia and a long jump nearer to South America than any
other inhabitable speck of land in the entire Pacific. This
unique location is highly important to the student of early
Pacific migrations, irrespective of his theories of migratory
routes and origins. If we presume that the first Pacific explorers set out from Asia, then this remote spot must have
been the one last discovered, and therefore the one with the
shortest period of human occupation. If, on the other hand,
the seafarers came from South America, then Easter Island
would be the nearest, the first reached, and possessing the
oldest culture in all Polynesia.

Until our carbon samples were analyzed, all datings of the
Easter Island culture were based on individual theories rather
than on archaeological facts. So far, carbon tests had brought
no Polynesian community anywhere back beyond 800 A.D. In
fact, Pacific scholars have long agreed that Polynesia as a
whole was the last major area in the world to be settled by
man, and that, for a number of reasons, all these islands remained undiscovered until about 500 A.D. On the specific
assumption that the migration went from west to east, it has
been concluded that the islands nearest Asia were first
reached and occupied at that time, whereas Easter Island
could not have been settled until the fourteenth century A.D.
at the very earliest, and according to many, not until 1500 or
1600 A.D. This is not very long before the European arrival in
1722. In such a brief period of human occupation there would
hardly have been time for stratigraphy or deposits on a barren
island, and due to these preconceived conclusions no one
attempted to dig.

Reversing the approach and assuming, as I did, that people
of another culture, from early South America, had found their
way into the Pacific before the present islanders, then the
time sequence too would be reversed, and Easter Island
would have been first instead of last. This suspicion was
verified through actual excavation. Even today we do not
know just when the first overseas voyager put his foot ashore
on Easter Island. But we do know, thanks to modern carbon-
14-dating tests, that by 380 A.D. (with a possible margin of
plus or minus one hundred years) organized labor was at
work on Easter Island. This is a thousand years earlier than

it should have been if Easter Island lay last in line. It shows that the particular island nearest to South America and farthest from Asia was already settled at the time when the first voyagers began to colonize the islands of the Polynesian ocean.

2: Nothing was found to contradict the general opinion that the ancestors of the present population reached Easter Island extremely late. What we found was that another people was there to receive them. This was perhaps our principal discovery. Archaeology revealed a clear-cut substratum of two distinct cultural epochs that antedated the final period of unrest and decadence concurring with the late arrival of the present population. Contrary to former suppositions, the history of Easter Island was not a brief explosive bloom of one coherent culture, but a restless exchange of three predeveloped cultural systems ending with complete decay.

3: Of the countless island settlements in the entire Pacific, Easter Island alone was acquainted with the highly specialized masonry technique otherwise typical of ancient Peru. If Easter Island were discovered from Peru, this distribution would be understandable, and this remarkable technique would be as old on the island as the first local colony. But the striking parallel to Peru has only been another problem to those who assumed that the first Easter Islanders came the other way, where similar masonry does not exist. It has, therefore, hitherto been proposed that this extraordinary form of masonry was the final and most recent achievement on Easter Island, gradually evolved quite independent of the outside world. But this preconception too did not stand up to archaeological testing. For our excavations revealed that this typical Peruvian type of masonry was characteristic of the *first* settlers on Easter Island, whereas the two subsequent cultural periods yielded superimposed structures of entirely different and inferior types.

4: The same reasoning was almost universal in regard to the Easter Island statues. Their purely local style has strengthened the common argument that they too are the result of local imagination, evolved independent of the great variety of similar statues in ancient Peru. Our field work revealed that the validity of this reasoning was based on inadequate information. Deviating types of early local statues were excavated by us and also found in rebuilt temple walls. Their discovery upset all existing ideas of local style and uniformity. Two of the most unaccountable specimens displayed more similarity to specialized pre-Inca statues in Tiahuanaco than to any other monument on the island or in the entire Pacific. The hitherto well-known busts of Easter Island were reduced to a secondary product of the island: they belong to the second epoch only, and to compare them with outside areas was therefore of little avail. But missing links were found beneath their base, and these important prototypes had been carved by the same first-epoch settlers who had introduced the highly specialized form of masonry.

5: To check the value of the occasionally propounded theory that Easter Island was first settled by statue makers from the Marquesas group, the basis for a chronological comparison was sought by our expedition. Carbon samples were obtained from underneath each of the two great statuary platforms in the Marquesas group, revealing that the Hiva Oa stone giants were put up about 1300 A.D. and those of Nuku Hiva two hundred years later. As opposed to the ancient pre-Inca statues of Peru, these Marquesan specimens are therefore of too recent origin to be prototypes of the Easter Island giants. On the other hand, by 1300 A.D. the fame of the second-epoch stone giants might most likely have spread from Easter Island to Hiva Oa. Such a contact would explain how the Polynesians of Hiva Oa were later able to repay the visit. For there is good traditional evidence to indicate that Hiva Oa in the Marquesas group was the home port of the warlike Polynesian seafarers that conquered Easter Island and began the third local epoch the last century before the coming of the Europeans. At any rate carbon datings reveal that stone statues, otherwise characteristic of ancient South America, spread into the easternmost fringe of Polynesia in a chronological sequence which again puts Easter Island first in line.

6: Consistent Easter Island traditions insist that *Ko te Ava o Iko* on Poike Peninsula was a man-made defense position made by the "long-ears," a people distinct from the present population. Science has disregarded the legend and identified the depression as a purely natural formation. Excavations, however, revealed that the natives were right; the depression had been skillfully transformed by man into an elaborate defense position, about 400 A.D. Nothing was found at the bottom of the trench to indicate an early war. Poike was therefore probably prepared as a place of refuge, like the *pare* on Rapa Iti, by a precautious and industrious people who feared that former enemies would follow in their wake. Wind erosion of centuries had been permitted to fill the lower portion of the trench when, about 1670 according to our carbon-14 tests, a huge pyre was lighted throughout its length. Native tradition insists that this pyre was lighted eleven generations ago. Pacific scholars reckon an average of twenty-five years to a Polynesian generation, which would bring us back to about 1680, only a decade off our own carbon date.

7: The genealogy of the present Easter Islanders points out certain individuals as descendants in direct line from the only surviving male long-ear. Traditions among these descendants, concerning the techniques employed with the second-epoch statues, were put to various tests, and many important practical problems were solved in connection with the carving, transport, and erection of the great statues.

8: During the last decades botanists have been able to prove genetically that Peruvian sweet potatoes, Peruvian cotton species, and Peruvian gourds have been transported to various Polynesian islands by pre-European voyagers. The Easter Island agriculture was based on the extensive cultivation of the Peruvian *kumara* potato when the first Europeans arrived. Another genetic proof of contact was found in the Peruvian *totora* reed, planted in all the crater lakes to serve as a principal raw material for building houses and boats, and for mats, hats, and basketry. Illustrations of *totora*-reed boats with masts and sails were also found among petroglyphs, roof-paintings, and sculptures on the island, and through the aid of oral tradition two types of reed vessels were built and tested at sea. A tightly tied *totora*-reed bundle will have the strength and buoyancy of any sturdy log, and reed ships may be constructed in a size feasible for any wooden ship, and thus capable of crossing any ocean.

Pollen borings were made in the *totora* marshes on Easter

Island and may, when the laboratory analysis is completed, yield further information on the early vegetation of the island.

9: Solar observations and discoveries in Orongo and Vinapu disclosed that the first-epoch architects, like the ancient Peruvians, had some reverence for the sun, as they made solstice observations and oriented principal religious structures accordingly.

10: Fresh blood samples were secured for the Commonwealth Serum Laboratories in Melbourne, and disclosed that serologically even the third-epoch population on Easter Island, like their close kin in all the rest of Polynesia, conform remarkably with the aboriginal population in North and South America, whereas they contrast with the Indonesians, Malays, Micronesians, Melanesians, and other southeast Asiatic peoples in such important hereditary genes as the A-B-O, M-N-S, and Rh blood factors. Nevertheless their language is somehow related to the Malay tongue, and a combination of all known facts makes it possible that the present Polynesian stock, including the third-epoch Easter Islanders, reached their present area from eastern Asia upon a long sojourn on the islands off the Northwest American coast, where the Japan Current sweeps the shore line with water from the Philippine Sea. A direct diffusion from Malay to Polynesian waters is not in accord with the genetic evidence of the Polynesian blood.

11: A number of hitherto unexplored habitation and refuge caves were examined on Easter Island, and the existence of secret storage caves was verified. The principal contents of the secret caves were small stone sculptures, although burials, paper manuscripts, pots, wood carvings, and modern trade goods occasionally occurred. The small stone sculptures were entirely different from all ancient and modern art hitherto known from Easter Island. The ripe, expressive style, complex motifs, and cultural aspect of these secret Easter Island stone sculptures are without known counterpart in any other Polynesian community or in ancient South America. A dating of these ethnographic artifacts was not possible. But in one instance disintegrated *totora*-reed mats and packages, showing the same age and degree of crumbling into dust, were found to envelope burials and associated sculptures. The burials in question must at least have antedated the introduction of Christianity, with compulsory interment at the cemetery, toward the end of last century. Style and motif of a number of sculptures clearly indicate an art form surviving from pre-European time, whereas others bear every evidence of acculturation. It is very likely, as native tradition states, that the whole system of secret caves and the custom of hiding transportable art treasures underground began with the civil wars. That is, at the close of the second epoch. Even short-ears made use of the secret caves. Much may indicate that the system survives today as a moderate form of ancestral worship, and that it had a new stimulus when missionaries introduced Christianity and cleared the native homes for religious symbols at the end of the last century. Although more sincere Christians hardly exist, the recesses of the hidden caves permit the acculturated Easter Islander, in the shade of the mighty statues, to pay silent respect to the memory of his ingenious heathen predecessors on the island.

Index

361

INDEX

INDEX

INDEX